METHODS *for* BEHAVIORAL RESEARCH

To Beverly, for more reasons than I am able to express

METHODS *for* BEHAVIORAL RESEARCH

A Systematic Approach

Paul D. Cherulnik

Sage Publications
International Educational and Professional Publisher
Thousand Oaks ■ London ■ New Delhi

For information:

Sage Publications, Inc.
2455 Teller Road
Thousand Oaks, California 91320
E-mail: order@sagepub.com

Sage Publications Ltd.
6 Bonhill Street
London EC2A 4PU
United Kingdom

Sage Publications India Pvt. Ltd.
M-32 Market
Greater Kailash I
New Delhi 110 048 India

Printed in the United States of America

Library of Congress Cataloging-in-Publication Data

Cherulnik, Paul D., 1941-
  Methods for behavioral research: A systematic approach / by Paul D. Cherulnik.
      p.   cm.
Includes bibliographical references and index.
  ISBN 0-7619-2199-0
  1. Psychology—Research—Methodology.   I. Title.
  BF76.5 .C465 2001
  150'.7'2—dc21   2001000100

This book is printed on acid-free paper

01 02 03 10 9 8 7 6 5 4 3 2 1

Acquiring Editor:	Jim Brace-Thompson
Editorial Assistant:	Karen Ehrmann
Production Editor:	Diana E. Axelsen
Editorial Assistant:	Cindy Bear
Typesetter/Designer:	Janelle LeMaster
Cover Designer:	Michelle Lee

CONTENTS

Chapter 11
The Researcher's Responsibilities as Scientist, Colleague, and Citizen

PREFACE

In psychology, the introductory research methods course has had two distinct "personalities" in recent decades. In some instances, it mainly has been about the nuts and bolts of research. At one time, that included a good deal of material on psychophysics, animal learning and motivation, and other specialties within traditional "experimental psychology." More recently, it has emphasized more general topics such as conducting a literature review, analyzing research data, and writing a research report.

Increasingly, in recent years, the research methods course has focused more on the logic of the scientific method. In this conceptual approach, different methods of doing research are compared in connection with how well they deal with a variety of problems that would make it difficult to interpret research results. Earlier examples of this approach often used statistical classification schemes. For example, between-subjects designs that compared different groups across varied conditions were contrasted with within-subjects designs that compared the same individuals on different occasions.

Later courses on the conceptual approach were often modeled, at least in part, after Campbell and Stanley's (1963) monograph. Campbell and Stanley divided research methods among the categories of pre-experimental, true experimental, and quasi-experimental, and considered their vulnerability to a variety of threats to internal and external validity.

Unfortunately for the textbook writer, instructor, and student, neither of these two versions of the course is adequate by itself. As difficult as it is to explain or learn just one of them in an undergraduate course, one really needs to know both to be able to do or to understand research adequately. Most research methods courses have, therefore, included some material from the "other" side while emphasizing one approach or the other. It is a daunting challenge to combine full-size versions of both into a manageable introduction to the subject of research methods, but that is what this book intends to do.

The structure for this enterprise will be a simplified model of the research process. It treats research as an ordered series of steps, as follows:

1. Formulating a *hypothesis* containing cause and effect constructs (e.g., TV violence causes aggression).

2. Specifying the *variables* that will be studied to test the hypothesis by transforming the cause and effect constructs in the hypothesis into independent and dependent variables using prescribed measurement operations (operationalization).

3. Creating a *research design* that specifies how the comparisons are to be made, either over time or across groups, to permit conclusions to be drawn about whether or not the hypothesis is true.

4. *Collecting* the data by making the observations prescribed by the research design.

5. *Analyzing* the data by making the appropriate statistical comparisons.

6. Drawing *conclusions* from the results of the statistical analyses.

7. Appreciating the *responsibilities* of the researcher to science, professional colleagues, and society as a whole.

The simplification in this model consists, first, of assuming that research proceeds in such a logical sequence. Sometimes, researchers have finished making their observations before the final version of the hypothesis suggests itself. Sometimes, the researcher is unaware of the most significant prior study in a given area of research until after the study has been completed, while the report is being prepared. This may change the conclusions materially.

It is also simplistic to assume that a single research study can be planned and carried out so flawlessly that it will by itself produce a useful test of the hypothesis. Quite often, a research study produces only evidence that the researcher doesn't yet fully appreciate the complexity of the problem, so that one or more further studies are needed to test the hypothesis satisfactorily.

Nonetheless, this is a useful model because it makes it possible to construct a table of contents for a book and a plan for a course that follow a logical sequence. Moreover, it encompasses all the basic questions that need to be considered in a study of research methods. Telling writers, instructors, or students that they'll know what it means when they get there presumes a greater tolerance for ambiguity than most of us have.

You may have noticed several references to the adequacy or quality of research in this discussion. One of the primary goals of the research methods course is to foster an understanding of what makes a research study in psychology adequate, or, to use the more appropriate term, valid. That is to say, what makes the study persuasive in the sense that one can trust the conclusions drawn from the results?

To that end, this text builds on the framework Campbell and Stanley provided more than 30 years ago. Their emphasis on the importance of useful generalizability in addition to valid causal inference (external validity in addition to internal validity), their descriptions of powerful designs for applied research where experimentation may not be possible (quasi-experiments), and their discussion of the problem of reactivity in psychological experiments seem as important to psychological researchers today as they were in the early 1960s.

Of course, Campbell and others have moved our understanding further since that time. They have added a fuller consideration of measurement issues (construct validity) and of the importance of decisions about statistical analysis (statistical conclusion validity), and have separated them from the internal and external validity issues (see Cook and Campbell, 1979). They have also increased the emphasis on external validity, as in Cronbach's (1982) UTOS formulation. Even in this text, innovations are introduced, such as the treatment of conceptual validity and the extension of Campbell and Stanley's system for representing designs to multivariate research problems.

Here, those methodological questions will also be combined with practical suggestions for carrying out and reporting research studies, including ways of dealing with validity problems constructively. All of it will be tied to discussions of actual studies that illustrate the issues and, it is hoped, help to bring them alive for the reader. Those studies are described first in Chapter 2 to illustrate the various sources of research hypotheses, and then referred to and discussed in more and more detail in later chapters in connection with the other steps in the research process.

This text makes every effort to treat all the issues involved in doing psychological research within a systematic framework. Although that requires learning a set of terminology and symbols, the effort pays off for the instructor and the student alike. Issues are connected so that later learning builds on what was learned earlier. As we know from the study of memory, connections and deeper understanding are keys to learning that will last.

None of this is easy to explain or to understand, but all of it is endlessly fascinating to some of us and ultimately crucial to every student and researcher in psychology. If the validity, or quality, of research cannot be evaluated adequately, none of us can know whether we can depend on the research results we read and hear about, and much of our own effort to find the answers to important scientific and practical questions about behavior will be wasted.

For the student, every effort has been made to facilitate studying and learning. In addition to the usual summary tables and diagrams interspersed throughout the text, there are several other features to watch for. At the beginning of every chapter, there is a summary known as a Quick Guide that will help to orient the reader to the intensive discussion that follows. In the chapters, there are Thinking About Research boxes that raise questions about research methods in interesting historical and contemporary contexts to make the material come alive. At the end of each chapter, there are review questions and exercises that will serve as self-tests as well as opportunities to engage the material in the chapter more deeply. Chapter 6 introduces a device known as the Validity Scorecard that makes it easier to evaluate the validity issues inherent in the use of a particular research design and to compare the strengths and weaknesses of different designs. A broader range of issues is addressed by the Study Analysis Form presented in Appendix A. Finally, a glossary is provided in Appendix B.

In addition to the study aids included in the text, students and instructors who use this book can take advantage of a related Web site at www.sagepub.com/ cherulnik. Copies of the Quick Guides that begin each chapter of the book can be downloaded for easier access as the student is reading the chapters. There are also blank copies of the Validity Scorecard and Study Analysis Form study aids. These can be downloaded and used for practice with the analysis of methodological strengths and weaknesses that is presented in this book. The Web site also provides access to several bulletin boards that can be used by students and instructors to share information about their successes and failures in using this text. Finally, there is an e-mail link to allow questions and suggestions to be addressed to me directly. I hope you will visit this Web site and find something there that helps you to make the experience of learning or teaching research methods more rewarding.

With all of this, it is the interest and effort of the reader that will determine, ultimately, what is learned. I hope that every reader has as much fun with these admittedly difficult questions as I have.

Even though my name is the only one on the cover, this book would not have been possible without the help of many other people. Jim Brace-Thompson at Sage had faith in the book and worked with incredible efficiency and good spirits to move the project along. Copy editor A. J. Sobczak helped me to improve my writing and my thinking. Diana Axelsen and her staff created this book from my manuscript with a degree of care and expertise that not only made the book much better but inspired me to do my best when the final author chores began to wear me down. Reviewers Dennis Doverspike, Julie Feldman, Ira Fischler, Kimberly Purdy, Ronald Rogers, and Douglas Waring contributed excellent suggestions for improving the sense and language of the text. My student assistant Tonya Roberts typed a first draft of most of the pages and took care of many of the other details involved in producing the original manuscript. Steve Brown's help with most of the artwork and the design of the cover helped make the manuscript look like a book. Finally, dozens of students who had to lug around photocopies of various drafts of the manuscript helped immeasurably with their comments and corrections. I hope that you will be in touch on the Web site for this book to help me make future editions even better.

Science as something already in existence, already completed,
is the most objective, impersonal thing that we humans know.
Science as something coming into being, as a goal, is just as subjectively,
psychologically conditioned as are all other human endeavors.

—Albert Einstein

AN OVERVIEW OF THE RESEARCH PROCESS

● A QUICK GUIDE TO CHAPTER 1: THE RESEARCH PROCESS

The process of doing research can be broken down arbitrarily into a series of steps, beginning with the formulation of the research hypothesis and ending with the writing of a research report. Throughout the process, the researcher must make choices among alternative means of answering the practical or theoretical question that prompted him or her to undertake the study in the first place.

Thus, there are many ways that any question about behavior might be answered. The researcher's decisions about how to do so go a long way toward determining the value of the particular answer that emerges from his or her study. The ultimate goal of any research study is to provide observations of behavior, under carefully selected contrasting conditions that will provide an unequivocal answer to the researcher's question. To the extent that the study succeeds in this, its findings are said to be valid.

The **validity** of research findings, then, is determined by the quality of the decisions made by the researcher throughout the process. Although it would be convenient to summarize the overall validity of a particular research finding, there are several different types of validity associated with decisions made by the researcher at different points in the research process. Because decisions made to improve one type of validity may affect another type differently, even adversely, there is value in considering the different types of validity separately.

For a researcher planning a study, or for a research consumer reading a report of a completed study, the analysis of specific validity questions and the aggregation of those analyses into an overall judgment of validity are crucial to maximizing the ultimate value of psychological research. Although the interests of the theorist and practitioner sometimes diverge, they (and we) are always concerned that research findings provide good answers to important questions about behavior.

Chapter 1 Quick Guide: Overview of the Research Process on the next page provides an overview of the steps in the research process. For each step, it reviews the validity criteria involved and identifies the section of a research paper that should contain the information needed to evaluate those criteria. The deeper meanings of the concepts summarized in Chapter 1 Quick Guide are explained more fully in this chapter, but an adequate understanding of them can be gained only by following them up in the subsequent chapters.

● A STEP-BY-STEP ANALYSIS OF THE RESEARCH PROCESS

In most cases, the goal of psychological research is to test a hypothesis. There are also other kinds of research, such as survey research, where the goal is to describe

Chapter 1 Quick Guide: Overview of the Research Process

Steps in the Research Process	Validity Criteria	Parts of the Research Paper

1. Formulate the hypothesis (see Chapter 2)	Conceptual validity
	    Unnecessary duplication?
	    Theoretical contribution?
		Introduction

2. Operationalize the hypothesis and its constructs (see Chapters 3 and 4)	Construct validity Are the independent and dependent variables adequate representations of the hypothesis constructs?	Method

3. Arrange the comparisons/ choose a research design (see Chapters 5, 6, 7, and 8)	Internal validity
	    Can we have confidence in a causal inference drawn from the results?
	
	External Validity
	    Can we generalize the results safely to target populations and settings?
		Method

4. Make the observations/ collect the data (see Chapter 9)	Relevant to construct validity	
5. Analyze the results (see Chapter 10)	Statistical conclusion validity Are the data described appropriately? Is the method of statistical inference appropriate?	Results
6. Draw conclusions	All validity issues	Conclusions/ discussion
7. Write the research paper (see Chapter 11)		All

a psychological property of some group of people, for example their attitudes toward a political candidate or a fast-food burger. With still other kinds, the goal is to describe the properties of some behavior, such as the stereotyping of a racial or ethnic group ("What do people believe about Azerbaijanis?"). In the more typical case, research starts with a hypothesis that suggests a cause for some behavior. "Exposure to televised violence causes aggressive behavior" is an example of a hypothesis for psychological research.

In this text, we will focus mainly on hypothesis-testing research (although some of the issues we will consider, such as measurement, are relevant to the other types as well). Our goal will be to develop an understanding of how to plan a research study that can provide the clearest possible evidence on which to base a decision about whether the hypothesis is true or false. Not all of us want to be researchers,

TABLE 1.1   The Seven Steps of the Research Process

1. Formulating the hypothesis
2. Operationalizing cause and effect
3. Arranging comparisons
4. Making observations
5. Analyzing the results
6. Drawing conclusions
7. Writing a research report

but even if we use knowledge about research methods only rarely to do our own research, it is important to have it when we read about others' research. All psychologists need to read the work of others.

There are differing views on testing scientific hypotheses. Some people would like to believe that good scientific research methods guarantee that eventually we will arrive at the truth, or a useful approximation to it. An alternative view—the one on which we'll be basing our analysis—holds that the rules governing the use of methods of scientific research are not so clear that following them guarantees a perfectly clear answer to a research question. A researcher must always choose among a variety of methods for testing his or her hypothesis, and the answer is always subject to evaluation, an evaluation that requires a good deal of technical knowledge. The best one can do is to try to get as close to the truth as possible, for a particular question about a particular behavior under a particular set of investigative circumstances.

To make the necessary technical knowledge a little easier to grasp, we will break down the process of research—from the formulation of the research hypothesis to the final decision about whether that hypothesis is true or false—into a series of smaller steps. In this chapter we'll get a brief introduction to the overall structure of the process and to each of the individual steps. We'll also be introduced to the underlying logic of the research process. The major purpose of this chapter is orientation. Detailed analysis will come later.

The step-by-step model we'll be using to understand the research process is shown in Table 1.1. As we consider each of the seven steps into which the model divides the research process, we will begin to learn some of the technical terms that are used to discuss research methods. This is the language of **methodology**, the field that studies research methods. (By the way, when new terms you should remember are introduced, they will be printed in boldface type, and you can look up definitions for them in Appendix A, a glossary that appears at the end of the book.)

As we go along, try to keep in mind that this model is just a convenience. It allows us to consider difficult questions in an orderly manner. In the actual practice of research, however, these "steps" are all interrelated—they depend on one another. In addition, they may not always occur in this seemingly logical order, for a variety of good reasons. For the sake of pedagogy and to facilitate understanding, however, the plan is to introduce these more complex questions gradually, as our base of knowledge grows broader and more stable.

Consider this, if you will, a seven-step program for those suffering, as I once did, from methodology anxiety. My salvation was a systematic analysis first published in 1963 by Donald Campbell and Julian Stanley. I have used the same strategy of organizing methodological questions into a coherent system of analysis so that you too can learn about methodology.

THE STEPS IN THE RESEARCH PROCESS ●

Step 1: The Hypothesis (see Chapter 2)

As mentioned earlier, most psychological research starts with a proposition that links some behavior the researcher wants to understand better with a possible cause—what some methodologists call the **putative cause**, or supposed cause. Again, "exposure to TV violence causes aggression" is an example of such a proposition or **hypothesis**. In this case, aggression is the behavior of interest and TV violence the putative cause.

Research hypotheses come from a variety of sources, among them personal life experiences, existing psychological theories, and the results of previous research studies. We'll consider how hypotheses are developed at greater length in the next chapter, but all hypotheses contain at least two elements. Those elements are a behavior, such as "aggression," and a putative or hypothesized cause of that behavior, such as "exposure to TV violence." (Some hypotheses are more complex, suggesting multiple causes for a behavior like aggression, and even multiple forms of aggression.)

These elements of hypotheses—cause and effect—will be referred to as the **constructs** around which the research study will be planned and carried out. In the form in which they appear in the hypothesis, they usually are not specific enough to allow the researcher to conduct an empirical (based on observation) test of the hypothesis.

After all, what is TV violence? Which shows are violent? Realistic "cop shows" as well as Saturday morning cartoons? How violent are they? Are some violent enough to cause aggression, but others not? Does it matter whether the violence on TV is real, as it is on the news or in a documentary, or whether it's fictional?

| Box 1.1 | *THINKING ABOUT RESEARCH* |

Science Doesn't Have a Monopoly on the Truth _____

If one gets to the point of believing that he or she understands the complex issues involved in scientific research, it is easy to feel superior to those who lack the same methodological sophistication. There may even be a temptation to believe that only those with scientific training can understand the way the world works. It is a temptation that should be resisted.

Consider the case of the "Kepler conjecture." The famous astronomer Johannes Kepler developed, in the 16th century, what he believed to be the most efficient method of stacking cannonballs. Kepler couldn't prove mathematically that he was correct, but the British navy needed to know.

More than 400 years later, mathematician Thomas Hales spent 10 years developing a 250-page mathematical proof of the Kepler conjecture that takes up three gigabytes of computer memory. He considered 150 variables that produce every conceivable stacking arrangement and found Kepler's "face-centered cubic" method to be the most efficient.

Although most of us probably couldn't understand the mathematics involved, that didn't prevent people who knew little about mathematics from proving Kepler to be correct years earlier than Hales did, in their own way. It turns out that the face-centered cubic is the method grocers traditionally have used to stack oranges. They place each line of oranges in the cracks of the line next to it to form the bottom layer, and each layer above in the "dimples" of the layer below to build the stack (see Figure 1.1).

Is science the only way to know the truth? Or is it just the only way to prove it? Do we know how long it took grocers to find the most efficient method of stacking oranges? Trial and error can be a long and costly process, and it doesn't guarantee the best solution if it finally works at all. But doesn't that describe the scientific approach as well? Consider how long it took to get from Kepler to Hales.

And what is aggression? An armed robbery? A bar fight? Spanking a child? A hard foul in a playground basketball game? A painful insult during a family argument? All of the above or just some? The most damaging, or even the least?

These are the kinds of questions that need to be answered before moving to the next step of the research process.

Step 2: The Operations for Measuring Cause and Effect (see Chapters 3 and 4)

To know where to go to observe the effects of a putative cause on the behavior of interest, one needs to specify what is meant by the two constructs in the hypoth-

Figure 1.1. Two depictions of the face-centered cubic stacking method that was first proposed by Kepler. On the left is a diagram that shows the generic solution to the stacking problem. On the right is a market in India where a grocer obviously solved the problem, most likely without any help from science.
SOURCE: Reprinted from *Mathematics: The Science of Patterns*, pp. 153 and 157, Devlin, © copyright 1997 by W. H. Freeman. Reprinted with permission.

esis. In our example, to carry out a research study the researcher needs to specify the **causal construct** by deciding exactly where and when exposure to TV violence occurs. The researcher also needs to specify the **behavioral construct** by deciding exactly what type of aggression to look for when violence does occur. It is necessary to choose a specific form of TV violence, and a few contrasting examples, so that their effects can be compared. To make the most sense of those comparisons, it is helpful if the level of violence can be measured precisely for those examples.

It is also necessary to choose a specific form of aggression that can be observed in the presence of those contrasting examples of TV programming and, again, one that can be measured precisely for its frequency or intensity. Because the specific versions of putative cause and behavior can vary in their amount of causal influence and in the amount of behavioral effect, respectively, they are referred to as **variables**. The variable based on the causal construct is known as the **independent variable**. It is the experience or event the researcher creates in different forms or levels, or finds in nature, whose effects on the behavior in question are studied. The variable based on the behavioral construct, the measure of behavior where its effect, if any, may be observed, is known as the **dependent variable**.

The process of moving from general constructs such as "TV violence" and "aggression" to specific variables such as "cartoon shows that contain 12 or more incidents of physical violence per half-hour program" and "instances of non-instigated physical violence in a free-play situation" is called **operational definition** or **operationalization**. That term was chosen by philosophers called epistemologists who study the methods of science. It refers to a method of defining constructs by specifying the operations by which the constructs are to be measured in a particular research study. Those operations result in the creation of the independent and dependent variables, the measured forms of the causal and behavioral constructs, respectively. This form of specification—or operationalization—of the constructs is necessary before the research can go any farther. The kind of research we're considering—empirical research—involves observing behavior directly. To do that, we need to decide exactly where to look and what to look for.

Step 3: Arranging Comparisons to Test the Hypothesis (see Chapters 5 through 8)

To test a research hypothesis, even when we know what specific variables to use, it is necessary to make some sort of comparison. The classic example is that of comparing how much of the behavior of interest is observed with and without the presence of the putative cause mentioned in the hypothesis. Is there more violence in the playground after children watch a violent cartoon show than after a period in which they don't?

In this example, one approach would be for two different groups of children to be observed, one that previously watched a violent cartoon show and one that did not. We will refer to this general approach as a **comparison among groups**. There actually are a number of different ways of testing the hypothesis by comparing different groups. We'll see later how the difference between comparing two groups created by randomly assigning similar individuals and comparing two groups that have a history of being together can affect the interpretation of the observations that are made.

We'll also consider still another way of evaluating the effects of a violent TV cartoon show on the aggressiveness of children's play: comparing the behavior of a single group of children before and after they watch a violent cartoon. In addition, we'll learn how the results of that **comparison over time** might be interpreted.

Of course, there are still more complicated ways to test the same hypothesis. It would be possible to observe several different groups of children who were exposed to cartoons that contained several different levels of violence, or even exciting nonviolent themes, to provide more information on how, if at all, TV violence affects aggression. It also would be possible to look at how different kinds of children—boys and girls, older and younger children, and so on—respond to TV violence of various sorts. Starting out with the simplest examples will make it easier to understand the basic concepts of methodological analysis. Once those concepts are understood, they can and will be applied to more complex examples.

Step 4: Making the Observations to Test the Hypothesis (see Chapter 9)

Once the plan for making the appropriate comparisons has been made, the next step is to carry it out. This is often referred to as the **data collection** phase of the research process. The research **participants**, once known as **subjects** (the term still is used and even seems more appropriate in some contexts, such as research with nonhuman species)—those whose behavior will be studied—are exposed to variations in the independent variable—present versus absent, more versus less, or whatever. During that exposure, or afterward, measurements of their responses need to be made.

Most psychological research uses **quantitative measurement** of participants' behavior. That is, the results of the observations that are made are expressed in numbers. Sometimes these numbers come from the participants themselves. They might rate their own mood from 1 (*negative*) to 10 (*positive*). The numbers could come from observers employed by the researcher (a good deal of research is more like a "mom-and-pop" operation in which the researcher works as his or her own observer). An observer could rate a participant's mood from 1 to 10 based on what could be seen (facial expression, for example), or might simply count how many times a certain behavior (such as a smile) occurred, or might record how much time was spent in a particular activity. Instruments can record behavior directly: buttons pushed by participants, electrodes attached to the participants' skin, or a beam of light that is interrupted by movement through it, to mention just a few examples.

There are also forms of **qualitative measurement**, which involve placing each participant in a category or group, based on what he or she says or what is observed—voter or nonvoter, smoker or nonsmoker, or whatever. Qualitative and quantitative measurement are discussed further in Chapter 3, because measurement is an important issue in constructing variables to represent the constructs in the research hypothesis.

Step 5: Statistical Analysis of the Observations (see Chapter 10)

Whatever the procedure followed, numbers or **data** are the result. These are the ratings, frequencies, durations, category counts, and so on. They are the values of the dependent variable that are used to evaluate the outcome of the study—the relationship between the independent and dependent variables.

That evaluation is based on work in a branch of applied mathematics known as **statistics**. Statistics provides ways of describing what the participants did—were there more instances of aggressive behavior in one group than another? More important, statistics helps us to decide whether a difference is large enough or consistent enough to support the judgment that the independent variable really did exert sufficient influence on the dependent variable, or that a relationship existed between the two that was large enough to either support or contradict the hypothesis.

Based on the statistical analyses that are carried out for a particular study, a judgment is made about whether the **research results** confirm, fail to confirm, or disconfirm the hypothesis (more about the differences among these conclusions later).

Step 6: Drawing Conclusions
From the Research Results

If the appropriate statistical analyses are carried out, the results of the research study should be fairly clear. For example, the study may show that one group was more aggressive than the other, or that group was less aggressive, or there was no difference between the groups.

Although some complex statistical analyses are far from cut and dried, it is usually the case that the results of a research study are fairly clear. There is a difference, or a relationship, or there is not. What those results mean is often not so clear. We will call this meaning the **research findings** to maintain a distinction between what is observed in a study and what is learned about the truth or falsity of the hypothesis. The problem in going from the results to findings is attributable to the nature of the research process itself.

Throughout the research process, choices are made. How should TV violence be represented? How should aggression be measured? How should participants be selected? How should comparisons be arranged? How should the observations be analyzed? Each of these choices—and, finally, all of them put together—affects the meaning of the results. To introduce the technical term that will dominate the discussion throughout most of this book, those choices affect the **validity** of the research findings. That is, they determine the meaningfulness or trustworthiness of the conclusions that may be drawn from the results.

As mentioned earlier, some believe that there is a scientific method that, if learned properly and applied properly, can ensure that research will provide a clear, unequivocal judgment on the truth or falsity of a research hypothesis. In other words, they believe that at each stage along the way, there is a correct choice that can and should be made. Many methodologists within the field of psychology would disagree with that position. Their study of research methods suggests another answer, that at best there are better and worse choices. More often than not, there are both good and bad consequences that flow from every choice. Our goal, therefore, is not to learn a perfect scientific method, but instead to understand the choices that researchers need to make and the consequences that follow from those choices.

In addition to considering how the methods used in research affect the conclusions that can be drawn from the research results, one needs to consider the scope of the findings. Even if we are sure that TV violence can exert a strong causal influence on aggression, it is not necessarily the only cause, or even one of the most important. Ending TV violence won't end aggressive behavior if there are many other causes of aggression, or many other viable hypotheses that also can explain aggression. Our conclusions need to recognize that reality and may benefit from the use of relatively new methods for studying behaviors, such as aggression, that are likely to have many causes. We will consider those methods in Chapter 8.

Step 7: Communicating the Research Findings (see Chapter 11)

Science, including psychology, has the goal of cumulative knowledge. The value of what is learned in a single research study extends beyond providing a test of a particular hypothesis. Current research has the potential to influence how scientists think about and how they investigate a problem in the future. To realize that potential, research findings need to be shared among colleagues. The means of choice, among many alternative means, is publication of the findings in a periodical known as a **scientific journal**. Such a report of findings, known as a **research article**, takes the basic form of a summary of the entire research process.

The **introduction** to a research article states the hypothesis and presents a justification for testing the hypothesis that places it in the context of existing knowledge and theory about the behavior the researcher is trying to understand. The **method section** of the article details the ways in which the hypothesis constructs were operationalized as the independent and dependent variables, the arrangements for comparisons to reveal the effects of the independent variable, and the selection of participants. The **results section** describes the statistical analyses conducted and their outcomes—the nature of the observations collected during the study and comparisons among them that are relevant to evaluating the research hypothesis.

Finally, the **discussion section** presents an argument for interpreting the meaning of the results and their implications for the truth or falsity of the hypothesis. Ultimately, of course, it is up to the readers of the article—armed, it is hoped, with sufficient knowledge of research methods—to draw their own conclusions about the research findings and about the causes of the behavior they are trying to understand.

CHOICES AND VALIDITY ●

Introduction

As mentioned above, our evaluation of the research process will be organized around the concept of validity. In the present context, validity refers to the confidence with which one can draw conclusions about the truth or falsity of a hypothesis from the results of a research study. In other words, one might ask, "To what degree of certainty do the results of this study allow us to decide that the hypothesis is true or false?" or "How confident can we be, based on the results of this study, in deciding whether the putative cause of the behavior being studied is or is not a causal factor in its occurrence?" The greater the degree of confidence or certainty, the more valid the findings. The degree of confidence or certainty, as we will see, depends to a large extent on the methods the researcher chooses to use.

Again, validity is not an all-or-none issue. The overall question about the validity of research findings summarizes a number of more limited questions. Each of the choices the researcher makes can be judged for how it affects a particular aspect of validity, and each of those judgments is made more difficult by the fact that the researcher's choice can have different, even opposite, effects on separate aspects of validity. In other words, a choice can make the interpretation of research results easier in one respect but, at the same time, more difficult in another. Each aspect of validity, therefore, needs to be considered separately before any overall judgment about the validity of the research findings can be attempted.

The rest of this book is devoted mostly to the consideration of these questions about validity. They will be treated individually and as higher-order groups of categories. The overall scheme for this analysis is shown in Table 1.2.

The table shows 24 separate validity issues. They are organized into five major categories, shown in boldface print because they will be the major focus of our discussion in this chapter. One of the five categories is subdivided further, for reasons that should become clear later.

I will not even try to explain all of this in this chapter, but I will try to make a good start, concentrating on the broader questions, or categories, and merely introducing the specific questions or issues. Before I start, however, some basic things must be said about the approach I am taking, here and throughout the discussion of these validity issues.

Our approach will be, for want of a better term, a negative one. It will focus on problems that make research results more difficult to interpret, or make them less useful for determining whether the research hypothesis is true or false. We will refer to these problems as **threats to validity**. This negative or problem-focused approach is reflected in the language used to present the 24 validity issues in Table 1.2—"lack," "non-," and so on.

We will evaluate the decisions that research psychologists make in terms of how well they eliminate potential threats to the validity (credibility) of the research findings. We will, in other words, be looking for weaknesses, rather than strengths, in research plans or research studies. Of course, if you would rather look on the bright side of things, it is possible to turn the analysis around to the positive direction, because the absence of weakness is strength.

TABLE 1.2   An Overall View of Threats to the Validity of Research Findings

I. **Threats to conceptual validity**
    1. Unnecessary duplication
    2. Theoretical isolation
II. **Threats to construct validity**
  A. The independent variable
    a. Inadequate operationalization
       3. Lack of reliability of the independent variable
       4. Lack of representativeness of the independent variable
       5. Lack of impact of the independent variable
    b. Treatment artifacts
       6. Demand characteristics in the research setting
       7. Experimenter expectancy effects on the behavior being observed
       8. Pretest sensitization to the treatments
  B. The dependent variable
    a. Inadequate operationalization
       9. Lack of reliability of the dependent variable
      10. Lack of representativeness of the dependent variable
      11. Lack of sensitivity of the dependent variable
    b. Measurement artifacts
      12. Strategic responding by the research participants
      13. Linguistic/cultural bias in the dependent measure
III. **Threats to internal validity**
      14. Extraneous effects (history)
      15. Temporal effects (maturation)
      16. Group composition effects (selection)
      17. Interaction of temporal and group composition effects
      18. Selective sample attrition (mortality)
      19. Statistical regression effects (regression to the mean)
IV. **Threats to external validity**
      20. Nonrepresentative sampling
      21. Nonrepresentative research context
V. **Threats to statistical conclusion validity**
      22. Inappropriate use of statistical techniques
      23. Use of a statistical test lacking sufficient power
      24. Mistaking a trivial effect for support for the research hypothesis

Conceptual Validity

Using our model (Table 1.1 on p. 4) as a guide, the first choice a researcher makes is what hypothesis to test. This might be the most difficult choice to evaluate. There are no established criteria for judging the worth of a research hypothesis. When one reads the introduction to a research article, it seems that the justification for selecting the hypothesis is either persuasive or is not. To some extent, that depends on how much the reader knows about the particular area of research. It also depends on whether the hypothesis was chosen based on a closely reasoned analysis of the existing theory and research on the subject at hand. It is more difficult to write a persuasive justification for a hypothesis that arose from a whimsical desire to find out "what would happen to the research participants' behavior if. . . ."

The less a research study duplicates previous studies unknowingly and unnecessarily, and the more a study fits together logically with other studies to test a potentially explanatory theory, the more valuable and meaningful its findings become (intentional duplication to double-check the results, known as **replication**, is a separate matter). We'll refer to these properties of research findings as **conceptual validity**. As with all other aspects of validity, the conceptual validity of research findings can vary from high to low, depending on the quality of the researcher's choices.

In the case of conceptual validity, the two most obvious threats to validity, highlighted in Table 1.3, are the choice of a hypothesis that results in **unnecessary duplication** of previous research and the choice of a hypothesis that lacks relevance to existing theory, or that suffers from **theoretical isolation**. Both these threats can be minimized by a thorough search of the existing research literature and a careful analysis of relevant theory. Chapter 2 is devoted to a detailed discussion of these topics.

The Validity Scorecard

Conceptual validity is the first in the series of categories of validity that will be introduced in this chapter. Once one understands them and the specific threats to validity they contain, which are considered in detail throughout the remainder of this book, it is possible to evaluate the findings of any research study, given sufficient information about it.

In fact, one is not limited to evaluating the findings of psychological research, although that is our main focus here. I use these principles almost every day as I read and hear about the findings of medical research, explanations for the state of our nation's economy, claims about the effectiveness of programs to reduce crime and drug use, ads for new products, and much more. Examples of the everyday use of methodological principles are described in some of the Thinking About Research boxes that can be found sprinkled throughout this book, beginning earlier in this chapter.

It can be difficult to keep straight all the separate issues that make up the complex question of validity. To make that a little bit easier, we will use a device called the **Validity Scorecard** (look ahead to the Quick Guide to Chapter 7 on page 210

TABLE 1.3   Threats to Conceptual Validity

 I. Threats to conceptual validity
          1. Unnecessary duplication
          2. Theoretical isolation
 II. Threats to construct validity
    A. The independent variable
       a. Inadequate operationalization
          3. Lack of reliability of the independent variable
          4. Lack of representativeness of the independent variable
          5. Lack of impact of the independent variable
       b. Treatment artifacts
          6. Demand characteristics in the research setting
          7. Experimenter expectancy effects on the behavior being observed
          8. Pretest sensitization to the treatments
    B. The dependent variable
       a. Inadequate operationalization
          9. Lack of reliability of the dependent variable
         10. Lack of representativeness of the dependent variable
         11. Lack of sensitivity of the dependent variable
       b. Measurement artifacts
         12. Strategic responding by the research participants
         13. Linguistic/cultural bias in the dependent measure
III. Threats to internal validity
         14. Extraneous effects (history)
         15. Temporal effects (maturation)
         16. Group composition effects (selection)
         17. Interaction of temporal and group composition effects
         18. Selective sample attrition (mortality)
         19. Statistical regression effects (regression to the mean)
IV. Threats to external validity
         20. Nonrepresentative sampling
         21. Nonrepresentative research context
 V. Threats to statistical conclusion validity
         22. Inappropriate use of statistical techniques
         23. Use of a statistical test lacking sufficient power
         24. Mistaking a trivial effect for support for the research hypothesis

for a preview of what it looks like). It converts the list of validity issues shown in Table 1.2 into a more user-friendly table. So far, we have considered only the first section of it— conceptual validity. Let's now move on to the rest.

Construct Validity

Following along in order through our model of the research process, the second area of concern about the validity of research findings has to do with how well the constructs in the hypothesis are operationalized as the independent and dependent variables.

This area of concern is labeled **construct validity**, although it is not the quality of the constructs themselves that is at issue here (that's the issue of conceptual validity), but how well the constructs have been adapted for a particular empirical study. Because the study is based directly on the independent and dependent variables, and only indirectly on the constructs, the quality of the variables obviously is very important.

Table 1.4 shows the threats to construct validity, again highlighted against the context of all the other threats to validity. You can probably tell just by looking at the table, and the fact that two chapters are devoted to construct validity, that this issue is complex. For one thing, both the causal and behavioral constructs in the research hypothesis must be operationalized, so both the independent and dependent variables must be evaluated for how well that process is planned or carried out. In addition, we will make that evaluation in two different ways.

First, we will consider how well several basic criteria of measurement are satisfied by the operational definitions of the independent and dependent variables. Second, we will evaluate each of the variables for the possibility that it is contaminated by unintended elements or **artifacts** as the result of its application in a particular research context.

Problems with measurement quality will be treated under the heading of **inadequate operationalization**. Both the independent and dependent variables can be compromised by a **lack of reliability**, meaning that they can lack stability or consistency over repeated administrations. A noisy lab where unpredictable distractions randomly alter the experience of some research participants and a poorly worded questionnaire that can be interpreted differently according to a participant's mood are two examples of potentially unreliable independent and dependent variables, respectively. Both variables can also suffer from a **lack of representativeness**, meaning that they can fail to measure some essential element(s) of their respective underlying constructs. A violent animated cartoon might be considered unrepresentative of TV violence in general, and a laboratory task in which electric shocks are delivered by remote control might be considered unrepresentative of aggression in general.

Finally, the independent variable may suffer from a **lack of impact**, so that its effects on participants are too weak to influence their behavior. A violent film that is so uninvolving that research participants pay little attention to the violence shown in it might not have sufficient impact to elicit more aggression than a nonviolent film, even if TV violence can cause aggression. The dependent variable may suffer from a **lack of sensitivity**, so that effects of the independent variable that might occur would go undetected. A playground supervised too closely by several intimidating adults might not provide the opportunity for aggression to be observed, even if aggression had been strongly instigated by a prior experience.

TABLE 1.4   Threats to Construct Validity

I. Threats to conceptual validity
       1. Unnecessary duplication
       2. Theoretical isolation
II. Threats to construct validity
  A. The independent variable
    a. Inadequate operationalization
      3. Lack of reliability of the independent variable
      4. Lack of representativeness of the independent variable
      5. Lack of impact of the independent variable
    b. Treatment artifacts
      6. Demand characteristics in the research setting
      7. Experimenter expectancy effects on the behavior being observed
      8. Pretest sensitization to the treatments
  B. The dependent variable
    a. Inadequate operationalization
      9. Lack of reliability of the dependent variable
      10. Lack of representativeness of the dependent variable
      11. Lack of sensitivity of the dependent variable
    b. Measurement artifacts
      12. Strategic responding by the research participants
      13. Linguistic/cultural bias in the dependent measure
III. Threats to internal validity
      14. Extraneous effects (history)
      15. Temporal effects (maturation)
      16. Group composition effects (selection)
      17. Interaction of temporal and group composition effects
      18. Selective sample attrition (mortality)
      19. Statistical regression effects (regression to the mean)
IV. Threats to external validity
      20. Nonrepresentative sampling
      21. Nonrepresentative research context
V. Threats to statistical conclusion validity
      22. Inappropriate use of statistical techniques
      23. Use of a statistical test lacking sufficient power
      24. Mistaking a trivial effect for support for the research hypothesis

Contamination by artifacts results in **confounding**. The independent variable can be confounded with three **treatment artifacts**. **Demand characteristics** can provide clues to the research hypothesis that influence research participants' behavior. **Experimenter expectancy effects** can also contaminate the dependent variable by providing unintended influence toward hypothesis confirmation

---

from the researcher. **Pretest sensitization** can distort the influence of the independent variable when the latter follows a preview of the behavioral measure used later to assess its effects.

The dependent variable can be confounded with two **measurement artifacts**. One is **strategic responding** on the part of research participants, who may seek to be helpful or to protect their self-esteem or self-image. The second is **linguistic/cultural bias**. Participants may fail to understand what is expected of them because of unfamiliar language or explanation.

| Box 1.3 | *THINKING ABOUT RESEARCH* |

Science Promotes a Healthy Skepticism

It seems clear that schoolchildren are endangered by the use of drugs. If they could be persuaded to resist peer pressure and other inducements to experiment with drugs that could hinder their development or get them in trouble with the law, how could anyone oppose an effort to do that? It's easy to see, then, why the D.A.R.E. program has become so popular.

Introduced in Los Angeles in 1983, D.A.R.E. (Drug Abuse Resistance Education) purports to discourage drug use among schoolchildren by educating them about the dangers of using drugs. Police officers visit schools to present students with information and to urge abstinence from drug use. More than 75% of the school districts in the United States have participated in the program, which currently costs hundreds of millions of dollars per year.

But does the program, however well-intentioned, really work? Or would the funds that are used to support it be better spent on new books, computers, or more teachers and smaller classes? The national council that oversees D.A.R.E., school administrators who authorize it, police departments that assign officers to it, and legislators who fund it believe wholeheartedly in the program's effectiveness. But does any or all of that make it so?

In 1998, a study conducted by researchers at the University of Illinois at Chicago compared the attitudes toward drugs and actual drug use among students who had been exposed to the D.A.R.E. program with a similar group who had not. They found no differences between the groups.

Does this mean that the D.A.R.E. program doesn't work? Think about the way the program was evaluated. Are there any reasons to be skeptical about the findings? Were these researchers claiming that they proved that the program doesn't work, and, if so, should we believe them?

How would you test the effectiveness of the D.A.R.E. program? Do you usually believe that programs work because the people who run those programs say they do? How should we evaluate government programs like D.A.R.E.? How do we? Why? Would these questions be any less appropriate if they were asked about corporate programs to increase worker motivation or management efficiency, or about university programs to improve the quality of higher education?

Research Design

After the independent and dependent variables have been created, following a consideration of and attempts to minimize the potential threats to construct validity for each, a research design must be chosen. That design will specify the participants who will be exposed to the treatments, as well as the times and places where the treatments will delivered. To test the hypothesis that exposure to televised violence causes viewers to behave more aggressively, one could ask a number of schoolchildren to list their favorite TV programs and ask their teachers how aggressive each of the children is. Alternatively, one could show a randomly chosen half of the students a violent cartoon program while the other half watch part of Disney's *Snow White*, then turn all the children loose on the playground and look for instances of aggressive behavior. Would the results of those different **research designs** (or any of the numerous other possibilities for testing the same hypothesis) shed equal light on the hypothesis?

Internal and External Validity

Two sets of criteria are commonly used to evaluate the implications of research design for the validity of research findings. They are referred to as potential threats to **internal validity** and **external validity**, labels provided by Campbell and Stanley way back in 1963. Every research design attempts to compare how two or more treatments or levels of the independent variable influence the dependent variable, with all other influences held constant. Those other influences, or **extraneous variables**, must be eliminated, or they must affect all the treatment groups equally if they are not to threaten the validity of the research findings.

Threats to internal validity are influences on the dependent variable, other than the independent variable, that the research design fails to hold constant. We will consider six types or categories of threats to internal validity (see Table 1.5). Threats to external validity are limitations on the generalizability of the research results beyond the subjects and research setting of a particular research study and, particularly, to the behavior in question as it occurs in its natural context.

Internal Validity

Research findings have internal validity to the extent that there is no reason to doubt that an observed difference among treatment groups, or relationship between independent and dependent variables, reflects a causal relationship. In other words, clear **causal inference** is achieved by eliminating threats to internal validity. Beginning in Chapter 5, we will examine in detail the six potential threats to internal validity that are listed in Table 1.5.

Extraneous events, or differences in **history**, are unintended influences on the dependent variable, besides the independent variable, that could affect the groups differently. For example, children who report preferences for violent TV programs and those who prefer nonviolent programs might have grown up in families that use different parenting styles, and those parenting styles might have influenced the children's level of aggressiveness and the TV programs they watch.

Temporal effects are changes affecting the dependent variable that are associated with the passage of time during the research study, in a manner similar to the

TABLE 1.5   Threats to Internal Validity

I. Threats to conceptual validity
       1. Unnecessary duplication
       2. Theoretical isolation
II. Threats to construct validity
  A. The independent variable
    a. Inadequate operationalization
       3. Lack of reliability of the independent variable
       4. Lack of representativeness of the independent variable
       5. Lack of impact of the independent variable
    b. Treatment artifacts
       6. Demand characteristics in the research setting
       7. Experimenter expectancy effects on the behavior being observed
       8. Pretest sensitization to the treatments
  B. The dependent variable
    a. Inadequate operationalization
       9. Lack of reliability of the dependent variable
      10. Lack of representativeness of the dependent variable
      11. Lack of sensitivity of the dependent variable
    b. Measurement artifacts
      12. Strategic responding by the research participants
      13. Linguistic/cultural bias in the dependent measure
III. Threats to internal validity
      14. Extraneous effects (history)
      15. Temporal effects (maturation)
      16. Group composition effects (selection)
      17. Interaction of temporal and group composition effects
      18. Selective sample attrition (mortality)
      19. Statistical regression effects (regression to the mean)
IV. Threats to external validity
      20. Nonrepresentative sampling
      21. Nonrepresentative research context
V. Threats to statistical conclusion validity
      22. Inappropriate use of statistical techniques
      23. Use of a statistical test lacking sufficient power
      24. Mistaking a trivial effect for support for the research hypothesis

effects of **maturation** on psychological development. An ongoing economic cycle might, for example, influence the incidence of violent crime in American society during the time that a research study evaluated the effect of a government policy requiring ratings for violent TV programs and TV sets to have a means of preventing children from watching violent programs (the "V-chip").

    Group composition effects occur when the **selection** of participants for the various treatment groups results in different types of people being exposed to different treatments. This can make it impossible to determine whether the differences in behavior among the groups, or lack of differences, reflected how much televised violence participants were exposed to or the pre-existing differences between the groups. Kids who watch violent TV programs might display more aggression toward their playmates because those who prefer violent programs have a more aggressive temperament that influences their behavior and their TV-watching habits.

An **interaction of temporal and group composition effects** would cause participants in different treatment groups to be influenced by different temporal cycles. Two large cities in different parts of the United States, one where there is an anticrime program of some sort and one where there isn't, might be quite similar in terms of occupations, education, and income at the beginning of a study of the effects of the anticrime program. They may be affected by different economic trends thereafter, however, so that one of the cities in a more depressed area would be compared to a second city that was experiencing better economic times. Thus, the populations that might have been "matched" for economic prosperity or unemployment rates at the beginning of the study might become "unmatched" by the end.

Selective sample attrition occurs when participants are lost from treatment groups through the course of a research study in ways that distort the picture of the research hypothesis given by the research results. One group of students might be shown violent TV programs during the same class period each day for 2 weeks, while another group watched programs containing no violence. Imagine that some members of the second group got so bored after a while that they began to cut class rather than watch more episodes of *The Brady Bunch*. They would also miss the session afterward during which aggressive behavior is measured. Their absence when the dependent variable finally was measured might make their group seem less aggressive than it really was. In that case, the TV programs or treatments would appear to be the cause of a difference in aggression between the groups when, in fact, an emergent difference between the students in the groups caused by selective loss or **mortality** of participants in one of the groups was the real cause.

Finally, **regression to the mean**, which will require more thorough explanation later, can occur when a large group of participants is tested to select the highest and/or lowest ones for participation in a research study. Later, after some treatments are administered, the same test might be administered as the dependent variable. The highest and lowest scorers on any test are the beneficiaries and victims, respectively, of random factors that influence scores on the test. When they take the test again, their scores are likely to "regress," or become less extreme and closer to the overall population mean. These **statistical regression effects** might then be mistaken for the effects of the treatments to which the groups were exposed, making the results of the study difficult to interpret.

Each of the six potential threats to internal validity involves selective effects across the groups or occasions being compared. Any influence on the behavior in question, intended or not, that affects equally all groups or occasions being compared is effectively held constant, just as if it hadn't occurred at all. Having equal effects means that a comparison among the effects of the treatments won't be affected, the extraneous effects canceling out each other. It is only selective effects, effects that occur in one group or on one occasion but not others, that we need to worry about. Selective effects of extraneous factors can be mistaken for effects of treatments or can cover up treatment effects. Internal validity depends on being certain that observed differences in behavior between participants exposed to different treatment were caused by differences in the treatments and nothing else. In other words, extraneous factors can interfere with valid causal inference.

External Validity

External validity, in brief, is about generalizability of research findings. The constructs in a research hypothesis have to be operationalized as the independent variable and dependent variable, as we have seen. A sample of participants and a setting and task must be selected as well. As a result, whatever is learned about the causes of the behavior in question in a research study is learned in a very specific mix of those elements.

The conclusions drawn about the research hypothesis from the results of the study—the research findings—have external validity to the extent that they hold under conditions different from those in the study itself. External validity is threatened, then, when the research findings are based on **nonrepresentative sample of units** (participants) and/or when they are derived from a **nonrepresentative research context**. In either case, doubt is cast on attempts to generalize the findings.

This is a very brief statement of a complex issue. The definition of external validity on which our analysis of research will be based requires a good deal more discussion. That discussion will be found in Chapter 5.

Statistical Conclusion Validity

Once the research results are in, after observations have been made under the conditions specified by the research design for the samples selected, the next step is statistical analysis. This usually starts with tabulation of the scores (numbers), treatment group by treatment group. Then **descriptive statistics** are used to summarize the data. The group **mean** (average) and **standard deviation** (measure of the range of scores, or the degree of variability around the mean) are the most common ways to do that. Finally, **inferential statistics** are used to compare

TABLE 1.6   Threats to External Validity

I. Threats to conceptual validity
        1. Unnecessary duplication
        2. Theoretical isolation
II. Threats to construct validity
  A. The independent variable
    a. Inadequate operationalization
        3. Lack of reliability of the independent variable
        4. Lack of representativeness of the independent variable
        5. Lack of impact of the independent variable
    b. Treatment artifacts
        6. Demand characteristics in the research setting
        7. Experimenter expectancy effects on the behavior being observed
        8. Pretest sensitization to the treatments
  B. The dependent variable
    a. Inadequate operationalization
        9. Lack of reliability of the dependent variable
      10. Lack of representativeness of the dependent variable
      11. Lack of sensitivity of the dependent variable
    b. Measurement artifacts
      12. Strategic responding by the research participants
      13. Linguistic/cultural bias in the dependent measure
III. Threats to internal validity
      14. Extraneous effects (history)
      15. Temporal effects (maturation)
      16. Group composition effects (selection)
      17. Interaction of temporal and group composition effects
      18. Selective sample attrition (mortality)
      19. Statistical regression effects (regression to the mean)
IV. Threats to external validity
      20. Nonrepresentative sampling
      21. Nonrepresentative research context
V. Threats to statistical conclusion validity
      22. Inappropriate use of statistical techniques
      23. Use of a statistical test lacking sufficient power
      24. Mistaking a trivial effect for support for the research hypothesis

groups or to evaluate the strength of the relationship between the independent and dependent variables.

At each step in the statistical analysis, a researcher is again faced with choices about how to proceed. We are fortunate that mathematicians have supplied us with a large number of useful statistics, but this bountiful variety presents a researcher with a more complex set of choices. The same data may lead to different

TABLE 1.7   Threats to Statistical Conclusion Validity

I. Threats to conceptual validity
       1. Unnecessary duplication
       2. Theoretical isolation
II. Threats to construct validity
  A. The independent variable
    a. Inadequate operationalization
       3. Lack of reliability of the independent variable
       4. Lack of representativeness of the independent variable
       5. Lack of impact of the independent variable
    b. Treatment artifacts
       6. Demand characteristics in the research setting
       7. Experimenter expectancy effects on the behavior being observed
       8. Pretest sensitization to the treatments
  B. The dependent variable
    a. Inadequate operationalization
       9. Lack of reliability of the dependent variable
      10. Lack of representativeness of the dependent variable
      11. Lack of sensitivity of the dependent variable
    b. Measurement artifacts
      12. Strategic responding by the research participants
      13. Linguistic/cultural bias in the dependent measure
III. Threats to internal validity
      14. Extraneous effects (history)
      15. Temporal effects (maturation)
      16. Group composition effects (selection)
      17. Interaction of temporal and group composition effects
      18. Selective sample attrition (mortality)
      19. Statistical regression effects (regression to the mean)
IV. Threats to external validity
      20. Nonrepresentative sampling
      21. Nonrepresentative research context
V. Threats to statistical conclusion validity
      22. Inappropriate use of statistical techniques
      23. Use of a statistical test lacking sufficient power
      24. Mistaking a trivial effect for support for the research hypothesis

conclusions about the research hypothesis depending on how those data are analyzed. The quality of the researcher's choices will determine the **statistical conclusion validity** of the research findings, or the degree to which the statistical analysis leads the researcher toward a correct conclusion about the truth of the research hypothesis. We will examine the quality of those choices in terms of three separate threats to statistical conclusion validity (see Table 1.7).

First, a researcher must choose a **statistical technique**. For example, the results of a study based on ratings of violence in children's favorite TV shows (the independent variable) and teachers' ratings of the children's aggressiveness (the dependent variable) could be analyzed in at least two ways. A correlation coefficient could be computed to show the relationship for the sample (e.g., +.58 or −.61). Alternatively, the children could be divided into groups with low, medium, and high tastes for violence, and those groups' average levels of aggressiveness could be compared to see whether they differ in the way that the hypothesis would lead one to expect they would.

That choice between two statistical techniques, correlation and group comparison, might make a difference in the conclusion one would draw from the results. The same data could lead to different findings. We'll be able to delve deeper into the consequences of making an inappropriate choice of a statistical technique later, after we've become more familiar with research design (the two topics are related).

Each of the descriptive and inferential statistical techniques that is available to psychological researchers makes some assumptions about the nature of the numbers that are being analyzed. For example, correlation requires that the sample of children involved display considerable variation on both the independent and dependent variables. If they were all rated just moderately aggressive, the correlation coefficient wouldn't "work." This violation of test assumptions (or any other) would seriously call into question any conclusion about the research hypothesis based on the correlation coefficient that was computed. A researcher can eliminate the threat of **inappropriate use of statistical techniques** both by choosing a statistical technique that is appropriate to the research design used in a particular study and by making sure that the assumptions about the measures being analyzed are satisfied by the data from that study.

A second threat to statistical conclusion validity concerns the way inferential statistics are used. The researcher who performs inferential statistical tests on research data must choose both a level of probabilistic certainty against which the results are evaluated and the size of the sample on which that evaluation is based. Both of those decisions are critical to avoiding the **use of a statistical test lacking sufficient power** to detect evidence for the research hypothesis when such evidence is present in the research results.

Finally, statistical tests don't tell us directly how large any of the differences are, if there are any. By **mistaking a trivial effect for support of the research hypothesis**, we may end up making an erroneous evaluation of the hypothesis. If TV violence makes a small difference, our findings have a different meaning than if it makes a great difference, especially if we need to make a political decision about how to weigh the danger of TV violence against a loss of constitutional freedom of expression, or even an economic decision about the value of the V-chip (although in other kinds of research these might be less important issues).

| Box 1.4 | *THINKING ABOUT RESEARCH* |

Psychological Research Can Have Personal Consequences _____

One of the most important decisions any person can make in his or her lifetime is about having children. The decision not to have children, or not to have more children, not only influences a person's posterity, but also, if that person is in a heterosexual relationship, entails a choice among methods of birth control. For a woman, this could mean the use of birth control medication (hormones) or tubal ligation. For a man, it could mean the use of condoms or surgical vasectomy. In addition, such a choice may create tensions in the relationship.

Bill McKibben, a best-selling author on various environmental subjects, decided with his wife to stop having children after their first, a daughter. Although McKibben's choice to have a vasectomy is somewhat unusual, because most couples choose other means of birth control, the McKibbens' decision is perhaps even more unusual for the decision process they followed in making the decision to have no more children.

In his recent book, *Maybe One*, Bill McKibben (1998) describes how he and his wife decided whether the environmental benefits of a decision to have only one child, their initial motivation, might be offset by negative effects on the psychological development of their daughter. A strong factor in their decision was the research literature the McKibbens found on the psychological development of only children. Only when they were satisfied, on the basis of their review of that research, that only children were just as well adjusted and successful as children reared with siblings did the McKibbens decide to have no more children.

Do you think it makes sense for people to make personal decisions on the basis of psychological research? As a student of psychology yourself, do you ever do so, or think that you might do so someday? Do you know of any examples of psychological research exerting a widespread influence on how people live their lives? Whether or not you know of an example, does such influence seem sensible or desirable to you? If so, could that make this book and this course more valuable to you?

THREATS TO VALIDITY AS QUESTIONS ●

At this point, we have a thumbnail sketch of the ways in which the choices made during the research process can affect the research findings. We will always have results—the data collected through observation of participants' behavior. The conclusions drawn from those results—the research findings—depend on the nature of the methods used to produce them.

We can't hope to understand the full meaning of all these issues at this point. The remainder of this book contains detailed explanations of each of these issues,

TABLE 1.8   Threats to the Validity of Research Findings in Question Form

   I. Conceptual validity (formulating the hypothesis): How much will an answer to the question posed in the hypothesis contribute to our understanding of the behavior in question?

  II. Construct validity (operationalizing cause and effect): How well do the independent and dependent variables studied in the research represent the constructs contained in the hypothesis?

 III. Internal validity (arranging comparisons): How certain can we be that any differences observed in the behavior of the treatment groups, or on different occasions, were caused by variations in the independent variable (the treatments themselves)?

 IV. External validity (arranging comparisons): How generalizable are the research results beyond the specific samples and context in which the research was carried out?

  V. Statistical conclusion validity (analyzing the results): How well does the statistical analysis that was carried out portray the research results?

including many nuances and examples that obviously would not fit in this introductory chapter. That information, together with your personal thoughts and discussions with your instructor and classmates, will help you to build a more robust understanding of this issue that will enable you to pursue your own ideas for research and to evaluate research done by others that is relevant to your work and your life. At this point, we have a blueprint that we can follow to build a strong and permanent structure.

Before we move on to do that, however, we're going to draw a slightly different picture of the research process. Perhaps, as architects use both floor plans and elevations to give their clients a better idea of what a structure will look like, we can combine different types of pictures of the research process to get a better idea of the structure we are going to be building during this course.

So far, the choices to be made during each of the steps in the research process have been discussed in terms of the threats to validity they pose. Because these are choices that researchers need to make in the course of planning a study, or that readers need to evaluate in deciding what to make of a study, these issues might be clarified somewhat further at this point if they were restated in the form of questions that researchers or readers might ask themselves in considering the variety of issues that contribute to the overall validity of research findings. Some examples of such questions are listed in Table 1.8, as alternatives to the label-based versions in Table 1.2. At this point, we will limit ourselves to the five major categories of validity issues. Later, as we deal with all 24 specific threats to validity in depth, you might try turning each of them into a question yourself. It might help you to better understand what they mean.

Review Questions and Exercise

Review Questions

1. What are the individual steps in the research process, and what happens during each one?

2. What does validity mean? What is a threat to validity?

3. What specific questions about validity, or threats to validity, are tied to the individual steps in the research process, and why?

Exercise

In your college library, or online if you have such access, find and read an interesting article in a recent psychological journal. Can you identify the steps the researcher(s) went through, the decisions they made, and the answers at which they arrived, at the various steps in the research process? What are the validity issues that are raised in this study?

FORMULATING THE RESEARCH HYPOTHESIS

● A QUICK GUIDE TO CHAPTER 2: THE HYPOTHESIS

The first step in the research process is formulating the **research hypothesis**. In psychology, the hypothesis usually ties together two **constructs**. In reverse order, the constructs are, first, some behavior of interest to the researcher and, second, its suspected or putative cause (later, as we've seen already, to become the dependent and independent variables, respectively). The constructs are tied together in a causal assertion; in our well-worn example, "exposure to televised violence causes aggression."

There is an important distinction to be made between formulating a hypothesis and choosing one. Although a researcher often becomes interested in a question about human behavior for personal reasons, the ultimate value of a research study depends on the researcher bringing methodological criteria to bear on the selection of the hypothesis to be tested. Good hypotheses, in other words, are made, not born.

A researcher's interest may arise out of a significant event in his or her life, or from reading about historical events or events in someone else's life, or it might be based on knowledge about previous research, whether his or her own or someone else's. That interest may provide the motivation to undertake the difficult work of conducting a research study, but it does not guarantee that the study is original or that it makes an important contribution to existing knowledge about the causes of the behavior in question.

The overall judgment of the quality of a research hypothesis is a judgment about its **conceptual validity**. Within that overall judgment are nested two constituent judgments about specific threats to conceptual validity. One concerns the question of whether the hypothesis avoids **unnecessary duplication** of previous research on the same question. The second evaluates the undesirable likelihood that the eventual research findings will stand in **theoretical isolation** from past research on the question.

The means of answering both those questions lies in the **literature review**. By determining what research already has been done, a researcher has a basis for judging what most needs to be done next. By presenting his or her documented argument in the introduction to the report of a completed study, the researcher makes it possible for the reader to make the same judgment independently. Fortunately, there are electronic retrieval systems available that make it possible to conduct an efficient search of the vast archives of published psychological research.

The Chapter 2 Quick Guide shows the structure of a research hypothesis, the potential threats to conceptual validity, and the means of improving or evaluating the latter.

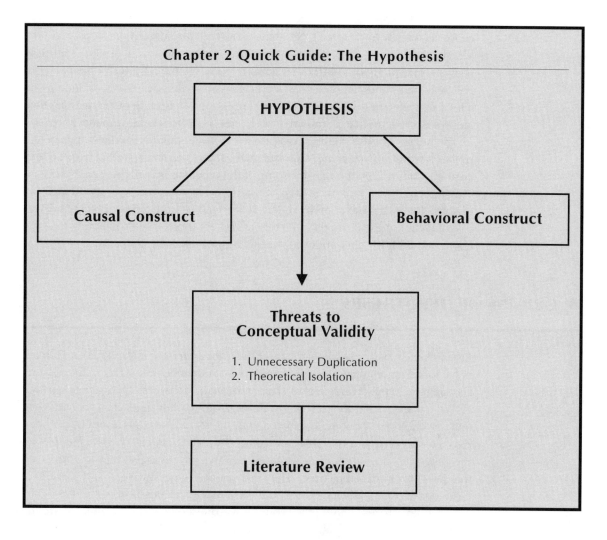

Chapter 2 Quick Guide: The Hypothesis

HYPOTHESIS

Causal Construct

Behavioral Construct

Threats to
Conceptual Validity

1. Unnecessary Duplication
2. Theoretical Isolation

Literature Review

INTRODUCTION TO THE CHAPTER ●

Computer software engineers are fond of the saying, "garbage in, garbage out" (it sometimes appears in print as GIGO, which can be pronounced "gee-go"). By GIGO, they mean that no matter how well a computer program works, if you use it to analyze faulty input (garbage), your output will be correspondingly useless (garbage).

The same logic could be applied to the research process. In the case of research, it would stress the primary importance of the research hypothesis. Research almost always starts with an idea that links some behavior with a possible cause, as we saw in Chapter 1. No matter how well the subsequent steps in the research process are carried out—operationalization, research design, statistical analysis, interpretation—without a good hypothesis, the findings of the research will be of little value. Finding out a lot that someone already knows, or finding out a lot about something that no one else cares about, or finding out something that ignores everything that is known already, are all hollow achievements at best.

The purpose of this chapter is to provide some guidelines for developing a hypothesis worth investigating. Unfortunately, such guidelines are likely to be less clear-cut than will be the case for some of the other steps in the research process. This first and very important step is one that has received less attention from methodologists to date than the others. It is arguably more a matter of art and less one of technical expertise than the others are, but there is still something to learn about and a lot to think about for the student of research methods.

● ORIGINS OF HYPOTHESES

Researchers in psychology get ideas for their research from many sources. Human behavior is something we see all around us—our own behavior, that of friends and acquaintances, the diverse cast of characters on the TV news, writers' fictional and real characters whom we get to know through our reading, and so on. To some extent, psychologists become fascinated with the same questions about human behavior as any other curious observer would. We are all interested in why people do the things they do, although, as we'll see, research psychologists may try to answer the questions in different ways. They use science to get answers, and use it in a more knowledgeable way than would the average curious observer.

Psychologists also have other sources for questions about behavior than are available to the general public. They read their own professional literature. There are articles in professional journals that report the results of research studies and occasionally propose theories that seek to organize and explain whole bodies of research. There are also edited books in which experts summarize and organize research studies addressed to specific questions about human behavior or specific psychological theories and sometimes attempt to build new theories or refine existing theories to explain them. Some psychologists' work gives them opportunities to observe the behavior of people with emotional problems, people who work in corporations that have organizational problems, husbands and wives trying to save their marriages, children having learning difficulties in school, and the many other clients served by the practitioners of psychology. Still others observe people and nonhuman animals who participate in their research studies.

In all, it is possible to identify at least seven sources of hypotheses for psychological research that may be used separately or in combination. They are

1. personal observation,

2. other people's experiences,

3. psychological theory,

4. previous research,

5. serendipitous research results,

6. new technologies, and

7. the need to solve practical problems.

In this chapter, or at least for the bulk of it, we will be considering some examples of each of these sources. As we go along, the examples will be numbered sequentially. For example, the first will be numbered **E1** for exemplar study number one. Table 2.1 shows the seven sources for hypotheses and the examples of each, including detailed references in the "APA style," the citation system promoted by the American Psychological Association and used fairly broadly in the social and behavioral sciences.

Sources of Hypotheses and Exemplar Studies

Personal Observation

Whether in their day-to-day lives as family members and citizens, or in their professional roles, psychologists observe at first hand examples of human behavior that inspire them to ask questions about the causes of human behavior that can be addressed by scientific research. Their observations raise preliminary questions about the causes of behavior that can then be developed into fruitful research hypotheses.

Julian Rotter (**E1**) was a prominent personality psychologist who based some of his best-known research on observations he made of clients he treated in psychotherapy. Some of those clients discussed disturbing events in their lives, such as breakups of important relationships, as if their own behavior had nothing to do with what happened. Using his knowledge of B. F. Skinner's principles of reinforcement as a base (and the more one knows about human behavior to start with, including psychological research and theory, the easier it is to formulate an insightful research hypothesis from personal observation or any other source), Rotter hypothesized a personality dimension that came to be known as locus of control, or I-E (for internal-external control).

Rotter developed a questionnaire, the I-E Scale, to measure people's standing along that dimension, and then he and others did hundreds of studies in which they demonstrated relationships between locus of control and specific patterns of behavior. For example, people toward the internal end, or "internals," who believe that they control the outcomes in their lives, were found to know more about their

TABLE 2.1 Sources of Research Hypotheses and Exemplar Studies

A. Personal observation

(E1) Rotter, J. B. (1966). Generalized expectancies for internal vs. external control of reinforcement. *Psychological Monographs, 80,* 1-28.

(E2) Friedman, M., & Rosenman, R. H. (1959). Association of specific overt behavior pattern with blood and cardiovascular findings. *Journal of the American Medical Association, 169,* 1286-1296.

(E3) Triplett, N. (1897). The dynamogenic factors in pacemaking and competition. *American Journal of Psychology, 9,* 507-533.

(E4) Aserinsky, E., & Kleitman, N. (1953). Regularly occurring periods of eye mobility and concomitant phenomena during sleep. *Science, 118,* 273-274.

(E5) Broverman, I. K., Vogel, S. R., Broverman, D. M., Clarkson, F. E., & Rosenkrantz, P. S. (1972). Sex-role stereotypes: A current appraisal. *Journal of Social Issues, 28*(2), 59-78.

(E6) Clark, K. B., & Clark, M. K. (1940). Skin color as a factor in racial identification of Negro preschool children. *Journal of Social Psychology, 11,* 159-169.

B. Other people's experiences

(E7) Darley, J. M., & Latané, B. (1968). Bystander intervention in emergencies: Diffusion of responsibility. *Journal of Personality and Social Psychology, 8,* 377-383.

(E8) Ceci, S. J., Loftus, E. F., Leichtman, M. D., & Bruck, M. (1994). The possible role of source misattributions in the creation of false beliefs among preschoolers. *Journal of Clinical and Experimental Hypnosis, 42,* 304-320.

(E9) Milgram, S. (1974). *Obedience to authority.* New York: Harper & Row.

C. Psychological theory

(E10) MacRae, J. R., Scoles, M. I., & Siegel, S. (1987). The contribution of Pavlovian conditioning to drug tolerance and dependence. *British Journal of Addiction, 82,* 371-380.

(E11) Festinger, L., Riecken, H., & Schachter, S. (1956). *When prophecy fails.* Minneapolis: University of Minnesota Press.

(E12) Harlow, H. F. (1958). The nature of love. *American Psychologist, 13,* 673-685.

(E13) Cartwright, R. D. (1974). The influence of a conscious wish on dreams: A methodological study of dream meaning and function. *Journal of Abnormal Psychology, 83,* 387-393.

D. Previous research

(E14) Dement, W. (1960). The effect of dream deprivation. *Science, 131,* 1705-1707.

(E15) Rosenthal, R., & Jacobson, L. (1966). Teachers' expectancies: Determinants of pupils' IQ gains. *Psychological Reports, 19,* 115-118.

(E16) Zajonc, R. B., & Markus, G. B. (1975). Birth order and intellectual development. *Psychological Review, 82,* 74-88.

illnesses as patients in a hospital and to prefer games of skill to games of chance, at least compared to "externals."

E. Serendipitous research results

(E17) Cherulnik, P. D., Way, J. H., Ames, S., & Hutto, D. B. (1981). Impressions of high and low Machiavellian men. *Journal of Personality, 49,* 388-400.

(E18) Seligman, M.E.P., & Maier, S. F. (1967). Failure to escape traumatic shock. *Journal of Experimental Psychology, 74,* 1-9.

(E19) Calhoun, J. B. (1962). Population density and social pathology. *Scientific American, 206,* 139-148.

(E20) Pavlov, I. P. (1927). *Conditioned reflexes.* London: Oxford University Press.

F. New technologies

(E21) Gazzaniga, M. S. (1967). The split brain in man. *Scientific American, 217*(2), 24-29.

(E22) Rosenzweig, M. R., Bennett, E. L., & Diamond, M. C. (1972). Brain changes in response to experience. *Scientific American, 226*(2), 22-29.

(E23) Haier, R. J., Siegel, B., Tang, C., Abel, L., & Buchsbaum, M. S. (1992). Intelligence and changes in regional cerebral glucose metabolic rate following learning. *Intelligence, 16,* 415-426.

G. The need to solve practical problems

(E24) Smith, M. L., & Glass, G. V. (1977). Meta-analysis of psychotherapy outcome studies. *American Psychologist, 32,* 752-760.

(E25) Frazier, F. W. (1985). *A postoccupancy evaluation of Contra Costa County's Main Detention Facility: An analysis of the first new-generation, modular, direct supervision county jail.* Unpublished doctoral dissertation, Golden Gate University, San Francisco.

Meyer Friedman is a cardiologist. One would expect that his observations, like those of most doctors, are probably focused mainly on his patients' physical symptoms and test results. When Friedman's upholsterer pointed out to him that the front edges of the chair seats in his waiting room had worn out very quickly, that suggested a research hypothesis to him that has subsequently generated many important studies. It led him to question whether his patients' heart problems might not be caused, in part at least, by a tendency to be so tense that they literally sit on the edges of their chairs.

That hypothesis led eventually to the discovery of the Type A personality. **Friedman and Rosenman (E2)** found a cluster of psychological characteristics—including competitiveness, sensitivity to time pressure, and hostility toward people perceived to be obstacles to goal attainment—that was related to a patient's likelihood of suffering a second heart attack.

Norman Triplett (E3) is credited in many textbooks with having published the first research article in the history of the field of social psychology, during the late 1890s. Triplett's hypothesis for that research was that persons working at a task in the presence of other persons performing the same task will work harder than if they were working alone. He developed the hypothesis from his observation that participants in bicycle racing, a personal interest of his and a popular sport at the time, raced faster when racing with or against others than when racing alone against the clock.

Triplett tested his hypothesis in a laboratory experiment, having college students turn a fishing reel as fast as they could, randomly alternating sessions where they worked alone with sessions in which two subjects worked side-by-side. For reasons we'll consider at length in a later chapter, the evidence from that controlled experiment that subjects would work harder in the presence of another worker was more persuasive than the results of bicycle races in which solitary racers might have been slower because they were less motivated to work hard, as Triplett thought, or because they were not such good athletes in the first place, or for some other reason.

In 1952, Eugene Aserinsky was a graduate student in psychology who spent a good deal of his time watching babies sleep in his research laboratory. One thing that caught his eye was that periodically the babies' eyes seemed to move rapidly beneath their eyelids, scanning up and down and side to side. Based on his observations, he hypothesized that those eye movements, referred to today as rapid eye movements or REM, accompanied repeated episodes of dreaming.

Aserinsky and Kleitman (E4) later tested that hypothesis by waking adult subjects in a sleep laboratory during randomly chosen periods of REM and non-REM sleep (identified through continuous electroencephalograph, or EEG, recordings). They found, as they had predicted, that those woken during REM sleep were much more likely to report that they were in the middle of a dream at the time than were those woken during non-REM sleep.

All of us probably think from time to time about the possible causes of behavior we observe directly. The examples we've just reviewed suggest that personal observations inspire many of the hypotheses that psychologists test in their research. Again, psychologists get opportunities to observe behavior—as therapists and researchers—that other people do not. Psychologists know things about behavior that may lead them to see different things than other people do even in ordinary settings—as in Triplett's take on the bicycle races of which he and many others of his day were so fond.

In addition to the cases where we know that the researcher's hypothesis arose from a personal observation, there are undoubtedly many others for which we have no certain knowledge but the inference that it did seems reasonable. Could **Inge Broverman's (E5)** research documenting gender-role stereotypes not have been stimulated to some degree by her own experiences as a woman? Or could **Kenneth and Mamie Clark's (E6)** classic study showing that black children preferred white dolls have been motivated by their personal experiences as African Americans?

Other People's Experiences

Many good hypotheses for psychological research are natural outgrowths of psychologists' interests in the world around them. An interest in the causes of human behavior often leads research psychologists to follow current events, to read about the lives of interesting people, and to seek out other sources of information where they can apply their theories or test them.

One of the best-known studies in social psychology arose in just that way. In 1964, in New York City, a young woman named Kitty Genovese was brutally murdered outside her home in a middle-class neighborhood. In the intense glare of the New York media spotlight, her story became a symbol of all that Americans feared was going wrong with our increasingly urbanized society.

One of the most noticed facts of the Genovese case was that the police investigation of the murder uncovered 38 witnesses to the crime, neighbors of the victim, none of whom had done anything to help her, not even call the police. When they heard about this, researchers **John Darley and Bibb Latané (E7)** formulated a hypothesis about why no one had helped. Borrowing the concept of "diffusion of responsibility" from other research in social psychology, they tested the idea that the more people who witnessed an emergency, the less likely any individual bystander would be to take responsibility for helping the victim.

They conducted a controlled laboratory experiment in which participants were led to believe that they heard someone having an epileptic seizure over an intercom from another room. That study found that the more other bystanders a participant believed there to be, listening in other rooms, the longer it took the participant to act and the lower the probability he or she would act at all.

Cognitive psychologist **Stephen Ceci (E8)** became intrigued with reports that adult women who were being treated in psychotherapy for a variety of problems, from obesity to depression, had recalled instances from their childhood where they had been sexually abused. These memories were characterized as repressed because they seemed to have been retrieved for the first time long after the incidents occurred, in some cases after several decades. These reports led Ceci and some of his colleagues to formulate the skeptical hypothesis that some of those memories might actually have been created by leading questions asked by psychotherapists who had developed their own hypotheses about the causes of their clients' problems.

Ceci's hypothesis has given rise to several studies. In one with children, a brief structured meeting with each child was followed up with an interview shortly afterward. In the course of asking the child about events that actually took place during the initial meeting, the experimenter asked a question about something that never really happened. Without much coaxing, the child typically "remembered" the fictitious event and then, in response to further probing, supplied specific, even vivid, details about it that had never even been suggested by the interviewer.

A well-known series of studies by social psychologist **Stanley Milgram (E9)** illustrates how an interest in historical events can stimulate research hypotheses. These studies, known well enough outside the field to have been portrayed in *The Tenth Level*, a 1976 television movie starring William Shatner, arose out of Milgram's curiosity about the reasons for the widespread participation of ordinary German citizens in the crimes perpetrated by the Nazis during the 1930s and 1940s. What circumstances could have caused those people to do the terrible things their government asked of them?

Milgram hypothesized that obedience should be expected when it is demanded by someone in a position of authority. Under those conditions, people might rely on the judgment of someone in authority to the point of abandoning their own personal standards of right and wrong. In Milgram's experiments, a large number and broad spectrum of ordinary Americans followed a lab-coated researcher's orders. They delivered severe electric shocks to an innocent fellow participant in order, according to their instructions, to further research on the effects of punishment or learning. Of course, no one was really shocked because the experiments were elaborate ruses to create false perceptions by the participants, but many wondered afterward whether the suffering on the part of the participants themselves, as they were obediently delivering the shocks, reported in great detail by Milgram, was justified.

These are just a few examples of the numerous cases in which important research hypotheses have arisen out of researchers' exposure to events in other people's lives. Although much of this research is developed in ways that tie it to existing research and theory, its original impetus—for reasons I'll expand on later in this chapter—comes from the dramatic events in ordinary people's lives as portrayed in the media and in books on history and biography.

Psychological Theory

There is good reason to argue, as I will argue later in this chapter, that building accurate theories of human behavior is one of the most important reasons for conducting psychological research. As published research studies proliferate, at the rate of many thousands per year, there is an increasing need to organize research findings and to provide direction for future research so that knowledge in the field is cumulative rather than confusing. That is the main function of theory, although I will have more to say about that later (for example, see the Thinking About Research Box 2.1 on page 47).

One of the oldest theories in psychology is Pavlov's (1927) analysis of classical or respondent conditioning. Pavlov explained how a dog could come to salivate at the sound of a bell through the repeated association of the bell with food. His theory labeled the bell and food as conditioned and unconditioned stimuli, and salivation in response to those stimuli as conditioned and unconditioned responses, respectively. Pavlov's theory provided a framework that can still be used today as the basis for investigating a wide variety of behaviors.

In fact, almost a century later, **Shepard Siegel and his colleagues (E10)** developed a program of research to investigate drug addiction that was based on Pavlov's theory. They injected rats with morphine and measured their responses to painful heat. That research showed that tolerance for drugs and withdrawal symptoms following addiction are both based on conditioned responses to the drug, at least in the case of the opiates. The body's struggle for homeostasis works against the anticipated physiological effects of the drug. It lessens the drug effect in the case of tolerance, and it creates the painful withdrawal symptoms that occur when the drug is anticipated but not received.

In the 1950s, Leon Festinger published his theory of cognitive dissonance. The theory held that a person felt discomfort as a result of entertaining mutually contradictory ideas; for example, believing that cigarette smoking is harmful but knowing that one is nevertheless a smoker. That discomfort, or dissonance, according to the theory, led to attempts to eliminate the contradiction by forgetting selectively or distorting information, or by a variety of other means.

Festinger and some of his students (E11) heard through the news media of a cult in Minnesota whose members believed that the end of the world was near but that they would be rescued from its destruction by extraterrestrials because of their faith. They planned a test of cognitive dissonance theory around that event. Assuming that the world would not really end, the researchers expected that the cult members' expectations that it would and the contradictory reality that it hadn't would cause them to experience dissonance. They predicted that rather than give up their beliefs, the cult members would reduce dissonance by convincing themselves even more strongly that they were correct (just mistaken about the date?) and by trying to recruit new converts whose faith would serve to bolster their own. That basically is what happened.

The epitome of theory-based research is the "critical experiment." That is a study that promises to provide evidence that would make it possible to choose among competing theories that explain the same phenomenon. In the 1950s, **Harry Harlow (E12)** conducted a series of studies with rhesus monkeys to investigate the basis for mother-infant bonds. His research was planned to pit two theories against one another: a theory that infants were drawn to their mothers by biological instinct and a theory that nourishment from the mother's breast reinforced the infant's attachment to her.

He took infant rhesus from their mothers and arranged for them to be reared by human caregivers instead. Once they were weaned, they lived in cages with wire figures that Harlow called "surrogate mothers" (see Figure 2.1). In one experiment, the infants were provided with a choice between two surrogate mothers. One bare

Figure 2.1. A photograph of a rhesus monkey clinging to a cloth-covered "surrogate mother" used by Harry Harlow in his research comparing reinforcement and instinct explanations for mother-child bonds.
SOURCE: Reprinted from *From Learning to Love*, Figure 8-6 (p. 110), Harlow, © copyright 1986 by Greenwood Publishers. Reprinted with permission of Greenwood Publishing Group, Inc., Westport, CT.

wire figure "fed" them via a baby bottle inserted in an opening in its "chest." The other was covered with soft terry cloth that reflected the infant's body heat but held no bottle.

Through the infants' preferences between the two figures, Harlow hoped to test the two competing theories of infant-mother attachment. If the infant preferred the feeding surrogate, the one with the bottle, that would be evidence for the secondary reinforcement theory, which held that an infant's love for its mother arose out of an association between the mother and gratification of hunger. If the infant preferred the terry cloth surrogate, that would be evidence for an innate need for contact comfort. In the end, contact comfort proved more important, as the monkeys stayed on the bare wire feeder only long enough to empty the bottle, and otherwise clung to the warm, cloth-covered "mother."

Rosalind Cartwright (E13) performed another critical experiment, this one to compare three different theories about the meanings of dreams. She woke sleeping subjects during REM sleep to question them about the content of their dreams. In sorting the dreams out, she counted the numbers of those that seemed to reflect unfulfilled wishes or repressed fears, in line with Sigmund Freud's theory about the symbolic functions of dreams; and she counted those that seemed to serve the function of mental housekeeping, dealing with unfinished business of the day, as a theory by Francis Crick and Graeme Mitchison predicted. Cartwright also counted those that seemed merely an extension of waking thought, as she herself had predicted. Not too surprisingly, the content of the dreams Cartwright's subjects reported supported Cartwright's own theory about the function of dreams.

These examples show how theories can provide researchers with hypotheses. Theories provide ways of understanding the causes of behaviors of interest so that empirical studies can be designed to learn more about them, as in the case of Siegel's work on drug addiction and Festinger's on beliefs of cult members. They also stimulate research that can provide evidence that allows us to choose among competing theories, as in Harlow's and Cartwright's research, so that future research can be based on even better theories, each time moving science a step farther than it had gone before.

Previous Research

Most researchers spend more time reading about the results of others' research than in doing their own. In keeping up with the literature in a particular field of study, researchers learn that certain questions they might be interested in have already been answered, that new methods have been invented to investigate those questions, or that new theories have been developed to explain what is known about them. They also get ideas about what questions they might want to try to answer in their own research. Sometimes minor changes to past studies promise to make important contributions to the field. That might involve studying different types of participants, measuring the behavior in different ways, using different research designs, or pursuing some other variation on the original theme. Other times, entirely new lines of investigation are suggested by the results of a past study.

Aserinsky and Kleitman's finding that REM sleep was associated with dreaming, from the study in which they woke sleeping subjects (**E4**), led researcher **William Dement (E14)** to hypothesize that REM sleep and dreaming were necessary for people to function normally. He tested his hypothesis in a study in which sleeping subjects were awakened every time they entered REM sleep. After three to seven nights of being deprived virtually entirely of REM sleep, Dement's subjects were allowed to sleep undisturbed for several nights. They spent more time in REM sleep on those nights than they had during a baseline period before the deprivation phase of the study.

After a hiatus of several nights, the subjects came back to the sleep lab. This time, for several nights they were awakened during non-REM sleep for the same periods they had been deprived of REM sleep earlier. After this non-REM deprivation phase, there was no change in REM when they were allowed to sleep through the night undisturbed. It seems from this research that REM sleep is necessary. When people are deprived of REM sleep, they catch up on it the first chance they get.

In 1906, a German psychologist named O. Pfungst (1906/1965) analyzed the case of a "wonder horse" named Clever Hans. The horse seemed to be able to answer its master's questions about mathematics, spelling, and more, by stomping its front hoof. Pfungst determined that the horse could not actually count or spell (quelle surprise!), but simply responded to subtle gestures by its master that caused it to stomp at the right times.

More than 50 years later, Robert Rosenthal and several colleagues extended Pfungst's research. They began to study whether similar communication takes place in psychological laboratories, classrooms, and other venues, wherever the persons in charge— experimenters or teachers for example—expect those in their charge, research participants or students, to act in a certain way. For one demonstration of this "expectancy" effect, **Rosenthal and Lenore Jacobson (E15)** led elementary school teachers to believe that some of their students were more capable than their previous academic performance indicated. After that, those "underachievers," actually chosen at random, performed better in school than they ever had, presumably because their teachers somehow signaled them to do clever things.

For another example, American social psychologists **Robert Zajonc and Gregory Markus (E16)** were inspired by a study done in the Netherlands by Lillian Belmont and Francis Marolla. An analysis of intelligence test scores for more than 350,000 Dutch 19-year-old men showed that scores declined as the men's family size and birth order increased. That is, the larger the man's family and the later the man was born into it, the lower his intelligence test score.

Zajonc and Markus used the same information to test a hypothesis that promised to help explain the mechanism by which family size and birth order influenced intelligence. Their "confluence" hypothesis held that a child's intellectual development was proportional to the average intellectual accomplishment of the other family members at the time of the child's birth. Parents know more than children do and thus contribute more to the child's intellectual growth. The more children already in the family, the lower the average accomplishment for the family as a whole and the less instructive for the new addition. Zajonc and Markus's analysis of the Dutch data supported that hypothesis for the most part.

Previous research studies obviously are valuable sources of hypotheses for new studies. Researchers sometimes extend the findings of previous studies to new areas of behavior, as Rosenthal and Jacobson did with Pfungst's analysis of the Clever Hans phenomenon. In other cases, they develop hypotheses to explain further what previous studies found, as Dement did for the initial research on REM sleep, and as Zajonc and Markus did for the Dutch findings about the relationship between family structure and intelligence test scores. Sometimes researchers test new populations, or test in new settings, or introduce some other variation that takes knowledge of the behavior in question a bit further.

Serendipitous Research Results

There are times when researchers set out to test one hypothesis only to observe something so unexpected in the course of their research that they become much more interested in an entirely different hypothesis. There's no telling how often this happens, but it has happened to me, and there are some well-known cases of it happening to other researchers as well.

In my case (**E17**), one of the most interesting and productive hypotheses I ever developed came about in exactly this way. I was working on a study to test the hypothesis that manipulative people, people who scored high on the trait of Machiavellianism, would try to make other people like them by looking them in the eye more. The participants, high and low Machiavellian men, were videotaped so that the direction of their gaze could be measured accurately, by playing the tape back repeatedly. While watching the tape over and over, timing the participants' patterns of gaze with a stopwatch, I came to believe that I could tell the high and low Machiavellians apart based solely on their looks.

That hypothesis seemed very unlikely to me at the time, based on what I believed then, but I tried it out anyway on a class I was teaching at the time. Based on promising results there, I carried out a full-scale study that showed that people could in fact tell the high and low "Machs" apart by looking at 1-minute samples of their videotapes or even from photographs made from the tapes.

A much better-known example of a hypothesis developed from serendipitous research results is one tested in research by **Martin Seligman and Steven Maier** (**E18**). It arose out of Seligman's unexpected observation while he was testing dogs for avoidance learning in a shuttle box. The shuttle box is a classic setup for training animals to escape electric shock by jumping over a barrier and then training them to avoid the shock by jumping when they hear a signal that has preceded the shock on a number of previous occasions. Seligman was surprised to find that his animals never learned to escape, much less to avoid the shock. They just curled up in a corner, hunkered down on the electrified wire grid floor, and suffered the pain of the shock.

In the course of trying to understand what he had seen, Seligman discovered that the animals had been used in a previous study in which they had been given painful electric shocks they could not escape. He hypothesized that they had learned from that earlier experience that they were helpless in such circumstances. That hypothesis was tested by Seligman and Maier, who found evidence for learned helplessness, a concept that has subsequently become a well-accepted explanation for depression in human beings (see Figure 2.2).

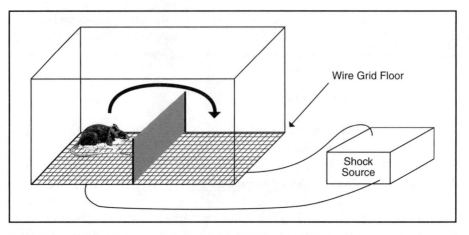

Wire Grid Floor

Shock
Source

Figure 2.2. The shuttle box apparatus used by Seligman and Maier in their research that led to the learned helplessness theory of depression.

John B. Calhoun (E19) developed a hypothesis about the effects of crowding from a serendipitous finding during a study of population growth in rats. In a protected environment (no predators, traps, or poison), with unlimited food and water, the population of rats Calhoun was studying stabilized at what was to him a surprisingly low number—about 150 on one-quarter acre. The reason was a very high infant mortality rate.

Based on that observation, Calhoun hypothesized that there were biological mechanisms to control population. He tested his hypothesis in a series of experiments in a special 10-by-14-foot environment containing feeders, water supplies, and nesting boxes (see Figure 2.3). At twice their natural population density, he observed a pattern of pathological behavior among the rats that he called a "behavioral sink." Dominant male rats and their harems of females took over the more isolated areas, while most of the colony crowded into the more central ones. In the crowded central areas, Calhoun observed aggression, withdrawal, sexual deviance, and the failure of normal instincts to build nests and nurture young.

One of the most famous examples of serendipity in the history of psychology gave rise to the seminal work of **Ivan Pavlov (E20)**. As a physiologist, Pavlov studied how digestive enzymes worked. To get material to study, he developed a technique for collecting saliva from dogs. The dogs were strapped into harnesses on tables in Pavlov's lab, food was put into their mouths, and saliva was collected through tubes inserted into the corners of their jowls. While observing this process, Pavlov was surprised to see dogs begin to salivate when his lab assistants approached them with the food, before the dogs had anything at all in their mouths.

That observation led Pavlov to hypothesize a form of learning that today we call classical conditioning (described in a little more detail earlier in this chapter). In many experiments conducted afterward, he showed that it was the repeated asso-

| Box 2.1 | *THINKING ABOUT RESEARCH* |

Can We Always Know What Research Already Has Been Done? _____

Meta-analysis is being recognized increasingly as an invaluable tool for psychological research, making it possible to add together the results of numerous studies in a more meaningful way than was previously possible (as illustrated by Smith and Glass's meta-analysis of psychotherapy outcome studies [**E24**]). There is a problem, however, that makes researchers somewhat uneasy about interpreting the results of meta-analytic studies. It is known as the "file-drawer problem."

Researchers who conduct meta-analyses have no sure way of knowing whether there are tests of the hypothesis in question other than those they are able to find. If they exist, those studies are assumed to be buried in the researchers' file drawers because they produced negative results (see Thinking About Research Box 3.2). That is because the results of such studies are so difficult to interpret that they are rarely published. Recently, a new and more troubling variation on the file-drawer problem has emerged.

Knoll Pharmaceutical Company is reported to have prevented publication of research on its popular thyroid drug, Synthroid. Betty Dong, a researcher at the University of California at San Francisco, found that the drug was no more effective than less expensive generic equivalents. Her study was funded by Knoll, under a contract that allowed the company to veto its publication.

Although Dr. Dong's research is available to the Food and Drug Administration, it remains a secret from other researchers (not its existence, obviously, but its details), as well as from physicians who read the research literature. How much of an effect does such repression of research results have on the development of scientific theory? How many researchers feel the need to accept funding under restrictions that give corporations with selfish interests control over the results of their research? As government funding of basic science declines, how much more scientific research will become the property of special economic interests? How does all of this affect a researcher's ability to evaluate the conceptual validity of a potential research hypothesis?

ciation of food with a neutral stimulus that caused the neutral stimulus to acquire the capacity to elicit a response previously made only to the food itself. By using stimuli that he could control, like a tuning fork, Pavlov was able to develop a better understanding of how classical conditioning works, after first encountering it so unexpectedly.

Conducting research in which behavior is observed directly is one of the hallmarks of scientific psychology. It not only provides answers to questions about behavior but also provides opportunities to observe behavioral phenomena the researchers might not yet know enough to look for. Those unplanned or serendipitous observations provide some of the best ideas for further research.

Figure 2.3. The artificial environment created by John Calhoun to study the effects of overpopulation on the behavior of rats.
SOURCE: From "Population Density and Social Pathology," *Scientific American*, 206, pp. 140-141, Calhoun, © copyright 1962 by Bunji Tagawa. Reprinted with permission.

New Technologies

Throughout the history of psychology, research has depended on the development of new technologies for studying behavior. Skinner's operant conditioning chamber, sometimes called the Skinner Box, is one well-known example. It increased the efficiency and flexibility of studying the effects of reinforcement on behavior to the point where many more researchers developed and tested hypotheses about it than would have otherwise. There are many more examples from learning and other areas of experimental psychology. There are also cases in which hypotheses could not be tested until requisite technologies were developed.

One example is the well-known work of **Michael Gazzaniga (E21)**, Roger Sperry, and others on the functions of the left and right cerebral hemispheres of the brain. A new medical technology was developed in the early 1950s to treat unusually severe cases of epilepsy. Surgeons cut the patient's corpus callosum (the

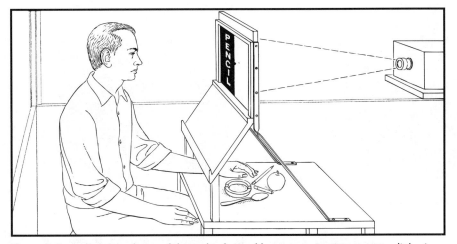

Figure 2.4. A diagram of one of the tasks devised by neuroscientists to test split-brain patients. Their research revealed the specialized functions of the left and right cerebral hemispheres.
SOURCE: From "The Split Brain in Man," *Scientific American*, *217*, p. 27, Gazzaniga, © copyright 1967 by Eric Mose, Jr. Reprinted with permission.

structure that connects the cerebral hemispheres) to prevent seizures from spreading from one side of the brain to the other. This callectomy or commissurotomy procedure prevented the cerebral hemispheres from exchanging information in the normal fashion. The existence of a small group of split-brain patients who had received this radical treatment gave neuroscientists the opportunity to devise experiments in which separate information could be presented to the left and right hemispheres. The participants' behavior in response to that information could be compared to test hypotheses about possible differences in the functions of those hemispheres.

In another case, **Mark Rosenzweig and others (E22)** were able to test hypotheses about the effects of experience on brain development only after suitable means had been devised to measure brain structure. They compared rats raised in standard laboratory cages, barren of anything except a supply of food pellets and a lick tube coming from a water bottle, with rats raised in enriched environments containing other rats and rodent toys (think hamster cage).

The hypothesis that increased environmental stimulation would enhance brain development had been around a long time. What had been lacking previously (Rosenzweig's study was performed around 1970) was adequate technology to compare brain development from one group of rats to another. With new methods that made that possible, these researchers were able to compare development in specific parts of the brain and in the different types of cells within those parts. They could measure the sizes of those cells and even compare levels of activity of the

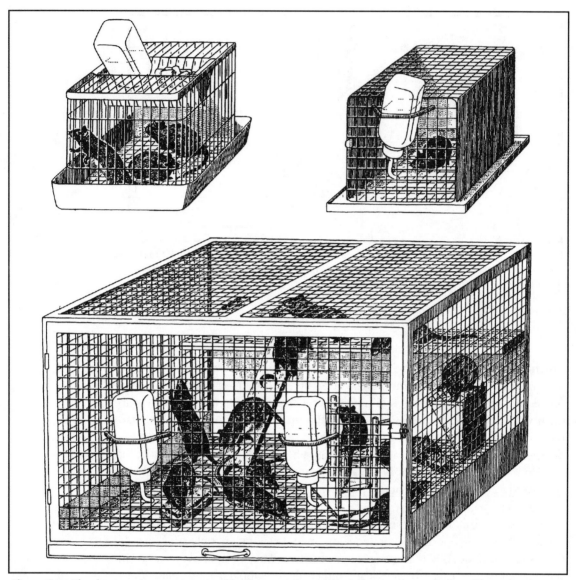

Figure 2.5. The three environments created by Rosenzweig and his colleagues to study the effects of early experience on brain development in rats.
SOURCE: From "Brain Changes in Response to Experience," *Scientific American*, *226*(2), p. 23, Rosenzweig, Bennett, and Diamond, © copyright 1972 by Bunji Tagawa. Reprinted with permission.

chemicals that make those cells function. All those comparisons showed the advantage of enriched environments for brain development in rats.

The PET (positron-emission tomography) scan is one of the latest technological innovations to provide psychologists with new research opportunities. It is a new type of imaging technique that reveals not only the structure of a brain but also the current levels of functioning in different brain locations. PET scans show patterns of blood flow, oxygen use, and glucose consumption, reflecting the effects of drugs and of chemicals produced in the body itself.

Richard Haier and his coworkers (E23) have tested people of varying levels of intelligence to compare how their brains function while they solve problems. Their more intelligent participants' brains used less glucose (i.e., expended less effort) while solving a given problem than did the brains of the less intelligent participants. As they learned to solve problems better with practice, more intelligent participants' glucose metabolism became more localized (i.e., they used their brains more efficiently) compared to that of less intelligent participants. Those research results were all based on PET scans of the subjects' brains.

Although it is particularly apparent in the area of neuroscience, new technologies are important to the development of research hypotheses in many other areas of psychological research as well. They may take the form of new personality tests or new computer software for statistics as well as PET scans and other high-tech devices. Good ideas about the causes of behavior may languish for long periods of time if the technology needed to test them is not available. At the same time, it has been pointed out that there is the danger that researchers will "look where the light is brightest, rather than where the object was lost." They may be tempted to test hypotheses that allow the use of a "sexy" new technology, even if those aren't the hypotheses that contribute most to the development of knowledge about the behavior in question.

The Need to Solve Practical Problems

Throughout the recent history of psychology, it has been customary to categorize research as basic or applied. Basic research is usually defined by the researchers' motivation to satisfy curiosity, extend knowledge, or build a better theory, with less regard for the usefulness of the findings to solve practical problems. Applied research is motivated more by a desire to solve practical problems than by desire to advance the science of human behavior. In applied research, hypotheses derive primarily from the recognition of a practical problem or need.

For example, **Mary Lee Smith and Gene Glass (E24)** wanted to find out whether psychotherapy is effective and which method of psychotherapy works best for various psychological disorders. Rather than study therapists and their clients directly, they used a technique called meta-analysis to evaluate the results of 375 previous studies. Meta-analysis, in effect, "adds up" the results of different research studies that test the same hypothesis. It determines the overall results as well as the ways in which differences among the studies (in this case, those differences included the type of therapy used and the client's diagnosis) affect that result.

Smith and Glass found that psychotherapy works and that different types work about equally well across the board. Although the categories of sources of hypotheses we've been considering may sound mutually exclusive, they aren't really. This study was prompted to some degree by the availability of new technology —in this case, the statistical technique called meta-analysis—in addition to the desire to find out something about psychotherapy that would be useful. This chapter has tried to describe studies in a way that sharpens the differences among the categories as much as possible, but real examples of research often cross those boundaries.

Another example of research that arose primarily out of a practical need is a study by **Frederick Frazier (E25)**. It comes from the field of environmental psychology and is an example of post-occupancy evaluation (POE). *POE* is a generic term for studies that evaluate how well new buildings, interior designs, parks, or any new environmental settings achieve their behavioral and other goals.

In 1981, a new jail was opened in Contra Costa County, in the town of Martinez in the San Francisco Bay area of California. It had been designed, partly on the basis of prior psychological research, to protect both its prisoners and corrections officers from discomfort, and especially from violence. Most county jail prisoners are not convicted criminals. They are accused persons waiting for arraignment or making arrangements for bail (the average stay at the old Contra Costa County jail was just 2 to 3 days), and courts have ruled that they have the constitutional right to be protected under those circumstances.

Frazier did his research to find out whether the jail worked the way it was intended to work. He inspected the records and reports kept in the jail and questioned the inmates and corrections officers about their perceptions of its comfort and safety. Many of these respondents had had previous experience with traditional jails. Their generally favorable responses, along with the official jail records, indicated that the "modular, direct-supervision" design used in Contra Costa County's new jail worked well. In that new design, about 50 prisoners shared an attractive, common living/eating/recreation space with two unarmed corrections officers, except for the time when they were asleep in their individual cells.

In recent decades, more and more research in psychology has tested hypotheses inspired by practical problems (don't be misled by the small number of examples considered here). This is due partly to a shift in criteria for research grants, particularly from governmental sources. At the same time, a good deal of this applied research also contributes to the development of psychological theory. Researchers often plan their applied studies that way. Some even believe that the best test of a scientific theory is one carried out in an applied setting such as a therapist's office or a jail, where the rich mix of variables that might influence the behavior in question can come into play. More will be said about that later in an extended discussion of internal and external validity.

Recycling the Examples

We've now seen more than two dozen examples of some of the varied sources of hypotheses for psychological research (recall that Table 2.1 provides a review of the sources and the studies discussed in connection with them, including complete references to the original articles). Although the studies and their hypotheses have been described in ways that highlight the differences among the various categories, any of them could have and probably did originate from more than one of those sources, as was earlier discussed in connection with the Smith and Glass study (**E24**). Likewise, these same examples could be used to illustrate other important points about the process of psychological research. And they will.

These exemplar studies were chosen not only because they tested hypotheses that originated mainly in personal observation, or psychological theory, or one of the other five categories. They were chosen because they also represent, as a group, both basic and applied research and a wide variety of content areas in psychological research, from the study of brain structure to the study of family structure, and because they will be useful later in the book as illustrations of the many choices that researchers must make in all the other phases of the research process —operationalization of constructs, research design, statistical analysis, and the rest. In addition, they were chosen because they might be interesting enough to persuade you at this early stage that psychological research methods are worth knowing about and that the questions and answers in psychological research are important enough to warrant acquiring the considerable knowledge that is required to do research well and to evaluate it intelligently.

These studies will be referred to repeatedly throughout the course of this book, adding more details in many cases as they become relevant to the discussion at hand.

BUILDING A BETTER HYPOTHESIS ●

Regardless of its source, any hypothesis can benefit from a process of development. From the time that it first excites a researcher's interest until it is finally tested in a research study, the research hypothesis can be refined from its original status as an expression of the researcher's curiosity or desire for information into a valuable link in a cumulative chain of scientific investigation.

At the outset, many hypotheses exist in the form of "what if . . .?" speculations. The researcher's encounter with some personal experience or news report, or a participant's unexpected behavior in a prior research study, or whatever, leads to a hypothesis such as the following:

TABLE 2.2   Threats to Conceptual Validity

---

1. Unnecessary duplication
2. Theoretical isolation

- What if men and women both watch an interaction of a dating couple? Will they differ in their interpretation of the participants' behavior?

- Do the patrons in a bar find members of the opposite sex more attractive as closing time approaches? (This hypothesis actually was suggested by a country and western song.)

- Does a stroke victim remember what happened before the stroke but nothing after the stroke because new memories are formed in a different part of the brain from where old ones are stored?

Conceptual Validity

There is nothing wrong with a researcher following up on such a speculation by conducting a formal study. Quite the contrary. Pure intellectual curiosity fuels much important research in psychology, carried out as it is by professors and students who stand to gain little more from it than the satisfaction of following through on their own interests. There is something, however, that a researcher can and should do while planning a research study that might increase the meaningfulness of its outcome—that is, its validity—beyond the satisfaction of the researcher's curiosity. That "something" begins with a literature review. By learning about prior research and theory that is relevant to his or her preliminary hypothesis, the researcher can answer several questions about potential threats to the usefulness or validity of the research findings.

Two of those questions directly concern **conceptual validity**—the term we will use for the quality of the hypothesis on which the research is based (see Table 2.2). The first question is, "Has this hypothesis already been tested in previous research?" If the answer if yes, the researcher can avoid **unnecessary duplication** by abandoning his or her plans to test the same hypothesis again. Of course, the hypothesis may be important enough to justify double-checking the results by repeating the study (replication, in research jargon). If there is a good reason, the researcher may retest the hypothesis using a sample from a different population of participants, or using a different way of measuring the participants' behavior, or with some other variation on the original study. At least under those conditions, the decision would be an informed one, and the new study would be undertaken deliberately to add something of value to knowledge of the behavior.

Somewhat more complex is the second question related to conceptual validity: "Does this hypothesis promise to add something valuable to knowledge of the behavior in question?" Previous research may have been carried out that is relevant to the original or preliminary hypothesis, or the hypothesis may fit into an existing theory that was developed to organize and explain other aspects of the behavior in question. In those cases, it might be desirable to modify the preliminary hypothesis so that it better fills in the most important gaps in knowledge that have been left by the previous research and/or serves as the best possible test of the existing theory. Such modification lessens the likelihood that the eventual research results will stand in **theoretical isolation** from the existing knowledge base, and thus makes the findings more meaningful or valid.

In addition to strengthening the conceptual validity of research findings by making it possible to avoid both unnecessary duplication and theoretical isolation, a thorough literature search can improve a study in other ways during the planning stage. Learning about prior work in a particular research area can provide a researcher with good ideas about how to represent independent and dependent variables in the new study.

The literature review can inform the researcher about technology that would be useful for carrying out the research, perhaps making the independent variable more reliable or increasing its impact, or making the measure of the participants' behavior more reliable or more sensitive. In these and other ways, researchers can benefit from the work of those who have gone before them. The quality of new work, its construct validity and more, can be improved, and the effort required to do the research can be lessened by borrowing good ideas and proven methods from the published research literature.

The Literature Review

How should a thorough review of the research literature be carried out? How can a researcher find relevant and useful information for planning a study in the vast archives of psychology and related fields? There is no clear blueprint for doing this, but there are some suggestions, based on experience, and some useful tools any prospective researcher should know about.

It should be kept in mind throughout this discussion that there is no substitute for experience in doing a literature search. Everyone who does this repeatedly, over a period of time, will develop a method that suits him or her best, as is true of any skilled activity. The research literature in psychology is vast (see the description of *Psychological Abstracts* below), and it is scattered; in addition, relevant items are sometimes found in publications in sociology, biochemistry, medicine,

| Box 2.2 | *THINKING ABOUT RESEARCH* |

A Hypothesis Is Not (Yet) a Theory

The elected Kansas Board of Education voted in August of 1999 to remove the theory of evolution from the state's list of required science topics. Fundamentalist Christians organized to elect half of the board's members because they believed that its eventual ruling would make it possible for local school boards to prevent evolution from being taught at all, thus eliminating the conflict with their belief in divine creation. Even though a committee of prominent scientists appointed by the board advised that understanding evolution was crucial to modern science education and the success of Kansas students in the modern world, and even though the presidents of all six state universities in Kansas asked the board not to drop evolution from the state's mandatory science curriculum, the board voted to do just that.

Apart from the religious question, some of the comments reported by media covering the board's discussion and decision revealed a fundamental and, I'm afraid, common misunderstanding of the scientific method. Both the chairperson of the Kansas Board of Education and a science teacher in the Kansas public schools were quoted as saying that evolution didn't need to be a required part of the curriculum because "it's only a theory."

Many laypeople confuse scientific hypothesis with scientific theory. A hypothesis is an educated guess about the cause of some natural phenomenon, such as the variety of plant and animal species around the world. A scientific theory is a summary and explanation of a body of scientific facts that have been collected to test that hypothesis (in the case of evolution, the facts include millions of living organisms and fossils). A scientific hypothesis is the starting point of the process, whereas a scientific theory is its ultimate goal. As long as those who plan and teach the science curriculum don't know the difference, the rest of the public isn't likely to either.

Have you heard people confuse a theory with a hypothesis? If so, did it ever seem that they did so intentionally to make a debating point? Do you understand the difference between the two, and will you be on the lookout for the error of equating them in future public debates?

and many other "neighboring" disciplines. Some tips therefore might be helpful to a newcomer.

One way to become oriented in that vast and scattered literature is by starting with secondary sources. **Secondary sources** are publications that describe, organize, and analyze the published journal articles, books, and book chapters (**primary sources**) in which researchers initially present their original research and theory. Secondary sources include textbooks. For a hypothesis about the effects of exposure to televised violence on aggression, one could consult an introductory psychology textbook, or a text for an introductory course in developmental or social psychology, or a text for a course (in the field of communication, perhaps) on the media's effects on human behavior. By doing so, one could fairly quickly get an idea of the scope of previous work in this area of investigation, trusting the textbook's author to be familiar enough with the literature to sample all the important areas within it and to highlight the most important studies in each of those areas.

Some of those secondary sources presumably would provide information about the topic. Those that did would provide varying amounts of information, depending on the interests of the author and the overall scope of the book. An introductory psychology text might contain only a few paragraphs on the effects of TV violence on aggression, whereas a text on the media's effects on behavior might devote a whole chapter or more to the subject. Almost any text that described a sample of the work that had been done in the area of interest would provide detailed references to the primary sources the author had consulted, the articles and books in which that work was published.

The next step would be to obtain as many of those items as possible in a nearby library, to obtain them from other libraries via interlibrary loan, to "download" them from electronic sources accessed through the Internet, or to get them from the authors via e-mail (or "snail mail" in the case of articles; many researchers are willing to provide "reprints" or photocopies of their publications to colleagues who request them). Each of those items would in turn provide its own list of references, and by following this bootstrapping procedure one could generate a large bibliography fairly quickly.

If the topic of the hypothesis was a popular one, like the effects of TV violence on aggression, the list might soon become too long to ever read each item. Under those circumstances, one might decide to settle for a sample that represented each of the subtopics one could identify in the area. This is probably what the author of the secondary source did in the first place. One might very well be retracing the author's steps, but it is important to do so. One needs to recognize that secondary sources are interpretations of the original research literature. A researcher needs to do his or her own analysis to be certain that the unrecognized biases of another reviewer don't throw the research off course.

Armed with an overview of one's chosen area of research and some familiarity with the technical terms used by researchers in that area, both of which one should be able to obtain from secondary sources, one could look for further information in the area of a particular hypothesis by consulting publications that are devoted to more detailed and more technical reviews. One such publication is the *Annual Review of Psychology*, which has been published for about 50 years. One volume is published each year, containing reviews of about 20 areas of research and theory, each review written by an acknowledged expert or experts in those areas. Some popular topics appear every few years, such as health psychology or personality and environmental psychology, each time with a slightly different slant depending on the particular interests of the review's author. Over longer periods, different topics are rotated, as the "hot" topics in the discipline change. More specialized topics are also included when new work warrants and when a suitable author can be enlisted, such as "Contemporary psychology in Spain" (Prieto, Fernandez-Ballesteros, & Carpintero, 1994). The reviews published in these volumes typically provide very long reference lists containing hundreds of items.

Other sources of detailed reviews include edited books on a wide variety of research topics that can be located through library catalogs (usually online these days, with electronic title, subject, and keyword search capabilities), or in the *Books in Print* title and subject volumes (also online in some libraries and on some computer networks, and also with electronic search capabilities). Two journals in psychology are devoted to literature reviews: *Psychological Bulletin* and *Psychological Review* (the latter emphasizes theory more than the former). Similar publications exist in related fields, such as *Personality and Social Psychology Review*. In addition, many journals occasionally publish issues devoted to a single research topic that can give a relatively quick thumbnail sketch of the state of the art.

One also can search directly for references to the original articles and books in which research studies and theories are published. For more than 80 years, the American Psychological Association has published *Psychological Abstracts*. In 1998, the 12 monthly issues contained more than 300 pages each. In each issue were listed references and summaries for 3,000 or so articles and books, grouped together by headings ranging from traditional subdivisions of scientific psychology such as developmental, social, and personality; to well-known applied fields like educational, industrial/organizational, and mental health; to more recently developed areas of interest such as forensic, sport, and military psychology.

The sheer size of *Psychological Abstracts* (more than 36,000 articles in a single year) makes it difficult to use. A search over a period as long as 5 or 10 years would require digging through a veritable mountain of paper. In 1998, the annual subject index alone comprised five separate volumes, and the author index three more. We can be thankful that computer technology has made the search of the primary literature less painful and more efficient. First with an online system called PsycINFO, and then with a CD-ROM–based system called PsycLIT, the mountain of *Psychological Abstracts* has been reduced to electrons in cyberspace or a few grams of plastic. At the same time, computer software has made it much easier to find the desired needle in the haystack of information those high-tech systems can hold.

We'll concentrate on PsycLIT, which is the computerized search (electronic retrieval) system I've used most, though it should be easy to adapt this discussion to PsycINFO if that's the system you find in your library. Depending on the particular library, you might need to check out one of the two PsycLIT CDs from behind the reference desk, or you might just log onto a network terminal. In either case, you'll find out that one CD contains citations and abstracts for journal articles published between 1974 and 1989, and the other contains the same information for journal articles from 1990 to the present and for book chapters and books from 1987 to the present (these dates are subject to change as the database is updated, which happens quarterly). Before those starting dates, you're stuck with *Psychological Abstracts* and other sources.

Searching the CD-ROMs is made possible through the use of special software created by a company called Silver Platter. The records of journal articles, book chapters, and books stored on the CDs contain information such as title, author, publisher, and date of publication. That information makes it possible to find the complete article, chapter, or book in your library or some other library, depending on the size of the library and the popularity of the publication. Each record also contains a description of the content of the item in question, either the abstract that is published along with most journal articles, a book publisher's blurb, a description of a chapter from the introduction to an edited book, or something of the sort. Some systems even provide links to the actual articles and chapters if the library subscribes to that service.

The idea is to find articles, chapters, and books that will provide information about research and theory that is relevant to the hypothesis at hand. That information will prevent unnecessary duplication of past research and will allow the researcher to plan a study that fills important gaps in the research literature and/or tests vital theories about the causes of the behavior in question. One can take several routes.

One can search using subject terms such as "aggression" and "media violence." During a search, a researcher can consult a thesaurus in printed form or, if it exists in digital form, on the computer screen (by pressing the appropriate function key). This thesaurus provides alternative and related terms that might lead one to additional relevant material. Combinations of terms, linked by conjunctions such as "and" and "or," can be used to narrow or to broaden the search until a reasonable number of items is located.

The search is carried out in the database by trying to match the terms you choose with the actual words, including authors' names, stored on the CDs. The software menu contains a series of commands—Find, Show, Mark, and Print (or Download). In the end, one can walk away with a record (on paper or on a diskette) of references to the articles, chapters, and books one would consult to better understand the place of one's hypothesis in the existing literature.

It is sometimes very useful to search the database using an author's name. Once one identifies one or more researchers who have made important contributions to a particular area of research over a period of years, it sometimes makes sense to conduct a search of those researchers' work. This search can turn up more information that might be relevant but is not necessarily identified by the usual terms of reference or topics that one might use in a search. (Researchers sometimes show off their creativity by devising titles that don't mention the topic of the research at all.)

The Silver Platter software contains many other features that we don't have time to discuss here. To learn more about the system, you need to practice on it. As you do, you can use various aids such as a tutorial available on some PsycLIT servers (the computer that runs the network) as well as printed reference guides at the computer or network terminal. You can get a very helpful booklet, *Searching PsycLIT*, from the American Psychological Association by calling (800) 374-2722 or (202) 336-5650 (Washington, D.C.) or by sending an e-mail message to psycinfo@apa.org. (These numbers and the Web address are subject to change.) The phone numbers also provide "hot line" assistance (useful if there's a telephone near your computer terminal) during normal weekday office hours (Eastern time).

Although it's no substitute for mucking around in PsycLIT (or PsycINFO or any other similar system) on your own, it might be helpful to go over a search I conducted some time ago, using PsycLIT. I was looking for research and theory related to one of my own research interests, the role of physical appearance in leadership. It might seem that a good way to start would be to look through the recent research on leadership to locate the studies and theoretical papers highlighting the role of physical appearance. If you had done that during July of 1996, using the PsycLIT CD containing research articles published between 1990 and that date, you would have found 1,635 articles categorized under the heading "leadership" by the Silver Platter software in the journals covered by PsycLIT. If you had searched that same CD using the term "leader*", you would have found that 2,504 articles related to leadership were published during that period. (The * is called the truncation symbol by Silver Platter, and in this case it matches any term beginning with "leader," including leader, leaders, leadership, and so on). A search of the current books and chapters database would uncover 1,265 more items using "leader*" as the search term.

Where would one go from that point? It would be very time-consuming, to say the least, to look at descriptions of 3,769 or more articles, books, and chapters on leadership to identify those that are relevant to the role of physical appearance in leadership. Fortunately, there is an alternative. One may enter both terms, connected with "and," (physical appearance and leader*), to identify only those articles or books and chapters that pertain to the possible connection between physical appearance and leadership. How many items would be identified that way? Only two articles published between 1990 and June of 1996, along with two books or chapters between 1987 and June of 1996!

Where would one go from there? Adding a search of the older records, articles from 1974 to 1989, using "physical appearance" and "leader*", would add only two more items to one's list. Remember, however, that each item turned up in a PsycLIT search has a list of references included in it. Then there are the textbooks, *Annual Review of Psychology* volumes, and other secondary sources as well. PsycLIT is a good way to find those, too, although in that case it is probably wise to stick to broader search terms such as "leadership" or "physical appearance." For a topic such as leadership, it could be very useful to look at similar sources in other disciplines where the subject is important. Those include political science, management, organizational behavior, and others.

Magazines, newspapers, and other publications also can be searched using indexes and electronic retrieval systems your reference librarian can show you. In addition, PsycLIT itself has further possibilities, using terms such as "physical attractiveness," "facial maturity," and others that you would turn up as you read the abstracts of articles categorized under the heading "physical appearance." The ultimate goal is to get to the point where you are confident that you have found the relevant literature, or enough of it to get a good start on a literature search that will support development of a conceptually valid hypothesis. Don't forget bootstrapping: Each item you find will have its own list of references to add to yours.

It obviously takes some experimentation with terms, combinations of terms, and software features (such as the truncation symbol) to be able to conduct an effective search using PsycLIT or a similar electronic retrieval system. One can narrow or broaden a search in many ways to produce a good working bibliography, assuming of course that the items to fill it exist. There is no substitute for a real interest in poking around in libraries. One "trick" that has worked very well for me is to look along library shelves or through the table of contents of a book or journal issue where I find an item identified in one of my PsycLIT searches. Where you find one item you can use, others are likely to be close by.

Another very useful tool for searching the research literature in psychology is the Social Science Citation Index (SSCI). Using increasingly powerful and available computer technology, SSCI is able to track the instances in which a given research article is listed among the references in other articles; that is, "cited." If one knows of an article that was influential in opening up the area of research one seeks to pursue, SSCI can provide a list of all subsequent articles that cite that seminal article. Of course, an SSCI search can be based on any article, as long as it was published no earlier than 1966, when the SSCI service was begun.

This method of "treeing" forward in time can be a valuable part of a literature search, especially when a key early article can be identified. The Seligman and Maier (1967) article reporting the first study of learned helplessness (**E18**) is a good example. Very often, current articles help a researcher to identify a good starting point for an SSCI search. An article might be cited often or prominently in those articles, or it might be identified explicitly as an important early contribution in their introduction sections.

In practice, unless the topic is extremely obscure, one is more likely to be overwhelmed by the amount of material to be read, organized, and applied to the research hypothesis at hand than to be disappointed by how little is known. The more there is, the richer the possibilities for making connections, borrowing techniques, evaluating theories, and the like. It is more difficult in a well-developed literature to do original research that will make a big difference in how much is known. In some ways, it is more exciting to strike out alone on the cutting edge of a problem that has received little previous attention. One needs to be certain that the problem hasn't been ignored because it's just not important enough, and that it will be possible to develop all the necessary materials without being able to borrow very much from predecessors. In either case, it is most important to know where one is so that one can develop a hypothesis that makes sense in the light of what has gone before.

However you do your literature search, the object is to end up with a good idea of where your hypothesis fits in the overall scheme of research in the area in which you want to work. You should be able to refine your hypothesis accordingly so that your study makes the greatest contribution possible to the current understanding of the behavior in question. Along the way, you may pick up some valuable pointers about how to measure the constructs in your hypothesis, which population to sample, how to arrange the comparisons you need to make, and more.

Once a researcher has some experience working in a particular area, with a good grasp of the relevant literature, the problem becomes one of keeping up with new work as it is published. A publication called *Current Contents* (there is one for the social and behavioral sciences, with others for related scientific disciplines) lists the contents of each of hundreds of journals on a weekly basis, along with addresses of authors to whom one can write for reprints or copies of their articles. Although the articles' titles are all one has to go on, for an experienced researcher *Current Contents* is an excellent way of keeping up with the literature.

Professional conferences are another good source of information about the cutting edge of research. At many conferences, leading researchers are invited to speak about their work, often before it is published, and will discuss it with interested colleagues, on the spot or later via e-mail. The Internet is rapidly emerging as another possibility. Interest groups of researchers exchange information electronically without the lag of months or years it takes to get new work published in professional journals or books. Some predict that the Internet will replace printed journals some day (some journals are already available online), but that's not likely to happen during the life of this book.

If you become primarily a reader of research, rather than a researcher, familiarity with the purposes and methods of the literature search should allow you to evaluate more intelligently the research reports you read. You will look for evidence in the introduction to a report that the researcher understands the place of his or her study in the larger area of research. Does the researcher make a good case for the originality of this particular hypothesis and for its importance as an addition to the existing literature and/or as a contribution to building a better theory? If so, one can read on with the confidence that other components of the research were built on a solid base of conceptual validity.

Once the hypothesis has been refined, based on the literature search, the researcher is ready for the next step in the research process. In our scheme, that involves converting the causal and behavioral constructs of the hypothesis into measurable independent and dependent variables. It is that process of operationalization, and the evaluation of how well it was done in terms of construct validity, to which we turn next.

Review Questions and Exercises

Review Questions

1. What is a research hypothesis?

2. What are the two elements that make up a research hypothesis?

3. What is conceptual validity, and what are the two questions a researcher needs to answer in evaluating the conceptual validity of research findings?

Exercises

1. Make a list of hypotheses about the causes of behavior that you would be interested in testing some day, along with the source of each one.

2. Go back to the journal article that you looked at for the exercise following Chapter 1 and identify the hypothesis it tested. What are the causal and behavioral constructs? Did the author(s) make a good case for each element of the conceptual validity of the hypothesis? If so, why? If not, why not?

3. Conduct a literature search based on the constructs in one of the hypotheses you would like to test some day.

CHAPTER **3**

SPECIFYING THE RESEARCH VARIABLES I
Operational Definition and Measurement

● A QUICK GUIDE TO CHAPTER 3: SPECIFYING THE RESEARCH VARIABLES I

Operationalization is the indispensable process of defining the general constructs in a research hypotheses in terms of concrete measurement operations. This process creates the specific **independent** and **dependent variables** that are actually studied in research. Operationalization must be evaluated for **construct validity**, a judgment about the quality of the measurement operations employed.

Two general criteria for measurement quality concern the **precision** of the measurement and the degree of **error** contained in the measurements that are made. The type of **measurement scale** used is an important determinant of measurement precision. Measurement scales range from the **nominal scale**, the least precise, through the **ordinal scale** and **interval scale**, in that order, to the **ratio scale**, the most precise. The property to be measured may limit the researcher's choice of the type of scale to be used.

Random error in both independent and dependent variables is reflected in the level of **reliability** or reproducibility of the obtained measurements. **Systematic error** in both variables can result from a **lack of representativeness**. In addition, treatments can suffer from a **lack of impact** because of insufficient contrast among them. The behavioral measures also can suffer from a **lack of sensitivity** in detecting any differential effects of treatments that might occur.

Remember that the purpose of a research study is to shed as much light as possible on the truth or falsity of the causal relationship stated in the research hypothesis. If the constructs aren't measured properly by the independent and dependent variables, the findings will lack construct validity. In that case, the research results will not be able to support with certainty any conclusion about the truth of the research hypothesis, because the variables used in the study don't properly represent the constructs specified in the hypothesis. That's why decisions about operationalization are crucial to the overall validity of research findings, as are all the other decisions made throughout the research process.

The Chapter 3 Quick Guide table shows the measurement-related threats to construct validity. For each one, the result obtained when using the treatment or behavioral measure intended by the researcher (which would have acceptable construct validity) is contrasted with the result when unacceptable measurement error is introduced into the intended variable. It should be noted that every research study compares at least two treatments, or levels of the independent variable, and may assess more than one behavior as well.

The validity issues involved in specifying the research variables that will represent the constructs in the research hypothesis are complex enough that our discussion of them will occupy two chapters, this one and the next. In this chapter, we

Chapter 3 Quick Guide:		
Measurement Threats to Construct Validity I		
Threat to Validity	*Intended by Researcher*	*Actual, If Contaminated With Measurement Error*
Independent Variable		
Lack of reliability	Treatment X	Treatment X plus or minus excessive random error
Lack of representativeness	Treatment X	Treatment that lacks an important component of the causal construct represented by Treatment X
Lack of impact	Treatments representing contrasting levels of the causal construct	Treatments that lack sufficient contrast to permit a determination of the effect of the causal construct on the behavior in question
Dependent Variable		
Lack of reliability	Behavioral measure O	Unreliable measures of participants' responses to treatments
Lack of representativeness	Behavioral measure O	Behavioral measure that fails to assess an important component of the behavioral construct represented by O
Lack of sensitivity	Behavioral measure O	Behavioral measure that lacks the sensitivity required to detect possible effects of treatments

will consider basic issues of definition and measurement. In the next, we will move on to problems that arise when these basic principles are implemented in research and, finally, an overview of the threats to construct validity.

INTRODUCTION TO THE CHAPTER ●

Let's assume that a working hypothesis has been established, preferably a conceptually valid hypothesis that does not unnecessarily duplicate previous research and that extends in meaningful ways the previous research and associated theory related to the behavior in question. The first step in turning that hypothesis into a useful research study is to specify the operations by which the constructs making up the hypothesis will be measured (the putative cause and the behavior presumed to be its effect).

In this chapter, we will consider the questions a researcher must answer in order to make useful measurements on which to base an investigation of the relationship between those constructs. Those questions are embedded in the larger issue of **construct validity**. The quality of the answers to those questions will determine the quality of the measurements that are ultimately made. The quality of those measurements, in turn, will help determine the value of the contribution made by the research study toward determining the truth or falsity of the research hypothesis—in other words, the validity of the research findings.

In formal terms, the cause and effect constructs in the hypothesis need to be transformed into the *independent variable* and *dependent variable*, respectively. The independent variable consists of precisely those variations or levels of the putative cause whose effects will be compared when the research study is carried out. Those variations are often referred to as the **treatments**. In our long-running discussion of the causes of aggression, the independent variable would be the levels of TV violence to which the research participants would be exposed. The dependent variable consists of precisely those measurements of behavior that will be used to determine the effects of the variations in the independent variable. In our example, the dependent variables are the measures of aggression used to evaluate the effects of TV violence.

In both cases, the basic issue is construct validity, the issue of the quality of measurement. Do we know precisely and accurately how much and what type of causal conditions are present on any given occasion, and do those treatments faithfully represent the causal construct in the research hypothesis? Do we know precisely and accurately how much and what type of behavior is present on the same occasion, and do those behavioral measures faithfully represent the behavioral construct in the research hypothesis? The more confidence we can have that the answers to those questions are in the affirmative, the more useful our test of the research hypothesis will be.

The notion that the meanings of scientific constructs need to be established through direct ties to valid measurement processes is known in science as **operational definition** or **operationalization** (Figure 3.1 is a visual depiction of the process of operationalization for one hypothesis, the familiar hypothesis that TV violence causes aggression.) One of the leading advocates of operationalization was physicist Percy Bridgman. Bridgman, in turn, was inspired by the school of philosophy known as **Logical Positivism** (its members are often referred to as "positivists"). In their efforts to create a philosophical basis for science, an *epistemology*, or system for knowing nature, the positivists stressed two points that are reflected in the label they chose for themselves.

Taking the phrase "logical positivism" apart, back to front, the positivists' first point was that scientific constructs must be defined by the observations that are used to measure them. This would mean that the attitudes, emotions, traits, memories, and other constructs studied in psychology would be defined solely by the

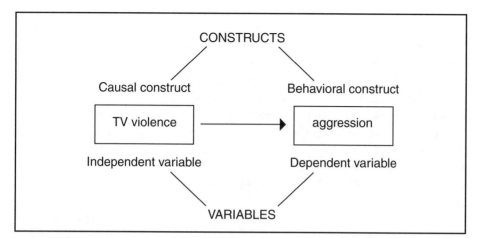

Figure 3.1. The process of operationalization.

specific questionnaires, rating scales, psychophysiological devices, or other measurement tools that were used to determine how much people liked broccoli, how afraid they were of dogs, what they remembered about a book they had read, or whatever.

For the philosophers, this was a positivist approach in the sense that the use of direct observation or measurement of the behavior or the experience referred to by the construct permitted the scientist to be positive about how much of it there was. Bridgman and others suggested the term "operational definition" because constructs were to be defined in terms of the operations used to measure them. There could be no excess meaning, no assumptions about what people were experiencing or what they were doing that went beyond what could be observed or measured. Tying constructs to measurement operations in this way is key to scientific research being objective, public, and repeatable.

The second point made by the logical positivists deals with the logic or inference that is used to link the construct with the particular technique used to measure it. Once we commit to using blood pressure as a measure of emotional arousal, we can be positive that we will know arousal when we see it, and that we will be able to tell less of it from more, using the very precise blood pressure scale. But this begs the question: By what logic or inference is blood pressure an appropriate measure of emotion? Why not use fingernail length, or hair color, or even what people tell us about how emotional they feel? The inference that blood pressure is linked to arousal is a logical conclusion based on accepted premises that describe the environmental factors that influence blood pressure, the neural mechanisms that regulate it, and so on.

Even given the requirements that constructs be defined in terms of the operations used to measure them—that they be specified as independent and dependent variables in terms of observations and that those observations be tied logically to the constructs they represent—the transformation from construct to variable can be carried out in any research study in a wide variety of ways. The researcher must choose among alternative operational definitions or measurement procedures. In addition, as in the other steps in the research process, those choices can be better or worse. If they are better, we will know more about the relationship between the antecedent conditions and consequent behaviors being studied. If they are worse, we will know less. In this chapter, we will consider a variety of criteria that distinguish better choices from worse ones. Those criteria allow us to evaluate the construct validity of variables, or how well they represent their respective constructs.

As is true of other aspects of validity, construct validity will be evaluated by the degree to which potential threats, in this case potential flaws in the measurement procedures and the logic of operationalization, can be ruled out. If you recall the preliminary discussion of this question in Chapter 1 (you can refresh your memory by taking another look at Table 1.2), you know that there's a fairly long list of potential threats to construct validity that need to be considered. These threats will not be considered until the next chapter, after we've reviewed the basics of measurement in this one. They will be introduced one at a time then, as they come up in the discussion. There will be a complete list later on in Chapter 4, when it should be easier to follow.

● MEASUREMENT SCALES

Before we embark on a tour of the many potential threats to construct validity, we will review some basic ideas about measurement in general and psychological measurement in particular. First, we're going to consider how different types of **measurement scales** afford varying levels of **precision** in measurement, although their use may be limited somewhat by the nature of the construct to be measured. Then we'll consider several **psychometric criteria**, so called because they are used to evaluate various aspects of psychological measurement. This background will prove helpful when we consider potential threats to construct validity.

Observation is often said to be the hallmark of science. Scientists trust what they see with their own eyes or instruments, rather than what seems reasonable or what they have been told by people who ought to know. This commitment to the **empirical method** of knowing the world—in preference to relying on reason that might be subject to personal bias or faulty logic, or received wisdom (faith)—makes good sense to most scientists, but it sounds easier than it really is. How, as psychologists, do we observe people's emotions, intelligence, or personalities?

How do we observe how much stress they're under, how much peer pressure they're subjected to, or how much parental love and affection they receive?

It seems fairly obvious that many of the behaviors psychologists would like to study, and many of the possible causes of those behaviors, cannot be observed directly. So how do we determine the type and amount of behavior, or the type and amount of a possible cause, that may be present in a particular setting?

One thing we need to understand is that **measurement** is, in general terms, a process by which some symbol is used to represent an event in nature. That event could be the violence portrayed in a television program or the aggression displayed by a viewer of that program. Any other event that might influence behavior, or any other behavior, could just as easily be used as an example of the events that might need to be measured in psychological research. In other contexts, of course, we measure the produce we buy in the supermarket, how much we like a particular movie, the growth of a child, and too many other things to mention here.

Among the exemplar studies we reviewed in Chapter 2, Rotter (**E1**, 1966) measured the I-E personality trait, Darley & Latané (**E7**, 1968) measured their research participants' responses to a staged emergency, and Frazier (**E25**, 1985) measured the level of violence in the Contra Costa County jail. The basic principles of measurement we'll be considering here could be applied to any specific form of measurement, although we'll focus on psychological measurement in our choice of examples, for obvious reasons.

The first thing we need to consider is the general point that the particular symbol that is used to represent a natural event when we measure it can determine the usefulness of that measurement. To some extent, the choice of that symbol depends on what is being measured, but to some extent it also depends on the judgment of the person doing the measurement. To understand how that choice is made and the consequences it may have for the outcome of the research, we will use a classification system first introduced by psychologist S. S. Stevens (1951) in one of the first research methods textbooks published for students of psychology.

Stevens described four measurement types or *measurement scales* that provide different amounts of information about an event by representing that event with a particular type of symbol. Those measurement scales can be arranged in order of the amount of information or precision of measurement that they afford (see Table 3.1). Our purpose here is to understand how those scales differ in informativeness or precision.

The Nominal Scale of Measurement

The simplest form of measurement utilizes what Stevens designated the **nominal scale** of measurement. A nominal scale, as its label implies, simply assigns a name or label to each event that is to be measured to designate one of its proper-

TABLE 3.1   Measurement Scale Properties

Characteristic	Name of Scale
A different score means a difference in the property being measured	Nominal
Previous characteristic, and a higher score means that there is more of the property being measured	Ordinal
Previous characteristics, and an equal distance along the scale indicates an equal difference in the property being measured	Interval (Equal-Interval)
Previous characteristics, and a zero point at which none of the characteristics being measured is present, making ratios of scale scores meaningful	Ratio

ties. For example, political scientists might measure registered voters' party affiliations by assigning each voter (event) the label Democrat, Republican, or Independent (property). More labels could be added to the scale (Libertarian, Socialist, etc.) without changing the basic fact that this form of measurement merely groups events (voters) together by assigning each of the different types of an event a different label, with each label being mutually exclusive of the others. A voter can be only one type, whether he or she reports to the researcher what that is or whether the researcher checks voting registration records to find out which type it is. Similarly, a biologist might measure the species membership of a plant or animal by labeling each individual organism (the "event" in this case) with a mutually exclusive term such as *Homo sapiens* that distinguishes it from different types or species.

Among our exemplar studies, the distinctions between Triplett's (1897) alone versus together treatments (**E3**), Clark and Clark's (1940) research participants' choices of a black or white doll (**E6**), and Cherulnik et al.'s (1981) research participants' guesses that a target person was a high or low Mach (**E17**) are examples of nominal measurement. Even if more categories were added, such as medium-high and medium-low, they would still constitute nominal measurements. That is because the judgments would be categorical, rather than judgments along a continuous scale.

It should be clear from these examples that nominal measurement does not tell us how much of any property is displayed by each of these events. Although some Republicans might be more committed Republicans than are others, we don't know that from a nominal measurement because all Republicans are labeled alike. In the same way, some people might be more extreme Internals than are other Internals, in Rotter's (1966) research (**E1**), but nominal measurement or categorization ignores those differences. It would be possible to determine the extent of such properties, in theory at least, and to assign a number that measures them, as we'll see below, so why not do that? In some cases, it isn't easy. Party affiliation can be determined easily from voter registration lists at the county courthouse, whereas information about degree of party affiliation would require direct contact with each registered voter to administer a survey or interview that some voters might not be eager to answer. In addition, such quantification may not be necessary. It certainly isn't if, for example, we ask the question how many registered Democrats, Republicans, and Independents there are in Oklahoma, compared to California. Not only can the degree to which someone is an Internal (or External, for that matter) be measured more precisely, using the score on Rotter's I-E Scale, but it must be before the nominal measurement or category assignment can be made. In practice, however, that information is rarely used.

Nominal measurement is sometimes called **qualitative measurement** because the measurements, even if they are expressed as numbers, don't reflect how much of the property being measured has been observed, only the type or quality of it. That distinguishes it from **quantitative measurement**, for which the symbols used are numbers that do indicate how much of the event in question was present, not just what type. Qualitative measurement is not used as much as quantitative in psychology, for reasons to be discussed more later, but it is sometimes very useful. For example, in a classic study by Gibson and Walk (1960), infants were placed in the middle of a platform. On one side there seemed to be a solid surface, while on the other side there appeared to be a steep drop-off (although a sturdy sheet of glass actually prevented the infant from falling). The structure was called the "visual cliff." In measuring the effects of various conditions on the infants being studied, the researchers simply designated the two contrasting routes available to the infant, the solid surface and the visual cliff. In measuring the infants' responses, then, they simply labeled each response according to the particular direction the infant chose.

Frazier (**E25**, 1985) compared qualitatively different jail designs for safety and comfort. That study is an example of nominal measurement of the independent variable.

Simply distinguishing between two possible responses is nominal measurement. All Gibson and Walk had to do was count how many tests and how many responses fell into each of the categories, just as political scientists count registered Democrats or dog show organizers count the number of Irish Setters registered to compete. In Gibson and Walk's case, that was enough. Their finding that very young infants avoided the visual cliff, even when their mothers tried to coax them in that direction, has been as influential in psychology as any study using the most precise form of quantitative measurement. The same could be said about research into the I-E personality trait, almost all of it based on nominal measurement of the trait—Internals versus Externals, or about Frazier's finding that some jail designs are safer than others.

The Ordinal Scale of Measurement

The three other measurement scales that Stevens (1951) described are all quantitative because they use numbers to indicate the amounts of the properties of events. They do not, however, all provide the same amount of information or precision in their symbols or measurements.

The simplest of these is the **ordinal scale** of measurement, so called because it orders the events being measured, or arranges them in order according to the amount of some property they all possess. The symbols that make up an ordinal scale are known as **ranks**. The event with the greatest amount of the property being measured is usually assigned the rank 1, the one with the next greatest amount 2, and so on.

Sometimes ordinal measurement, or rank ordering, is used because no more precise measurement is available. In the absence of a yardstick or tape measure, one could measure the lengths of pieces of wood by placing them alongside one another, then arranging them in order from longest to shortest and assigning them ranks in that order. I recall an elementary school gym teacher of mine who made up basketball teams by lining us up in order of height, then separating the members of each adjacent pair between two teams to equalize the teams for height. He didn't know exactly how tall we all were, but he still ended up with pretty evenly matched teams (on height, anyway) without taking a lot more time to apply more precise measurement.

The ratings of psychotherapy outcomes in the studies reviewed (meta-analyzed) by Smith and Glass (**E24**, 1977), as well as the grades received by the schoolchildren in Rosenthal and Jacobson's (1966) study of teacher expectancies (**E15**), are examples of ordinal-level measurement. They indicate which outcomes were better and which worse, and which students did better and worse, respectively.

The Interval Scale of Measurement

We could measure height more precisely if we just had the right tools, but what about school performance? Can we really know more than that one person knows more than another? Do we have a tool that can tell us how much more? We will pursue that question further as we go on.

The next higher level of precision is found in the **interval scale**, or **equal-interval scale**, of measurement. Here, again, the symbols are numbers that indicate amounts, but these numbers don't just designate more or less. They tell us something about *how much* more or less there is of some property of the events being measured. In the physical world, the scale we usually use to measure temperature, the Fahrenheit scale, is a good example of interval measurement. Each

---

| Box 3.1 | *THINKING ABOUT RESEARCH* |

Not All Numbers Are Alike

In the aftermath of a recent catastrophic earthquake in Turkey, much of the media attention focused on the very heavy casualties. About a week after the quake, more than 12,000 deaths had been confirmed by Turkish government officials, and many more victims were feared buried in the rubble. This tragedy was also the occasion for remembering other earthquakes of historic proportions, including one in China in which more than 600,000 people died.

One reason for the high numbers of casualties in the worst earthquakes is the severity of the quakes themselves. The intensity of an earthquake is measured on the Richter scale, which has a range from 1 to 10. The Turkish earthquake measured 7.4, and the one in China registered 8.0.

The damage and casualties that occur during an earthquake also depend on factors other than the intensity of the quake itself, including soil conditions, population density, and building construction methods. Even so, it seems difficult to reconcile the seemingly small difference in scale values between 7.4 and 8.0 with such a great difference in the amount of damage and loss of life.

Part of the explanation lies in the nature of the Richter scale itself. We are accustomed to scales like those for length and weight, which have equal distances among scale units (the difference between 6 and 7 inches is the same as the difference between 13 and 14 inches, etc.). The Richter scale is quite different. It is a logarithmic scale, which means that each whole number on the scale represents 10 times the magnitude of the whole number below it, and within each of those intervals, each tenth of a unit represents a greater increase than the tenth below it. Even more striking, an increase of one unit on the Richter scale represents that the amount of energy released during the more powerful earthquake is 31 times as great as that released during the lesser one. The difference in power between earthquakes that register 8.0 versus 7.4 on the Richter scale is much greater than a comparison of the numbers, 8.0 versus 7.4, would make it appear to someone unfamiliar with the properties of the scale.

What questions should we ask when we hear about a comparison of measurements made in unfamiliar scale units like those of the Richter scale? What do we need to understand about measurement to understand the magnitude of earthquakes, tornadoes, hurricanes, and other natural phenomena? Can you think of other examples that raise similar questions?

---

pair of adjacent numbers on that scale represents an equal difference in temperature between objects whose temperature might be measured.

Temperature is defined in this case as the amount of kinetic energy in the molecules in the substance being measured—that is, the speed with which atoms are moving around inside them. If one substance measures one degree Fahrenheit warmer than another, the additional energy in, or speed of, the atoms that make up that substance is always the same, no matter where the two measurements are along the Fahrenheit scale (5 degrees vs. 6 degrees, 37 degrees vs. 38 degrees, etc.). In other words, the scale has equal intervals.

Interval measurement permits a more precise comparison of events than simple rank ordering, where the difference between two ranks might be 1 degree or 100 degrees. The same, of course, is true of basketball teams. A team whose tallest player (rank = 1) is 7 feet, 2 inches tall is quite different from one whose tallest player is 6 feet, 2 inches tall (also rank = 1).

But what about interval measurement in psychology? Psychologists would obviously know more about an individual's intelligence if it were measured on an interval scale than if it were rank-ordered. Unfortunately, however, interval-level measurement of intelligence (and many other psychological properties) turns out to be highly problematic.

Before we try to understand more about the measurement of intelligence, consider how a researcher in social psychology might measure how much one person likes another. One way would be to give that person a rating scale like this one:

1	2	3	4	5	6	7
DISLIKE			NEITHER LIKE NOR DISLIKE			LIKE

The person would circle a number at the point on the scale that best represents how much he or she likes some other person (sometimes referred to as a "target" person). That number would represent or measure the degree of liking for the other person, from 1 at the DISLIKE end of the scale to 7 at the LIKE end. But do we know that the differences between adjacent points on the scale (1 and 2, 2 and 3, and so on) represent equal changes in the amount of liking, the way that the differences or intervals on the Fahrenheit temperature scale are equal? Unfortunately, we don't. We probably can say safely only that a rating of 1 represents less liking than 2, and 2 less than 3, and so on. That is unfortunate, because not only do the numbers on interval scales tell us more about the events we've measured than do ranks, but they also are useful in a more practical sense.

Once measurements have been made in a research study, they are used to evaluate the hypothesis being tested. To do that in psychology, measurements usually are subjected to statistical analysis (a topic we will consider in detail in Chapter 10). In most statistical analyses, the numbers that have been assigned to the events that have occurred (the behaviors that have been observed) are added up or summed, then averaged and manipulated in a variety of other ways. There are forms of statistical analysis that don't require those arithmetic manipulations, but they are less informative than those that do and, therefore, are less widely used. The problem with the statistics that require summing, averaging, and so on is that ordinal numbers from rating scales—like the one for liking discussed above—can't legitimately be treated that way.

To add and average numbers meaningfully, the numbers need to come from a scale with at least interval properties (an even more precise measurement scale, the ratio scale, will be discussed below). To see why, let's look at an example. Let's say we wanted to measure how much Americans like Communism, or, as a social psychologist might put it, their attitudes toward Communism. We might use a rating scale like this one:

1	2	3	4	5	6	7
COMMUNISM IS BAD			COMMUNISM IS NEITHER GOOD NOR BAD			COMMUNISM IS GOOD

Like the numbers from the attractiveness rating scale discussed earlier, the numbers people circled on this scale would represent their attitudes, from 1 for bad to 7 for good. But what do those numbers mean to the people who mark the scale? Because measuring their attitudes essentially involves them holding the scale up to themselves to see what they're like, their view of the scale is important.

We can probably safely assume that the people whose attitudes we measure will see the intervals on the scale as representing more positive attitudes toward Communism as they run from left to right. In other words, we can assume that they understand that the response to which we would assign a 2 is more favorable to Communism than the one we would assign a 1, and so on up to 7. But how different would 1 and 2, 3 and 4, and so on appear to them?

If they were educated during the Cold War, as I was, to believe that Communism is a totally evil political system, they might see 2 as being a long way from 1 because it implies that Communism isn't all bad. The other steps or intervals on the scale might seem smaller because they just represent increments of "badness," not the giant step from completely bad to not so bad. That's just one example of how this scale might function for a particular individual. To that hypothetical person, the scale might actually look like this, with the intervals shrinking progressively as we move up the scale, from 1 to 7:

1	2	3	4	5	6	7
COMMUNISM IS BAD			COMMUNISM IS NEITHER GOOD NOR BAD			COMMUNISM IS GOOD

Imagine, for the sake of this argument, that this is the case. Then what if we measured the attitudes of 10 people who all read the scale that way, and their responses were as follows:

Person Number	Response
1	3
2	4
3	1
4	2
5	6
6	3
7	2
8	3
9	1
10	2

How could we determine their average attitude? If we just added their responses as they appear above and averaged them, we'd get 2.7 as the average. How far from 1 toward 10 is 2.7? Arithmetically, it's less than one-third of the way from bad to good. But in terms of these individuals' readings of the scale, if they read it the way we're guessing they might, it might actually be more than halfway to good. Because the scale intervals are not equal, adding and averaging the measurements obtained from that scale distorts the true nature of the events being measured. In that case, 2.7 doesn't really mean what we'd expect 2.7 to mean. Only an equal-interval (or more precise) scale can produce measurements than can be legitimately treated as "real numbers."

There are ways of producing rating scales such as the attitude and attractiveness scales discussed above that provide measurements that have interval properties. They happen to take a lot more time and effort than just drawing a line and dividing it ad hoc into a number of equal segments. For that reason, and because of some disputes about how well these methods actually work, they are used vary rarely in psychological research.

Frazier's (1985) evaluation of the modular direct-supervision design for jails (**E25**) utilized ad hoc rating scales administered to inmates and corrections officers. Broverman et al.'s (**E5**, 1972) subjects rated the "average adult man" and "average adult woman" on a variety of ad hoc rating scales, and there are innumerable examples in social psychology and other research fields. On the other hand, Siegel and his colleagues (Macrae et al., 1987) measured the effect of morphine on rats using the interval-level Fahrenheit scale of temperature as an indicator of pain tolerance (**E10**).

Does that mean that psychologists who use scales that don't have equal intervals can't analyze the results with statistical methods based on arithmetic manipulation? Can they describe their results only by counting how many times each response is observed and analyze them only by using statistics designed for use with nominal or ordinal measures? Some mathematicians believe that treating ordinal data as though they were interval does no real harm to the results of statistical analyses. For obvious reasons, most research psychologists are eager to believe they're right.

The Ratio Scale of Measurement

The final and most precise measurement scale is known as the **ratio scale**. When the numbers assigned to events have the properties of a ratio scale of measurement, they have all the properties of interval scale measurements. Each interval on the scale is equal in size, so that the arithmetic operations required in most statistical analyses can be performed with confidence. They also have one additional property—ratio scales have true zero points. That means that a measurement of zero on a ratio scale means that there is a complete absence of the property being measured in the event being observed.

Defining a ratio scale might start most profitably by explaining why interval (and other) scales lack true zero points. When we measure the temperature of something as zero degrees Fahrenheit, that does not mean that there is zero (no) heat present. After all, Fahrenheit measurements of temperature can go below zero. If we were to measure someone's physical attractiveness as zero, using a rating scale that starts at 0, rather than 1, that would not mean that the person had no attractiveness or beauty.

In scales that lack true zero points, the zero points are arbitrary. On the Fahrenheit temperature scale, 0 is 32 degrees (Fahrenheit) below the point at which water freezes. On the Celsius temperature scale, 0 is the temperature at which water freezes. On both scales, there are much lower temperatures. People who might be rated 0 on a scale of physical attractiveness could still be more attractive than unfortunate people with deformities, even if the scale doesn't include negative numbers, as the Fahrenheit and Celsius temperature scales do.

A scale that has a true zero point—a ratio scale—automatically has all the properties of other scales of measurement. It has equal intervals, its scale values indicate rank order, and different values on the scale indicate a difference in the property being measured. As shown in Table 3.1, each of the four types of scales has the properties of those below it, with nominal being the lowest on the hierarchy, followed by ordinal, interval, and ratio. A ratio scale carries that name because its true zero point means that valid ratio comparisons can be made among the measurements it generates.

The second-tallest member of a basketball team is not necessarily twice as tall as the fourth-tallest member, and 40 degrees Fahrenheit is not twice as hot (by any standard) as 20 degrees Fahrenheit. Four inches, however, *is* twice as long as 2 inches, and 9 pounds *is* three times as heavy as 3 pounds, and so on. That's because a measurement of 0 inches actually does mean no length and 0 pounds actually does indicate no weight. The comparisons that can be made using ratio-scale measurement (remember the crucial role of comparison in testing a research hypothesis) are considerably more precise and useful than those made with other types of measurement scales.

Some ratio scales are obscure and necessary only for specialized purposes such as scientific research. On the Kelvin temperature scale, for example, there is a true zero point. Zero degrees Kelvin means absolutely no heat, no movement at all of the atoms within the molecule whose temperature is being measured. Needless to say, the average person never encounters an object whose temperature is even close to zero degrees Kelvin. There are many ratio measurement scales, however, that are much more familiar. As indicated above, when we measure distance or time, we use ratio scales. Measurements of 0 inches and 0 seconds mean none of the property, distance or time, was detected. Something never moved or never got started.

Ratio scales are used quite commonly in psychological research. A rat's performance in a maze might be measured by the amount of time it takes to get from the start to the end, or the effects of physical appearance on a person's self-concept might be measured by the length of time the person looks in a mirror. The degree to which two people like one another has been measured by the freely chosen distance between them as they stand side by side, and the effects of arousal have been studied by varying the distance between a man standing at a urinal in a public bathroom and the person standing beside him, then measuring the time it takes the man to begin to urinate. Time and distance typically are measured on ratio scales.

Among our exemplar studies, Pavlov (1927) measured the volume of saliva secreted to assess the strength of conditioning (**E20**). Dement (1960) measured the amount of time his subjects spent in REM sleep (**E14**), and Rosenzweig et al. (1972) counted and weighed brain cells and tissue to determine the effects of enriched environments on rats (**E22**). Volume, time, and weight are all ratio measurements.

Although it is important to understand as much as possible about the four types of measurement scales, we ought not lose sight of the most important point. We are accustomed to using numbers as though they have a fixed, universal meaning. Our experience in learning mathematics may have led us to believe that 1 is always 1, $(3 - 2) = (8 - 7)$, $4/2 = 2$, and so on, but Stevens's analysis of measurement scales makes it clear that being in Platoon No. 1, ranking number one in a high school graduating class, having a temperature of 1 degree Fahrenheit, and being 1 inch long represent properties of objects or events being measured by four very different 1's.

When we assign a number to represent some property of an event, to measure that property of that event, the rules by which we assign the number (the scale we

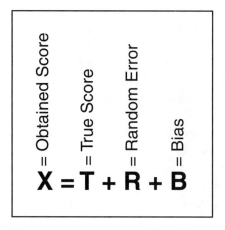

Figure 3.2. True score test theory.

use to measure the property) determine the meaning of that number. Our measurements need to be interpreted and used with those rules—the scale of measurement—in mind.

TRUE SCORE TEST THEORY ●

Another basic fact about measurement needs to be kept in mind as well. It is known as **true score test theory**. Don't let the term "test" throw you off. True score test theory applies to more than scores on tests like IQ tests and personality tests. For its purposes, and ours, any measurement device—formal test, rating scale, stopwatch timing—is a test, and any measurement derived from it is a score. Any measurement made by a researcher of the state of an independent variable or dependent variable, in other words, constitutes a score.

True score test theory can be summarized, as in Figure 3.2, in an equation:

$$X = T + R + B.$$

(Others may use slightly different symbols, but the theory remains pretty much the same in different versions.) In this equation, **X** stands for the **obtained score**, the measurement or observation that is actually made. This could be the score a television program received for the amount of violence it contains, or the rating a child received from his or her teacher for displaying a particular level of aggressive behavior on the playground.

T stands for the **true score** in true score test theory. In the examples above, the true score is the actual amount of violence or aggression that occurs. In general, it is the actual amount of a particular property that is present in the event being measured. It is important to understand that "true score" is a hypothetical term. There is no way to determine how much violence there is in a TV program or how aggressive a child is except to use some form of measurement, and measurements are obtained scores, not true scores. If it were possible to obtain the true score directly, there would be no need for measurement and no reason for us to be considering all the difficulties it entails.

Because the result of any actual measurement is **X**, **T** must be something else. The fact that **X** and **T** are not equal in the true score test theory equation, because **X** equals **T** plus two other quantities, should make it even clearer that the true score is not measured but assumed.

The TV program contains a certain degree of violence, and the child exhibits a certain degree of aggression in his or her behavior. Those are the properties that need to be measured to test the hypothesis that TV violence causes aggression, and they do exist in some real sense. True score test theory is all about how to be sure that the measurements of those properties, or obtained scores (**X**s) represent as accurately as possible the actual properties themselves, or true scores (**T**s). The goal of measurement, then, in the terms of true score test theory, is for **X** and **T** to be equal, or at least as close as they can possibly be. The **T** term is used to help us to understand the problem, even though it doesn't really exist.

There are, unfortunately, many reasons why measurements might not accurately reflect or agree with true scores. One category of reasons is represented by **R** in the true score test theory equation. **R** stands for **random error**. When we measure some behavior, we need to recognize that our measurement is influenced by a variety of factors. One of them is the actual property we are measuring. Some of the others are short-lived influences on the measurement process whose effects fluctuate randomly over time.

Consider the problem of measuring intelligence. (Our discussion of intelligence is purposely simplified to highlight the measurement issues we're considering here, notwithstanding other important issues in understanding intelligence that must be left to other texts and other courses.) One element of that measurement might be a question on an intelligence test about the meaning of a word. If the person whose intelligence is being measured defines the word correctly, his or her intelligence test score (**X**) goes up. If the answer is incorrect, the score goes down.

The person's answer, however, does not depend solely on how much he or she knows (**T**, actual intelligence). It might depend also on when the question is asked. If it is asked when the person is well-rested, alert, highly motivated to do well, and concentrating on the question, the answer might be correct. If the same question is asked on a different occasion, when the person is tired, bored, resentful at having to take the test, or daydreaming about something more exciting, the answer might be incorrect. The person's state of mind and motivation are random (**R**) factors that could influence that person's intelligence test score in either a positive or a negative direction.

The measurement obtained (**X** = obtained score) therefore depends not only on the property being measured (**T** = true score = person's actual level of intelligence) but also on random influences whose effects vary over time (**R**). Recall that Zajonc and Markus's (1975) study of the effects of birth order and family size on intelligence (**E16**) was based on a comparison of IQ test scores, and Haier et al. (**E23**, 1992) used IQ scores as their independent variable in comparing brain function between more and less intelligent subjects.

Imagine another example. A sample of a television program is presented to participants in a research study of aggression. The sample was selected because it contained a very high level of violent content. In this case, the sample's score for violent content measures the amount of violence to which research participants are supposed to be exposed when they view it. The same sorts of random influences that might operate to distort a measure of a person's intelligence, however, also can influence a measure of violence in TV programming.

If an individual happened to be distracted by some personal problem or even a commotion in the hallway while watching the program, its actual violent content might be diluted by the lack of attention. On the other hand, if the person exposed to the program had recently gone through a traumatic violent experience, the program might have an exaggerated impact. Again, these are random events with respect to the person's experience in the research study.

Random influences change the nature of a person's behavior or of an event he or she experiences (the subjective experience, in the example used here). They are, first of all, distortions of the true properties of the events in question (how intelligent the person is or how violent the content of the program is) that cause the measurement of those events (**X**s) to misrepresent the true properties (**T**s).

They are also, however, random distortions. Because the measurement is made at an arbitrary point in time, there is no way to tell in advance how the measurement will be distorted, if at all. Over repeated occasions, these random fluctuations will cancel each other out, so that the average of many repeated measurements will equal the hypothetical true value.

A person's average IQ score over many repeated testings, or a person's measured experience of a TV program over many repeated viewings, will average out to be accurate reflections of the person's intelligence or the program's content. Alert days and dull days, daydreamy days and anxious days, are interspersed randomly throughout most of our lives. Over numerous instances, then, there will be as many overestimates as underestimates based on random errors of measurement. (We will see more in the next chapter about why random errors may still constitute a threat to the validity of research findings.)

The second reason that measurements do not accurately reflect the underlying properties being measured is **bias (B** in the true score test theory equation, as we're symbolizing it here). Unlike random factors, which can be expected to balance out, so that repeated measurements will average out to the true score value, biases are sources of **systematic error**. Biases distort measurements so as to *consistently* overestimate or underestimate the actual property being measured (true score).

Some biases are rooted in the individual who makes the measurement. Some people, for example, are more reluctant than others to make judgments of another person. When asked to mark a rating scale to report their judgment of how intelligent or honest another person is, they stick to the middle portion of the scale. Other people are especially generous in their ratings, using the favorable end of the scale for everyone they rate. Still others rate everyone low. Assuming that the people or events being rated have properties that vary along the entire scale, these individual rating patterns are biased. They are known as the **central tendency bias**, **leniency bias**, and **strictness bias**, respectively.

Other biases are rooted in the measuring instrument itself. In research I have conducted over a period of several years, I have asked research participants to rate, on each of a series of traits, strangers presented to them in photographs. At the beginning, I thought it was a good idea to include trait adjectives that covered a wide spectrum of favorability, from very positive ones like "intelligent" to very negative ones like "dishonest."

I learned gradually that people who were asked to judge the character of strangers hardly ever chose the most negative traits if they were asked to select a fixed number of adjectives to describe each target. If they were asked how much of the trait the person had, they were reluctant to say that any stranger had a lot of a very negative trait. This is another type of leniency bias, one that is characteristic not of specific individual raters but of the measuring instrument given to all raters. When I substituted less extreme negative terms for those that hardly anyone ever used, the measuring instrument was improved. Broverman et al.'s (1972) study of gender-role stereotypes (**E5**) and other similar studies would face the same potential problem of leniency bias.

A more socially significant example of bias residing in the measuring instrument can be found in measures of intelligence. People who take IQ tests are asked to define words and idiomatic expressions, among other things. To make it possible to give appropriately high scores to the small number of people with the most intelligence, IQ tests have to include some fairly difficult questions about obscure words or expressions. But how are those test items to be presented? One common method is to present the word or expression in a sentence, so that it is encountered on the test in a context in which it is actually used.

If everyone who was tested came from the same background, they might all be equally familiar with the context that is chosen for a given word. In a country like

| Box 3.2 | *THINKING ABOUT RESEARCH* |

Going Into Battle Without a Helmet _____

When England first entered World War I, during the second decade of the 20th century, its soldiers wore cloth caps on their heads when they were on the field of battle. As the war progressed, British military officials became more and more concerned about their troops' vulnerability to damage to their heads from bullets, shrapnel, and the like. Eventually, metal helmets were designed, manufactured, and issued to the British troops in the field.

After the metal helmets were introduced, however, the incidence of head injuries was greater than it had been before. What could explain an increase in head injuries following the switch from cloth to metal head protection?

If you want a clue to help you solve this mystery, you might ask yourself whether the rate of head injuries was the right way to measure the effects of the switch to metal helmets. What other measure could one use to assess their value? Don't read the next paragraph until you're ready to give up trying to figure it out on your own.

As it turns out, the reason head injuries were more frequent with helmets than caps is that helmets worked. When the British soldiers wore cloth caps in battle, those who were struck in the head by projectiles were usually killed. When, later in the war, the troops wore metal helmets, their wounds were less likely to be fatal, and thus more likely to be recorded as head injuries rather than deaths.

Does this seem to you like a problem with construct validity? If so, what particular threat to construct validity does it represent? Does it highlight the importance of valid measurement in answering a research question correctly?

---

the United States, however, with its different regions, ethnic groups, social classes, and other sources of diversity, what is familiar to the person who writes an intelligence test question may not be equally familiar to all the people who take the test.

If this is true, then test scores will underestimate the true intelligence of those who come from backgrounds very different from that of the question writer. They might even overestimate the intelligence of those from very similar backgrounds, who have an unfair advantage of getting better clues (for them) to the meaning of the term they are to define.

Unlike random measurement errors, biases like this one don't cancel themselves out across different measurement occasions. Instead, they produce consistent differences between obtained score (X) and true score (T), within the limits of any accompanying random variations. Some people consistently score lower than they should, and other people higher, no matter when or under what conditions they are measured.

The existence of random error and systematic error or bias will cause a measurement to be inaccurate. The true nature or degree of the property being measured will not be reflected in the measurement or observation that is made. Fortunately, there are ways of minimizing both random and systematic errors. Along with a constructing a more extensive catalog of those two types of error, we'll take a look at those remedies later on in this chapter. Unfortunately, none of those remedies can be implemented so neatly that its use will guarantee the elimination of a particular source of error; however, there are ways to determine how well they work.

● PSYCHOMETRIC CRITERIA

Random and systematic errors of measurement can be estimated by a number of qualitative and quantitative techniques. They permit evaluation of measurement accuracy according to a number of so-called **psychometric** (or psychological measurement) **criteria**. That is, we are going to measure the quality of our measurement. Before we look at specific criteria, the point needs to be made that the criteria are evaluated by estimating not the degree to which random error or systematic bias is present but the degree to which each is absent.

Psychometric criteria are usually broken down into two major groups known as **reliability criteria** and **validity criteria**. Although that distinction is useful in some ways, it is maintained here mainly because these terms are widely used; students may need to know them to be able to communicate with others about these issues. What is more important to understand, at this point, is that reliability and validity are both categories of criteria for evaluating the quality of psychological measurements. Each is assessed in order to determine, albeit somewhat imprecisely in some cases, the degree to which those measurements are contaminated with error.

The more reliable a measurement is, the less it is subject to random errors. That is, a more reliable measurement produces a smaller range of fluctuation (due to random influences) of individual measurements from one measurement to another. The more valid a measurement is, the less it is subject to systematic error or bias. That is, a more valid measurement reflects more clearly the underlying property of an event that is being measured, contaminated less by unintended influences on the measurement.

If a measurement is valid, then, the random fluctuations due to imperfect reliability are centered on the true score or actual value of the property being measured by the obtained scores. If not, that "center" is displaced from its true value by the bias in the measurement process. Neither reliability nor validity assessments reveal directly the nature of any error in the measurement being assessed, or the magnitude of that error. By determining how good a particular form of measurement is, in some way, each indicates indirectly how much error must be present, preventing that measurement from being even better.

Reliability Criteria

Because random error causes measurements of a property to vary from one occasion to another, although the property itself presumably does not vary, the assessment of reliability focuses on the **stability** of multiple measurements. Of course, if the property itself changes over time, that fluctuation would be reflected in the measurement, along with any lack of stability in the measurement itself. The classic method for assessing stability is the **test-retest method**. It involves measuring a number of examples of the property in question on successive occasions and then determining the degree to which those measurements agree across those occasions.

Imagine a device for measuring intelligence, an IQ test. To assess stability, it would be administered to a sample of people (events) to determine each one's level of intelligence (properties). Then, after some time had elapsed, it would be administered to the same sample again. The degree of agreement between the measurements taken on those two occasions would be determined using a statistic known as a **correlation coefficient**. In that particular case, the statistic is known as the **coefficient of stability**. It summarizes, in a single number, the degree to which the individuals in question are found to keep their same relative positions in the sets of measurements obtained on those separate occasions.

Imagine that there are 20 people whose intelligence is measured twice in an assessment of the reliability of an IQ test. Table 3.2 shows what the results of the assessment might look like. The group is small enough that you might be able to tell without statistics that those who score relatively high when tested the first time also score relatively high the second time, and those who score relatively low the first time stay relatively low when tested again. The results of this example of test-retest assessment of reliability would be analyzed statistically, using the most common method of estimating correlation, calculation of the Pearson product-moment coefficient. In this case, that coefficient is found to take the very high value of .97.

This coefficient, like most correlation measures, can vary from 0 to 1.00. A coefficient of 0 indicates no relationship between the two sets of scores, whereas 1.00 indicates a perfect relationship, meaning that there is no change at all in the relative positions of individuals (higher or lower than one another) between the two sets of scores.

A correlation coefficient can be either a positive number or a negative number. A positive coefficient, indicated by a plus sign or (more commonly, as in this example) by the lack of any sign, indicates that individuals with high scores in one set have high scores in the other. A negative coefficient, always preceded by a minus sign, indicates that those whose scores are high in one set score low in the other, and vice versa. Of course, a coefficient with a low value, near 0, means that there is little relationship, whether the sign is positive or negative.

TABLE 3.2   Results of a Test-Retest Study of Reliability

Person number	1st Score	2nd Score
1	97	100
2	102	102
3	101	99
4	111	114
5	105	103
6	117	115
7	98	99
8	104	105
9	122	121
10	100	99
11	106	105
12	118	120
13	105	103
14	102	100
15	95	98
16	120	120
17	105	107
18	117	120
19	99	98
20	101	100

Another way of showing the relationship between two variables is through the use of a **scatterplot**. See Figure 3.3 for the scatterplot that shows the measurements presented in Table 3.2. The fact that the points for those 20 pairs of measurements look a lot like a straight line is consistent with the very high value for the correlation coefficient calculated from the same data.

The reliability of any measurement can be assessed in this way. Examples might include ratings of aggression in schoolyard play, measures of violence in a TV program, the rate of keypecking by a pigeon being reinforced on a particular schedule, the length of your foot according to a shoe store sizing device, and many others.

Some technical adjustment in the assessment technique might need to be made, depending on the specific property being measured.

If a particular IQ test were administered to a group of people on two separate occasions, a few weeks apart, the people involved might remember their answers from the first occasion and repeat them on the second. That would inflate the coefficient of stability and thus overestimate the reliability of that measurement device. One solution is to create two different forms of the test, using similar items. One of these **parallel forms** would be administered on the first occasion, the other on the second. A correlation coefficient then would be calculated from those two sets of scores.

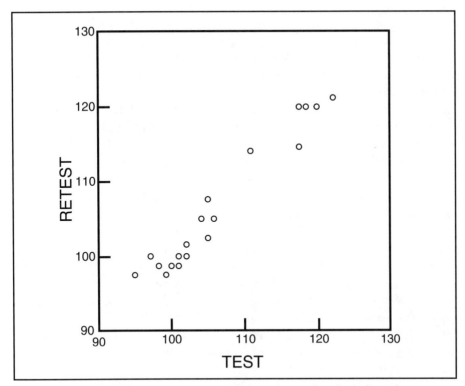

Figure 3.3. A scatterplot showing the test and retest scores for a hypothetical assessment of the stability of scores on an IQ test.

Of course, this coefficient might underestimate the stability of scores on the test because the two forms themselves would be at least slightly different, perhaps affecting the relative standing of the individuals being tested. By chance, items on the first test might be easier for some, and those on the second test easier for others. Given a choice between the two approaches, most researchers would probably favor the parallel forms method because it is more conservative. By this reasoning, which is typical of science, it's better to have too little faith in a reliable measurement than to have too much faith in an unreliable one.

Another alternative is to calculate a coefficient of **internal consistency**. In this method of assessing reliability, a group of individuals is tested (measured) just one time. Their answers to all the various individual questions on the test are split into two halves to determine whether there is consistency within the test, from one part to another. These "micro-occasions" can be the first and second halves of the test, the odd- and even-numbered items on the test, or even, using complicated statistics impossible to explain here, every possible half-and-half split. The result is a correlation coefficient that looks like any other (range of 0 to 1, positive or negative), but it doesn't tell us about stability of responses over time, just consistency of responses within the test.

As mentioned earlier, a further complication in assessing the reliability of psychological measurements is that the property being measured itself might not be completely stable. Most psychological theories of intelligence would lead us to believe that a person's intelligence would not change over a period of weeks, unless some unusual event intervened. But what about depression? Could that change in a few weeks? Or anger? That could change in a few minutes. When we consider the reliability of a measurement, therefore, we can't assume that fluctuation from one occasion to another is necessarily a reflection of random error. Both the property being measured and the interval between measurements need to be considered when evaluating a reliability coefficient.

In the end, in any specific context it is necessary to make a summary judgment about the reliability of measurement from a correlation coefficient. How high a value will be judged to indicate an acceptable level of reliability? How low a value indicates serious problems with random error? There are no hard and fast rules to follow, only guidelines based on past experience. There have been enough intelligence tests and studies of their reliability to establish guidelines for evaluating the reliability of a new test. Other forms of psychological measurement may be less well understood. Researchers concerned about the reliability of their measures can consult with colleagues by reading their published papers or talking with them at professional conferences, or in other ways collect information that will give them guidelines to follow in their own work.

It should be clear by now that measures of reliability don't measure random error directly. A higher reliability coefficient means that less random error must have occurred. If there were no random error in a measurement, reliability would be perfect—a correlation of 1.00.

Validity Criteria

Bias, or systematic error, in psychological measurement is discovered through psychometric assessments of validity. Biases and validity criteria are more diverse than their counterparts in the case of reliability, both in the types of error considered and in the methods of assessing them. Validity criteria traditionally have been organized into four categories, and we will follow that approach here.

Face Validity

The first validity criterion is known as **face validity**. It assesses the systematic error that may arise when a measure does not seem plausible to the person being measured.

Imagine that you showed up to take the SAT or ACT test as a high school senior and were told that the first part of the test required that you grab hold of a device that measured grip strength and then squeeze as hard as you could. The gauge on that device would then be read by the examiner, and the appropriate number factored into your SAT or ACT score. Is it possible that a measure of grip strength could reveal your academic aptitude? Most people would probably doubt it, although Francis Galton, a 19th century scientist, believed that it did, along with a number of other physical capacities, like reaction time, not usually thought today to be indicators of intelligence.

Let's assume that Galton was right, just for the sake of this argument. If so, the SAT or ACT testers people would need to know your grip strength to properly evaluate your academic aptitude. But how would average high school seniors respond to that part of the test? If they thought it was inappropriate, unfair, or even ridiculous, how hard would they try? If they didn't do their best, their SAT scores would be biased, underestimating their true academic aptitude. This example makes it clear how a lack of face validity can introduce systematic error into a measurement, even if it results from the use of an otherwise sensible measurement procedure (test).

Of course, there's another side to face validity—maybe even two sides. First, there are psychological measures that are constructed purposely to not be face valid. For reasons we'll address at greater length later on, some psychologists believe that we can learn more about people's motives by asking them to tell a story about an ambiguous picture than by asking them directly. Their fantasies may reveal what they would be reluctant to tell, or may not even know themselves in a conscious sense.

Second, some measures are good because they predict behavior well, even if they don't seem plausible. A former professor of mine did psychological research for the Air Force during the Korean War. He discovered that the success of pilot trainees could be predicted from their answer to a question about whether their mothers were afraid of heights. The pilot trainees probably doubted the relevance of the question when they answered it, but their answers were good measures of their aptitude for flying just the same (one aspect of it, anyway). Of course, they could have been asked whether they themselves were afraid of heights, but how many gung-ho pilot trainees, no matter how acrophobic, would have admitted that, even to themselves?

Content Validity

A second criterion for evaluating systematic measurement bias is known as **content validity**. To understand what it means, we need to start with some assumptions. The first is that the construct we want to measure may be complex, made up of multiple parts. The overall composition of the construct is sometimes referred to as its **domain**. If our measure is to reflect the construct accurately, then it must address each of the areas within the domain of that construct. To the extent that it does not, it lacks content validity and thus will be a biased representation of

---

Box 3.3 | THINKING ABOUT RESEARCH

What Does That Test Score Really Mean? _____

Affirmative action is a controversial method for redressing the hardships caused by discrimination based on race, gender, and other social characteristics. In cases in which standardized tests are used to select qualified applicants, affirmative action may involve accepting minority candidates who score lower on the tests than some of those in the majority group who are *not* accepted. But how valid are those tests as measures of the ability in question?

From 1979 to 1996, the University of Michigan law school admitted black, Hispanic, and American Indian students under its affirmative action program. Although those students' scores on the standardized Law School Admission Test (LSAT) were lower on average than those of white applicants, surveys revealed that their performance following graduation was similar in most respects to that of their white classmates.

Minority graduates passed their bar exams at the same rate and evaluated their career accomplishments similarly. By 1990, they were even earning just as much money.

What does all of this tell us about the use of the LSAT as a measure of law school applicants' abilities? Why does the test predict less success for minority students when they actually achieve just as much? What specific threat(s) to its construct validity should concern law schools that use the LSAT, minority law school applicants, and all those who believe in fair treatment?

By the way, the University of Michigan was sued in 1999 for allegedly discriminating against white law school applicants by admitting less qualified minority students. On *methodological* (not legal) grounds, is the school guilty?

---

the construct. That is, it will systematically misrepresent the property it purports to measure.

Consider tests to measure intelligence as an example. Most IQ tests focus on academic aptitude. Most of the questions on those tests address people's skills with words and numbers. Some people argue that intelligence consists of a much broader domain of aptitudes, from being able to understand mechanical systems, to being able to manage interactions with other people, to being able to understand and control one's own emotions. To the extent that those people are correct in maintaining that the domain of the construct "intelligence" encompasses many more areas than those represented on most IQ tests, the tests have poor content validity.

If that is true, scores on IQ tests are biased. The high scores of those with strong academic aptitudes but little aptitude for anything else overestimate their true intelligence. Those whose academic aptitudes are lower than their other aptitudes earn lower scores than they should, given their "true" intelligence.

Intelligence may be more complex than some other constructs, but many construct domains are complex enough that content validity needs to be addressed. Of course, the same IQ tests that stress academic aptitude would have higher construct validity if a narrower definition of intelligence were used. In that case, there would be a smaller construct domain to be sampled.

Face validity and content validity are both assessed qualitatively. That is, face validity and content validity are usually judged yes or no, good or bad, based on a visual inspection of the measure in question and a comparison between it and the construct as it is understood by the evaluator. There are no correlation coefficients, or any other statistics or numbers, that can be used to symbolize the degree to which a measure is face valid (free from biases introduced by lack of face validity) or content valid (representative of the domain of the construct being measured). The best one can do is to evaluate the measure and characterize it with some label like "good" or "poor." (By the way, what type of measurement scale would you say is being used in such assessments of face validity and content validity?)

Content validity can be assessed using quantitative methods including the use of factor analysis (which we'll discuss in more detail later in the book); these methods assess the content structure of a measure. Those methods still don't yield measures of content validity that are as clear-cut as the correlation coefficients used to assess reliability or the other aspects of validity discussed below. In the end, they are generally used as the basis for qualitative judgments. Some fairly recent developments in statistics promise to move us closer to the point of quantitative evaluation of content validity eventually, but they are far beyond the scope of this book.

The best a researcher can do at this point is to examine the construct carefully, using whatever research and theory are available, then design a measure that represents or samples the entire domain of the construct. The reader of research, or critic, must judge the degree to which the researcher has accomplished that task successfully.

Criterion-Related Validity

The most widely used assessments of validity, however, are quantitative. They make use of the same measures of correlation that are used to assess reliability. One of them, **criterion-related validity**, is based on the reasoning that if a measurement is biased, it ought not to be correlated highly with other measures to which it is related theoretically. This is, again, an indirect approach, in that those correlations do not measure criterion-related validity directly. The higher those correlations are, however, the less likely it is that the measure is contaminated with bias.

Take the example of intelligence again. If intelligence is intellectual aptitude—if that is the construct IQ tests are supposed to measure—then scores on an IQ test should correlate positively and highly with measures of intellectual performance.

Individuals with higher IQ scores should make higher grades in school, for example. They should also score higher on tests of intellectual achievement like the SAT or ACT following high school, or the GRE, LSAT, MCAT, and other such tests following college.

The higher the correlations between IQ scores and those measures of intellectual achievement, each known as a **validity coefficient**, the less likely that IQ tests are biased. If they didn't measure what they were supposed to, the argument goes, they wouldn't correlate with the other behaviors to which they ought to be related.

As in the case of reliability coefficients, validity coefficients are judged against standards developed in particular areas of measurement. Because so many factors besides intelligence are important in determining a student's grades (motivation, psychological adjustment, health, etc.), even a perfectly reliable and valid measure of intellectual aptitude would be expected to correlate only moderately strongly with grade point average (GPA). For that reason, validity coefficients generally are lower than reliabilities.

It should also be pointed out that there is a relationship between reliability and validity. To the extent that a measure has less-than-perfect reliability, its validity coefficients will be limited accordingly. The more a measure of a construct fluctuates around the true value of the property being measured, the weaker the observed relationship between that measure and others will be, all else being equal. In other words, the more subject the measure is to random errors, the more difficult it is to predict related behaviors from it. In fact, validity coefficients can be "adjusted" statistically to take account of the level of reliability of the measures in question, providing what some believe to be more accurate estimates of the true validity of the measures in question.

Criterion-based validity coefficients are usually divided into two groups or categories. If the measure whose validity is being assessed is obtained some time before the criterion measure it is correlated with, the coefficient is referred to as a measure of **predictive validity**. An example would be evaluating the validity of (validating) an IQ test given during students' elementary school years by correlating those IQ scores with the students' high school GPAs determined several years later.

If the measure in question is correlated with a criterion measure obtained at about the same time, the coefficient is called a measure of **concurrent validity**. An IQ test could be administered and a student's current GPA determined on the same day, for example.

In addition, the designation of one measure as the test and another as the criterion is completely arbitrary. Just as the achievement test could serve as the criterion for evaluating the validity of the IQ test, the IQ test could conceivably serve as the criterion for assessing the validity of the achievement test. Choices of predictive or concurrent criteria are made at the discretion of the researcher and judged according to the quality of the logic of his or her arguments supporting those choices.

It is also important to understand that any validity coefficient (or reliability coefficient, for that matter) holds only for that group of individuals whose scores are used to calculate it. For the researcher, this means that one cannot assume that a measure found to be valid (or reliable) in someone else's research will necessarily be so in one's own. The more similar the two research contexts, including characteristics of the participants, the more likely the same evaluation would result, but one can never be certain.

It is possible for a measure to be biased for one particular group but not another. Questions on a standardized test might be written in such a way that to do well, one needed experience with words or phrases or situations that are more familiar to white test-takers than to those from minority groups. In that case, whites' answers might reflect their academic aptitudes differently than minorities' answers do. Both groups' scores might be closely related to some performance criterion, as the scores should be, but white students' scores might be higher overall than those of minority students, so that the score predicting success for minorities would be lower, just as the framers of "affirmative action" programs seemed to understand (see Thinking About Research Box 3.2). If fair-minded voters understood this, affirmative action programs might still be in effect where laws have been changed to end them.

Construct Validity

So far, we have considered the issue of bias or validity in psychological measurement from three perspectives. First, we considered the possibility that measurement might be biased because the person being measured has doubts about the method that is used (face validity). Then we saw that bias can be introduced when a measure neglects part of what it should be measuring, part of the domain of the construct (content validity). Third, we saw that validity coefficients can reveal biases by failing to establish strong relationships between the measure in question and other measures or criteria to which the construct ought to be related (criterion-related validity). We now consider a fourth possibility, that the measurement we obtain depends upon the particular method by which it was obtained, thus biasing its assessment of the underlying property it is intended to measure.

This final approach to bias and validity has been labeled **construct validity**. That term may be somewhat confusing here, because it is the label we have already used to refer to the overall question of how well measurements or variables represent the constructs being measured. The term is used so widely in psychology and other fields, however, that it would be foolish to try to rename it here. Try, therefore, to remember that the construct validity that is being considered here is one part of the larger question of construct validity.

This more limited version of construct validity is based on the argument that part of any measurement results from the underlying property of the event being observed, while part is due to the method of observation. This is a recapitulation of true score test theory. The contribution of the property being observed is **T**, and the contribution of the method of measurement a type of measurement bias (**B**).

There is no way of proving this directly, but in 1959 Donald Campbell and Donald Fiske suggested an indirect way of doing so. Their suggested method is known as the **multitrait-multimethod matrix**. It involves measuring each of two or more properties (the traits) using the same two or more methods for each, all with the same group of individuals. Then correlations are calculated for each possible pair of measures, creating a trait × method table or matrix.

As a hypothetical example, imagine that one were to administer two measures of emotional stability (trait A) and two measures of sociability (trait B) to the same group. I picked these two traits because recent factor analytic studies suggest that they are uncorrelated (independent) dimensions of personality. Each one would be measured by a standardized personality test that asked the participants questions about themselves (method 1). Each one would also be measured by asking the participants' best friends to rate them on 10-point scales, such as calm-excitable and outgoing-shy (method 2). The "intercorrelations" among those four sets of measures would then be displayed in a table (matrix) like the one shown in Table 3.3a.

In Table 3.3a, the hypothetical results of this hypothetical study suggest the following conclusions. First, the correlation coefficients in parentheses are reliability coefficients that represent correlations between measurements of the same trait by the same method on two separate occasions (the test-retest method) and pretty much set the upper limits for correlations in this table. When the same trait is measured in two different ways, self-report versus friend's rating, the correlations are positive and moderately high, .71 for sociability and .68 for emotional stability in this hypothetical example. Here, we begin to get the idea that the amount of the property that is detected changes with the method of detection or measurement that is used. That is indicated by the correlations between different methods of measuring the same constructs being conspicuously lower than the reliabilities for those individual measures (.71 vs. .92, and .68 vs. .95 in this hypothetical example).

Because the two traits are theoretically and empirically (based on previous research) independent of one another, we would expect measures of them to be uncorrelated—and they are, essentially, when the two traits are measured by different methods (.03 and −.01). But when those independent traits are measured by the same method, the correlations are substantially higher, .32 and .27. Here, again, we see that the method of measurement makes a difference. Even when we're measuring two different things, our measurements will be somewhat similar if they are made using the same method. Presumably, there are unique biases in these different forms of measurement that are responsible for that similarity.

This multitrait-multimethod matrix provides evidence that the method used to measure a trait determines to some extent the value that is observed. That bias is

TABLE 3.3a A Sample Multitrait-Multimethod Matrix of Correlation Coefficients

	Trait A		Trait B	
	Method 1	Method 2	Method 1	Method 2
Trait A: Sociability				
Method 1: Self-report	(.92)[a]	.71[b]	.32[c]	−.01[d]
Method 2: Rating by a friend		(.89)[a]	.03[d]	.27[c]
Trait B: Emotional Stability				
Method 1: Self-report			(.95)[a]	.68[b]
Method 2: Rating by a friend				(.88)[a]

TABLE 3.3b An Ideal Multitrait-Multimethod Matrix of Correlation Coefficients

	Trait A		Trait B	
	Method 1	Method 2	Method 1	Method 2
Trait A: Sociability				
Method 1: Self-report	(1.00)[a]	1.00[b]	0.00[c]	0.00[d]
Method 2: Rating by a friend		(1.00)[a]	0.00[d]	0.00[c]
Trait B: Emotional Stability				
Method 1: Self-report			(1.00)[a]	1.00[b]
Method 2: Rating by a friend				(1.00)[a]

a. These correlations show the reliabilities of the four measures (two traits times two methods). In each case, there are two sets of scores that are obtained by applying the same measure of one trait on two separate occasions.
b. These correlations show the relationships between sets of scores obtained by measuring the same trait twice, using the two different methods of measurement (self-report and rating by a friend).
c. These correlations show the relationship between scores for the two different traits (sociability and emotional stability) obtained by applying the same method of measurement to each.
d. These correlations show the relationship between scores for the two different traits obtained from the two different methods of measurement.

referred to as **method variance**, whereas the pure reflection of the trait itself is referred to in the language of construct validity as **trait variance**.

This point is relevant to any measurement, not just the measurement of personality traits. The point is that there is always the possibility that a measurement reflects the method used to make it as well as what is being measured. Only a test like the one represented in Table 3.3a can reveal the extent of the problem.

In some cases, there could be much less method variance mixed up in the measurements than is the case here. In other cases, there could be much more. Construct validity increases as the amount of trait variance increases relative to the amount of method variance. Perfect construct validity would be reflected in the same low correlations between sociability and emotional stability whether measured by the same or different methods, and correlations between the different measures of each individual trait that were just as high as their respective reliability coefficients.

The ideal (hypothetical) outcome is shown in Table 3.3b. In the ideal outcome, all four measures (two traits times two methods of measurement) are perfectly reliable, there is perfect agreement between measures of the same trait obtained from different methods of measurement, and there is no relationship between measures of different (unrelated) traits made with the same method. When using this method to assess construct validity, the closer the actual multitrait-multimethod matrix (Table 3.3a) to the ideal matrix (Table 3.3b), the greater the construct validity of the method of measurement in question for the trait being measured.

Review Questions and Exercise

Review Questions

1. What is the purpose of operationalization? What are the products that result from it?

2. What role does measurement play in the process of operationalization?

3. What are measurement scales, and how do their characteristics affect operationalization?

4. What does true score test theory tell us about the process of psychological measurement?

5. Identify the psychometric criteria and explain how they are used to evaluate random error (reliability) and bias (validity) that can distort psychological measurements?

Exercise

1. Go back to your work on Exercise 2 following Chapter 2. How did the researchers whose articles you examined operationalize the constructs in their hypotheses? What measurement scales did they use? What steps, if any, did they take to ensure the adequacy of their measurement operations? How would you evaluate the construct validity in that study, and why?

CHAPTER **4**

SPECIFYING THE RESEARCH VARIABLES II
Artifacts and Construct Validity

● A QUICK GUIDE TO CHAPTER 4:
SPECIFYING THE RESEARCH VARIABLES II

An **artifact** is an unintended or extraneous element that is presented to research participants along with an independent or dependent variable. The effects of artifacts, if any, combine with those of the variables created by the researcher to influence the research participants' behavior. That makes it impossible to separate responses to the artifacts from responses to the variables themselves. Thus, it is said that the variables and artifacts are **confounded**, meaning that they are so mixed up together that their effects are inseparable. This makes any interpretation of the research results problematic; the research findings are ambiguous, or lack validity.

In the case of the independent variable, artifacts are more likely when a study is conducted under **reactive arrangements** Because the resulting **reactivity** makes participants aware that they are being studied, they may engage in hypothesis-seeking behavior and/or attempt to play the role of a good participant. They also may respond defensively because of their apprehension about being evaluated.

In a reactive setting, there are three **treatment artifacts** that can create confounds by providing participants with cues to the research hypothesis. One is **demand characteristics**, or cues to the research hypothesis in the research setting provided by the task, the instructions, or an obtrusive behavioral measure. Another is **experimenter expectancy effects**, or cues provided through the behavior of an experimenter who is aware of the research hypothesis. The third is **pretest sensitization**, or cues from the pretreatment administration of the same dependent measure used later to assess the effects of treatments on the participants.

In the case of the dependent variable, there are two principal factors that can create confounds through their influence on the participants' responses to the behavioral measure(s). One is **strategic responding**, where, particularly in a reactive setting, the intent of the measures is so obvious that many participants respond in ways intended to assist the researcher. They may also try to make themselves look good, or, in other words, to act in a socially desirable manner. The second is a **linguistic/cultural bias** that makes it difficult for participants to understand the intended meaning of the dependent measures. In both cases, the danger is that participants' responses, as assessed by the dependent variable, will reflect not only the effects (if any) of the treatments to which they were exposed but also the inseparable influence of the **measurement artifacts**.

The Chapter 4 Quick Guide shows the artifacts that can contaminate both independent and dependent variables. As in the Chapter 3 Quick Guide, the researcher's intent is contrasted with the possible **confounding** of artifact with variable.

Chapter 4 Quick Guide: Artifacts		
Threat to Validity/ *Treatment Artifact*	*Intended by Researcher*	*Actual, If Confounded* *With Treatment Artifact*
Independent Variable		
Demand characteristics	Treatment X	Treatment X plus situational clues to the research hypothesis
Experimenter expectancy effects	Treatment X	Treatment X plus experimenter expectancy cues for participant responses
Pretest sensitization	Treatment X	Treatment X plus pretest cues for participant responses
Dependent Variable		
Strategic responding	Behavioral measure O	Behavioral measure O plus participant's response strategy
Linguistic/cultural bias	Behavioral measure O	Behavioral measure O plus the effects of any linguistic/cultural bias

INTRODUCTION TO THE CHAPTER ●

Beyond Measurement

In the previous chapter, we considered basic issues in psychological measurement. We saw how measurement involved the assignment of symbols, usually numbers, to the psychological properties of events. We also saw how different rules for that assignment or measurement resulted in different measurement scales that provided different amounts of information about the properties being measured.

We then reviewed true score test theory and the psychometric criteria that have been developed to evaluate psychological measurement in line with that theory. We discussed criteria for evaluating the degree to which random error renders psychological measurement unreliable as well as validity criteria to assess the degree to which psychological measurement is contaminated with bias.

We saw that the independent and dependent variables on which research is based are, essentially, measured versions of the **constructs** in the research hypothesis. As such, their quality and impact on the validity of research findings depend on the quality of measurement operations that define them. Flaws in those measurement operations constitute threats to construct validity in a particular study and, therefore, threats to the overall validity of the research findings.

But there is more to construct validity than measurement quality. After measurement operations are chosen to create the variables in a research study, they need to be put to use in a particular context. The nature of the research participants, the setting in which the research is carried out, and the procedures by which it is carried out are all relevant to construct validity as well. Their relevance needs to be considered before we are in a position to understand fully how construct validity can be evaluated. We need to consider how the administration of the treatments that constitute variations in the independent variable and the administration of the behavioral measures that constitute the dependent variable can give rise to biases that threaten construct validity.

Biases that are introduced as a result of the administration of treatments or behavioral measures are known as **artifacts**. They are sometimes known as "experimental artifacts," although I'll introduce a more limited definition of experimental research very soon and flesh out its details in later chapters. Awareness of artifacts goes back only a few decades, although psychometric analysis has been around a lot longer. In fact, only fairly recently has it been widely recognized that studying the factors that cause human behavior can itself influence, in important ways, the behavior being studied. In a fairly short period of time, however, methodologists have gained a good deal of understanding about artifacts and ways of dealing with them.

Reactivity and Artifacts

The first research methods in psychology (along with their underlying philosophy of science) were borrowed from the natural sciences, particularly from physics. The most prominent of those methods is the **experiment**. In an experiment, the researcher creates contrasting events or conditions and observes their effects (in psychology, participants' responses) in order to learn whether those events can cause the effects predicted in the research hypothesis. In methodological parlance, this is called the **manipulation** of the independent variable.

A compelling example of the power of the experimental method, in real life as well as in scientific research, was provided some years ago by the late Nobel laureate in physics, Richard Feynman. When he was appointed to a presidential commission charged with discovering the cause of NASA's *Challenger* disaster (in which that manned space vehicle exploded shortly after liftoff, in 1986), he conducted an experiment on national television during one of the commission's hearings. He put small O-rings, made of the same material as the large ones that joined together the sections of the *Challenger* rocket, into his glass of ice water. When he took them out, he showed that they were brittle and broke easily. This experiment provided evidence for the hypothesis that the unusually cold winter temperatures on the morning of *Challenger*'s final, fatal launch from its base in Cape Canaveral, Florida, ultimately were responsible for the accident.

There are good examples of the use of the experimental method in psychological research among our exemplar studies. One is Ceci et al.'s (1994) study in which researchers created false memories in their young participants (**E8** in Table 2.1). Another is Seligman and Maier's (1967) study in which some dogs were randomly selected to be given exposure to electric shock prior to avoidance training (**E18**).

For much of the history of scientific psychology, researchers pretty much took for granted the superiority of experimental research as well as their ability to conduct valid experiments. They had faith in the methods of the physical sciences and in the philosophical rationale that underlay them. It is still not uncommon for people to make reference to "the scientific method," with the connotation that its use is an unassailable guarantee of arriving at the truth. As will become clearer much later on, the fact that early research psychologists studied mainly nonhuman species under **laboratory** conditions probably added to their sense of security in what they were doing.

Beginning around the 1950s, however, researchers who were studying human behavior under less secure conditions began to become aware of difficulties in adapting the methods of the natural sciences to the needs of scientific psychologists. They became concerned about the possibility that when research participants are aware that their behavior is being studied, they may react very differently from the way they would under similar circumstances when they do not feel they are being observed. Unlike the physicist's atomic particles or ball bearings, the subjects in psychological research often know and care about what's happening to them. Even when they don't, as may be the case with very young children, rats, and dogs, they are able to be influenced by unintended messages they receive from researchers. As many believe is true of most research participants, Clever Hans (see Pfungst, 1906/1965) was not trying to cheat, only to adapt to the situation in which he found himself.

Reactive arrangements in a research setting, then, are conditions that make participants aware that they are being studied and threaten to alter their responses to events occurring there. Consider an everyday example. The man who delivers my mail is subject to periodic assessment of his job performance by his bosses at the U.S. Postal Service. I'm not privy to the details of the measuring instruments used, but they seem pretty detailed, based on my observation of the evaluator. Every few months or so, the evaluator walks in the gutter, trailing just behind the letter carrier, making periodic entries on a form on the clipboard he carries.

I don't know how well my letter carrier scores on these occasions, but I can't help but wonder if he does his job the same way when somebody is following and evaluating him as when he is alone. Measurement under those circumstances seems likely to create a setting that is highly reactive, so that any conclusions about the causes of the behavior that is observed are commensurately suspect. Is he a good letter carrier, obeying the Postal Service rules governing how he should do his job, or an apprehensive one concerned about receiving a favorable evaluation? Does any letter carrier dare to cut corners or dawdle while a supervisor is following, taking notes? Do research participants act the same way when they know that their behavior is being studied as they do in their everyday lives?

Artifacts

The participants in psychological research are often aware that the events occurring around them are meant to test them in some way, and that their behavior is under scrutiny. As a result, they may not take those events or requests for information at face value and may not simply react to the treatments and behavioral measures administered by the researcher.

Any influence on participants' behavior other than the treatment to which he or she is exposed is known as a **treatment artifact**. We will consider three treatment artifacts that are potential threats to construct validity because they can make the treatments, as administered, biased representations of the causal construct in the research hypothesis. **Demand characteristics** are unintended sources of information about the research hypothesis that can influence the responses of participants to treatments. **Experimenter expectancy effects** are unintended communications from researchers to research participants that can alter the participants' behavior. **Pretest sensitization effects** occur when a pretreatment assessment of participants' behavior influences their responses to the events that follow.

Any element of the behavioral measures administered to research participants that distorts their measured responses to the treatments is known as a **measurement artifact**. One type, **strategic responding**, occurs when behavioral measures allow participants to respond in ways that they believe will confirm the research hypothesis or create a desired impression on the researcher. Another type, **linguistic/cultural bias** causes misunderstanding among research participants about the meaning or intent of the behavioral measures administered to them. Both of these measurement artifacts threaten construct validity because they cause the behavioral measures as administered to be biased representations of the behavioral construct in the research hypothesis.

Both treatment artifacts and measurement artifacts, then, constitute additional potential threats to construct validity beyond those posed by inadequate operationalization. Our analysis of construct validity therefore will include both types of threats, for both the independent and dependent variables in a research study.

TABLE 4.1   Logic of Analysis of Construct Validity

Constructs in the Research Hypothesis	Variables Representing Construct	Variables as Administered to Participants	Categories of Threats to Construct Validity
Causal construct	Independent variable	Treatments	Inadequate operationalization
			Treatment artifacts
Behavioral construct	Dependent variable	Behavioral measures	Inadequate operationalization
			Measurement artifacts

The logic of that analysis is shown in Table 4.1. The whole group of threats to construct validity that we will be considering in the remainder of this chapter is shown in Table 4.2.

Experimental Versus Nonexperimental Research

Of course, sometimes the causal events or influences in the hypothesis cannot be created or manipulated by the researcher, at least not in a realistic way. Consider the question of how a tornado or a hurricane affects people's fear of natural disasters, or Gazzaniga's (1967) research assessing patients who already had the callectomy surgery (**E21**), or Friedman and Rosenman's (1959) research in which some patients developed the Type A personality without any interference from the researchers (**E2**). For those cases, the effects of naturally occurring events might have to be studied in nonexperimental research, unless some sort of approximation or simulation of the causal event can be created, as Feynman did so cleverly.

The behavior of research participants is sometimes not measured directly, particularly in nonexperimental studies. Participants are not asked to fill out questionnaires or rating scales, as they were in Broverman et al.'s (1972) stereotyping studies (**E5**) and Cherulnik et al.'s (1981) research on appearance and personality (**E17**). Nor is their task performance observed directly, as in Triplett's (1897) studies of the effects of competition (**E3**) and Gazzaniga's (1967) split brain studies (**E21**). Instead, existing records of participants' past scores on IQ tests might be examined, as in Zajonc and Markus's (1975) studies of birth order and intellectual development, or records of past violence examined, as in Frazier's (1985) comparison of different jail designs (**E25**).

Many of the implications of conducting experimental versus nonexperimental research will be discussed in later chapters. Our interest here is in how well the

TABLE 4.2   Threats to Construct Validity

I. Threats to conceptual validity
   1. Unnecessary duplication
   2. Theoretical isolation
II. Threats to construct validity
   A. The independent variable
      a. Inadequate operationalization
         3. Lack of reliability of the independent variable
         4. Lack of representativeness of the independent variable
         5. Lack of impact of the independent variable
      b. Treatment artifacts
         6. Demand characteristics in the research setting
         7. Experimenter expectancy effects on the behavior being observed
         8. Pretest sensitization to the treatments
   B. The dependent variable
      a. Inadequate operationalization
         9. Lack of reliability of the dependent variable
         10. Lack of representativeness of the dependent variable
         11. Lack of sensitivity of the dependent variable
      b. Measurement artifacts
         12. Strategic responding by the research participants
         13. Linguistic/cultural bias in the dependent measure
III. Threats to internal validity
   14. Extraneous effects (history)
   15. Temporal effects (maturation)
   16. Group composition effects (selection)
   17. Interaction of temporal and group composition effects
   18. Selective sample attrition (mortality)
   19. Statistical regression effects (regression to the mean)
IV. Threats to external validity
   20. Nonrepresentative sampling
   21. Nonrepresentative research context
V. Threats to statistical conclusion validity
   22. Inappropriate use of statistical techniques
   23. Use of a statistical test lacking sufficient power
   24. Mistaking a trivial effect for support for the research hypothesis

variables used in a research study represent the constructs of a research hypothesis. In principle, it is the same question we asked in the previous chapter about the measurement of behavior and its causes. We need to know how well a measure of TV violence reflects that underlying construct when exposure to TV violence is the independent variable in a study. We also need to know how well a measure of aggression reflects that construct when level of aggression is the dependent or outcome measure in a study. Furthermore, we need to know how the conditions under which the treatments and behavioral measures are administered affect research participants' responses to them.

THREATS TO CONSTRUCT VALIDITY: ●
INTRODUCTION

Given what we know now about measurement scales, measurement error, and artifacts, how can we evaluate the choices of independent and dependent variables to represent the causal and behavioral constructs of a research hypotheses? In the final section of this chapter, we will apply all those concepts to that task. Table 4.2 provides an overview of that process, bringing together the concerns addressed both in Chapter 3 and earlier in this chapter. It lists a number of threats to the validity of research findings caused by flaws in the operational definitions employed in a research study—threats to construct validity, in other words. Each of them will be discussed in turn below.

Although this issue has been discussed already, it's been a while, so it's probably a good idea to make sure that the big picture is still clear. Every researcher must make choices about the particular forms of the independent and dependent variables that will represent the cause and effect constructs whose relationship is the subject of the research hypothesis. The quality of those choices, like the choice of hypothesis and all the other choices a researcher must make, will affect the quality of the research findings. It will affect, in other words, the confidence one can place in the conclusions that are drawn from the research results about the truth of the hypothesis. Construct validity is the label for the quality or adequacy of the choices of independent and dependent variables. As previously mentioned, Table 4.2 lists a number of criteria by which construct validity can be evaluated. The rest of this chapter will be devoted to a review of those criteria, the factors that influence how a research study measures up against them, and the ways in which a researcher can improve the validity of his or her research findings as measured against these criteria.

THREATS TO CONSTRUCT VALIDITY: ●
THE INDEPENDENT VARIABLE (TREATMENTS)

We will start with the choice of treatments. These are the specific forms in which the contrasting causal conditions suggested by the research hypothesis are represented in an empirical study. In general, treatments are meant to take different val-

---

Box 4.1 *THINKING ABOUT RESEARCH*

How Do We Know We've Measured the Right Thing?

One of the most difficult methodological issues to understand is the meaning of "negative results." When a hypothesis predicts a relationship between independent variable and dependent variable, or a difference between treatment groups, and no relationship or no difference is actually observed, what do those negative results mean? Although scientists accept positive results—evidence of a relationship or a difference—as proof that the research hypothesis is tenable, they do not so readily accept negative results as proof that there is no relationship or no effect. Why is that?

A recent case from the realm of agronomy makes the point dramatically. Billions of dollars are being spent by large corporations such as Monsanto to produce genetically engineered crops. The new "gen-en" seeds promise larger yields, resistance to parasites (reduced use of pesticides and herbicides), and lower-cost food, especially attractive prospects for developing countries. But what are the dangers, if any?

New transgenic plants have to undergo extensive testing to prove that they are safe. But if those tests reveal no harmful effects, does that

mean that the plants are really safe? One such plant, Bt corn, was developed by inserting a gene that causes the plant to produce a substance that kills corn borer pests. Having passed the required safety tests, it now accounts for almost 25% of the 80-million-acre U.S. corn crop.

Recent evidence, however, shows that pollen from Bt corn plants that is deposited on nearby milkweed plants is poisoning monarch butterflies. Why wasn't this effect known before Bt corn went into widespread use? Was it simply because no one thought to look for it? Does that clarify the problem with negative results? Does it illustrate how the failure to find an effect might only mean that the specific effects researchers chose to look for weren't found—not that no effects occurred that were consistent with the hypothesis? Once an effect is observed, we might be reasonably certain that it occurred (depending on how it was observed). If an effect is not observed, might that mean only that it was not detected? How many unforeseen environmental (and other) problems arise this way?

---

ues along the dimension known as the independent variable. For example, in a test of the hypothesis that exposure to televised violence is a cause of aggressive behavior, the treatments might be samples of television programs that portrayed different levels of violence. Those treatments would be administered to participants to determine whether the level of aggressive behavior the participants displayed varied with the level of violence to which they were exposed.

Consider the example of Harlow's (1958) research on the nature of mother-infant love (**E12**), from the file of exemplar studies in Chapter 2. The wire and cloth surrogate mothers represented the two points on the independent variable of motherly nurturance that Harlow wanted to compare. Those treatments were reinforcement associated with feeding and contact comfort.

A researcher might choose to compare some of the putative cause with none of it, or to compare more of it with less of it, or to compare two or more different types of it. In any of those cases, the value of the study would depend on the researcher's ability to know (i.e., to measure) how much of a given causal factor was present on a given occasion. If the level of the independent variable is not known, how can its relationship to the behavior in question ever be determined?

Inadequate Operationalization of the Independent Variable

We will consider three principal threats to the *construct* of research findings under this heading: **lack of reliability of treatments**, **lack of representativeness of treatments**, and **lack of impact of treatments** (see Table 4.3). Beyond those, however, one would also want to consider the precision with which treatment events are measured. As we've seen, measurement can be imprecise qualitative or nominal-scale measurement, such as the comparison between pressures toward obedience and no pressures in Milgram's (1974) research on obedience to authority (**E9**). It also can be the most precise ratio scale measurement, as in a comparison between 4 hours of food deprivation and 8, 12, and 24 hours in study of the effects of motivation on maze learning in rats.

Lack of Reliability of Treatments

In a research study, treatments are presented repeatedly to individual participants or groups. Treatments lack adequate reliability if they vary so much from one occasion to another as to introduce a degree of variability in participants' responses that would cloud the relationship between the treatments and related behaviors.

If a videotaped presentation of selected television program material were presented on repeated occasions, one would expect considerable stability or consistency across participants' experiences. But what about a conformity experiment where confederates of the experimenter act out different scenarios, and these scenarios constitute the contrasting treatments? The researcher needs to be concerned about whether repeated administrations of the same conformity treatment are sufficiently similar. Extensive training of the confederates would seem to be required for adequate stability. If direct observations could be made of the confederates' behavior, some sort of reliability coefficient could be used to evaluate stability. Although criteria for judging such a coefficient (how large a coefficient is sufficient?) are not as well established as in the case of a standardized psychological test, they can be useful.

TABLE 4.3   Threats to the Construct Validity of the Independent Variable: Inadequate Operationalization

I. Threats to conceptual validity
        1. Unnecessary duplication
        2. Theoretical isolation
II. Threats to construct validity
  A. The independent variable
    a. Inadequate operationalization
      3. Lack of reliability of the independent variable
      4. Lack of representativeness of the independent variable
      5. Lack of impact of the independent variable
    b. Treatment artifacts
      6. Demand characteristics in the research setting
      7. Experimenter expectancy effects on the behavior being observed
      8. Pretest sensitization to the treatments
  B. The dependent variable
    a. Inadequate operationalization
      9. Lack of reliability of the dependent variable
      10. Lack of representativeness of the dependent variable
      11. Lack of sensitivity of the dependent variable
    b. Measurement artifacts
      12. Strategic responding by the research participants
      13. Linguistic/cultural bias in the dependent measure
III. Threats to internal validity
      14. Extraneous effects (history)
      15. Temporal effects (maturation)
      16. Group composition effects (selection)
      17. Interaction of temporal and group composition effects
      18. Selective sample attrition (mortality)
      19. Statistical regression effects (regression to the mean)
IV. Threats to external validity
      20. Nonrepresentative sampling
      21. Nonrepresentative research context
V. Threats to statistical conclusion validity
      22. Inappropriate use of statistical techniques
      23. Use of a statistical test lacking sufficient power
      24. Mistaking a trivial effect for support for the research hypothesis

The more automated the presentation of treatments to research participants, or the better trained those involved in that presentation, the more reliable the treatments should be. The more subject to the moods, thoughts, and other psychological states of those involved in presenting the treatments, the greater would be the need for attention to possible inadequacies in their reliability.

In addition, as was discussed earlier in this chapter, the researcher needs to be concerned about possible sources of random error beyond those that may be introduced by the experimenter and apparatus employed in the study. If participants can be isolated from extraneous sights and sounds that could distract them or otherwise interfere with the effects of the treatments, their experiences would more consistently represent those intended by the researcher. Laboratory research has the distinct advantage of providing such isolation, in addition to control by trained experimenters and automated equipment, whatever other issues it may raise (see the discussion of treatment artifacts below).

Lack of Representativeness of Treatments

An intelligence test can fail the test of content validity because it does not represent adequately all the important aspects of the construct labeled "intelligence." In the same way, the independent variable or treatments whose effects are being studied can fail to represent adequately all the important aspects of the causal construct being studied. Just as the construct of intelligence has a domain of content that any variable representing it must sample thoroughly, so does the construct of television violence have its domain of content that must be represented adequately.

Consider a study of how a charismatic leadership style affects those who are exposed to it. Charismatic leadership has been defined in a number of very different ways. According to one definition, a charismatic leader is one who provides new ideas to a group. Another definition emphasizes the leader's interpersonal style. A researcher might choose to use the latter definition, intentionally ignoring the "ideas" area of the domain. Still, it would be necessary for the sake of representativeness to identify all the various elements of interpersonal style that were involved in charismatic leadership, such as smiling and speaking in an animated manner. Then the contrasting examples of leadership style that served as treatments would be constructed so as to include each of those elements.

The process of operationalization involves separating the domain of a causal construct into its constituent elements. Then, an independent variable must be designed to represent that construct so that each treatment contains appropriately varying degrees of each of those elements. Only in that way can a researcher ensure that the validity of the research findings will not be threatened by lack of representativeness.

Calhoun's (1962) research on the role of population density in social pathology in rats (**E19**) also raised the issue of representativeness of treatments. Does an indoor pen with restricted feeding and nesting sites, and paths that artificially concentrate the population in one area, represent the conditions of high population density that exist in nature, for rats or for people?

| Box 4.2 | THINKING ABOUT RESEARCH |

Timing Is Everything _____

In their research on the bogus pipeline, Sigall and Page (1971) demonstrated how people are reluctant to admit that they are prejudiced. (See Chapter 9 for a more complete description of this work.) When their research participants were convinced that the researcher had a special type of lie detector that would reveal their true feelings, they were more likely to admit to holding racist attitudes.

The bogus pipeline, however, is too unwieldy a procedure to be used routinely when attitudes toward minorities are the target of the dependent measure in a research study. It can be administered only in a laboratory, following a long and convoluted explanation, to one research participant at a time.

Recently, social psychologists devised a more practical means of outflanking people's reticence about revealing their prejudices. They call it the Implicit Association Test (IAT). It is administered by computer and can be taken on the Internet (you can look it up using your Web browser and try it yourself if you like; the URL is http://www.yale.edu/implicit).

Participants are timed as they classify names (for example, Jamal and Chip) into the categories black and white, then classify words (for example, love and war) into the categories good and bad, and finally group good and bad words with black and white names in all combinations. Latent prejudice supposedly is revealed when a participant takes longer to group good words with black names than with white names.

Which threats to construct validity does the IAT seem to eliminate? Can you think of how it might be used in hypothesis-testing psychological research? If the IAT receives a lot of media exposure, will that lessen its value as a research tool? Is this as good a way of estimating the prevalence of unconscious prejudices among white Americans as its inventors have claimed?

Lack of Impact of Treatments

When a college student seeking a career in clinical psychology takes the Graduate Record Examination (GRE), the pressure is on. Only a very high score will give that student a good chance to be admitted into a doctoral program. How does that "pressure" affect the student's performance? How could that pressure be represented as a treatment in an experiment? It is difficult to create an experience in a laboratory for the purpose of studying the relationship between pressure and performance that would have an impact on research participants comparable to that experienced by the aspiring clinical psychologist taking the GRE.

On one hand, participants may believe that nothing that happens to them in an experiment is likely to affect their lives as much as will their score on the GRE. At the same time, we know that it is possible for research participants to experience that kind of impact, as they did in Milgram's (1974) famous studies of obedience to

Figure 4.1. The home page of the Web site on which one can take the Implicit Association Test (IAT), an indirect measure that can be used to assess a variety of sensitive attitudes. The Web site is also a source of information about research that has been done using the IAT. SOURCE: Reproduction of the home page at URL http://www.yale.edu/implicit/. Materials on this site © by IAT Corp. Reproduced with permission of IAT Corp.

authority (**E9**). When they do, there is the question of whether it is ethical to cause research participants to experience that degree of emotional upheaval. This is one area where research that is carried on outside the laboratory has an advantage. When Festinger et al.'s (1956) subjects who expected the world to end (**E11**) found out that it hadn't ended after all, one suspects that the impact on them was very great indeed.

In any case, researchers need to be concerned about the degree to which the treatments they create to represent the causal construct they are studying produce a realistic impact on their research participants. This requirement is known as **mundane realism**; that is, seeming like real life. One way to deal with this problem is through a procedure known as **pilot research**. Preliminary versions of the treatments can be administered to small groups of participants to find out what impact they actually have. Those pilot participants can be observed and questioned, like the participants in the focus groups used by market researchers. The pilot participants' responses to the treatments then can be assessed to evaluate the impact of those treatments. That process is usually referred to as **debriefing** in scientific research.

Based on the evaluation from a pilot study, treatments can be altered or fine-tuned until they seem to have the desired impact. Then, the final, corrected treatments can be administered in the full-scale research study. Such a process of developing effective treatments will also benefit from a researcher's experience in studying a particular research problem over a period of time in a number of separate studies. Although it is desirable to minimize any waste of time and money in research, it seems inevitable that a researcher will learn from past efforts, including mistakes.

Pilot research also can be used to evaluate treatments' reliability and representativeness. Participants' responses can be used to determine whether treatments have consistent effects across the occasions on which they are administered, and whether the participants experience the intended elements of the construct. Again, these assessments may not compare favorably in their precision with psychometric assessments of intelligence tests or the like, but they do provide one method of addressing the question of whether the causal construct in the research hypothesis has been operationalized adequately in the independent variable. In addition, pilot research can be useful for testing research equipment, perfecting the timing of a research session, and other purposes.

Treatment Artifacts

So far, we have considered some of the important measurement issues in constructing an independent variable, or set of treatments, to represent the causal construct in a research hypothesis. Now it is time to consider threats to the validity of research findings that might arise out of the actual presentation of those treatments to research participants (see Table 4.4 for a list).

Treatment artifacts are the result of participant and experimenter motivations and actions. They are also the product of the setting in which the treatments are administered. Treatment artifacts may become combined with the effects of the treatments so that it is impossible to know where one leaves off and the other begins.

TABLE 4.4   Threats to the Construct Validity of the Independent Variable: Treatment Artifacts

I. Threats to conceptual validity
      1. Unnecessary duplication
      2. Theoretical isolation
II. Threats to construct validity
  A. The independent variable
    a. Inadequate operationalization
      3. Lack of reliability of the independent variable
      4. Lack of representativeness of the independent variable
      5. Lack of impact of the independent variable
    b. Treatment artifacts
      6. Demand characteristics in the research setting
      7. Experimenter expectancy effects on the behavior being observed
      8. Pretest sensitization to the treatments
  B. The dependent variable
    a. Inadequate operationalization
      9. Lack of reliability of the dependent variable
      10. Lack of representativeness of the dependent variable
      11. Lack of sensitivity of the dependent variable
    b. Measurement artifacts
      12. Strategic responding by the research participants
      13. Linguistic/cultural bias in the dependent measure
III. Threats to internal validity
      14. Extraneous effects (history)
      15. Temporal effects (maturation)
      16. Group composition effects (selection)
      17. Interaction of temporal and group composition effects
      18. Selective sample attrition (mortality)
      19. Statistical regression effects (regression to the mean)
IV. Threats to external validity
      20. Nonrepresentative sampling
      21. Nonrepresentative research context
V. Threats to statistical conclusion validity
      22. Inappropriate use of statistical techniques
      23. Use of a statistical test lacking sufficient power
      24. Mistaking a trivial effect for support for the research hypothesis

Such a combination of effects is known as a **confounding**. The separate effects of the treatments and the treatment artifacts cannot be determined. This confusion makes it impossible to explain research results with any confidence, rendering the research findings ambiguous and useless in judging the truth of the research hypothesis.

Demand Characteristics

One of the pioneers in studying treatment artifacts was Martin Orne, a psychiatrist who was wrestling with the problem of understanding hypnosis. He was trying to determine whether hypnosis was an involuntary trance state or a voluntary attempt to cooperate with the request of the hypnotist. To do that, Orne (1959) created situations like police sting operations. People who supposedly had been hypnotized were led to believe that they were temporarily beyond the surveillance of the hypnotist, while they were actually being observed without their knowledge. When the hypnotist seemed to have gone off somewhere, supposedly hypnotized subjects came out of their "trances." When they heard the hypnotist's footsteps in the hall, returning to them, they went back to the hypnotized state.

Orne concluded from these studies that participants in studies of hypnosis, at least, don't merely respond to the researcher's instructions—they determine for themselves what they should do, and where and when. They can do so, according to Orne, because they have preconceptions about what a hypnotized subject should do. Those preconceptions are bolstered by information they receive directly from the hypnotist and the setting.

Orne went on to consider the implications of his findings about hypnosis for much of psychological research in general. If participants in hypnosis are likely to do what they believe the hypnotist wants them to do, creating the illusion that they are in a trance state when, in fact, they are not, might not participants in other types of psychological research do the same? This hypothesis led Orne and others to devise demonstrations that participants in psychological research are motivated to fulfill the role of assisting the researcher in advancing the cause of science.

Eventually, evidence of other participant motives surfaced, most notably the desire to appear to be a competent, good person, even if the researcher is looking for a different pattern of behavior. The important point is that participants can't be relied upon to accept at face value the experiences that the researcher provides. They bring their own agendas with them, raising considerable doubt about the true nature of the conditions they experience and the true cause of whatever behaviors the researcher observes.

The label Orne chose for this phenomenon was *demand characteristics*. In his terminology, participants' motives, whether altruistic or self-protective, led them to search for cues to the meanings behind what the researcher arranged for them to see and hear. In this game of cat and mouse between the researcher and the research participant, the meanings that participants construe become mixed up with, or confounded with, the events that are intended to constitute the independent variable.

Thus, the causal construct in the researcher's hypothesis is misrepresented, if not in the conditions intended by the researcher, then in those actually experienced by participants. As a result, the behaviors observed by the researcher are artifacts of an unintended complex of events. As artifacts, they cannot be attributed with any certainty to the experimental treatments. They are the products of the treatments administered by the researcher combined with an indeterminate combination of subject motives and perceptions. They therefore provide a shaky basis, at best, for drawing conclusions about the truth or falsity of the research hypothesis.

If demand characteristics are to be taken seriously as a threat to the validity of research findings in psychology, there needs to be some indication that participants are motivated to "help" researchers confirm their hypotheses or to respond strategically in some other way. There also needs to be some indication that the research setting presents some cues on which subjects could base actions directed at the motives involved. Unfortunately for researchers, but fortunately for those who study the artifacts themselves, as threats to the validity of research findings and as interesting behavioral phenomena in their own right, there are strong indications of both.

Orne once asked subjects to do an endless (really!) series of simple math problems. When it looked like they might never quit, he told them to tear each page into tiny pieces once they'd finished with it. After more than 6 hours, he gave up because he saw no sign that there was any limit to their willingness to help him in his research.

Again, a confounding of treatment with experimental demand makes it impossible to interpret the subjects' behavior in such a way as to determine the truth of the research hypothesis. In our ongoing example, was it the violent TV program that caused participants to behave more aggressively, or the fact that the participants who were exposed to it had decided that the researcher expected them to respond aggressively and did so in response to that perceived expectation, rather than in response to the TV program itself? Did Cartwright's (1974) research participants report the actual content of their dreams in response to her explicit instructions (**E13**), or did they censor or invent what they reported out of implicit motives quite apart from the instructions they received?

When a research participant goes to a psychological laboratory to participate in an experiment, he or she enters a reactive setting. It is usually quite clear that the researcher will be studying how participants respond to the events that occur there. Under those conditions, we can expect, based on Orne's and others' work, that participants might try to cooperate to help the researcher confirm the research hypothesis, or that they might try to behave in a way that makes them look competent or good.

The **experimental demand** for cooperative behavior and the evaluation apprehension that is so problematic in a laboratory is very unlikely to occur in field research. When people's behavior is studied unobtrusively in the public places they are accustomed to inhabiting in their day-to-day lives, there are no demand characteristics. Unfortunately, there is also less control over the events that people experience, so that operationalization of the causal construct in the research hypothesis is often less precise and less repeatable (reliable). There are cases, however, in which field experiments minimize reactivity while apparently risking little negative trade-off. Rosenthal and Jacobson's (1966) study of teacher expectancy effects (**E15**) is a good example.

Experiments conducted in the field, as well as nonexperimental research that takes advantage of natural exposure to possible causes of the behavior in question, are less subject to demand characteristics and other artifacts, but they are more vulnerable to threats to construct validity arising out of inadequate operationalization. In response to this dilemma, many psychologists have chosen to do their research in the laboratory and to try to combat the problem of demand characteristics using the method of deception. They tell research participants an elaborate "cover story" that purports to explain the purpose of the experiment. In fact, it misleads the participants about the experiment's true purpose and thus makes them unlikely to try to control the behavior that is actually being studied, because of its relevance either to the research hypothesis or to their own self-esteem.

The effectiveness of such deceptions can be tested to some degree by debriefing participants, when their participation has ended, about their perceptions of the events they have experienced. Some methodologists, however, perhaps having Orne's analysis of the cooperative hypnosis participant in mind, have expressed doubts about the effectiveness of deception or debriefing in circumventing research participants' strong motivations to be helpful to science and to be respected.

The researcher does, in such cases, seem to be subject to the catch-22 of depending on research participants to abandon their hidden motives in order to reveal the truth during debriefing, when such honesty cannot be relied on during the experiment itself. Of course, very young children, such as those studied by Ceci et al. (1994, **E8**), and nonhuman participants are less likely to form and test their own hypotheses, thus obviating the demand characteristics problem. Similarly, it is safer from demand characteristics artifacts to study behaviors such as REM sleep (**E14**) or glucose utilization in the brain (**E23**) that are unlikely to be controlled by subjects no matter what their motives might be.

Experimenter Expectancy Effects

The evidence that researchers provide cues, however unwittingly, that participants can use to determine how to do what is expected of them goes back to that horse in Germany around the turn of the 20th century. A German named Wilhelm von Osten owned the horse that seemed to be able to count, to spell, and so many other non-horsey things that he became known as Clever Hans. If one were to re-cast Osten's sideshow into a research study in psychology, it would seem to demonstrate that horses have a far greater capacity for learning than is generally believed. An early German psychologist named Pfungst was skeptical, as scientists generally are, often to the consternation of those who think they already know answers to questions. Because Hans was able to "answer" questions put to him by people other than his owner, it seemed clear that his performances weren't ordinary fakes. But were they really evidence of intelligent behavior?

In a series of studies, Pfungst (1906/1965) was able to show that Hans wasn't responding to his questioners' queries, but to subtle movements they weren't even aware of making. When Hans wore blinders, he was less able to answer the usual questions. The same was true when the questioner moved farther away. When the questioner didn't know the answer (a date in history, for example), Hans didn't know it either. Through careful observation, Pfungst discovered that by leaning forward, or raising an eyebrow, or dilating a nostril, the questioner cued Hans to start and stop clopping with his hoof, thus guiding him to the right answer.

Does this seem relevant to modern psychological research? It is, according to many methodologists, especially Robert Rosenthal of Harvard University, who revived Pfungst's work about 40 years ago. They believe that a researcher's expectations for the performance of research participants can influence those participants' behavior in much the same way as Clever Hans's behavior was influenced by the expectations of his questioners. The modern term for this phenomenon is *experimenter expectancy effects*. The first formal studies of them were carried out to test the possibility that they are responsible for artifacts in psychological research. As more was learned about these effects, they gradually became a subject of research in their own right, generating a literature of more than 450 studies, by Rosenthal's count, as of 1990 (Rosnow & Rosenthal, 1997).

Rosenthal's early studies (Rosenthal, 1969) illustrate the problem that experimenter expectancy effects pose for the validity of psychological research findings and also their intrinsic interest as a psychological phenomenon. In one study, research methods students were assigned to collect data for a research study as a class project. The study purportedly tested the hypothesis that people could tell how successful someone was just by looking at a photograph of that person. Rosenthal and his colleagues (the real researchers in this case) cut photographs out of a college yearbook and pasted them side-by-side on cardboard rectangles in randomly selected groups of three. The student experimenters tested other students by holding up one card at a time and asking them to identify which of the three people shown in the photographs was a successful person.

The experimenters themselves were led to believe that one of the three was a successful person. That one was supposedly identified on the back of the card, the side they were looking at while they tested their research participants. The participants they tested, of course, would have had no real clue as to which photograph to choose, since not even the people who chose the photographs knew how successful the people in them really were. They were more likely, however, to guess the one that the experimenter believed was the correct choice. You might call them a bunch of Clever Participants.

In another study that followed pretty much the same format, student experimenters conducted a study of maze learning in rats. This time, half were told their rats (the research participants) had been specially bred to be "maze bright" (good at learning mazes). The other half were led to believe their rats were "maze dull." In fact, pairs of littermates were divided randomly between the student experimenters.

When the students brought their results back to Rosenthal, their expectations had become a reality. The rats labeled maze bright had learned faster than those labeled maze dull. Experimenters' expectancies produced an artifact, a result caused by something other than the independent variable. Of course, in this case there was no treatment at all, no real difference between the groups of rats. The only possible cause of the difference in performance between the two groups of rats was how the experimenters treated them based on their expectations, a treatment artifact.

Interestingly, decades before Rosenthal and others realized the importance of experimenter expectancy effects in behavioral research, some earlier researchers acted as though they already knew that the problem existed. In Ivan Pavlov's research on classical conditioning (1927, **E20**), the researcher was prevented from "communicating" with the canine participants by a shield that blocked the line of sight between them. I discovered this by accident while reading the 1928 edition of Pavlov's *Conditioned Reflexes*. It contains a drawing of the laboratory arrangement, reproduced in Figure 4.2.

Another example of Rosenthal's early work on the experimenter expectancy effect, the study listed as **E15** among our list of exemplars, is probably the one that put this issue on the map and caused it to spread far beyond the discipline of psychology. A San Francisco school principal, Lenore Jacobson, heard of Rosenthal's work and wondered if teachers' expectations for their students' performance had similar effects to those experimenters have on their research participants.

She and Rosenthal administered a nonverbal test of intelligence to several classes in each of several grades in her school. The teachers of those classes were told that it was a test that could identify underachievers, students whose aptitudes were greater than their current academic performance indicated. In fact, the test was a sham. The researchers selected several children in each class at random and informed their teachers that test scores had indicated that these students should soon "bloom" into their true potential. After retesting all the students 8 months later, they discovered that those students' IQs had increased more than those of

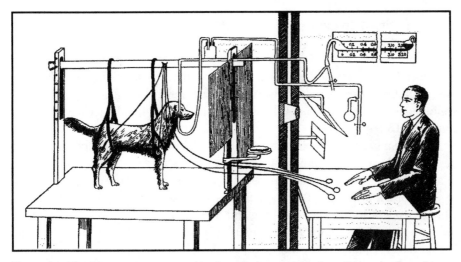

Figure 4.2 The laboratory setup used by Ivan Pavlov to study "conditioned reflexes" in dogs. The drawing shows how screens prevented visual contact between the researcher and the dog.
SOURCE: Reprinted from *Lectures on Conditioned Reflexes* (Vol. 1), p. 271, Pavlov, © copyright 1928 by Lawrence and Wishart. Reprinted with permission.

other students. Those gains held up after two whole school years, presumably long after the students left the classrooms of their experimentally biased teachers.

Treatments are often administered to research participants by experimenters who have been informed about the research hypothesis, or who have had the opportunity to draw their own inferences about the research hypothesis in the course of administering the treatments. Those experimenters may develop expectancies for the participants' behavior. If the research is conducted in a setting where it is possible for the experimenters to unintentionally communicate those expectancies to participants, the results of the study might be biased accordingly.

When that happens, differences in the behavior of research participants exposed to different treatments might result from the experimenters' expectancies via exposure to the unintentional cues they produce rather than differences in the treatments themselves. Where that is possible, results that appear to confirm the hypothesis must be interpreted cautiously. If the results are responses to experimenter expectancies rather than to the treatments, or to some confounded combination of the two, the validity of the research findings is compromised.

In some studies, research participants may respond to natural events that are not produced by the researcher. Treatments may be administered in a laboratory by some automated device such as a tape recorder or computer, or in a laboratory or field setting by an experimenter who truly has been kept unaware of the research hypothesis or of the intent of the treatment being administered to each individual participant. In those cases, the likelihood of experimenter expectancy effects can be greatly reduced.

One area of research where the threat to validity of participant and researcher motives and expectancies has long been recognized is in testing the effects of drugs. In fact, the name for the unintended influences that might become confounded with the effects of the drugs themselves is familiar: They are called **placebo effects**.

To prevent placebo effects in drug trials, the **double-blind procedure** is used. Research participants are randomly chosen to receive either the drug being tested or an inert substance that is administered in the same way as the drug (as a pill, or an injection, or however). Both participants and researchers are kept unaware of ("blind" to) which doses are the drug and which are the placebo imitation of the drug. An elaborate system of code numbers is administered by a researcher who has no direct contact with either group.

An interesting outcome of a placebo drug trial is currently (as this book is being written) being reported in a television ad campaign for the drug Detrol, which is used to treat too-frequent urination or "overactive bladder." When compared with a placebo for its effectiveness in reducing the frequency of urination, the drug is reported to be roughly twice as effective. In tests, the number of accidents dropped by two a day for the research participants given Detrol and by one a day for those given the placebo. Thus, even in a double-blind test, participant expectancies and motivation produced half as much impact as the drug itself.

The more interesting results, however, come from comparisons of side effects. Participants taking Detrol reported three to four times the frequency of dry mouth, indigestion, headache, and other side effects of the drug. It makes sense, based on our previous discussion, that participants in a drug trial would expect the drug to alleviate their problem, whose nature they would be well aware of. They would not, however, expect the specific side effects of the drug, which they would have no way of knowing about in advance.

Pretest Sensitization

A special kind of treatment artifact can occur in the administration of research treatments when a pretest is used. A pretest is a measure of subjects' behavior that is made before any treatment is administered to them, usually to get a "baseline" measure of the behavior being studied. In a **pretest-posttest research design**, the same measure is administered again after the treatment, for comparison against the pretest.

In a reactive setting, where the research participants may already be searching for cues to the "right" thing to do, a pretest can serve to sensitize them even further. It can give the participants a clearer idea of which behavior is being studied. It can also provide a basis for using the second administration of that measure, the posttest, to do what seems to be expected or will be perceived favorably under the circumstances.

Cognitive psychologists have studied a phenomenon known as **conceptual priming** that sheds some light on how pretest sensitization might work. In conceptual priming, a few key words that are related to a concept serve to bring the concept to mind, and it then influences a person's subsequent thought processes. In some of the research on conceptual priming, the concept is brought to mind through a task that requires the research participant to make meaningful sentences out of scrambled lists of words.

In one study (Bargh, Chen, & Burrows, 1996), the concept was the stereotype of elderly people. Each "scrambled sentence" contained a key word that could re-mind one of the stereotype. The sentences, however, did not refer directly to the elderly, so that the participants were kept unaware of the subtle effects the task had on them. For example, one sentence was "Oranges are from Florida." Another was "Sunlight makes raisins wrinkle." Can you tell what the key words were in those sentences?

The key words, "Florida" and "wrinkle," along with others, influenced partici-pants in a later task seemingly unrelated to the scrambled sentences task. In the second task, they were more likely to judge the elderly in stereotypic terms as slow, weak, and failing. Does this seem so different from giving research partici-pants a test measuring the behavior being studied and then providing them with some experience that might influence that behavior? Not so different that we don't need to worry about the pretest subtly creating a mindset that could cause that subsequent experience, the treatment, to have a different effect than it would oth-erwise (in the absence of a pretest).

In the research on conceptual priming, the debriefing of participants is a crucial requirement. Careful questioning of participants must demonstrate that they were unaware of the purpose of the research and, especially, of the connection between the scrambled sentences task and the judgments they were asked to make later. Unless the possibility that participants' behavior was caused by a treatment artifact is ruled out in this way, the results cannot be interpreted with any confidence as evidence for conceptual priming.

Although a similar kind of debriefing could be used with pretested research par-ticipants, the most effective remedy for pretest sensitization is the elimination of the pretest. In many cases, it is unnecessary, as we will see in the discussion of re-search design in Chapters 5, 6, and 7. Where a pretest is needed, it is sometimes possible to disguise it, or to obtain the pretest measure without the research partic-ipants being aware of it, or to use an equivalent measure different from the one used as the posttest. All of these are promising antidotes to problematic pretest sensitization effects.

| Box 4.3 | *THINKING ABOUT RESEARCH* |

Documenting Behavior Can Change It _____

One of the most fascinating films I've ever seen, and not just because it deals with psychological themes, is independent filmmaker Michael Apted's documentary series beginning with *7 Up* (1962). It began with filmed interviews and activities of 7-year-old English boys and girls, about half a dozen of each from three different social strata in English society. The same children were interviewed every 7 years, at ages 14, 21, and 28, with the exception of a small number who chose to drop out of the project at various points along the way. In November of 1999, *42 Up* was released as the most recent installment in a series of films that included *28 Up* (1984) and *35 Up* (1991).

The original purpose of Apted's project was to examine social class differences among British children. The films also reveal much about the degree of consistency and inconsistency in people's personalities across their life spans, and they tell us some about the reasons for stability and change in people's lives.

A different issue was raised in *42 Up*, one that seems very relevant to our examination of meth-ods for psychological research despite the seemingly wide methodological gulf between documentary filmmaking and the kind of research we're examining in this book.

Several of the remaining participants in Apted's project seem to have had their lives changed as a result of appearing in the series of films. One who became a successful physicist regrets being more famous for his part in the films than for his scientific work. Another, who once had fairly serious psychological problems, managed to get elected to public office partly on the strength of publicity about the films.

How would you describe in methodological terms the effect of these "research participants" being "studied" in this way? Are there specific examples of formal psychological research where such a problem would be especially likely to be encountered? Does this mean that Apted's work or such research is worthless? Even if it is worth less because of this problem, what does it have to recommend it that might partially offset the problem?

● THREATS TO CONSTRUCT VALIDITY: THE DEPENDENT VARIABLE (BEHAVIORAL MEASURES)

The researcher must also choose a dependent variable to represent the behavioral construct in the hypothesis. It will consist of one or more measures that can be used to record the behavior of research participants before, during, or following their exposure to the treatments. This choice is subject to a set of threats to the validity of the research findings very similar to that of the choice of treatments. We turn now to a description of each of those threats, with analysis of their causes and remedies. Try to tolerate the inevitable redundancy with previous discussion of threats to the construct validity of treatments. It is intended to reinforce understanding of the basic issues involved in both.

Inadequate Operationalization of the Dependent Variable

This section will discuss three significant threats to construct validity that parallel those discussed in connection with the independent variable. They are **lack of reliability of the dependent variable**, **lack of representativeness of the dependent variable**, and **lack of sensitivity of the dependent variable** (see Table 4.5). Each of them is related to the basic principles of psychological measurement discussed in Chapter 3. Of course, as was true of treatment operationalization, precision of measurement is also an asset here. Quantitative measurement is ultimately more useful in most cases than qualitative, and quantitative measurement that has interval or ratio scale properties is more useful than ordinal measurement.

Lack of Reliability of Behavioral Measures

As we know already, if the same measuring device is applied to the same property of the same event on repeated occasions, a different measurement will be observed each time. If the variation in those measurements is large, the usefulness of that measure will be compromised as a result. We won't know a high level of aggression when we see it. The same aggression will look like a high level sometimes, but not so high other times, and very high still others. In such a case, how can we ever find out how TV violence affects aggressive behavior? Reliability of this kind, stability, is the most basic prerequisite for good measurement.

One way to increase the reliability of behavioral measurement is to broaden the scope of the measuring device. We can make more detailed observations of a subject's behavior, tapping multiple occurrences of aggressive behavior for example, rather than just one. If we do that, it is less likely that our view of the same degree of aggressive behavior will be different on different occasions. In the case of standardized tests, just making the test longer by adding additional (relevant) questions will generally increase reliability coefficients.

Every measure or test is a sample of a more extensive pattern of behavior, and the larger the sample, the more it is that we will find out about the total pattern. The more reports during REM sleep Aserinsky and Kleitman (1953) collected dur-

---

TABLE 4.5   Threats to Construct Validity of the Dependent Variable: Inadequate Operationalization

---

I. Threats to conceptual validity
       1. Unnecessary duplication
       2. Theoretical isolation
II. Threats to construct validity
  A. The independent variable
    a. Inadequate operationalization
       3. Lack of reliability of the independent variable
       4. Lack of representativeness of the independent variable
       5. Lack of impact of the independent variable
    b. Treatment artifacts
       6. Demand characteristics in the research setting
       7. Experimenter expectancy effects on the behavior being observed
       8. Pretest sensitization to the treatments
  B. The dependent variable
  a. Inadequate operationalization
       9. Lack of reliability of the dependent variable
     10. Lack of representativeness of the dependent variable
     11. Lack of sensitivity of the dependent variable
    b. Measurement artifacts
     12. Strategic responding by the research participants
     13. Linguistic/cultural bias in the dependent measure
III. Threats to internal validity
     14. Extraneous effects (history)
     15. Temporal effects (maturation)
     16. Group composition effects (selection)
     17. Interaction of temporal and group composition effects
     18. Selective sample attrition (mortality)
     19. Statistical regression effects (regression to the mean)
IV. Threats to external validity
     20. Nonrepresentative sampling
     21. Nonrepresentative research context
V. Threats to statistical conclusion validity
     22. Inappropriate use of statistical techniques
     23. Use of a statistical test lacking sufficient power
     24. Mistaking a trivial effect for support for the research hypothesis

---

ing their research (**E4**), the more stable would be their estimate of the frequency of dreaming during REM. The more problems Gazzaniga (1967) asked split-brain patients to solve (**E21**), the more reliable his estimate of the differences between left and right hemisphere functions would be.

Another reliability issue associated with behavioral measurement is known as **interrater reliability**. Behavioral measurement is often accomplished by a subjective rating of some behavior, such as a child's aggressive behavior on a play-ground. There are advantages to having such ratings made by more than one observer. Individual observers' frames of reference might color their judgments in idiosyncratic ways (see the discussion of response biases in Chapter 3), but those would "average out" among a group. If more than one rater is used, however, the level of agreement among raters becomes an issue. Fortunately, it can be assessed with a complex version of a correlation coefficient that essentially averages the correlations among all possible pairs of raters.

Furthermore, interrater reliability can be improved by training raters to follow a common set of guidelines. It can also be improved by videotaping the behavior to be rated so that each rater sees it from the same visual perspective. Because multiple raters are used to eliminate the possibility that a single rater would see things strangely, it is important for multiple raters to agree substantially on what they see. As usual, past research can provide guidelines for judging the adequacy of any interrater reliability coefficients obtained.

Lack of Representativeness of Behavioral Measures

Measures of behavior also need to sample adequately the domain of the behavioral construct in the research hypothesis, in the same way as treatments need to sample the causal construct. In other words, they need to have adequate **content validity**. The first step in ensuring that they do is to clearly define the construct itself. What sort of behavior is to be considered aggression? Is it just hitting? Does a verbal insult also constitute aggression? Is hiding a playmate's favorite toy, or telling a destructive lie about a classmate to a third party, an indirect form of aggressive behavior? Once these sorts of questions have been answered, a measure can be constructed that samples each area of the final construct domain. This should prevent the measure from failing to sample one or more of those areas, thus lacking representativeness in reference to that construct.

Complex constructs raise still another measurement issue. If the measure developed to tap such a construct combines observations of a number of separate behaviors into a single score, it may obscure differences among participants' responses to the treatments. One set of experiences (treatment) might be followed by an increase in physical aggression, while another was followed by an increase in verbal aggression, and a third by an increase in indirect aggression. If the measure of aggression used in the study added up all three types of aggression into a single score, the participants exposed to the treatments that created those different experiences could receive similar scores even though they behaved in different ways.

If each treatment group received a high score for one type of aggression and low scores for the other types, the three groups would have similar overall scores even though the treatments had different effects. Statistical techniques exist that can be applied to such measures to determine whether they are unitary, and can legitimately be combined into a single score, or whether they are composites of in-dependent components. In the latter case, participants can be given a separate subscore for each independent component (sometimes called a *subscale score*), permitting a clearer picture of the effects of treatments to be obtained by evaluat-ing each type of response separately.

Lack of Sensitivity of Behavioral Measures

As important as it is for a treatment to have sufficient impact to provide a fair test of the research hypothesis, it is equally important for a behavioral measure to be sensitive enough to detect any differences in behavior across different treatments that might occur. Imagine a medical study to compare the effectiveness of several antibiotics. If insufficient doses of the antibiotics are given to research subjects, the treatments will lack sufficient impact. Even an effective drug will appear to have no effect. In such a case, conclusions drawn about the relative effectiveness of the drug will be worthless. At the same time, if the effectiveness of the drug is mea-sured in such a way that only very large differences in the numbers of bacteria that survive the test doses of the medication are detectable, the outcome measure will lack sufficient sensitivity. Real differences in effectiveness might not be observed even though they occurred.

A microscope used in such a medical experiment would have to have sufficient optical power to detect differences of a size that would be reasonable to expect in the particular research context. In the same way, a behavioral measure must be sufficiently sensitive to detect differences in behavior that are of reasonable size. Unfortunately, there is no established scale for behavioral measures that corre-sponds to the 10×, 20×, and so on magnification scale that is used to compare opti-cal instruments. Neither is there a measuring scale for estimating the "size" of be-haviors in the way that the size of bacteria or viruses can be estimated.

This is another reason to conduct pilot research, in which one can gauge the po-tential for a measuring instrument to detect changes of the type that occur in re-sponse to the treatments. Unfortunately, it might be difficult to determine whether the problem lies in the impact of the treatments or the sensitivity of the measures. In either case, a failure to find a hypothesized relationship may reflect less on the truth of the hypothesis than on the adequacy of the methods used to test it. If there is a problem, of course, one can make changes in both to try to give the hypothesis a fair test. Again, though, if the hypothesis is just not true, no amount of legitimate tinkering can be expected to work.

Measurement Artifacts

We have already seen how research participants search for clues to the re-searcher's hypothesis, especially in a highly reactive research setting such as a psychological laboratory, where they are likely to suspect that their current experiences have been created so that the researcher can study their responses. On the flip side of that problem is the susceptibility of behavioral measures to be biased by *strategic responding*. If the measures used to determine the nature of participants' responses to treatments have transparent meanings to participants, it is possible for participants to pursue the undesirable strategies to which demand characteristics and experimenter expectancies can also contribute.

In addition, there is the potential problem of *linguistic/cultural bias*. Participants' backgrounds may cause them to misunderstand the measures in such a way that their responses give an inaccurate account of their behavior in response to the treatments administered to them. These measurement artifacts are shown in Table 4.6.

Strategic Responding

It is common for a researcher to ask participants to report how happy they feel, or about their attitudes or impressions in regard to a particular person or situation, or for some other response to particular events that have occurred. To comply, participants might have to choose a point on a rating scale, or one of a group of statements provided by the researcher. These so-called self-report behavioral measures or questionnaires provide participants with a great deal of latitude for strategic responding.

A participant might believe that he or she knows the researcher's hypothesis and be motivated to "help" by responding as the researcher is supposed to expect. Alternatively, the participant might "know" which response will be evaluated most favorably by the researcher and be motivated to seek a favorable evaluation, or the participant might be predisposed to be lenient or critical or noncommittal. In each of these cases, self-report measures make it easy to select the response that will do the job. There is no way for the researcher who uses such measures to know how much the participants' responses reflect their true feelings, attitudes, or impressions, and how much those responses reflect strategic response biases to cooperate or look good or whatever.

Alternative behavioral measures are not so vulnerable to such response biases. If the researcher observes the participants' facial expressions, how close they stand to another person, or how much of some food they eat from a variety of choices during a taste test, the likelihood of strategic responding will be reduced somewhat. The participant may still be aware of the general purpose of his or her encounter with the researcher and of being under scrutiny. In addition, the participant can control facial expressions and other actions to some degree. The significance of those behaviors to the researcher, however, probably will be less obvious, and strategic efforts to control them less successful.

TABLE 4.6   Threats to the Construct Validity of the Dependent Variable: Measurement Artifacts

I. Threats to conceptual validity
    1. Unnecessary duplication
    2. Theoretical isolation
II. Threats to construct validity
  A. The independent variable
    a. Inadequate operationalization
      3. Lack of reliability of the independent variable
      4. Lack of representativeness of the independent variable
      5. Lack of impact of the independent variable
    b. Treatment artifacts
      6. Demand characteristics in the research setting
      7. Experimenter expectancy effects on the behavior being observed
      8. Pretest sensitization to the treatments
  B. The dependent variable
    a. Inadequate operationalization
      9. Lack of reliability of the dependent variable
      10. Lack of representativeness of the dependent variable
      11. Lack of sensitivity of the dependent variable
    b. Measurement artifacts
      12. Strategic responding by the research participants
      13. Linguistic/cultural bias in the dependent measure
III. Threats to internal validity
    14. Extraneous effects (history)
    15. Temporal effects (maturation)
    16. Group composition effects (selection)
    17. Interaction of temporal and group composition effects
    18. Selective sample attrition (mortality)
    19. Statistical regression effects (regression to the mean)
IV. Threats to external validity
    20. Nonrepresentative sampling
    21. Nonrepresentative research context
V. Threats to statistical conclusion validity
    22. Inappropriate use of statistical techniques
    23. Use of a statistical test lacking sufficient power
    24. Mistaking a trivial effect for support for the research hypothesis

For example, one researcher tested the hypothesis that attractive college students would be more vain not by asking them whether they were (would they admit it?), but by observing how much time they spent looking at their reflections while they walked past a campus building with a mirrored facade. Another researcher assessed the political attitudes of citizens of Hong Kong, while it was still a British colony, by dropping stamped letters in the streets that were addressed to fictitious groups with names that indicated differing political orientations (pro-Communist, pro-independence, etc.). Differences in the percentages of letters addressed to the various groups that passersby took the trouble to drop into mailboxes were taken as indications of the population's political leanings at the time.

There are some drawbacks to using **unobtrusive measures** of behavior. When research participants are asked directly how they feel or what they think, the researcher can select participants who are representative of a particular population. When a researcher watches people who walk past a particular building, however, or tests those who walk down a particular street and notice a lost letter on the pavement, the participants, not the researcher, choose whether they will be included in the study.

When participants say they are or aren't vain, or that they support British rule or a return to Chinese control, they may or may not be telling the truth, but at least we know what question they were asked. It isn't quite so obvious that people who look at their reflections in a building's facade are "telling" us they're vain, or that those who choose to drop a lost letter in a mailbox support the organization to which the letter is addressed.

These examples of nonreactive behavioral measures also point up the significance of the setting in which research is carried out. Students walking to class on a college campus or office workers running an errand at lunchtime are unlikely to know that a researcher is observing their behavior, or is even present. Compared to research participants in a psychological laboratory, then, they are less likely to be motivated to respond strategically (as we recognized in the earlier discussion of demand characteristics and experimenter expectancy effects).

Another alternative to self-report measures of behavior is to use **archival data**. These are measures of behavior that are collected by governmental or other organizations for their internal purposes but that are accessible to researchers and reflective of people's responses to events that may be important causes of behavior. The FBI's Uniform Crime Statistics, a factory's records of worker absenteeism and turnover, and sports teams' won-lost records at home and on the road are just a few examples of archival data that have proven useful in psychological research. It seems very unlikely that the behavior of the criminals, workers, and athletes involved was influenced in any way by the researchers who ultimately used those data to test their hypotheses. Much more information about data sources and settings for research will appear in Chapter 9.

Linguistic/Cultural Bias

A second source of concern over measurement artifacts is limited to those measures of behavior that present research participants with verbal questions and require verbal responses. Such measures depend on participants being able to understand the meaning of the questions and to communicate their responses accurately.

To do so, the participants must be familiar with the language itself. They must know the meanings of words and the grammatical structure. They must also be familiar with the culture. The questions likely will contain idioms and references to people, places, and things, references that mean more to people who grew up in the culture of origin than to recent immigrants, or even to minorities who are segregated from the majority culture by language, neighborhood, activities, or other aspects of their experience.

For this reason, as we have already seen, intelligence tests are widely believed to underestimate the true intelligence of African Americans and certain linguistic minorities. Along with many academic achievement tests, they stress facility in using "the" language. Questions are embedded in a cultural context that is more familiar to test takers whose backgrounds are similar to those of the highly educated question writers than to some others. It might even be true, although less attention seems to have been paid to this possibility, that such tests overestimate the abilities of those most attuned to the mainstream culture and most similar in background to the test makers who represent it.

Although the questionnaires, rating scales, and other verbal measures used in psychological research have not been studied for susceptibility to linguistic/cultural bias in the detail that intelligence tests have, their use raises the same concerns. Whether research participants are drawn from college student populations or from the general public, the considerable ethnic, regional, socioeconomic, and linguistic diversity in American society make it imperative that those who construct such measures take the possibility of linguistic/cultural bias into account. One way to do that is to design the measures with input from prospective participants that will ensure their understanding. Another is to substitute nonverbal measures. Participants' actions and movements can be used to measure their responses to treatments without resorting to language at all. Many examples have been discussed in this and previous chapters, and many more will be discussed in Chapter 9.

● SUMMING UP CONSTRUCT VALIDITY

It is important, amid all the detail—technical jargon, mathematical concepts, philosophy of science, and the rest—to be sure that we keep our eye on the shell that contains the pea. Construct validity refers to the quality, on a continuum from best (not perfect) to worst, of the choices a researcher makes among alternative ways of operationalizing the constructs in the research hypothesis.

It is necessary to move from the abstract cause and effect constructs of the hypothesis to the corresponding concrete independent and dependent variables.

The researcher must specify precisely what the treatments will be, how he or she will measure whatever differences in the behavior of the research participants may occur, and the setting where participants will actually come into contact with variations of the hypothesized cause. Those are the treatments created by the researcher or selected from conditions that already exist in nature to represent a range of values on the independent variable. Only then can related differences in participants' behavior can be measured, if they indeed occur.

The ways in which cause and effect are portrayed in the independent and dependent variables are important factors in determining the degree of certainty with which conclusions can be drawn from the results of the research, the actual numbers that represent participants' responses to the treatments. The quality of those portrayals, or the accuracy with which the hypothesis' constructs are operationalized, determines construct validity and contributes to the overall validity of the research findings. Treatments and behavioral measures must be as reliable and representative as possible. Treatments must not be contaminated by demand characteristics, experimenter expectancy effects, or pretest sensitization effects that engage irrelevant participant motives. Treatments must have sufficient impact to produce a measurable effect on participants' behavior (assuming the hypothesis is true).

Behavioral measures must be reliable, representative, and sensitive. They must also minimize opportunities for strategic responding and avoid misunderstanding resulting from linguistic/cultural bias. All efforts to minimize potential threats to construct validity increase the confidence of researchers and research consumers alike in the conclusions drawn from the research about the truth of the research hypothesis.

Of course, as complicated as the issues involved in construct validity obviously are, they are just one component of an overall judgment about the validity of research findings (conclusions). It will be helpful to revisit some of these issues in Chapters 5, 6, and 7, in the context of research design, and then again in Chapter 9, where we consider the vast array of behavioral measures or data collection techniques available to the psychological researcher.

Review Questions and Exercise

Review Questions

1. In what ways does inadequate operationalization of the independent and dependent variables threaten construct validity?

2. What are artifacts, and in what ways does the confounding of artifacts with the independent and dependent variables threaten construct validity?

Exercise

Go back to your work on Exercise 2 following Chapter 2. How well did the researchers operationalize the constructs in their research hypotheses? What opportunities, if any, did the researchers allow for artifacts to contaminate their variables? How would you evaluate the potential threats to construct validity of the independent and dependent variables in those studies? What reasons do you see for the existence of those threats to construct validity that you do find?

ARRANGING THE COMPARISONS I

An Introduction to Research Design

● A QUICK GUIDE TO CHAPTER 5:
AN INTRODUCTION TO RESEARCH DESIGN

Hypothesis-testing research is based on comparison. To conclude that a putative cause actually does influence the behavior in question, the researcher must observe the behavior in the absence of that cause as well as in its presence, or in the presence of varying levels of the factor that is suspected as its cause. The way those comparisons are arranged in a particular study, also known as the **research design**, plays an important role in determining the validity of the research findings.

There are two major types of research design. The researcher can utilize a **between-subjects design** that makes **comparisons among groups** exposed to different amounts of the independent variable representing the hypothetical causal factor. Alternatively, using a **within-subjects design**, the researcher can make a **comparison over time**, in which a single group is exposed to different forms or amounts of the independent variable. In addition to those variations in the way participants are exposed to the **treatments** (variations in the independent variable), there are further elaborations of research design based on whether or not the participants are assigned to groups or occasions at random by the researcher, and on the amount of control the researcher has over the presentation of treatments and the setting in which they are presented.

The researcher's decisions about how to arrange the comparisons on which a research study will be based have far-reaching implications for the interpretation of the research results. There are at least six separate threats to the **internal validity** of research findings at issue. They help to determine the degree of certainty with which one can draw a **causal inference** from the results. There are at least two threats to the **external validity** of the findings, or the **generalizability** of the results beyond the specific circumstances of a particular study, that are also contingent on research design. In addition, construct validity depends heavily on research design. The reliability and representativeness of the independent and dependent variables, as well as the reactivity of the research setting and the likelihood of associated artifacts, are all affected by the design created by the researcher to compare the effects of the treatments on the behavior in question.

The Chapter 5 Quick Guide shows the six threats to internal and two threats to external validity that are discussed in this chapter. They are identified and then presented in the form of questions that need to be asked about the research findings. This is not an exhaustive list, but merely a start toward understanding the methodological implications of research design.

Chapter 5 Quick Guide: Threats to Internal and External Validity Related to the Choice of a Research Design

Question About the Research Findings

Internal Validity

Extraneous events (history)	Are participants exposed to events, other than the treatments, whose effects on their behavior could obscure the effects of the independent variable?
Temporal effects (maturation)	Does the behavior of participants change with the passage of time in ways that could obscure the effects of the independent variable?
Group composition effects (selection)	If different groups are used to compare the effects of treatments, could pre-existing differences among the groups obscure the effects of the independent variable?
Interaction of temporal and group composition effects (maturation × selection interaction)	Could changes in participants' behavior over time that are related to pre-existing differences among groups obscure the effects of the independent variable?
Selective sample attrition (mortality)	Could differences among groups that are the result of the selective loss of participants during the study obscure the effects of the independent variable?
Statistical regression effects (regression to the mean)	Could changes in participants' responses to the behavioral measures that are caused by regression toward the mean obscure the effects of the independent variable?

External Validity

Nonrepresentative sampling of units	Are the participants in the research study so unrepresentative of those whose behavior needs to be understood as to preclude generalization of the research results from the former to the latter?
Nonrepresentative research context	Is the context in which the research study was carried out so unrepresentative of contexts where the behavior in question takes place as to preclude generalization of the research results from the former to the latter?

INTRODUCTION TO THE CHAPTER ●

A recent television "news magazine" show featured a story about controversy (what else!) over a vitamin-based treatment for Down syndrome. On one side of the debate was a woman advocating the treatment. Her own daughter was afflicted with Down syndrome. She appeared with several of her followers, who also were parents of children with Down syndrome. All of them claimed that their children had benefited greatly from the disputed drug-vitamin treatment.

On the other side were doctors and government officials who argued that there was no scientific evidence that the treatment worked. They also expressed concern about unresolved questions about possible long-term side effects. In interviews, parents of children with Down syndrome who had been persuaded by these skeptical arguments explained why they had decided to not give the drug-vitamin combination to their children.

Recast in the language of psychological research, these two groups were disagreeing over the evidence regarding a research hypothesis. Was the drug-vitamin therapy in question effective in treating Down syndrome? The principal reason for the dispute lay in the method by which the evidence for the efficacy of the treatment was collected. In the terms you will be encountering and learning to understand in this chapter and the next two, it is a question of **research design**. (This and many other important terms in this chapter and subsequent ones were first introduced in Chapter 1, but they will be boldfaced again so that we don't lose track of their importance or the fact that brief definitions of them can be found in Appendix B.)

Research design has to do with the choices researchers face among alternative arrangements for making the comparisons that are necessary for understanding the effects of a treatment on the behavior of those who are exposed to it. What effect did the drug-vitamin treatment for Down syndrome have on the children to whom it was administered? That's the question at the heart of the debate. Why couldn't the parties agree about whether the changes observed in children who received the treatment (the "research" results) support the hypothesis that the treatment is effective?

The principal reason in this case appears to be that they lacked appropriate comparisons for deciding on the truth of their hypothesis. It wasn't clear whether the children who received the treatment ended up better off as a result of it than they would have been without it—the **within-subjects design** type of comparison. Nor was it clear whether the children who received the treatment were really better off than other children with Down syndrome who didn't—the **between-subjects design** type of comparison.

In this chapter and the next two, we will learn how to arrange comparisons that can make it possible to draw valid conclusions from research results. We will consider both kinds of comparisons, the two categories of research designs. Some designs compare participants before and after they receive the treatment, **comparison over time** (the first example above), and others compare participants who receive the treatment with others who don't, or compare recipients of different versions or amounts of the treatment, **comparison among groups** (the second example above).

Within each of those categories, we will consider a variety of ways that comparisons can be made—different research designs. In the next chapter, we will learn a method for representing the basic elements in every research design. In each case, there will be one or more treatments representing values of the independent variable chosen to operationalize the causal construct in the research hypothesis. There will also be one or more administrations of a measure of the behavior that is observed in association with each treatment. We will use a system of notation in which a relatively small number of symbols can be combined to describe a very large number and wide variety of research designs.

Chapters 6 and 7 will examine samples of the two types of research designs, those that compare a single group over repeated occasions and those that compare across different groups. We will describe them and analyze them for their vulnerability to each of the potential threats to internal and external validity. Chapter 8 will consider ways of expanding the basic designs to accommodate more complex research hypotheses.

In this chapter, you will learn what to look for in those research designs. Earlier, we considered threats to construct validity that could be used to evaluate the adequacy of the independent and dependent variables chosen to represent the cause and behavior constructs in the research hypothesis. Now we will consider threats to the validity of research findings that are associated with the choice of a research design. Continuing with the approach first made popular by Donald T. Campbell and Julian C. Stanley in the 1960s (Campbell & Stanley, 1963), we will consider two sets of threats to validity that should guide the researcher's choice of a research design and the reader's evaluation of the conclusions drawn from others' research results.

Threats to the **internal validity** of research findings make it difficult to determine whether any **treatment effects** (behavioral differences associated with exposure to different treatments) were caused by the differences in the treatments or by some other unintended influence. Threats to the **external validity** of research findings make it difficult to generalize any behavioral differences associated with exposure to different treatments beyond the specific individuals and circumstances in the research study itself. When there are no differences in behavior among treatment groups, threats to internal and external validity make it difficult to know whether the lack of differences implies no causal influence of the treatments, and whether the same lack of differences would be observed in other individuals under different circumstances or whether it is limited to the particulars of the study in question.

● THREATS TO INTERNAL VALIDITY

For a large part of the history of scientific psychology, researchers were concerned almost exclusively with one consequence of research design (the arrangement of comparisons to test their hypotheses). They wanted above all else to achieve certainty in determining whether any differences that were observed in the dependent variable across the occasions or groups being compared were caused by corresponding differences in the treatments with which those differences were associated. We are going to refer to those concerns with **causal inference** as concerns with internal validity.

If research results show differences in behavior associated with differences in treatments over time or across groups, is that evidence of a causal relationship between the independent variable (treatments) and dependent variable (behavioral measures)? To the extent that comparisons over time or across groups are arranged so that differences in the dependent variable could have been caused only by the associated differences in the independent variable, the research findings have internal validity.

To the extent that there may have been other causes, known also as **alternative explanations** for those differences, or **rival hypotheses** for those differences, there are threats to the internal validity of the research findings.

This section will examine six specific threats to internal validity that need to be considered in the choice of a research design. In other words, these are six possible alternative explanations or rival hypotheses that must be ruled out before a researcher can be confident in drawing a conclusion from the research results about the existence of the causal relationship between the constructs that are specified in the research hypothesis (see Table 5.1). To achieve internally valid research findings, one must be certain that the only difference in experience between the groups whose behavior is being compared is that intended by the researcher. In the classical language of science, Latin, the requirement is known as *ceteris paribus*; all else (besides the difference in treatments) must be equal.

Extraneous Events (a.k.a. History)

Research participants in different treatment groups or on different occasions may be exposed to events, other than the treatments being studied by the researcher, that are capable of influencing the behavior that is being measured to test the hypothesis. If so, those **extraneous events** may be responsible for any differences that are observed over time or across groups, or any lack thereof. To the extent that those extraneous events or that *history* (to use Campbell and Stanley's original term) might have been present, the status of the causal relationship between the treatments and those differences is cast into doubt. The inference that

TABLE 5.1   Threats to Internal Validity

I. Threats to conceptual validity
> 1. Unnecessary duplication
> 2. Theoretical isolation

II. Threats to construct validity
> A. The independent variable
> > a. Inadequate operationalization
> > > 3. Lack of reliability of the independent variable
> > > 4. Lack of representativeness of the independent variable
> > > 5. Lack of impact of the independent variable
> > b. Treatment artifacts
> > > 6. Demand characteristics in the research setting
> > > 7. Experimenter expectancy effects on the behavior being observed
> > > 8. Pretest sensitization to the treatments
> B. The dependent Variable
> > a. Inadequate operationalization
> > > 9. Lack of reliability of the dependent variable
> > > 10. Lack of representativeness of the dependent variable
> > > 11. Lack of sensitivity of the dependent variable
> > b. Measurement artifacts
> > > 12. Strategic responding by the research participants
> > > 13. Linguistic/cultural bias in the dependent measure

III. Threats to internal validity
> **14. Extraneous effects (history)**
> **15. Temporal effects (maturation)**
> **16. Group composition effects (selection)**
> **17. Interaction of temporal and group composition effects**
> **18. Selective sample attrition (mortality)**
> **19. Statistical regression effects (regression to the mean)**

IV. Threats to external validity
> 20. Nonrepresentative sampling
> 21. Nonrepresentative research context

V. Threats to statistical conclusion validity
> 22. Inappropriate use of statistical techniques
> 23. Use of a statistical test lacking sufficient power
> 24. Mistaking a trivial effect for support for the research hypothesis

the treatments caused the observed changes or differences in behavior, or failed to if no effects are observed, can't be made with very much confidence in such a case.

The first task in research design is therefore to arrange the comparisons in a way that will prevent the influence of extraneous events. Remember, they're definitely not extraneous to the behavior being observed, just to the hypothesis being tested. In fact, only events capable of influencing that behavior—**plausible rival hypotheses**—need be considered.

Extraneous events are extraneous because they're not the causal events mentioned in the hypothesis. They're not intended to be part of the treatments chosen by the researcher to represent those events. They're events that either must be prevented from reaching the research participants or must be present equally on all the occasions or in all the groups being compared. In the language of research design, extraneous events must be controlled (either eliminated or held constant) for the true effects of the treatments (independent variable) on the behavior in question (dependent variable) to be understood. Without adequate control over extraneous events, the research findings will lack internal validity because accurate causal inference will be impossible. It will not be possible to know with certainty whether observed differences were caused by the treatments or by extraneous events.

Do you recall the discussion in Chapter 2 of Triplett's (1897) research on the effects of competition on performance (**E3**)? Initially, Triplett compared the times recorded at various distances by bicycle racers who rode alone, or who were paced by a series of other riders, or who competed head-to-head with another racer. The riders who competed posted the fastest times, paced riders were second fastest, and riders who rode alone were the slowest. Were those differences caused by the "dynamogenic factors" (competitive motivation) suggested as the putative cause in Triplett's hypothesis? Triplett believed that the three different race conditions he compared, which represented different levels of that independent variable, caused the differences in performance. But were the effects of those treatments really caused by competitive motivation?

Perhaps the crowds that watched those races, in the indoor arenas known as velodromes, gave racers more encouragement in competitive races where they could root for one rider against another. They might have rooted less vocally for riders to keep up with their pacers. Riders who rode alone might have aroused the least crowd excitement. If this were true, crowd noise could have been an extraneous event that varied systematically along with the race arrangement, on which Triplett focused. If so, it would be impossible to know how much of the differences in riders' performances to attribute to each.

Another possible extraneous event that could have contributed to some degree to the differences in performance across those three types of bicycle races is slipstreaming. When a bicycle racer follows another rider, he or she benefits from the decreased wind resistance the first rider produces. Both the riders who had pacers and the ones who raced against competitors had opportunities to benefit from slipstreaming. It could have enabled them to ride faster, or conserve energy, or both. Of course, the solitary, unpaced racers could not benefit from slipstreaming.

Triplett did not rely on his comparison of bicycle racers to prove that competitive motivation improves performance. He recognized that crowd noise, slipstreaming, and other uncontrolled extraneous events could have contributed to or

Figure 5.1. A velodrome, a banked track on which bicycle races are held. Triplett's interest in the effects of competition, as he framed the question, began with his observation of bicycle races on a track like this one. Triplett worked at Indiana University, which is located in Bloomington, a hotbed of bicycle racing to this day (although this track is in Manchester, England).
SOURCE: Photograph © copyright Nick Rosenthal. Reprinted with permission.

even produced the effects observed in that comparison. He constructed a device (see Figure 5.2) that allowed one or two people to perform a task that required turning the handle on a fishing reel to move a loop of fishing line between the reel and a pulley. The experiment he conducted using this apparatus, in which participants performed the fishing reel task repeatedly, sometimes alone and sometimes alongside another participant, ruled out the alternative explanations that a comparison among naturally occurring bicycle races could not.

Seligman's original observation that dogs failed to learn to escape electric shock, also discussed in Chapter 2, shows that extraneous events not only can create effects that might be mistaken for the effects of treatments administered by the researcher but also can mask effects those treatments otherwise would produce. As Seligman and Maier demonstrated in their research (1967, **E18**), dogs that were not previously exposed to the extraneous event of inescapable severe electric shock did learn to escape and then to avoid shock in a shuttle box. Negative reinforcement operated to strengthen those responses when extraneous events didn't operate to prevent it.

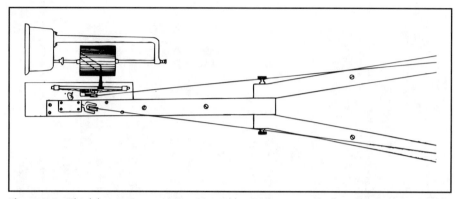

Figure 5.2. The laboratory apparatus created by Triplett to study the effects of competition using an experimental research design.
SOURCE: Reprinted from "The Dynamogenic Factors in Pacemaking and Competition," Triplett, *American Journal of Psychology*, 9 (1897), p. 519.

Finally, the case discussed at the beginning of this chapter, of parents reporting improvement in the speech and movement of their children with Down syndrome, provides a classic example of the threat of extraneous events. This special case, which is especially problematic in medical research, is known as the **placebo effect**. Recall our discussion of placebo effects in Chapter 4. When a drug or other medical treatment is administered to someone who is ill, that person receives the treatment in question along with the expectation that the treatment will work. That expectation is an extraneous event, in our terms. It is conveyed by the party administering the treatment and perhaps by others as well.

When patients' responses to medical treatments are compared against responses of patients who believe they received treatment but actually got a shot or pill that contained no active disease-fighting ingredient (the placebo), there is sometimes significant improvement in both groups. The placebo treatment ("sugar pill") can be effective, sometimes almost as effective as the real treatment. For this reason, medical research must show a treatment to be more effective than a placebo, in a "double-blind" study where neither the research participant nor the experimenter knows who is receiving the real treatment and who is receiving the placebo. It is not enough to show just that the treatment is more effective than no treatment at all for it to be approved for actual use with patients.

The placebo effect can be a very potent extraneous event. It may very well have been important in the case of parents who gave their children with Down syndrome children a vitamin treatment they believed would help or even cure them. No comparison was made with children who got a placebo treatment (an inert substance their parents believed was the cure) to determine whether it was expectations or the vitamin treatment itself that caused whatever improvement the parents claimed to see.

Box 5.1   *THINKING ABOUT RESEARCH*

Putting Research Design on Ice

The National Hockey League (NHL) recently conducted a research study. It wanted to know whether a proposed method for resolving tie games would work. Although this may not be as important as finding out how the brain works or how genes influence personality development, it is important to the NHL and its fans (personally, I admit that I might trade a couple of good theories about human behavior for tickets to watch the Sabres play in the Stanley Cup finals).

For most of the NHL's history, games that were tied after three 20-minute periods of play ended just that way. As the game expanded to more cities, and as the amount of money involved increased proportionately, dissatisfaction with ties grew. Eventually, the league added a 5-minute sudden-death overtime period, but most games that were tied at the end of regulation time stayed that way through the overtime as well. Various solutions to that "problem" have been suggested, including a shootout after the overtime in which five players from each team, or more if necessary, would face the goaltender one-on-one, until the tie is broken.

In the 1998-1999 season, the NHL tested another possible solution. The overtime period would be played with each team short one player, four skaters per team instead of five, to open up more scoring opportunities, and both teams would be guaranteed one point in the standings for the tie in regulation, to make them more willing to risk a loss by opening up the play during the overtime period. The test was conducted in the American Hockey League, the highest minor league of professional hockey, and the results were that more tied games were settled by a goal in overtime than had been before.

What was the source of the NHL's hypothesis? What research design did it use? Why do you think it chose the AHL for the trial instead of the NHL or a different minor league? Are you skeptical that the results of the AHL "study" mean that the tie problem will be solved by instituting the four-on-four rule in the NHL? If so, why?

Extraneous events can be prevented from occurring in a variety of ways. The research can be isolated from many potential extraneous events by conducting it in a laboratory setting. In a laboratory, the researcher can determine which events occur by following a carefully scripted protocol. In addition, laboratory sessions typically are brief, so that the opportunity for extraneous events to occur is limited. A laboratory setting also makes it easier for the groups exposed to the events of interest, the treatments, to be compared with a similar group that is not (see the discussion of group composition effects below).

Temporal Effects (a.k.a. Maturation)

Research designs that follow participants over extended periods of time are common in evaluations of educational or social programs. In studies that take considerable time to run their course, researchers must consider the possibility that the behavior they are observing might be changing as the result of some time-linked process that has nothing to do with the independent variable they are studying. When such **temporal effects** do occur, they may be mistaken for the effects of the independent variable, or they may mask the effects of the independent variable by influencing the behavior being studied in the opposite direction from the influence of the treatment.

Researchers who study the effectiveness of psychotherapy (recall the work of Smith and Glass [1977, **E24**] discussed in Chapter 2) need to be especially concerned about this problem. Many forms of psychopathology, including depression, anxiety, phobias, and even schizophrenia, are self-limiting or cyclical. In other words, people who suffer from these problems often improve without any treatment, at least temporarily. Perhaps, as the triggering event for the disorder fades into the past, its effects fade as well.

If a potential treatment for one of these problems, psychotherapy or any other, is tested by simply monitoring clients' responses over a period of time after the treatment is administered, the effects of the passage of time alone could be mistaken for the effects of the treatment that was administered. This is especially true if the treatment is administered when the client's problem is at its worst, at the "bottom" of the cycle, which is a common time for someone to seek help. A comparable group of clients who received no treatment might improve just as much, on average, as the group receiving treatment.

A different sort of temporal effect is fatigue. Participants in a research study may be exposed to the same event over and over again, or they may be asked to perform the same task repeatedly. Especially if a high level of attention or effort is required of them in the process, their behavior may change because of a natural loss of attention or energy.

I saw this happen many years ago in dissertation research by a graduate student in my department. He wanted to compare the effectiveness of various schedules of reinforcement (think Skinner) in maintaining the behavior of children. He chose a task that required children to drop marbles into a container, and he used M&M's candy as reinforcement. When he looked at the records of his participants' behavior to compare the effects of a number of different schedules of M&M reinforcement, he saw in every group what students of learning call *extinction*. The children tired of the boring marble-dropping task so quickly that no kind of reinforcement made much difference. With a more interesting task that resisted the (temporal) effect of fatigue, it might have been possible to see the effects of the reinforcement schedules and, ultimately, to compare them.

The evaluation of the previously discussed vitamin therapy for Down syndrome also raises the issue of temporal effects as a rival hypothesis for the improvement claimed for some of the cases (no wonder there was so much disagreement about it!). The principal advocate for the treatment showed videotapes of her own child as evidence for the treatment's effectiveness. She pointed out how much better the girl talked and walked after receiving the vitamins than she had before.

The videotapes also showed, however, that the girl was much younger when the therapy started than when the later observations of improvement were made. It is possible that at least some of the improvement in her speech and her movement was caused by the normal **maturation** process (an alternative label for temporal effects) that occurs in all children. A 6-year-old child typically talks and walks better than he or she did at age 3, whether or not he or she has Down syndrome, and whether or not he or she received the therapy whose effectiveness was at issue in this case.

In summary, some studies, by virtue of their duration, the participants being studied, and the nature of the treatment and behavior being studied, must take into account the possibility that "maturational" processes can change the behavior in question, independent of the effect of the treatments being studied. If those temporal effects are not ruled out as alternative explanations for changes in the behavior, or as rival hypotheses for the observed difference among treatment groups, the inference that the treatment caused the behavior to change cannot be drawn with confidence. In that case, the finding lacks internal validity.

Temporal effects can be avoided in a variety of ways. The briefer the study, the less opportunity there is for temporal cycles to occur. Of course, not all research problems lend themselves to being studied in brief laboratory sessions. If a study must take place over an extended period of time, the more measurements that are made of the behavior in question, the more likely it is that the effects of the treatments, if any, will be able to be separated from temporal cycles (much more will be said about this in Chapter 7). Again, in some cases, a comparable group that is not exposed to the treatments being evaluated can be observed throughout the same time period. If that is possible, any temporal changes in that group can serve as a point of comparison for the group receiving the treatment.

Group Composition Effects (a.k.a. Selection)

When comparisons are made among groups, it is important from the point of view of clear causal inference that the units that make up those groups be comparable in any respect that might be relevant to the behavior being studied. We use the term *units* because in addition to human and nonhuman animal research participants, research can also compare groups of countries, factories, football teams, or any other units whose collective behavior could be the subject of a psychological research hypothesis. For example, a researcher might want to find out whether football teams that play in domed stadiums enjoy a greater home field advantage than those that play outdoors.

In any case, if one group in a study comparing different techniques for remembering were more intelligent, or if the workers in one factory in a study comparing different management policies were more experienced, the effects of the treatments could not be identified with confidence as the cause of treatment group differences. Nor could a lack of differences be attributed to ineffective treatments with any degree of certainty. **Group composition effects**, also known as the effects of **selection**, could cause differences among treatment groups or mask them.

Imagine a study undertaken to test the hypothesis that the Head Start program increases children's readiness to begin school in the first grade. A researcher might choose to compare children in a local Head Start program with a group of children the same age who didn't attend Head Start. If it were found that the children in the Head Start group were better prepared to start school at age 6, how sure could we be that those children weren't higher in academic aptitude or intelligence to start with? Maybe their parents were more interested in seeing them do well in school. They may have not only found Head Start openings for them, but also exposed them even earlier in life to educational toys and TV programs, and read to them, and did other things that helped them to be ready for school.

Think about Frazier's evaluation (1985, **E25**) of the effectiveness of the architectural design for the Contra Costa County Main Detention Facility (CCCMDF). He found that modular direct-supervision jails such as CCCMDF were safer for inmates and staff than traditional jails designed with corridors lined with cells (see Figure 5.3). But were the inmates or corrections officers in the different kinds of jails equally likely to behave violently in the first place? The modular direct-supervision design placed unarmed corrections officers in among 50 or more inmates who had a good deal of freedom of movement within their module. For that reason, considerable efforts were made to screen potentially violent inmates out of the module populations at CCCMDF and other modular direct-supervision jails (they were put in separate "locked-down" cell blocks), as well as to train corrections officers to deal proactively with the special circumstances they would face in such a jail. As a result, it's hard to tell whether the design of CCCMDF (treatment) caused the difference in its occupants' behavior, or whether the special composition of those groups of inmates and officers was responsible for the inmates behaving less violently than their counterparts in traditional jails.

Still another example of the group composition problem can be found in Triplett's (1897) study comparing the performance of unpaced, paced, and competitive bicycle racers (**E3**). If those three groups were composed of different individuals, as seems possible if not likely, how do we know that they were all equally capable riders? Maybe the best riders chose to ride in competitive races, while the less talented or more poorly trained or less experienced ones rode alone against

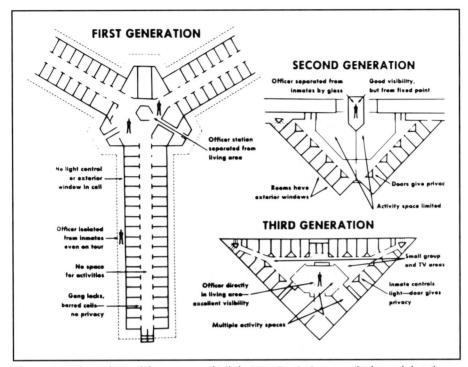

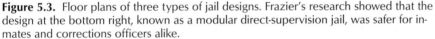

Figure 5.3. Floor plans of three types of jail designs. Frazier's research showed that the design at the bottom right, known as a modular direct-supervision jail, was safer for inmates and corrections officers alike.
SOURCE: Reprinted from "Building Better Jails," Wener, Frazier, & Farbstein, *Psychology Today*, (June, 1987), p. 48, © copyright 1987 by *Psychology Today*. Reprinted with permission.

the clock. If so, the fact that times were faster in competitive races might have had more to do with the quality of the riders than with their competitive motivation. Or maybe the best riders rode alone against the clock. If so, the faster time in competitive races would have actually understated the true effects of competitive motivation. Either way, the possibility of group composition effects makes clear causal inference impossible (as we will see later, this would not be true of Triplett's fishing-line-winding experiment).

There is one sure way of eliminating group composition effects as a threat to internal validity. If the available pool of research participants can be divided randomly among the groups to receive the different comparison treatments, we can be sure that the groups will be equivalent in all respects, including any that might be relevant to the behavior being studied but not known to the researcher. It is possible that some relevant characteristic of the subjects might be divided unequally among the groups by chance, but that possibility that can be dealt with through the use of the techniques of statistical inference that will be discussed in Chapter 10.

For all intents and purposes, **random assignment** prevents group composition effects. If random assignment is not possible, other remedies are available in research design. Studying a single group of participants over different occasions, such as before and after being exposed to a treatment (the within-subjects approach, again) eliminates group composition effects as a problem. The members of a single group are compared to themselves. In Chapters 6 and 7, you'll learn more about the reasons that random assignment is not always possible, as well as the available remedies when it is not.

Interaction of Temporal and Group Composition Effects (a.k.a. Maturation × Selection Interaction)

It might seem that comparing children who have been through a Head Start program with children who haven't, to determine the effects of the Head Start program on school readiness, isn't such a big problem after all. It may have occurred to you already that one way to deal with group composition effects is by determining whether the two groups are actually different in some relevant way (intelligence, parents' prior efforts on their behalf, etc.) before the period during which the Head Start vs. no Head Start comparison takes place.

If there are no differences, then it seems that group composition can be discounted as a plausible rival hypothesis for any differences in school readiness that are observed. If there are differences, perhaps they can be used to determine how much of any observed difference in school readiness is due to pre-existing group composition differences and how much to Head Start (in Chapter 8, you'll learn more about this possibility). As another alternative, subgroups of the Head Start and No Head Start groups that are similar in characteristics known to be relevant to school readiness could be selected for comparison.

This approach, determining the pretreatment status of the groups being compared to rule out or adjust for group composition effects, is sometimes referred to as **matching**. Unfortunately, it doesn't always work. One reason is that a researcher might not be aware of a potentially influential difference. It is also possible that two (or more) groups that appear to be matched on some relevant characteristic at the point when they are first exposed to the treatments being compared in a research study may not stay matched on that characteristic for the duration of the treatments because of an **interaction of temporal and group composition effects**.

Children in Head Start might be different as a whole from children who don't participate in the program. It might be possible, nevertheless, to find a group of children not enrolled in a Head Start program who are just as intelligent, or just as familiar with educational games, or just as favorably disposed toward learning as a group of the same age who are enrolled in the Head Start program that is to be evaluated. If the parents of the Head Start children are truly more ambitious for them, and if a better foundation for their future encounter with school already has been laid at home, their rate of development might also be faster.

In other words, a temporal trend might already have been started by their parents' concern and efforts on their behalf. That trend might not have made them so different from other children their age by the time they enter Head Start that a matched group couldn't be found. Any superiority they show over non–Head Start children at the time they leave the program, however, might be due to that pre-existing temporal trend rather than the Head Start program itself. Their more rapid development might continue while they are in the program, independent of anything Head Start does for them. That makes for a troubling alternative explanation, or problematic causal inference, in trying to explain any difference that might be observed between the groups at the end of the test period.

The reason that this threat to internal validity is labeled the interaction of temporal and group composition effects (or **maturation × selection interaction**) is that temporal effects in this case differ with the composition of the group. *Interaction* is a statistical term that refers to one way that two causal factors can combine to produce an effect. If each one of the factors has a different effect when the other factor changes, the two factors are said to interact.

For example, the level of a person's anxiety about performing a task has a different effect when the task is simple (when the most obvious response is correct) than it does when the task is complex (when the person must discount the most obvious response and look further to respond correctly). On a simple task, the higher the anxiety, the better the outcome. On a complex task, increased anxiety can lead to poorer performance, as the person forecloses prematurely on less obvious, but correct, responses. The effects of anxiety and task complexity therefore interact.

In the Head Start example, as it is described above for the purposes of this explanation, the temporal or maturational effect that produces an increasing readiness for school may be different (greater) when a group is composed of Head Start children than when a group is composed of non–Head Start children. If so, the temporal effect (the change already in process) and the group composition effect (the children's parents' past efforts on their behalf) would interact. The interaction between temporal and group composition effects for this hypothetical Head Start study is explained further in Chapter 7.

By the way, the alternative combination of two causal factors is when their contributions are independent of one another: Each one affects the outcome the same way regardless of the state of the other. For example, physical attractiveness affects others' responses to a person regardless of age (for most of the life span, anyway).

Age also affects those responses, regardless of the person's attractiveness. The effects of attractiveness and age simply add together (or subtract from one another). That kind of relationship between causal factors, where the effect of either one doesn't depend on the nature of the other, is referred to as an **additive relationship**. This subject will receive greater attention in Chapter 10.

The remedies for group composition effects can also be effective for a possible interaction between temporal and group composition effects. Random assignment to groups and comparisons over different occasions within the same group can be used where they are possible. When they are not, as in the Head Start example and other similar program evaluation studies, one of the remedies for temporal effects can be used. A long series of behavioral measures that begins well before the treatment and extends well past it may make it possible to separate temporal trends from effects of the treatments.

Selective Sample Attrition (a.k.a. Mortality)

Some research studies require lengthy commitments from their participants. A study of memory might require participants to spend some time memorizing a list and then to return to have their memory tested repeatedly over a span of hours, days, or even weeks. Longitudinal research in developmental psychology might follow participants for years or even decades to track changes in their behavior. Some social psychologists have asked their participants to return for separate experimental sessions several times in order to make it less obvious that a particular experience they had in one laboratory was intended to influence their subsequent behavior in another, or to study group processes that develop slowly over time.

In these and other cases where research participants are studied over extended periods of time and, especially, on repeated occasions, researchers run the risk that some of the participants available for testing at the outset of the research will no longer be available at the end of the study. This is known as sample attrition. What is more troubling, however, is the possibility that the attrition will be selective. The participants who are lost may not be a cross section of one or more of the groups being compared. In the case of **selective sample attrition** (also known as **mortality**), a change will take place in group composition. That change can distort the meaning of the results by promoting a faulty inference about the causal relationship between the treatments on participants' behavior.

Consider the classic longitudinal study of the effects of high intelligence ("genius") on development conducted by Lewis Terman beginning in the 1920s (see Terman & Oden, 1959). Terman followed his participants for most of his professional life, from the time they were young children until when they were middle aged. His findings that they were better adjusted, more successful, and healthier than people of average intelligence surprised (and probably disappointed) many of those who learned about them.

One question is vital to interpreting these results: During the period of that study, over the decades during which Terman contacted his participants repeatedly to learn about what was happening in their lives, did he manage to stay in touch with every one of them? Did some move without sending him their forwarding address? Did some neglect to return his phone calls or answer his letters? There must have been some attrition in a study like Terman's.

But which participants were lost? Were they a random sample of those he started with? Or is it possible that those who ran into trouble in their lives found it more difficult or more embarrassing to provide updates to Terman when he requested them? If we don't know that that did not happen, then the validity of the inference that high intelligence caused the list of positive outcomes observed by Terman is threatened by the possibility that the participants he did manage to follow throughout his study were more successful than people of high intelligence generally are. Selective attrition of those whose lives turned out worse might have contributed to the rosy picture Terman saw. If all the participants had been retained, the results might have looked different.

A similar question might be raised about the classic study of disconfirmed expectations by Festinger et al. (1956, **E11**). As you may recall, the researchers studied a "doomsday cult" whose belief that the world was about to end and that they would be rescued at the last minute by aliens in spaceships had been widely publicized. Based on Festinger's cognitive dissonance theory, the researchers predicted that after doomsday passed without the world ending or the rescue ship arriving, the cult members would rationalize what happened (e.g., they got the date wrong or their faith saved the world) rather than give up their beliefs.

But what if some of the members couldn't manage to do that? They might have quit and disappeared, leaving behind a selective group who did what the researchers predicted. That could have misled the researchers into overestimating the causal influence of rationalization on the beliefs of all those who might be exposed to events that contradicted their expectations.

Selective sample attrition is an especially troubling problem in any research study in which the participants are exposed to treatments that favor one or more groups over others. Such a study might compare a better technique for studying with a worse one, a better form of psychotherapy with a worse one, a better sales training program with a worse one, or whatever. If the study lasts long enough, and if the participants are free to leave when they choose, then those who are exposed to treatments associated with learning less, being more anxious, failing more often, being embarrassed, or in some other way having an unpleasant experience, are more likely to drop out. Because that would leave biased samples in those groups, consisting of those participants who did better or who suffered less, the value of effective treatments would be underestimated by the results that are observed. The difference observed between treatment groups would be less than if those who had the worst experience with the negative treatments had stayed around to respond to the behavioral measures throughout the study.

Studies comparing teaching methods, psychotherapy techniques, social programs, or other interventions that take a long time to administer and have substantial dropout rates obviously are prime candidates for invalid causal inferences resulting from selective sample attrition. In such studies, selective sample attrition can be prevented in a number of ways. If participants' behavior is assessed at the outset of the study, dropouts can be compared with those who remain (beware of pretest sensitization effects, of course). That comparison can clarify the true effect of the treatment. Limiting the duration of the study and using participants who have less freedom to "wander away" before the study is completed are other preventive measures. Students living on a college campus probably are easier to round up when they're due to return for a follow-up session than are people living more independently out in the community. Of course, nonhuman participants can be kept under lock and key until they're needed again.

Statistical Regression Effects
(a.k.a. Regression to the Mean)

The final threat to internal validity that we will consider is one that a researcher needs to be concerned about only under a special set of circumstances. It can occur when the groups of participants compared in a research study are selected because they achieve extremely high or low scores on a measure of some aspect of their behavior. If the effects of treatments to which they are exposed are evaluated by administering that same measure to them again following their exposure, a change can be expected in the group's average score as a result of a statistical phenomenon known as **regression to the mean**. That change is independent of, and can combine with, any treatment effects that might occur. It reflects **statistical regression effects** as well as, or instead of, treatment effects.

Think back to our discussion in Chapter 3 of the random errors that can cause fluctuations in the results of any behavioral measurement. When the same measurement of a given behavior fluctuates randomly over different occasions, those random errors cause any single obtained measurement to overestimate or underestimate the existing amount of whatever property is being measured. If you could take your next research methods test a number of times (God forbid!), without one testing affecting another (amnesia?), your score would fluctuate even though your knowledge of the subject matter stayed the same (relax, it's a thought experiment).

One day you might be well rested, optimistic, and primed to do your best. Another day, you might take the test after getting little sleep, while wondering why you're majoring in psychology in the first place (it happens to almost everyone), and have trouble concentrating. Thus, random errors caused by normal fluctuations in the previous night's sleep, motivation, distractions, and the like would cause your score on the test to be better or worse than it ought to be. Over a number of testing occasions, furthermore, such random errors would balance or cancel each other out (that's what "random" means here).

Now imagine that a large group of students took that test at the same time. There probably would be a small number of them who got very high scores and a small number who got very low scores. We would hope (professors always do, at any rate) that the first group contained students who had learned the material for the test very well, and the second group students who had learned very little of it. But what about random errors? Doesn't it make sense that the students who got the highest scores were more likely to have been influenced by favorable random errors that made their scores higher than they should have been than by unfavorable random errors? And that those who got the lowest scores were more likely to have been influenced by unfavorable random errors that caused their scores to underestimate their actual knowledge than by favorable ones? If not, think about it some more and discuss it with your friends in class until it does. To follow the argument here, you need to understand why it is more likely (not certain, just more likely) that a student who got 100% or close to it had a good day and that one who failed the test had a bad one.

Imagine further that the same groups of students took the same test again later, after taking an "experimental" study skills workshop. Even if the workshop had no effect on their performance, differences in the random errors that would affect their scores would cause the average score of the high group to come down somewhat and the average score of the low group to rise. Because the errors are random and cancel themselves out over repeated occasions, those who had their best day the first time are less likely to have another one the second time, and those who had their worst day are less likely to have another one as well. Not all the high group will get lower scores, and not all the low group will get higher scores the second time around, but some will. More high scorers probably will do worse the second time than will do even better, and more low scorers probably will do better than even worse. All of this is because of random factors.

This movement of the highest- and lowest-scoring parts of the whole group toward the overall average of the group is known as regression (movement back) to the mean (average). If the effects of treatments are evaluated by comparing groups that initially score very high and/or very low on some measure of behavior by administering the same measure to them again, after their exposure to the treatment, the groups' averages will be affected by this statistical regression in addition to any possible effect the treatments might have.

If both high and low groups are studied and the treatment is expected to make them more similar, regression will work to make the treatment look more effective than it really is. If the treatment is expected to make the groups more different, its effectiveness will be underestimated. If just one group is studied, a hypothesized increase in the scores of a low group, or a decrease in the scores of a high group, will be exaggerated by the occurrence of statistical regression effects. Regression effects will work against confirmation of the opposite hypothesis, that a low group will get worse or that a high group will get better.

Imagine that a researcher chose groups of gifted children or learning-disabled children on the basis of very high or low scores on an academic aptitude test, then put either group in a special educational program (treatment) to help them with their special needs. An evaluation of the effects of the program using scores on the same academic aptitude test would be complicated by statistical regression effects. Gifted children could be expected to get worse and learning-disabled children better as a result of regression to the mean alone.

Government officials and corporate executives who take over organizations when their performance is either at a peak or a very low point run into the same issue when their leadership is judged by subsequent changes in the organization's performance as measured by the same performance criterion. Peaks are more likely to reflect positive random errors and low points negative ones than the reverse, and later measurements are likely to reflect different random errors that somewhat balance out the first. Thus, a leader who takes over at a time of peak organization performance looks less effective than he or she really is, because performance tends to regress from that point toward the organization's long-term average. A leader who takes over at a low point in the performance curve looks better for the same reason. Of course, in both cases regression effects are superimposed over the effects of the leader's actual contribution.

If groups are not selected for the very highest or lowest scores, statistical regression effects will not be a problem. All of those in the group can be studied, or moderately high and low groups can be studied. Or groups can be selected using one measure and evaluated later using another, or an average of multiple indicators can be used both times. If none of those alternatives is possible, there are ways of adjusting the final comparisons for likely statistical regression effects so as to avoid arriving at a faulty causal inference. In other words, there are statistical solutions to the problem of statistical regression effects.

Summing Up Internal Validity

When the data are all in and the results have been analyzed (if the independent and dependent variables have adequate construct validity and the analyses have adequate statistical conclusion validity), the researcher will know whether or not the participants' behavior showed the hypothesized effects of the treatments to which the participants were exposed. The predicted changes over time or differences among groups may or may not have been detected by the statistical test conducted. But will it be possible to conclude with certainty that evidence of differences over time or across groups were caused by the treatments, or that an

TABLE 5.2   Eliminating Threats to Internal Validity

Threat	Preventive Measures
Extraneous events	Physical isolation (laboratory) Careful protocol Brief duration Comparable group exposed to everything but treatment
Temporal effects	Brief duration Long series of behavioral measures Comparable group not exposed to treatment
Group composition effects	Random assignment to treatment groups Within-subjects research design
Interaction of temporal and group composition effects	Random assignment to treatment groups Within-subjects research design Long series of behavioral measures
Selective sample attrition	Pretest measure for comparing dropouts with non-dropouts Brief duration Use of "captive populations"
Statistical regression effects	Avoid study of most extreme groups Use of alternative pretest Use of multiple criteria for selection and behavioral assessment

absence of differences reflected a lack of causal relationship between the independent and dependent variables?

The confidence that the researcher and, ultimately, the rest of the scientific community can have in such a causal inference depends on the extent to which the six threats to internal validity we have just considered can be ruled out through the use of a research design that provides the necessary comparisons. If extraneous events, temporal effects, group composition effects, the interaction of temporal and group composition effects, selective attrition, and statistical regression effects can be ruled out as alternative explanations or rival hypotheses for the differences or absence of differences that were found, the treatments are left as the only plausible explanation. In such cases, the results of the study can be taken as convincing evidence for the truth or falsity of the hypothesis (in Chapter 11, we'll discuss why falsity actually is more difficult to determine than truth). Ways of using research designs to accomplish that goal will be described in Chapters 6 and 7, but the threats to internal validity and preventive measures are listed in Table 5.2 as a

---

| Box 5.2 | THINKING ABOUT RESEARCH |

Just Because Mozart Was a Genius . . . _____

The governor of Georgia is spending public funds to provide CDs of Mozart's music to every new mother in his state. In Florida, children in state-run preschool programs are required by law to listen to classical music every day.

Those policies are based on psychological research showing that listening to music by Mozart improves cognitive performance. The findings of that research are sometimes referred to as the "Mozart effect," and the results are often interpreted as being analogous to the observed effects of enriched environments on brain development in rats (found by Rosenzweig and his colleagues, 1972, **E22**).

The research from which the Mozart effect was induced was actually done with college students, not infants or toddlers, and the positive effect of listening to Mozart was limited to performance on one specific test of spatial imagery. Listening to Mozart was not shown to affect cognition in general, much less brain development (which, of course, is mostly in the distant past for people of college age). Moreover, the observed effect lasted for only a few minutes.

Should we expect, then, that infants and preschoolers will benefit in profound and far-reaching ways from listening to classical music? In what ways, if any, should we be concerned about the external validity of the findings, or interpretation, known as the Mozart effect? Or should we just savor the irony that good psychological research can so often be rejected out of hand as a basis for public policy, while questionable research can exert as much influence as it has in this case?

---

reminder of what to look for. First, though, we must consider the related issue of external validity.

Before we go on, though, it needs to be pointed out again that not every event other than the treatment needs to prevented from occurring altogether, or from affecting participants at all times or in all groups. The only extraneous events a researcher needs to be concerned about are those capable of influencing the behavior in question, and influencing it selectively, in some groups or on some occasions, so as to mimic or mask the effects of the treatments. The same logic applies to temporal effects, sample attrition, and the rest. The experimenter wearing a different tie, for example, probably won't affect the memories of the participants.

Nor will a change of season cause children with Down syndrome to have higher IQ scores, so far as we know. In the language of methodology, only plausible rival hypotheses need to be ruled out when choosing the arrangement of comparisons over time or across groups that constitute a research design. All other things are never exactly equal (we can't take *ceteris paribus* literally), but only certain other things really need to be.

THREATS TO EXTERNAL VALIDITY ●

The Problem of External Validity

External validity is a subject that has been debated hotly among analysts of research methods in psychology. On one side, such figures as Donald Campbell, Egon Brunswik, and Lee Cronbach have elevated the importance of generalizability from obscurity to a status equal to that of causal inference and other validity issues. They have argued that certainty about cause and effect has value only if the causal relationship in question can be expected to occur outside the specific parameters of the research study in which the researcher observed it. This is especially important, to those who agree with this position, when the research participants are nonhuman organisms, or people from an atypical group such as an introductory psychology class, or when the research is conducted in an artificial laboratory setting where the participants' task has no direct counterpart in the real world. In either case, they believe, the generalizability of research results is too limited.

Brunswik (1956) argued for an approach he called representative research design. He argued that researchers need to test their hypotheses in multiple studies that sample the variety of ways the test could be conducted. If the predicted relationship is observed in the various populations of organisms, and with different procedures for manipulating the independent variable and assessing the dependent variable, that would establish the generalizability of the causal relationships that were observed.

Decades later, Cronbach (1982) developed his own scheme for understanding external validity. He developed the acronym **UTOS** to remind researchers of four aspects of research design whose generalizability needed to be considered. UTOS stands for Units, Treatments, Observations, and Settings.

In most psychological research, the **units** studied are individual organisms— the research participants, be they rats, pigeons, or people. In some cases, of course, the units are cities or countries or groups performing tasks, or even units of time during which the behavior being studied might occur. The *treatments* are, as we've used the term all along, the events to which participants are exposed. They are variations in, or degrees of, the suspected cause of the behavior being studied. *Observations* are the specific behavioral measures applied to the subjects to be able to compare the effects of the various treatments. **Settings** are the combinations of place and time, including the task and its duration and consequences, in which the treatments are administered and the observations made.

On the other side of this debate, there are those who argue that the Campbell-Brunswik-Cronbach concerns about external validity are exaggerated. The best-known representative of this opposing view is Douglas Mook, who made the argument very eloquently in a 1983 article in *American Psychologist*. Mook argued that generalizability is an important issue only in applied research, where the object is to predict whether the behavior observed in a research study would occur in some specific group of people in some specific setting. It would be as if a video game manufacturer wanted to understand the factors that influenced people's attraction to one of its games. In that case, the manufacturer should study people who are potential customers for the game, in a setting like the one in which people would be most likely to be exposed to the game. In this applied (marketing) research, the degree of similarity between the research sample and the target group, and between the research setting and the target setting, would affect the accuracy of the prediction.

Mook argued that generalizability may be much less problematic in basic psychological research. There, he contends, generalization to real life is neither intended nor meaningful. If a research study is conducted to test a theory, then the question is whether a prediction drawn from the theory will be confirmed by the results of the study. Whether the prediction is tested in the lab (to simplify for the purposes of the present argument, "lab" is shorthand for an artificial setting and task and a captive population of lab animals or introductory psychology students) or in the real world makes no real difference in this case, according to Mook. The researcher is interested in predicting to the lab, not from it to the real world.

A researcher who asks whether a treatment can produce a hypothesized effect is not concerned with generalizability. Evidence that the effect can happen is all the researcher wants to see. Evidence that a theoretical prediction fails is equally probative whether the sample and setting are real or artificial. In fact, lab research can provide the most powerful evidence for a theory, Mook suggests, because it can show that a prediction from the theory holds even in the most unlikely combination of participants and settings, far removed from those that might have inspired the theory in the first place.

Although many researchers, particularly among those who concentrate on basic research and theory building, agree with Mook, his arguments leave some questions unanswered. If a theory were tested only with samples and settings that are found exclusively in the research studies that test it, would the theory be as good an account of the causes of the behavior in question as if it had been tested with those samples and settings in which the behavior occurs in nature? Do we risk creating an experiment-based science that predicts the outcomes of further experiments but not behavior in the real world?

Furthermore, can't we expect a theory to lead to more successful application —even though that may not be the original goal of the theory or the research conducted to test it—if the theory is supported by data collected from samples like those to whom the application is to be directed, in settings like those where the application will be carried out? Mook argues that successful application is based on understanding, or good theory, not on generalizing observations. But could we ever learn from studies of reinforcement conducted with pigeons in operant conditioning chambers that people who enjoy an activity even though no one else cares how well they do at it are sometimes less likely to engage in it after they are offered rewards for good performance?

It is always more confusing when there are two sides to an issue, especially when both sides have persuasive proponents and committed constituencies. It is probably true in most such cases, including this one, that each side can learn something valuable from the other. Laboratory research with captive samples can be invaluable in the development of useful theories about human behavior, even if the behavior typically is observed in nature in very different organisms and circumstances. Seligman and Maier (1967, **E18**) may have made a better start on the learned helplessness theory of depression, as Mook suggested, because they studied nonhuman organisms in a traditional laboratory setting using a shuttle box. It is not necessary or even desirable to judge the value of research based on a simple count of the similarities in samples, settings, and tasks compared to real life.

But what about the argument that theories would be stronger—especially if used to predict behavior in natural settings with typical actors, or to create effective real-life applications—if the research used more natural samples and settings as well? Seligman's subsequent research (see Peterson & Seligman, 1984) on the attributional styles used by college students also seems to make that point convincingly. Attribution can be studied only in humans. Consistent with other arguments in this text, when alternative research approaches have different strengths and weaknesses, the most effective resolution is to use both and compare the results. Isn't it more prudent to be skeptical about external validity when sample and setting are atypical, even in basic research, than to assume that less representativeness is better?

In any case, we will be evaluating research designs and specific research studies for the representativeness of their samples and settings. In the hope that it will be easier to understand, I divided Cronbach's four concerns about generalizability between our discussions of construct validity and external validity. We have already dealt with the question of generalizing from the particular treatments and observations chosen to represent the hypothesized cause and effect for a research study. In the discussion of construct validity in Chapters 3 and 4, the threats of nonrepresentative treatments and measures correspond to Cronbach's concerns about the generalizability of treatments and observations. We will deal with the two remaining issues, generalizability across units and settings, below (see Table 5.3).

Our general position, then, will be to favor representativeness over nonrepresentativeness. That is not to say that representative research is superior in all respects. It needs to be kept in mind that greater representativeness is sometimes achieved at the cost of weakened causal inference, less reliable measurement, and other threats to validity. Nor is it to say that judging representativeness will be easy. Mook (1983) judged Milgram's (1974) well-known obedience experiments (**E9**) to

TABLE 5.3   Threats to External Validity

I. Threats to conceptual validity
    1. Unnecessary duplication
    2. Theoretical isolation
II. Threats to construct validity
    A. The independent variable
        a. Inadequate operationalization
            3. Lack of reliability of the independent variable
            4. Lack of representativeness of the independent variable
            5. Lack of impact of the independent variable
        b. Treatment artifacts
            6. Demand characteristics in the research setting
            7. Experimenter expectancy effects on the behavior being observed
            8. Pretest sensitization to the treatments
    B. The dependent variable
        a. Inadequate operationalization
            9. Lack of reliability of the dependent variable
            10. Lack of representativeness of the dependent variable
            11. Lack of sensitivity of the dependent variable
        b. Measurement artifacts
            12. Strategic responding by the research participants
            13. Linguistic/cultural bias in the dependent measure
III. Threats to internal validity
            14. Extraneous effects (history)
            15. Temporal effects (maturation)
            16. Group composition effects (selection)
            17. Interaction of temporal and group composition effects
            18. Selective sample attrition (mortality)
            19. Statistical regression effects (regression to the mean)
IV. Threats to external validity
            20. Nonrepresentative sampling
            21. Nonrepresentative research context
V. Threats to statistical conclusion validity
            22. Inappropriate use of statistical techniques
            23. Use of a statistical test lacking sufficient power
            24. Mistaking a trivial effect for support for the research hypothesis

be nonrepresentative of the conditions faced by Germans who obeyed the Nazis' orders to exterminate Jews and others, because research participants need not fear punishment if they disobey. It is not clear from my reading of history, however, that fear of punishment was an important factor in the minds of those German citizens who obeyed an immoral authority.

Logically, Brunswik's (1956) suggestion makes sense, that researchers sample various treatments and measures to determine empirically the scope of generalizability. The difficulty of testing hypotheses in a sufficiently long series of studies to accomplish that goal, however, probably rules it out as a viable option for most researchers. Perhaps we need to test many fewer hypotheses so that we can use more representative research designs, but that view is probably not going to become popular any time soon.

Some will say that this text favors the interests of applied psychologists over those of basic researchers, but I consider this to be the correct, albeit debatable, position to take at this point in time. Do not be surprised if your instructor, or something else you read, argues against it, or if you yourself come to believe otherwise after giving this important issue due consideration.

Nonrepresentative Sampling of Units

The participants in a research study may differ—in age, gender, cultural background, species, or some other characteristic that is relevant to the behavior being studied—from others to whom a researcher may wish to generalize the observed effects of treatments. By "relevant," I mean that there is reason to believe that units that differ in such a characteristic also differ in the relationship between the treatments being studied and the behavior being measured. In that case, the **nonrepresentative sampling of units**, or lack of representativeness of the participant sample, constitutes a threat to the external validity or generalizability of the research findings.

This is an issue that clearly arises in considering Harlow's (1958) choice of rhesus monkeys to study the development of infant-mother bonds (**E12**). If one is interested in the social development of orphaned infant rhesus monkeys, there is no problem with the representativeness of Harlow's sample. But what if one is interested in the social development of human infants, in questions about the possible benefits of breast-feeding, the merits of various child care arrangements or parenting styles, or the like? The question of whether the same instinctive tendencies Harlow observed in the rhesus exist in humans—and, if so, whether they play as great and as inevitable a role in human development—is critical in judging whether Harlow's results can be generalized to humans. It seems clear that he thought so, but was that an act of faith or of reason, and what should a reasonable reader of Harlow's work conclude?

A similar question could be raised about Siegel's (MacRae et al., 1987) research on opiate addiction in rats (**E10**). Can we generalize to the human opiate addict the results of studies on rats showing that classical conditioning can explain tolerance and withdrawal effects following repeated administration of morphine? Should we be concerned about the fact that humans can have difficulty stopping the use of drugs that don't produce tolerance or withdrawal effects, not to speak of activities like gambling and shopping? Does that suggest that the mechanisms of addiction might be different in humans than in rats?

The method routinely used to test the safety of new pharmaceutical drugs is interesting in this regard. Promising drugs are first tested on nonhuman organisms, often in very large doses so that any toxic effects are sure to be detected. If a drug passes that test, then it is tested in human patients in studies called clinical trials. This two-tiered approach makes use of nonhuman species to protect humans from harmful side effects, but it requires human tests to prove the drug is safe and effective for its intended users. It is a conservative approach that may err on the side of preventing drugs that are dangerous to other species, but not to humans, from being approved or even from being tested on humans. It also recognizes that salutary effects on rats, for example, may not generalize to humans. Animal research alone is not considered sufficient to prove that a drug is safe and effective for use in humans.

Medical research also provides a cautionary example. Until recently, clinical trials were conducted almost exclusively with men, although drugs were being developed to treat illnesses suffered by both men and women. Women have become concerned, and rightly so, that the drugs they need have not been tested adequately for them.

Research with human participants also needs to be evaluated for the threat of nonrepresentative sampling. When Darley and Latané (1968) staged false medical emergencies to study the effects of various conditions on the helping behavior of bystanders (**E7**), they studied college students. Their hypotheses, if you recall the discussion in Chapter 2, were based on the behavior of witnesses to the murder of Kitty Genovese. Is the behavior of college students, who may be living sheltered lives on a college campus, a good guide to understanding how residents of a dangerous urban neighborhood will respond to similar circumstances? Perhaps not, if college students perceive the world as a less dangerous place, if they have more altruistic motives, or if they differ in any other respect that could affect their responses to the needs of a stranger in an emergency.

The study of the effects of family size and birth order on intelligence by Zajonc and Markus (1975, **E16**) raises the issue in yet another way. Their results were based on observations taken from the military records of Dutch men and women, but their conclusions were universal. Darley and Latané were trying to understand the behavior of a *particular group of people* by studying a somewhat (maybe even very) different group, but Zajonc and Markus were trying to understand the intellectual development of *all people* to develop a general theory of intellectual development by studying one specific group. Moreover, Zajonc and Markus chose the Dutch not because they believed them or their culture to be especially representative of human beings in general, but because interesting data bearing on their hypotheses happened to be available for the Dutch. One can't blame these researchers for their choice. Research participants often are chosen as targets of opportunity. One needs to question (not reject, but examine) the conclusions reached by Zajonc and Markus. Perhaps before a large investment is made in a publicly funded American program of intervention based on their findings, their results should be checked out in an American sample.

Some very good models to follow exist for researchers who are concerned about the generalizability of their results. Stanley Milgram's research on obedience to authority (1974, **E9**) is one. Concerned about whether his observations of unexpectedly high levels of obedience could be generalized beyond the selective college student population at Yale University, Milgram rented offices in Bridgeport, Connecticut, and advertised for participants in local newspapers. Eventually, he conducted 18 separate studies and managed to include people from all walks of life in his samples. When he realized that all of his studies had been conducted with male participants (perhaps out of 1950s chivalry?), he repeated the experiment once more with female participants to establish even further the generalizability of his results.

When Festinger and his colleagues traveled across the country to study at first hand the response of cult members to a failed doomsday prophecy (1956, **E11**), instead of staging a simulation in their university laboratory, they demonstrated a concern with generalizability that is common in field research. Many psychological researchers rightly see cult members, criminals, and others whose behavior they seek to understand as inaccessible to them. Field research is sometimes possible, however, in the adventurous form of participant observation used by Festinger as well as in safer forms such as Frazier's evaluation of the behavior of jail inmates from institutional records. Researchers need not always depend on college students to stand in for people so different from themselves.

To reiterate briefly, when the units studied in research differ in some relevant way from those to which one wishes to generalize the research results, one needs to be concerned about whether nonrepresentative sampling of units constitutes a threat to external validity. But how is representative sampling to be accomplished? In some cases, the population of units to which research results need to be generalized is a small, homogeneous one. In those cases, choosing a **random sample** of the units for study can ensure representativeness of the sample. Picking numbers out of a hat or any procedure that gives each unit in the population an equal chance of being selected will work.

If the population is large and diverse, a more complex procedure is required. The population must first be divided into subpopulations on the basis of seemingly relevant characteristics such as gender, age, IQ, or whatever. Then a random sample needs to be drawn from each subpopulation that is proportional to its size. This will produce a **stratified random sample** that will be representative of the original population. This is the way that our normally accurate political polls are done.

Public Announcement

WE WILL PAY YOU $4.00 FOR
ONE HOUR OF YOUR TIME

Persons Needed for a Study of Memory

*We will pay five hundred New Haven men to help us complete a scientific study of memory and learning. The study is being done at Yale University.

*Each person who participates will be paid $4.00 (plus 50c carfare) for approximately 1 hour's time. We need you for only one hour: there are no further obligations. You may choose the time you would like to come (evenings, weekdays, or weekends).

*No special training, education, or experience is needed. We want:

Factory workers	Businessmen	Construction workers
City employees	Clerks	Salespeople
Laborers	Professional people	White-collar workers
Barbers	Telephone workers	Others

All persons must be between the ages of 20 and 50. High school and college students cannot be used.

*If you meet these qualifications, fill out the coupon below and mail it now to Professor Stanley Milgram, Department of Psychology, Yale University, New Haven. You will be notified later of the specific time and place of the study. We reserve the right to decline any application.

*You will be paid $4.00 (plus 50c carfare) as soon as you arrive at the laboratory.

— —

TO:
PROF. STANLEY MILGRAM, DEPARTMENT OF PSYCHOLOGY, YALE UNIVERSITY, NEW HAVEN, CONN. I want to take part in this study of memory and learning. I am between the ages of 20 and 50. I will be paid $4.00 (plus 50c carfare) if I participate.

NAME (Please Print). . . . .

ADDRESS . . . .

TELEPHONE NO. . . . . Best time to call you . . . .

AGE . . . . OCCUPATION . . . . SEX . . . . . .
CAN YOU COME:

WEEKDAYS . . . . EVENINGS . . . . . . WEEKENDS . . . .

Figure 5.4. For his well-known research on obedience to authority, Stanley Milgram recruited diverse samples participants, using newspaper advertisements like this one. SOURCE: Reprinted from *Obedience to Authority*, Milgram, p. 15, © copyright 1974 by Stanley Milgram. Reprinted by permission of HarperCollins Publishers, Inc.

Of course, none of this addresses models of human behavior tested on and/or generalized from nonhuman populations. In that case, representativeness can be judged only on the basis of a comparison of the underlying physical and behavioral processes in the nonhuman species and in humans—a very difficult judgment indeed! But we're already familiar with the position of Mook and others that generalizability across units may be irrelevant to a good deal of theoretical or basic research.

Nonrepresentative Research Context

The last of Cronbach's (1982) questions to be addressed concerns the generalizability of research results across research settings. Research evidence is collected in a particular time and place, with its peculiar array of apparatus and materials. We will refer to all of that as the **research context**. A good deal of psychological research is conducted in settings known as laboratories. They may contain the specialized technical equipment the term *laboratory* suggests, or they may just be ordinary rooms with tables and chairs. They are laboratories because they serve as the settings for research, and they are used because they are convenient. They are often down the hall from the researcher/professor's office, and easily located by the college student participants who are to be studied. More important, they are used because they isolate the participants and the events they experience from outside influences that could threaten the internal validity of the research findings.

Laboratory research sessions usually are brief. College student participants rarely can be persuaded to attend for more than an hour or two. Nonhuman participants certainly are available for indefinite periods, but fatigue is a concern, and the research assistants who "run" those animals may not be as available as the animals themselves. As a result, laboratory studies usually are designed so that the events being studied and their behavioral consequences take place within a short span of time.

Laboratory studies often are built around pieces of apparatus or tasks unique to the research setting. Participants rarely are asked to do things that are exactly like everyday activities. The research experience is more typically a new one for the participant. This is as true for nonhuman participants tested in mazes as it is of the human participants in Milgram's obedience experiments. Neither group is likely to have been anyplace exactly like the laboratory, nor does such a place actually exist elsewhere.

Consider Rosenzweig et al.'s (1972) study of the effects of enriched environments on brain development in rats (**E22**). Were the mobiles spinning overhead and the activity wheels in which the animals exercised representative of the natural environmental conditions that might enhance brain development in a rat? Are these the kinds of experiences that would be most enriching for human infants? Perhaps some experiences that would benefit human infants greatly, such as hearing an adult speak, could not be evaluated in the context in which Rosenzweig's research was conducted.

Triplett's (1897) laboratory study (**E3**), in which participants ran fishing line around fishing reels and pulleys in the presence of another subject or alone, raises similar questions. Did the context Triplett created in a laboratory contain the essential elements of real-life competitive contexts such as the bicycle races that he was trying to understand? He used a task that people may not normally think of as competitive. It provided no feedback to participants about their level of performance or how their performance compared with others', and it provided no reward or recognition for superior performance. Might not such a context result in behavior that differs from what would be observed when the task is perceived on the basis of past experience to be a competitive game or sport, when it is clear to participants who does well or poorly, or who wins and who loses, and when the winners profit from their victories?

As is the case with the representativeness of the units studied, the problem with a **nonrepresentative research context** depends on how one wants or needs to generalize the research results, as well as on the nature of the treatment-behavior relationship one wants to generalize. Researchers in psychology have often made the assumption that the laboratory tasks they invent capture the essence of whole classes of human behavior. The very strangeness and artificiality of the setting is assumed by Mook and his followers (see Mook, 1983) to convey unlimited generalizability or universality for the cause-effect relationships discovered there.

Skinner's operant conditioning chamber is a good example. Skinner took his very simple response-reinforcement arrangement as representative of virtually every complex form of learning humans encounter, from learning language to mastering college coursework. He took his schedules of reinforcement as representative of most contingencies in people's daily lives, from working for hourly wages to gambling on slot machines. He was not discouraged about the differences between a pigeon pecking at a plastic disc when randomly selected pecks are followed by measured amounts of grain and the behavior of a visitor to Las Vegas dropping quarters into a slot machine. Rather, he saw the two settings as similar in the essential elements that control behavior. He sought a good theory above all, as Mook argued is appropriate in basic research.

Some researchers seek to generalize to specific settings rather than to all settings. When Seligman and Maier demonstrated that dogs given inescapable electric shocks later failed to learn to escape shock in a shuttle box (1967, **E18**), they believed that their results could be generalized to the development of depression in humans. Again, despite the obvious differences in experiences and responses between their dysfunctional dogs and depressed people, they saw essential similarities between the two contexts that justified generalizing from their research in the laboratory to the real world of psychological disorders.

The question of whether research results can be generalized to specific real-world contexts is sometimes referred to as the question of **ecological validity**. Another example of the problem of generalizing from a laboratory setting to a real one is seen in Ceci et al.'s (1994) research on misleading post-event information (**E8**). When a child in an experiment is intentionally misled about the occurrence of a trivial fictitious event in the very recent past, the child may later report a false memory of that event and even supply details that make the report believable. The ecology validity question raises concerns about a child being asked leading questions by a police investigator. The child could be asked about a presumed traumatic event in the distant past, the occurrence of which is consistent with at least weak corrobative evidence. In such a circumstance, might a child be influenced to report a memory for that event even though the event never occurred?

The introduction to this section of the chapter examined Mook's argument about the generalizability of research results from the specific context in which they occurred to a broad class of related contexts, or to a specific context of pressing interest. That position holds that researchers can create universally generalizable results in laboratory contexts that resemble many other contexts in the abstract, though perhaps no others in their particulars. Another argument is virtually the mirror image: It holds that the greater the formal similarity between the research setting and the setting to which the research results are to be applied, the greater the confidence one can have in that generalization.

Social psychologist Philip Zimbardo (Zimbardo, Banks, Haney, & Jaffe, 1973) studied the influence of social roles on the behavior of prison inmates and guards by creating the closest approximation he could to an actual prison in the basement of a Stanford University building. Rosenthal and Jacobson (1966), in their study of the effects of teacher's expectancies (**E15**), and Frazier (1985), in his study of the impact of the modular direct-supervision jail design (**E25**), went one step further. They did their research in an actual school and an actual jail, respectively.

Summing Up External Validity

Some would argue that the external validity problem is insoluble. After all, psychology is largely the study of the differences among people and of how different environmental conditions influence behavior. Given that, the idea that one can blithely generalize research results from one group of people (the participants) or one set of environmental conditions (the research context) to another, as if behavior should be constant across such variations, seems illogical on its face.

Following that line of thought, it would seem that our only choice is to follow Brunswik's (1956) suggestion that all research hypotheses be investigated in systematically selected samples and settings so as to determine empirically the limits on the generalizability of the research results. This is not the position of most scientific psychologists, but they don't all assume unlimited generalizability either. Instead, many follow the admonition of Cronbach and others to consider differences in units and settings when attempting to generalize research results.

A final point about external validity has to do with the practical reasons why people want to generalize research results rather than the logic of doing so. When a researcher finds that mice and rats that are administered massive doses of the chemical phenolpthalein, once the active ingredient in over-the-counter laxatives such as Ex-Lax™, develop many more cancerous tumors than similar animals that don't receive the drug, the logic of generalizing to human users of laxatives seems clear. Humans are different enough from mice and rats, and the amounts of phenolpthalein they ingest in everyday use are different enough (relative to their size) from those administered in the research study in question, to create serious logical doubts about the generalizability from one combination of units and setting conditions to the other.

On the practical question, however, the answer might be quite different. In addition to the questions about the external validity of the research results, one must weigh the value of phenolpthalein to its users against the possible risk of developing a deadly disease. Other solutions to constipation are available. They include diet, other laxatives (the makers of Ex-Lax™ have since formulated an effective laxative without phenolpthalein), and exercise. That might make it prudent to generalize from the mouse in the laboratory to the person taking Ex-Lax™ in spite of the logical flaws inherent in doing so.

● CONCLUSION

Our discussion of the evaluation of research designs has focused thus far on the criteria by which they can be evaluated. We considered six possible threats to internal validity, or concerns about drawing causal inferences from observed treatment-behavior relationships. We also considered two possible threats to external validity, or generalizing from the units and contexts in which relationships were observed to other combinations of units and contexts. Although these aren't the only possible threats to internal and external validity, they are important ones, and it is hoped that they provide a sufficient sample to clarify the basic nature of the problems of internal and external validity.

Before we move on to a look at some of the actual designs psychologists use in their research, and their strengths and weaknesses in terms of internal and external validity, a point needs to be made about the relationship between the two general categories of criteria discussed in this chapter. As should become clearer in our consideration of actual research designs, the control required to make causal influences more certain and improve internal validity by eliminating rival hypotheses mitigates against studying behavior in participants and in settings that facilitate generalizing the research results to people's day-to-day lives. Internal validity considerations favor nonhuman participants, laboratory isolation, and specialized apparatus. Threats to internal validity can also be minimized by studying college student participants who are kept in the dark about the true purpose of the research and are studied in brief experimental sessions that elicit objectively measurable responses. On the other hand, consider research that seeks to maximize external validity, particularly generalizability to the typical contexts where people engage in behaviors that are of practical importance to themselves and others. It would seem that such research would best be conducted with human participants, in actual settings for work or relationships or other important human activities, over extended periods of time. Besides considering internal validity and external validity separately and how to maximize each of them, we need to keep in mind the trade-offs between the two that might be required in planning research.

Review Questions and Exercise

Review Questions

1. What is research design?

2. In general, how can threats to validity be introduced (either mimicking or masking the effects of treatments) or ruled out, depending on the researcher's choice of a research design?

3. What are the six separate threats to internal validity, and how can each of them lessen confidence about drawing a causal inference from the results of a research study? How can they be minimized?

4. What are the two separate threats to external validity, and how can each of them limit the generalizability of the results of a research study? How can they be minimized?

5. In what ways are the measures that must be taken to strengthen causal inference (eliminate threats to internal validity) and the measures that must be taken to strengthen generalizability (eliminate threats to external validity) incompatible with one another?

Exercise

For each of the threats to internal and external validity, sketch a possible research study in which that threat could occur. You may use examples from this book or from texts you have used in other psychology courses or other social science courses, or you may use your own imagination. In each case, determine under what conditions the threat could plausibly arise and how it could be minimized.

ARRANGING THE COMPARISONS II
Designs for Psychological Research

● A QUICK GUIDE TO CHAPTER 6: DESIGNS FOR PSYCHOLOGICAL RESEARCH

There is no limit to the number of different **research designs** that can be used in psychological research. To a certain extent, the nature of the research problem dictates how many groups need to be compared, or how many occasions. The research problem also determines, to some degree, how the groups or occasions are to be selected, the setting in which the study will take place, the behavioral measures that will be used, and more.

Still, researchers have choices. It is possible to categorize research designs, to characterize the basic dimensions along which they differ, and to analyze the implications of those differences for the validity of the research findings. Researchers and consumers of research both need to understand the implications of those choices.

Pre-experimental research designs lack sufficient or appropriate comparisons to rule out serious threats to internal validity, making causal inferences based on the research extremely problematic. In general, they can be more useful in generating hypotheses than in testing them.

True experimental research designs maximize internal validity through the use of two design devices. First, the groups or occasions that are compared are rendered equivalent before treatments are administered, by the **random assignment** of participants to groups or by randomly selecting occasions. Second, in a true experiment, the treatment variations are the result of **manipulation** by the researcher, who administers them in a controlled environment. These techniques preclude unintended differences in the experiences of research participants among groups or occasions, ruling out several of the most serious threats to internal validity.

Quasi-experimental research designs utilize naturally occurring groups, or occasions, to test hypotheses about the causes of behavior. This may introduce weaknesses in internal validity in some designs of this type. It may also strengthen external validity by sampling participants and occasions more representatively, and by studying treatment effects over longer time frames and in their natural contexts. It may strengthen construct validity by utilizing more realistic treatments and assessments of behavior. The Chapter 6 Quick Guide shows the defining characteristics of the three types of research designs considered in detail in Chapters 6 and 7.

Chapter 6 Quick Guide: The Defining Characteristics of the Three Types of Research Designs

Pre-Experimental Research Designs

1. Lack adequate comparisons
2. Are extremely vulnerable to threats to internal validity
3. Are more useful for developing hypotheses than for testing them

True Experimental Research Designs

1. Make use of random assignment of units to comparison groups
2. Allow experimenters to control the timing of treatments and behavioral measures
3. Are commonly used in laboratory settings with captive populations
4. Are free from threats to internal validity
5. Are vulnerable to treatment and measurement artifacts and to threats to external validity
6. Are popular among basic research scientists

Quasi-Experimental Research Designs

1. Substitute extensive measurement series for random assignment of units and control over timing of treatments and measures
2. Are free from threats to construct validity (especially treatment and measurement artifacts) and threats to external validity
3. Exploit natural events and existing behavioral measures to test hypotheses about the causes of behavior
4. Are popular among applied researchers

INTRODUCTION TO THE CHAPTER ●

The purpose of this chapter is to introduce a sample of specific research designs. They will be used to demonstrate how the threats to internal and external validity discussed in Chapter 5 can be evaluated. As was suggested earlier, these are not the only designs available to psychological researchers. They were selected for two reasons. One is that they are in common use in psychological research. That should become clear as we observe that many of our exemplar studies use these designs. In addition, these designs have pedagogical value. They provide opportunities to make important points about the relationship between research design and threats to validity. That will help establish in greater detail how research results and research findings are related. In other words, it will help to show how research design is an important factor in interpreting research results.

TABLE 6.1   Creating a Research Design

1. Deciding whether to compare among groups ("between-subjects" designs) or over time ("within-subjects" designs)
    a. If, among groups, participants can be randomly assigned to create treatment groups, or they can be members of pre-existing (intact) groups
    b. If, over time, occasions can be selected at random, or a naturally occurring series of occasions can be studied
2. Deciding how to administer the treatments
    a. How many and which values of the independent variable
    b. Manipulated or naturally occurring treatments
3. Deciding how to administer the behavioral measure(s)
    a. How many times
    b. When (especially, pretest or no pretest)

First, we will have to become acquainted with a way of representing different types of research designs so that they can be evaluated and compared efficiently. That "notation system" allows us to represent in a useful way the decisions a researcher must make to test his or her research hypothesis (that decision process is summarized in Table 6.1). Then we will look at three categories of research designs that will be represented using that notation system. We will examine some examples of those designs and consider some of their strengths and weaknesses in a preliminary way. In the next chapter, we will continue that discussion more systematically and in more detail.

● THE NOTATION SYSTEM

A notation system is a set of symbols that can be used for the purpose of representing ideas in an abstract way. The system we will be using comes, again, from Campbell and Stanley (1963). They developed it to represent designs that can be used in psychological research. I will expand on their pioneering efforts. As we go through the system point by point, you can refer to Table 6.2 for an overview.

It might seem difficult at first to understand why you need to make the effort required to learn these new symbols. I have found that in the long run it is much easier to understand research design in this way. The notation system provides a mental shorthand. In the terminology of the study of human memory, it makes it easier to process the information. Of course, it does take time and effort to learn any new system in the first place, but once you learn it, you will realize the same benefits from it that I have. It will leverage your study time and effort to provide a deeper

TABLE 6.2 Diagramming Research Designs: The Notation System

1. **X**—a treatment; subscripts can be used to designate different treatments, either numerically or descriptively
2. **O**—a behavioral measure (observation); subscripts can be used in the same way as for treatments
3. **G**—at beginning of a line, designates one group of research participants (organisms, or groups, or other units); numbered from top to bottom in designs with multiple groups
4. **Left-to-right order**—indicates temporal sequence or chronology, with events at the left occurring first and those that line up one below the other occurring at the same relative time for their respective groups
5. **R**—the group of participants represented on this line was created by random assignment of units from the entire sample tested
6. **-------** (between lines in designs with multiple groups)—groups of participants were pre-existing or intact groups
7. **Blank space**—if aligned temporally (left-to-right) with treatment (X) or measure (O) in other group(s), indicates absence or lack of same

level of understanding and a great facility in thinking about research design. As you will see in the next chapter, knowing this system also will make it easier to analyze the validity of psychological research findings.

Representing the Treatment(s)

In this system, the symbol "X" is used to designate a treatment. Thus, X is some event or combination of events to which research participants are exposed for the purpose of determining its/their effects on the behavior being studied. X represents some value of the independent variable, an operationalization of the causal construct contained in the research hypothesis. It could be a sample of violent or nonviolent TV programming, a particular neighborhood noise level, a method of parental discipline, or a type of reinforcement schedule, among other things.

If a group of research participants is administered no treatment at all, for the purpose of comparing their behavior to that of a group that receives some treatment (X), a blank space or no symbol at all will be used to reflect that no-treatment "control" condition (more will be said later about the concept of control).

If different forms of a treatment are used, to compare the effects of multiple variations of the independent variable, subscripts can be used to identify them. For example, X_v and X_{nv} could be used to designate violent and nonviolent TV programs. Alternatively, X_4, X_8, X_{12}, and X_{24} could be used to designate four different treatments in a study of the effects of motivation on learning, where they would indicate variations in the duration of food deprivation, from 4 to 24 hours. In Triplett's (1897) laboratory study of coaction based on the fishing reel apparatus (**E3**), X_A could be used to designate performance "alone" and X_T performance "together" with a second participant.

Representing the Behavioral Measures

The behavioral measure that is chosen to determine the effects of treatments (X's) on the subjects who are exposed to them is represented by the symbol "O" (as in observation). Some research designs compare groups that are measured with groups that are not, and occasions on which measurements are taken with occasions on which they aren't. The absence of measurement therefore needs to be represented in the notation system, just as the absence of treatment sometimes does. It is represented in the same way, by a blank space in the corresponding location.

Finally, just as different treatments can be designated with subscripts, different behavioral measures can as well. Usually, the same measure is applied to all groups on all occasions, so the subscript is used to identify the group and/or occasion for each application of the measure. In this way, the observations of aggressive behavior by subjects who viewed violent and nonviolent TV programs could be designated O_v and O_{nv}. The time taken by participants in the study by Darley and Latané (1968, **E7**) to respond to an emergency, compared across "virtual groups" of 2, 3, and 6 individuals, could be designated O_2, O_3, and O_6.

In the next chapter, nominal numerical subscripts will be used for generic forms of research designs to make it easier to refer to them as we discuss the strengths and weaknesses of the designs. In other words, O's will be numbered just to make it easier to keep them straight in our minds. In such cases, we will number from left to right. Measures taken at the same time will be numbered from top to bottom, from first group to last.

Representing Groups of Participants (Units)

Combining X's and O's, one could represent a simple research design as follows:

$$X \quad O_1$$

$$O_2$$

This would describe a comparison between two groups of participants. They could be two groups of children with Down syndrome, one of which received an experimental vitamin treatment (X) and one which received no special treatment at all. Both groups would be evaluated after the treatment given to the first group had an opportunity to take effect, using the behavioral measure designated O. The measurement of the treated group is arbitrarily designated O_1 in this case, and the measurement of the untreated group O_2.

To keep the groups straight, we're going to add another symbol. We will use G_1 and G_2 to identify the two groups, as follows:

$$G_1 \quad X \quad O_1$$
$$G_2 \qquad\quad O_2.$$

Of course, if there were more than two comparison groups, as there often are in psychological research, we would use a different number for each one, from "G_1" for the first group to "G_n" (n stands for the total number of groups) for however many groups there were. Subscripts can be as large as necessary for the treatments (X's) and measures (O's). Again, for the sake of simplicity, we'll always number groups from top to bottom in every design, as we did in this example, and treatments and behavioral measures from left to right and top to bottom. This will become more clear as the designs get more complicated.

Representing the Temporal Dimension of Research Design

When you see the symbols combined, when the notation system as a whole takes form, it makes sense that blank spaces as designate no treatment or no behavioral measure administered to a particular group. The meaning of blank spaces becomes even clearer when the next element in the notation system is identified. That is the position of a symbol on its line in the diagram of a design, from left to right.

That position indicates when an element of the design was encountered. When treatments or measurements occur at the same time, the X's or O's are aligned so that one is directly below the other. An X or an O on one line can have a blank space directly above or below it on another line. That means that the group whose line has the blank space in it did not receive any treatment or behavioral measure at the time when one was administered to the group that does have an X or an O on its line.

Any symbol to the left of another precedes it in time; if it is to the right of another, it follows that one. If an O precedes X on a given line, that O may be called a **pretest** because the measurement is made before ("pre") the treatment. If an O follows an X, it may be called a **posttest**.

Consider this design:

$$G_1 \quad O_1 \quad X \quad O_3$$
$$G_2 \quad O_2 \qquad\quad O_4$$

Pretests (O_1 and O_2) are administered to both groups. Group 1 receives a treatment, while Group 2 does not. Groups 1 and 2 are both tested at the same point in time, after Group 1 received the treatment—posttests O_3 and O_4. Of course, in the case of Group 2 it is essentially post-nothing.

Designating the various administrations of the behavioral measure with numerical subscripts makes it easier to talk about the results. For example, we might want to discuss how the difference between O_1 and O_3 compares with the difference between O_2 and O_4.

This is what we would do in the case of Dement's (1960) study of the effects of dream (REM) deprivation (**E14**). In that study, diagrammed above, there were two groups, one deprived of REM sleep (G_1) and one not deprived (G_2). The hypothesis was evaluated by comparing the differences between pretest and posttest measures of REM sleep (O_1 vs. O_3 in G_1; O_2 vs. O_4 in G_2). There was an increase in REM sleep in G_1, after deprivation. G_2, who weren't deprived, showed no difference between pretest and posttest.

Representing the Method Used to Assign Participants (Units)

A final pair of symbols in this notation system is used to indicate how the groups in the research were constituted, if there is more than one group. We will consider two possibilities. One is that the units included in the study were randomly assigned to the comparison groups. In this case, the entire pool of available research participants, or groups, or whatever units are chosen for study, might be assigned identification numbers and the numbers then picked out of a hat or from a table of random numbers that can be found among the appendices of most statistics textbooks. To create two groups, every other subject or unit chosen by its lottery number could be assigned to Group 1, and the next one to Group 2, with the process continuing until all have been assigned. To create three groups this way, it would be every third one, and so on. If this method of **random assignment** is used, as it was by Rosenthal and Jacobson (1966), who randomly selected schoolchildren to be identified as "bloomers" (**E15**), the symbol R will appear on each line of the design diagram, as in this example:

$$G_1 \quad R \quad X \quad O_1$$

$$G_2 \quad R \qquad O_2$$

In some research studies, it is difficult or even impossible to use the method of random assignment. Consider a study comparing the effectiveness of alternative teaching methods in a public school. In that case, the only practical approach probably would be to teach existing classes with the different methods that need to be compared. To divide the entire group of students into comparison groups using random assignment would disrupt the school routine, so it probably would not be allowed by school administrators.

But students may not have been assigned to those classes randomly in the first place. They may have been assigned according to estimates of their abilities ("tracked"), or because of pre-existing relationships among the children, or alphabetically, or for some other reason. In any case where pre-existing or **intact groups** are compared, meaning that the researcher was unable to assign units to them randomly and may not actually be privy to the rule by which they actually were assigned, the lines designating the experiences of the different groups in the research design are separated in the diagram of the design by dashed lines, as in this example:

$$G_1 \quad O_1 \quad X \quad O_3$$
$$\text{-----------}$$
$$G_2 \quad O_2 \qquad O_4$$

Summarizing the Notation System

With this notation system, consisting of the symbols X, O, blank space, G, R, dashed lines, and left to right (temporal) sequence, we can represent a wide variety of research designs. If one applied this system to every research study ever conducted in psychology, there would be a very, very large number of different diagrams to consider. Some research designs are very complex and some very original. Fortunately for us, methodologists (with Campbell and Stanley leading the way) have already developed a much more manageable inventory of basic research designs that can be customized to produce a study to test virtually any hypothesis. They have grouped the designs together in a way they will help us to understand how the choice of a research design affects the internal, external, and other types of validity of the research findings.

DESIGNS FOR PSYCHOLOGICAL RESEARCH ●

The remainder of this chapter consists of a presentation of some of those research designs—a kind of basic catalog. The next chapter will show how to evaluate their strengths and weaknesses against the threats to internal, external, and construct validity discussed in Chapters 3, 4, and 5. That is the next important element in the process of learning both how to interpret the meaning of published research results and how to plan new research.

Pre-Experimental Research Designs

The first category of research designs we will consider is something of an anomaly. For reasons that should be clear by the time you reach the end of the next chapter, these designs should be used rarely, if ever, in psychological research. They are included here not because you need to use them in your research but because understanding them will help demonstrate what you need to know about research design and validity.

These designs lack appropriate comparison groups or sufficient comparisons over time to pass most of our validity tests for research designs, but they actually are used quite often. In psychological research, they often serve the function of generating hypotheses for studies that can be carried out later, using more powerful research designs. Recall from Chapter 2 how observation of behavior can be a valuable source of research hypotheses. These designs are also used in studies conducted by untrained researchers and, especially, by those who seek a basis for false claims they make, perhaps for what they have accomplished or what they are trying to sell. The reasons for their use are an important part of understanding how they work, as is true of all the designs we will be considering in this chapter and the next.

We will consider four of these **pre-experimental research designs**, two based on comparisons over time (remember, within-subjects is the traditional label) and two based on comparisons among groups (between-subjects). They are shown in Table 6.3.

Pre-Experimental Designs That Compare Over Time (Within Subjects): PT Designs

PT1: The One-Shot Case Study. This design is easily diagrammed.

$$\boxed{\text{X} \quad \text{O}}$$

As you can see from the minimalist diagram, the one-shot case study is a fairly simple proposition, and therein lies much of the difficulty with it. In this design, there is only one group, or in some cases, just a single individual. The behavior of that group or individual is assessed (O) following its exposure to some event or experience (X). In practice, this kind of study more often proceeds in the reverse temporal order; that is, the behavior is noticed first, and then the researcher searches backward in time for its cause.

William Jefferson Clinton assumed the office of president of the United States in January of 1993. Observations of the American economy during the following 4 years revealed a high level of prosperity and stability, based on many statistical measures. Many of those who voted in the 1996 presidential election attributed

---

TABLE 6.3   Pre-Experimental Research Designs

Pre-experimental designs that compare over time

PT1	One-shot case study

$$X \qquad O$$

PT2	One-group pretest-posttest design

$$O_1 \quad X \quad O_2$$

Pre-experimental designs that compare among groups

PG1	Static-group comparison design

$$G_1 \quad X \quad O_1$$
$$\text{- - - - - - - - - - - - - - -}$$
$$G_2 \qquad \quad O_2$$

PG2	Correlational design

$$r_{xo}$$

NOTE: PT research designs are pre-experimental designs (P) that make comparisons over time (T). PG designs are also pre-experimental (P), but they compare among groups (G).

---

those positive conditions to the Clinton presidency. That evaluation of the country's economic performance (O) during the Clinton presidency (X) follows the form of a one-shot case study.

Many other historical studies do the same, and many studies of other types, as mentioned above, also are retrospective. An effect occurs—a war, a recession, an economic recovery—and the "researcher" looks for an antecedent event that may have caused it.

Sigmund Freud's case studies of his neurotic patients (and other clinical case studies in psychiatry, medicine, and neuropsychology) are similar, in design at least. The patients presented with symptoms, and Freud, using the techniques of psychoanalysis, searched for the antecedent causes. In the same way, a neuropsychologist who observes a person displaying odd behavior following a head injury searches for the specific brain damage that could explain the behavior.

In some college and university business programs, alternative approaches to management, leadership, and other presumably important factors in business success are studied through the use of one-shot case studies. Analyses of successful companies are believed to be a good way of determining which approaches work well in practice. In fact, many people in the field of business education believe the case study approach to be better than more methodologically rigorous studies of the sort that we'll consider later, for reasons to be discussed later.

The next chapter will analyze the vulnerability of the one-shot case study to specific threats to internal and external validity, but it is probably clear already that the design offers too few points of comparison—none, in fact—to allow alternative explanations to be ruled out sufficiently. Could the researcher have overlooked other reasons for economic prosperity or a war? Isn't the U.S. economy cyclical, so that it is bound to be robust sometimes, whether or not a particular president is elected or a particular government policy implemented? The use of one-shot case studies in psychological research, therefore, should be limited to instances where unforeseen events of potential relevance to a behavior of interest are followed up by an assessment of the behavior. Although such research may be of theoretical interest, it is more likely to be conducted for practical reasons rather than to build scientific theories. It can help the survivors of a traumatic event, be used to monitor the performance of an organization, or something of the sort.

If it does have any value in building scientific theories of behavior, it is as a preliminary step, to identify hypotheses that merit more extensive and systematic testing with more sophisticated research designs. Although they might have had more ambitious goals for their research, Cartwright's (1974) study of dream content (**E13**) and Calhoun's (1962) study of the effects of population density (**E19**) could be characterized as preliminary studies in this sense.

We will see that there are ways of making the results of such a study much easier to interpret by adding more points of comparison, sometimes with very little additional effort on the part of the researcher. As mentioned earlier, however, the design is often used by those who are more interested in taking credit or placing blame to serve their own interests than in finding the truth of a matter.

> *PT2: The One-Group Pretest-Posttest Design.* This design can be
> diagrammed as follows.

$$O_1 \quad X \quad O_2$$

This design, like the one-shot case study, involves just a single group or unit. In this case, however, the researcher has available for comparison some measures of the behavior in question taken on two separate occasions, before and after the hypothesized causal event. This is an example of how the one-shot case study can sometimes be elaborated, if a pretest measure of the behavior (O_1) can be obtained.

This may happen in at least two different ways. In Dement's (1960) study of the effects of dream deprivation (**E14**), the researchers were able to foresee the value of obtaining a baseline measure of the participants' level of REM sleep. It was the

---

| Box 6.1 | *THINKING ABOUT RESEARCH* |

True Experiments Need Not Be Far Removed From Everyday Life _____

One enduring controversy among those concerned with the methodological questions raised by psychological research concerns the role of the laboratory experiment. On one hand, some who are the equivalent of methodological fundamentalists argue that anything short of true experimentation that maximizes internal validity is not science at all. On the other are those who argue that experimentation strips away so much of the context of behavior that it can provide no real understanding of behavioral causes.

The latter position has gained stature recently, as the range of validity issues considered by researchers has expanded to the scope represented in this book. This is especially true in the areas of psychology that are most involved in applying their research. Examples of the value of simple true experiments—even those not rigidly controlled by researchers so as to minimize all types of threats to validity—still can be found today. One compelling example is to be found in

the work of James Pennebaker of the University of Texas on the effects of writing about one's emotions.

In a typical study, Pennebaker (see Pennebaker, Kiecolt-Glaser, & Glaser, 1996) randomly divides into two groups a sample of medical patients afflicted with a serious illness. One group is asked to write about their feelings concerning their illness, while the other group goes on with their normal treatment regimen. Follow-up measures show that those who write suffer less and improve more with the same treatment.

Which research design does Pennebaker use in this and similar studies? How would you characterize the internal validity of his findings? What about construct validity concerns? External validity? Are you as impressed with the scientific and practical value of true experimental research in this particular instance as I am?

---

only way to gauge whether REM deprivation would change the participants' brain activity during sleep. Fortunately, the participants were available to provide that needed baseline or pretest measure. A one-shot case study design would have been worthless for Dement's purposes.

In other cases, where research is based on public or organizational records, the required measurements may simply be on file, so that a researcher who did not anticipate the need could still acquire the pretest data, after the fact of the hypothesized causal event and perhaps even after the recording of posttest measures. For example, the effects of a new school curriculum might be evaluated by comparing students' scores on standardized achievement tests before and after the new curriculum is instituted. Those tests are given at regular intervals in many schools. As another example, a corporation might compare sales of a particular product line before and after a new advertising campaign. "Pretest" sales records probably would exist whether or not a researcher was interested in using them in a particular study.

You might have realized by now that one of the examples of a one-shot case study in the previous section could just as easily be described as a one-group pretest-posttest design. The economic performance of the Clinton administration could be evaluated by comparing economic indicators at the time President Clinton took office with the same measures at the end of his first term. The "study" would then be a one-group pretest-posttest design rather than a one-shot case study. The discussion in the next chapter will clarify the difference and demonstrate the importance of a researcher's choice of research design.

Even where the one-group pretest-posttest design is feasible, it would leave many questions unanswered. Did any change that occurred in the group that was studied also occur in other groups that weren't exposed to the presumed cause of the change? Had some earlier event started a change that seemed to have occurred between the pretest and posttest? Again, detailed analysis of the strengths and weaknesses of the design is left for the next chapter.

Of course, in the cases of other potentially important causal events—such as wars, high school murder epidemics, and tornadoes—that give no warning, there may not be pretest information available. If the effects of these events need to be studied by examining specific behavioral measures that are not available for the time preceding the event in question, the one-group pretest-posttest design would not be feasible.

Pre-Experimental Designs That Compare Among Groups (Between Subjects): PG Designs

PG1: The Static-Group Comparison Design. This design can be diagrammed as follows.

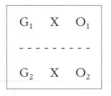

The first example we will consider of a pre-experimental design that compares among groups is the static-group comparison design. It includes two or more groups, although the generic diagrams will always be based on the simplest cases, two groups in this case. As the dashed line in the diagram clearly shows, the groups are self-selected or intact—the participants or units are not randomly assigned to groups. The groups are exposed to variations of some event/experience/treatment suspected of being a causal agent, in this case X or no X, and the behavior believed to be influenced by that cause is assessed afterward in both groups at approximately the same time (O_1 and O_2).

Did those states that raised their speed limits when allowed to by federal law experience higher rates of automobile fatalities thereafter than those states that left their speed limits at the pre-existing lower levels? Did those corporations that downsized by reducing their corps of middle-level managers become more profitable than the corporations that did not? Did children with Down syndrome who received the controversial drug-vitamin therapy discussed earlier experience cognitive development superior to those who did not? All these hypotheses could be tested using the static-group comparison design, and many similar hypotheses have.

In fact, five of the exemplar studies introduced in Chapter 2 utilized the static-group comparison design. Most of the studies reported by Rotter (1966, **E1**) and Friedman and Rosenman (1959, **E2**) compared groups that could be classified as different personality types. Personality types are always intact groups; a researcher can't randomly assign people to be different personality types. Festinger et al. (1956, **E11**) compared doomsday cult members who happened to be (weren't randomly assigned to be) in different settings when the cult's prophecy failed. Frazier (1985, **E25**) compared pre-existing populations of inmates in different types of jails. Zajonc and Markus (1975, **E16**) compared 19-year-old Dutch men from different types of families.

All the designs we will consider that are based on comparisons across groups can be expanded to include additional groups within the same general framework. In this case, those would be intact groups that were administered behavioral measures only following the causal event under investigation. As always, the design remains the same, both in the label assigned to it and in the analysis of its vulnerability to threats to internal and external validity, regardless of how many groups are studied.

For example, the effects of increased speed limits could be evaluated by comparing a group of states that did not raise their speed limits to a number of other groups that raised theirs to varying levels. If four groups were compared, representing the varying levels to which different states raised their speed limits, the design of the study could be diagrammed as follows, where the +'s indicate the level of increase and the absence of X indicates no increase at all:

$$\begin{array}{lcc}
\text{G1} & \text{X+++} & O_1 \\
\hline
\text{G2} & \text{X++} & O_2 \\
\hline
\text{G3} & \text{X+} & O_3 \\
\hline
\text{G4} & & O_4
\end{array}$$

This is still a static-group comparison design, even though there are four groups instead of two. The same principle—more groups under same guidelines = same design—holds true for other between-groups designs as well. In fact, among our exemplar studies, Friedman and Rosenman (1959, **E2**) compared three groups: Type A, Type B, and chronically anxious. That study could be diagrammed as follows:

$$G_1 \quad X_A \quad O_A$$

- - - - - - - - - - - -

$$G_2 \quad X_B \quad O_B$$

- - - - - - - - - - - -

$$G_3 \quad X_{CA} \quad O_{CA}$$

Zajonc and Markus (1975, **E16**) compared many different sizes of families and birth orders.

The static-group comparison design also has its problems. The most important one concerns the fact that the groups that are compared may behave differently from one another independent of the causal factor being studied. The citizens of states that raise their speed limits less might be more concerned about traffic safety, or they might be more careful drivers. Can you think of any comparable problems with interpreting some of the other static-group comparison studies discussed above?

> *PG2: The Correlational Design.* This design can be diagrammed very simply as follows.

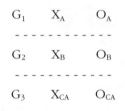

$$\boxed{r_{xo}}$$

Talk about disconfirmed expectancies! Given your experience so far with the notation system introduced earlier in this chapter, this can't be something you expected. The correlational design, which is widely used in psychological research, actually is an extension of the static-group comparison design, PG1. Because its use is based on one of the seminal accomplishments in statistics, the invention of the correlation coefficient by Karl Pearson in England about a century ago, it deserves a place and notation of its own in our analysis.

In a *correlational study*, as a hypothesis-testing study using this design is usually called, many participants or units are measured for two characteristics. One is a presumed cause of some behavior (X), referred to as the predictor. The second is the behavior it is presumed to cause (O), the criterion. The correlation coefficient is then used to summarize the relationship between X and O. (Correlation was discussed earlier, but the details of correlation are left to Chapter 10.) That's what r_{xo}

designates, the correlation (r is the symbol for the correlation statistic or coefficient) between X and O.

A study testing the hypothesis that intelligence influences school achievement could use correlation to determine the relationship between IQ and achievement test scores for a group of students. That would be a correlational study. So would a study of the effects of urban life that was based on the correlation between the size of a community and the walking speed of its residents, or one examining the correlation between the population density of an area and the crime rate there, for all the census tracts in a large city.

Among our exemplar studies, Haier et al.'s (1992) research on the effects of intelligence on brain efficiency (**E23**) is a good example of the use of the correlational design. In that study, participants' IQ scores were correlated with the rate at which glucose was metabolized in their brains while they performed a complex task they had just learned.

The correlational design is an extension of the static-group comparison design in the sense that each of the pairs of measures (X and O) that are obtained and that go into calculating the correlation coefficient constitutes a separate unit. There may be dozens, hundreds, or even thousands of such units. There are usually too many to diagram this design in the same way as we have the others. This design also shares some of the problems of the static-group comparison design. Are there other factors that can influence the behavior being studied? For example, is crime more prevalent in more densely populated census tracts because the people who live there are poorer?

True Experimental Research Designs

When scientific psychology committed to the methods of the natural sciences about a hundred years ago, the paragon of those methods was considered to be the experiment. Observation and operational definition were the most fundamental principles of "the" scientific method (today, methodologists and philosophers of science tend to take a more relativistic view of science, as you'll see in Chapter 11). The ultimate or best use of observation and operational definition was believed to be in experimentation. Many research psychologists still hold that belief.

The special properties of an experiment can be defined in a number of different ways. Rather than attempt to choose the best definition, I will use more than one. This may not be clear in the short run, and using multiple definitions makes it more difficult to say clearly and succinctly what an experiment is. In the long run, though, this use of multiple definitions should increase understanding of what makes an experiment an experiment, as well as what makes it something different from other scientific methods and something special (if not ideal in an absolute sense, or perfect, as it was once believed to be).

Two of the defining characteristics of **true experimental research designs** are **random assignment** (discussed earlier) and **manipulation** of the independent variable, and the two go hand in hand. To be able to assign participants randomly to comparison treatment conditions, the researcher must be able to determine to whom, when, and where different treatments will occur. That is true whether different groups are exposed to different levels of the independent variable or treatment (including no-treatment groups) in between-subjects designs, or whether participants are exposed to different treatments on different occasions in within-subjects designs. To be able to exercise that **control**, in contrast to research that studies the effects of naturally occurring events, the researcher must be able to manipulate the independent variable. That is, he or she must be able to create the various treatment conditions when and where random assignment requires them.

The researcher must control conditions, other than the treatments meant to be compared, that might affect the behavior under study, or those other conditions must be held constant (again, *ceteris paribus*). Random assignment controls for group composition, and manipulation of the independent variable controls for the possibility that causal factors other than the treatments will occur coincidentally during the course of the research study.

Experimental control, as it's often called, is achieved most often by studying captive populations (including students in introductory psychology courses), in isolated settings generally known as laboratories that are maintained by the researcher specifically for the purpose of experimental control. All of this usually means that research participants are isolated from possible extraneous influences on those aspects of their behavior the researcher wants to study, and this is achieved by removing participants to the laboratory and by limiting the time during which such influences can occur.

With those general principles in mind, we will consider five different true experimental designs, two that compare over time and three that compare among groups. They are shown in Table 6.4.

True Experimental Designs That Compare Over Time (Within Subjects): TT Designs

Within-subjects research designs are used in psychological research principally for one reason: They reduce the effects of individual differences on the observations or measurements obtained. As the psychological study of personality has shown so clearly, people differ widely in any characteristic or performance that might be observed. The effects of treatments sometimes can be difficult to estimate because of the variable responses by participants exposed to each one. If all participants are exposed to all treatments, as they are in within-subjects designs, one participant's response to one treatment can be compared with his or her response to another, making the effects of the treatments clearer because that participant's

---

TABLE 6.4   True Experimental Research Designs

True experimental designs that compare over time

TT1   Equivalent time samples design

$$X_1O_1 \qquad X_0O_2 \qquad X_1O_3 \qquad X_0O_4 \qquad \text{etc.}$$

TT2   Equivalent materials samples design

$$M_aX_1O_1 \qquad M_bX_0O_2 \qquad M_cX_1O_3 \qquad M_dX_0O_4 \qquad \text{etc.}$$

True experimental designs that compare among groups

TG1   Pretest-posttest control group design

$$\begin{array}{cccccc} G_1 & R & O_1 & X & O_3 \\ G_2 & R & O_2 & & O_4 \end{array}$$

TG2   Posttest-only control group design

$$\begin{array}{cccc} G_1 & R & X & O_1 \\ G_2 & R & & O_2 \end{array}$$

TG3   Solomon four-group design

$$\begin{array}{ccccc} G_1 & R & O_1 & X & O_3 \\ G_2 & R & O_2 & & O_4 \\ G_3 & R & & X & O_5 \\ G_4 & R & & & O_6 \end{array}$$

NOTE: TT designs are true experimental designs (T) that compare over time (T). TG designs are true experimental designs (T) that compare among groups (G).

unique personal characteristics are reflected in all of the responses being compared.

This approach can even be helpful if the research participants are nonhumans or organizations. For different reasons, obviously— genetics and experience in the first case and organizational culture in the second—there can be considerable variation in both of those types of units in response to the same treatments.

TT1: The Equivalent Time Samples Design. This design can be diagrammed as follows.

$$X_1O_1 \qquad X_0O_2 \qquad X_1O_3 \qquad X_0O_4 \qquad \text{etc.}$$

The single group studied in the equivalent time samples design is exposed to different levels of the independent variable on different occasions. Those experimental treatments must be manipulated by the researcher so that they can be scheduled randomly. That is what makes the occasions, or time samples as they're called in this case, equivalent. Just as random assignment of participants to groups provides control over group composition effects by creating equivalent groups, random scheduling of treatments across occasions controls for extraneous events by creating equivalent time samples.

Don't be misled by the design diagram that shows treatments X_1 and X_0 (a no-treatment condition) alternating with one another in a predictable pattern. That just makes the diagram simpler to write out. The key to this design, the feature that makes the study a true experiment, is the nonsystematic or random scheduling of treatment conditions over time. It is also important to recognize that this design can accommodate any number of treatments and any number of repetitions or occasions while retaining the essential character of the equivalent time samples design, just as between-groups designs can accommodate any number of groups. As usual, the most basic form of the design is shown in the diagram we use.

This design has been used frequently in studies of operant conditioning. A pigeon is reinforced for pecking at a plastic disc for a period of time, then the reinforcement is withdrawn, and then it is reintroduced. If those occasions are selected randomly with regard to the other relevant events in the pigeon's life (if there are any!—see Chapter 7), the study is a true experiment. The same design has been used to study the effects of reinforcement on human behavior, especially in institutionalized populations, where it is known as behavior modification.

When this design is used to study operant conditioning, in pigeons or people, it is sometimes referred to as an ABA design. First (A, or X_0), the behavior is observed as it occurs under normal conditions, without any experimental manipulation of reinforcement. This is also known as the "baseline" condition. Then reinforcement is administered, and the behavior is observed again (B, or X_1). Finally, the reinforcement is withdrawn to determine how the behavior changes in its absence (A, or X_0, again). In our notation system, the diagram might be this:

$$X_0O_1 \quad X_1O_2 \quad X_0O_3$$

or

$$X_AO_1 \quad X_BO_2 \quad X_AO_3$$

More complicated studies that compare the effects of different schedules of reinforcement during equivalent time periods are still based on the same design, even though the diagram might have to be expanded. For example, a comparison among continuous reinforcement, partial reinforcement, and no reinforcement might be diagrammed as follows:

$$X_0O_1 \quad X_cO_2 \quad X_0O_3 \quad X_pO_4 \quad \text{etc.}$$

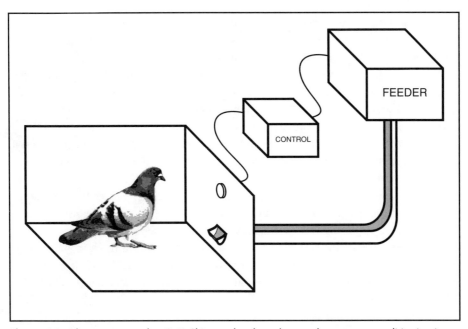

Figure 6.1. The apparatus that B. F. Skinner developed to study operant conditioning in his laboratory at Harvard.

Our exemplar studies include several examples of the equivalent time samples design. Pavlov's (1927) conditioning research (**E20**) alternated presentations of the CS (tone) with and without the US (food). Gazzaniga's (1967) research with split-brain patients (**E21**) alternated presentations to the left and right cerebral hemispheres. Aserinsky and Kleitman (1953) woke sleeping research participants during REM and NREM sleep (**E4**). Triplett's (1897) laboratory research on coaction alternated together and alone performances on the fishing reel apparatus (**E3**). Broverman et al. (1972) alternated male, female, and self judgments (**E5**). In every case, the same participants were exposed to each of the treatments in a random sequence. In this case, the prevalence of this design among our exemplars is a true indication that TT1 is a popular design in psychology, particularly in basic scientific research. It is, for reasons reviewed in the next chapter, deservedly popular.

TT2: The Equivalent Materials Samples Design. This design can be diagrammed as follows.

$$M_a X_1 O_1 \quad M_b X_0 O_2 \quad M_c X_1 O_3 \quad M_c X_0 O_4 \quad \text{etc.}$$

This second within-subjects true experimental design is used to compare participants' responses to a variety of equivalent materials or tasks presented in random order in association with different treatments.

For example, a study of memory might be conducted to test the hypothesis that words participants thought about (encoded) more deeply would be easier to remember. The same group of participants might be asked to memorize a list of words they thought about only to the extent of deciding whether the first letter of the word was a consonant or vowel. On other occasions, they might be asked to memorize a list they thought about more deeply, by deciding whether the word referred to an animate or inanimate object.

The researcher might want to expose the participants to each of the treatments, shallow encoding and deep encoding, more than once, to get a clearer picture of their effects. If so, it might be a good idea to use different lists of words on those different occasions. This would prevent exposure to one treatment from influencing the next (because the subjects already were familiar with the list). It would also increase the generality of the results across different lists of words. This study could be diagrammed as follows:

$$M_a X_s O_1 \quad M_b X_d O_2 \quad M_c X_s O_3 \quad M_d X_d O_4$$

In this diagram, M_a, M_b, M_c, and M_d would represent four different lists of words. X_s and X_d would represent instructions designed to get participants to use shallow and deep encoding strategies, respectively. O_1, O_2, O_3, and O_4 would represent administrations of a standardized memory measure (such as free recall) after each treatment, generating a score such as percentage of correct responses.

Researchers interested in the effects of a person's physical appearance on impressions of their character (including myself) have also used the equivalent materials samples design. Photographs of individuals representing varying levels of physical attractiveness (the treatments; e.g., high, medium, and low) can be presented in random order to a single group of participants. To establish the generality of the effect, two or three examples (photographs of the "target persons") of each level of attractiveness could be presented. Each of the target persons (photographs) would be rated on a standardized questionnaire for a number of personality dimensions. The study could be diagrammed as follows:

$$M_a X_h O_1 \quad M_b X_m O_2 \quad M_c X_l O_3 \quad M_d X_h O_4 \quad M_e X_m O_5 \quad M_f X_l O_6$$

M_a through M_f would be the individual photographs presented to the participants. X_h, X_m, and X_l would stand for the high, medium, and low levels of attractiveness they represent, and O_1 through O_6 would represent the impressions measured in response to each of the photographs on a standardized questionnaire. Comparing the sum of O_1 and O_4 with the sum of O_2 and O_5 and with the sum of O_3

and O_6 would reveal any differences that existed among responses to the three levels of attractiveness that constituted the treatments (X's) in this study. Comparing O_1 with O_4, O_2 with O_5, and O_3 with O_6 would reveal differences associated with the materials samples, the specific individuals chosen to represent each treatment or level of attractiveness. In such a study, a longer series, say 12 photographs, would ordinarily be used, and the order of the treatments and materials pairs would be randomized rather than alternated.

Among our exemplar studies, Cherulnik et al.'s (1981) research on impressions of high and low Machiavellian men (**E17**) used the TT2 design. Several examples (M_a, M_b, etc.) of high and low Machs (X_H and X_L) were shown to subjects in random order. After each one, a standardized measurement was taken, either an identifi- cation of the target's Mach status or the choice of trait adjectives to describe the target.

Clark and Clark (1940) used the TT2 design in their study of black children's racial identities and preferences for black versus white dolls (**E6**). Two dolls (materials) of each color (treatments) were used in that study. How would you design that study?

True Experimental Designs That Compare Across Groups (Between Subjects): TG Designs

The more common form of experimental research in psychology involves comparisons among groups or between subjects. Exposing people sequentially to different treatments can cause complications in which the lingering effects of one treatment alter the effects of those that follow. It is often easier, therefore, to interpret comparisons between groups than to interpret comparisons within groups. The examples of within-groups experimental designs described above are rare though valuable exceptions, used more often with nonhuman than with human research participants (their prevalence among our exemplar group notwithstanding). We will consider three true experimental research designs that compare among groups. The first two are widely used in research in psychology. The third has been used primarily to understand how the other two work.

TG1: The Pretest-Posttest Control Group Design. This design can be diagrammed as follows.

G1	R	O_1	X	O_3
G1	R	O_1		O_3

In contrast to the pre-experimental static-group comparison design, the two groups in this design are constituted by the method of random assignment. As we've seen, this is a key feature of the experimental method. In addition, both groups are assessed on the dependent variable before Group 1 is exposed to the treatment (i.e., pretested), as well as afterward (the posttest).

Social-psychological research on attitude change utilized a variation on this design. Some studies tested the hypothesis that a factual message attributed to a knowledgeable source would be more persuasive than one attributed to a non-expert. Randomly constituted groups would first be questioned about their attitudes on an engaging issue, perhaps the desirability of using nuclear power to produce electricity. Then the groups would be asked to read a brief essay on the subject. Researchers usually chose an issue on which prospective participants were likely to have non-neutral attitudes. Then the essay or message could be constructed to advocate the opposite position from theirs. One group would be informed that the essay was written by an authoritative source or expert, while the other group would learn that the author (of the same name) was respectable but not particularly knowledgeable on the particular subject at hand. Then both groups would be asked about their attitudes toward the subject of the essay (the attitude object) a second time. In this case, the design might be diagrammed as follows:

$$G_1 \quad R \quad O_1 \quad X_e \quad O_3$$
$$G_2 \quad R \quad O_2 \quad X_{ne} \quad O_4$$

X_e and X_{ne} stand for expert and nonexpert source in this case. The hypothesis would be evaluated by comparing the amount of attitude change between the two groups ($O_3 - O_1$ with $O_4 - O_2$). If communicator expertise were an influential factor, as hypothesized, $O_3 - O_1$ would be greater than $O_4 - O_2$.

By the way, as you may have guessed already from our prior discussion, the pretest-posttest control group design can accommodate comparisons between treatment and no treatment groups, between two contrasting treatments (as in the attitude change example above), or among more than two treatment and/or nontreatment groups. As long as the groups are constituted by random assignment and all groups are tested before and after any treatments are administered, the research design is the same.

It should be clear by now that for this design to be used, the researcher must be free to assign participants randomly to groups and to schedule the administration of behavioral measures and treatments at will. These constraints make this design much more likely to be used in a laboratory setting, where the researcher has control of what happens, to whom it happens, and when. The attitude change research that used this design was conducted in the laboratory.

The "laboratory" can sometimes be set up in a school or a factory. If researchers are allowed to reassign students or workers from their existing groups, and to disturb the organization routine by introducing special events in order to study their effects on the participants' behavior, the result is the same. Schools, factories, and other organizations often monitor the behavior of their members for their own

---

Box 6.2 | *THINKING ABOUT RESEARCH*

Research Design and Judgments of Cause and Effect _____

One prominent example of the growing contribution that psychological research is making to the field of medicine is the recent finding that there is a relationship between heart disease and depression. Researchers have found that people who have heart disease are more likely to be depressed, people who are depressed are more likely to develop heart disease, and people who have both heart disease and depression tend to die sooner than those with heart disease alone.

But what causes what? One explanation holds that biochemical changes associated with depression cause heart disease. This seems consistent with what we know about the effects of stress hormones on heart disease. Another explanation holds that people who are depressed neglect their health. For example, they

may forget to take their blood pressure medication, or they may fail to make prudent decisions about what they eat, or to exercise, and therefore they may become more vulnerable to heart disease. A third possibility is that having heart disease causes people to become depressed. It certainly can't be much fun.

What kind of research design do you think produced the evidence of a relationship between heart disease and depression? What are the key validity issues in interpreting evidence based on that design? What kind of research could deal effectively with those validity issues and make it possible to determine which of the explanations for the relationship between heart disease and depression is correct?

---

purposes. Schools perform periodic administrations of standardized achievement tests, factories often maintain continuous records of productivity, and computers may include software that could monitor the speed and accuracy of white-collar workers using them. In such cases, researchers do not need to introduce special behavioral measures to test their hypotheses in those settings.

Rosenthal and Jacobson's (1966) research on teacher expectancies (**E15**) used the TG1 design. In that case, the pretest was used not only for comparison with posttreatment IQ but also as part of the cover story that led the teachers to believe that some of their students had been shown by the IQ test to be potential stars in the classroom.

TG2: The Posttest-Only Control Group Design. This design can be diagrammed as follows.

G1	R	X	O_1
G2	R		O_2

This design contains all the elements of the pretest-posttest control group design except for the pretest. The participants are assigned to groups at random, but their behavior is assessed only after the treatment occurs.

In some cases, pretests make no sense. Even when researchers are capable of scheduling a pretest, in laboratory studies or in studies conducted in other settings that permit researchers such a degree of control. Consider the example of research to determine whether misleading information can cause children to report memories of events that never occurred. If such a study compared children who had been given such information with children who had not, would it make any sense to compare their memories for the suggested event before the suggestion was even made?

Does it ever make any sense to assess the behavior in question before any treatments are administered, even if it is possible to do so, in a true experimental design? Because the groups are randomly constituted, the only reason to compare them with a pretest is to know exactly how much of a change the treatment has produced, rather than simply the relative effects of different treatments. Did Rosenthal and Jacobson (1966, **E15**) need to test children to find out whether those randomly selected to be identified as bloomers had higher IQs than the others? Didn't random assignment guarantee that they would be no different at the beginning of the study? Unless it is important to know exactly where the groups started and ended up, the pretest is unnecessary and, as we will see later, even worse than that.

The posttest-only control group design is very popular in psychological research. The three examples among the exemplar studies are probably fewer than the number we would have found if we had chosen 25 studies at random from the psychological research literature rather than choosing them to make specific methodological points. Harlow (1958) randomly assigned infant rhesus monkeys to be fed by cloth or wire surrogate mothers, then tested their preference between the two when there was no food around (**E12**). Seligman and Maier (1967) randomly assigned dogs to be exposed to inescapable shock or not, then tested their performance in the shuttle box (**E18**). Rosenzweig et al. (1972) randomly assigned rat pups to impoverished, standard, or enriched laboratory cages, then assessed the differential effects of those environments on their brain development (**E22**).

The posttest-only control group design can accommodate any number of treatment or no treatment groups, as long as the rules of random assignment of participants to groups and posttest-only assessment of behavior are observed for all of them.

TG3: The Solomon Four-Group Design. This design, diagrammed below, shows more variation among groups and involves more groups.

$$
\begin{array}{ccccc}
G_1 & R & O_1 & X & O_3 \\
G_2 & R & O_2 & & O_4 \\
G_3 & R & & X & O_5 \\
G_4 & R & & & O_6 \\
\end{array}
$$

If you look closely, you can see that the Solomon four-group design is an amalgamation of the other two between-subjects experimental designs. Groups 1 and 2 represent the pretest-posttest control group design, and Groups 3 and 4 the posttest-only control group design. The rather specialized purpose of the Solomon four-groups design is to compare the results of the other two designs so that we can understand how they work.

Both the pretest-posttest control group design (TG1) and the posttest-only control group design (TG2) can be used to evaluate the effects of a treatment, X, administered to one of the two randomly constituted groups in each design. The behavior of the group exposed to the treatment is compared to the same behavior in the group in which the treatment is absent. For now, we'll set aside the other, equivalent uses of these designs to compare one treatment with another or more than two different treatment conditions.

The pretest-posttest control group design permits the researcher to observe the amount of change from before the treatment to after it. It complicates the comparison, however, by introducing the possibility that the pretest will sensitize subjects to the treatment and therefore alter the "normal" effect of the treatment. Recall from the discussion of construct validity that this problem is limited to studies where the pretest and posttest utilize identical measures and both are administered to participants directly. Adding the two groups of the posttest-only control group design allows the researcher to compare the effects of X when there is no pretest with the effects when a pretest is given. If the pretest doesn't distort the effects of X (i.e., if $O_3 - O_4$ is not different from $O_5 - O_6$), then the additional information afforded by the pretest about the amount of change can be used without the accompanying concern about pretest sensitization.

A study of attitude change by Rosnow and Suls (1970) demonstrates the importance of assessing pretest sensitization in this way. This study followed the attitude change paradigm described in the earlier discussion of the pretest-posttest control group design. Rosnow and Suls found, however, that the effects of a persuasive communication were increased when a pretest was administered. The pretest apparently alerted research participants to the fact that the essay they would read was intended to cause their attitudes to change. The pretested participants indicated greater changes in their attitudes, presumably because of that perceived experimental demand.

In attitude change research, then, the posttest-only control group design would appear to offer a more accurate picture of the effects of variations in the nature of a persuasive communication. As we'll see in a more complete discussion in the next chapter, the posttest-only control group design is actually preferable to the pretest-posttest control group design in most cases.

Quasi-Experimental Research Designs

For most of the history of scientific psychology, it has been accepted that experimental research, with its twin assets of random assignment and manipulation of the independent variable by the researcher, is the ideal method—if not the only acceptable method—for psychological research. Some researchers believe this so strongly that they avoid studying important questions about human personality, sex differences in behavior, and other subjects that do not lend themselves to experimental research. This is one reason that so much psychological research has been carried out in laboratory settings with nonhuman participants: These situations make experimental control even easier to accomplish.

This received wisdom began to be challenged a few decades ago, for a variety of reasons. One reason was the growing interest among research psychologists in applied questions. Studying how students learn in school, how well various forms of psychotherapy work, how to motivate factory workers, and other applied problems meant leaving behind the safety (methodologically speaking) of the laboratory. In many cases, applied research meant giving up control over the assignment of participants to groups and over the timing of events whose effects on behavior needed to be studied. Lack of the ability to control the assignment of participants or the timing of events made the use of true experimental designs impossible.

There are more affirmative reasons for the development of a growing interest in what has come to be called quasi-experimental research. One is the gradually increasing concern about artifacts in experimental research. Random assignment and manipulation of an independent variable, especially in a laboratory setting, bring intimate contact between researcher and participant and thus an acute awareness of hypotheses and of scrutiny. That makes demand characteristics effects and experimenter expectancy effects more likely to occur. Because **quasi-experimental research designs** can be more easily implemented in natural settings and can use existing data that don't require direct assessment of subjects, treatment and measurement artifacts can be minimized.

Finally, as applied concerns have become more common and as they have become more important sources of research hypotheses in psychology, some research psychologists have seen external validity becoming a more important criterion for evaluating research results. The results of research conducted in natural settings with minimal interference by the researchers typically are less vulnerable to threats from external validity than are the results of traditional laboratory experimentation.

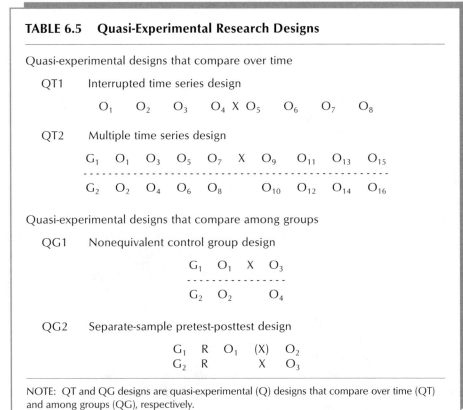

TABLE 6.5   Quasi-Experimental Research Designs

Quasi-experimental designs that compare over time

QT1   Interrupted time series design

O_1 O_2 O_3 O_4 X O_5 O_6 O_7 O_8

QT2   Multiple time series design

G_1 O_1 O_3 O_5 O_7 X O_9 O_{11} O_{13} O_{15}
- -
G_2 O_2 O_4 O_6 O_8 O_{10} O_{12} O_{14} O_{16}

Quasi-experimental designs that compare among groups

QG1   Nonequivalent control group design

G_1 O_1 X O_3
- - - - - - - - - - - - - - - - -
G_2 O_2 O_4

QG2   Separate-sample pretest-posttest design

G_1 R O_1 (X) O_2
G_2 R   X O_3

NOTE: QT and QG designs are quasi-experimental (Q) designs that compare over time (QT) and among groups (QG), respectively.

More will be said about all of this in the next chapter. For now, let's become acquainted with some basic quasi-experimental designs, two of the within-subjects variety and two of the between-subjects type. All four are shown in Table 6.5.

Quasi-Experimental Designs That Compare Over Time (Within Subjects): QT Designs

QT1: The Interrupted Time Series Design. This design involves one group and a series of measurements, as diagrammed below.

O_1 O_2 O_3 O_4 X O_5 O_6 O_7 O_8

The interrupted time series design evaluates the effects of an event that is experienced by one group of units on a series of measures of a behavior it is hypothesized to affect. Thus, there are two main elements in the design—the series of measures, represented here arbitrarily as a symmetrical series of eight, O_1 to O_8, and the event surrounded by them, X. In many cases, they are independent of one another. As was mentioned above, a factory may keep records of the productivity of its workers, just as a school may keep records of the achievement of its students, as a matter of institutional routine. Should a researcher wish to study the effects of a new management style in the factory or a new teaching method in the school, the relevant series of measures can be used for that assessment, even though it was not collected for that particular purpose.

When the design is used in this way, rather than as a planned series of measures for the specific purpose of evaluating the effects of some event in a research hypothesis, the series of measures might not be a symmetrical four before X and four after. The researcher might have to choose measures from a much longer series that typically would extend farther back in time from X than forward (it's easier to look up old records than to wait around for new ones). The key point is that the research design is an interrupted time series design if there is a series of measures that is extensive enough to distinguish any possible long-term trends in the behavior being studied that might be mistaken for effects of the treatment whose effects are being studied.

As you might expect, the interrupted time series design is very popular in social sciences like management, economics, and political science. Researchers in those fields are often interested in the effects of singular events like elections, wars, interest rate increases, and the like. They want to know how those events can influence "behaviors" such as stock trades, worker productivity, and political preferences that routinely are monitored periodically over long periods of time.

None of our exemplar studies was conducted using the interrupted time series design, even though it is used occasionally in psychological research and in related fields of interest to psychologists. Its importance to researchers in psychology, and to our examination of research methods in psychology, has more to do with its potential and with the lessons it can teach us than with its actual use. That point should become clearer when we discuss it further in Chapter 7.

QT2: The Multiple Time Series Design. This design is an extension of the interrupted time series design, as diagrammed below.

G_1	O_1	O_3	O_5	O_7 X O_9	O_{11}	O_{13}	O_{15}
G_2	O_2	O_4	O_6	O_8 O_{10}	O_{12}	O_{14}	O_{16}

Despite the availability of a long series of measures that can help clarify the role of the event or treatment in question, the results of research conducted with the interrupted time series design sometimes can be ambiguous. Over the extended period of time covered by a time series design, many changes can occur in the setting in which the research takes place. It is usually a complex setting with many events and trends that might affect the behavior in question. The addition of a comparison group for which the same series of measures is available, but which is not exposed to the event/treatment whose effects are being studied, can be useful in clarifying the relationship between the treatment (X) and any change in the series of behavioral measures being used. That is what the multiple time series design has to offer.

A study by Rindfuss, Reed, and St. John (1978) provides an interesting example of the use of the multiple time series design. They tested the hypothesis that the 1954 U.S. Supreme Court decision declaring racially segregated schools unconstitutional (*Brown v. Board of Education*) would cause Southern whites to have fewer children. Using government statistics from the period, they were able to show that the existing pattern (time series) of monthly birth rates among white citizens of Southern states that had segregated schools and had once belonged to the Confederacy was upset for a period of approximately 1 year following the court decision (treatment) compared to before it.

What if there had been a coincidental downturn in the U.S. economy, or a war, or some other coincidental event that could have had a similar effect on fertility rates? The researchers looked at additional time series for states that had legally segregated schools in 1954 but hadn't been part of the Confederacy, and for states that had never had legally segregated schools. They found a smaller downturn in fertility rates in the former and none at all in the latter, despite the fact that all the states shared the same exposure to the national economy, the Soviet threat, and any number of other major events that might have influenced fertility rates. As we will see again in the next chapter, that is the major advantage of the multiple time series design over the (single) interrupted time series design.

None of our exemplar studies used the QT2 design, and it is very rarely used in psychological research. It is important, however, for what it can teach us about research methods and, potentially, about human behavior.

Quasi-Experimental Designs That Compare Among Groups (Between Subjects): QG Designs

QG1: The Nonequivalent Control Group Design. This design is diagrammed as follows.

$$
\begin{array}{llll}
\text{G1} & O_1 & X & O_3 \\
\text{-----} & \text{-----} & \text{-----} & \text{-----} \\
\text{G2} & O_2 & & O_4
\end{array}
$$

You can see that the nonequivalent control group design is identical to the pretest-posttest control group design (TG1) in every respect but one very important one: The two groups are not randomly constituted. This design is very useful in settings where the researcher is unable to reassign participants from intact groups, such as students in their normal classes, workers in their usual work groups or shifts, and the like. Unlike the pre-experimental static-group comparison design, a pretest is administered, making pretreatment measures available in this case.

Consider a case in which a psychologist working in industry might be called on to plan an evaluation of the effects of a new training program for workers doing a particular job. Perhaps the organization was dissatisfied with the workers' productivity, or there may have been problems with quality control. One part of the evaluation could consist of comparing the quantity or quality of the workers' output before they went through the new training program with their performance after the training. Another could involve a comparison with a second group of workers doing the same job, on a different shift in the same factory or at another of the same company's factories, in a different location. The performance of these other groups could be assessed at the same two points in time, but they would not have any exposure to the new training program in between.

Together, those comparisons would constitute the nonequivalent control group design. The measurements included in the design would make it possible to determine whether the two groups were similar in their performance at the onset of the study (O_1 vs. O_2), whether the group given the new training showed a change in performance (O_3 vs. O_1), and whether any change that might have occurred in the training group (G_1) was greater than the corresponding change in the no-training group (G_2, O_4 vs. O_2).

The nonequivalent control group design could be used in many such "program evaluation" or "policy evaluation" studies, in schools, government agencies, and the like. Because new programs are often introduced with considerable advance planning and notice, pretest measures usually can be obtained. Of course, they are often available in the records an organization keeps routinely to monitor its performance, though records that would seem to make a time series study possible might not be available for the particular groups to be evaluated. In addition, many large organizations, such as manufacturing corporations and school systems, have multiple units that can be compared if the new program is introduced in selected units and withheld or delayed in others. There may be several factories or shifts, schools or classes, or the like.

This design is not represented in our group of exemplar studies either, for reasons we'll discuss in detail in the next chapter. For now, you might recall the studies we've looked at already that used the static-group comparison design (PG1). Think about whether they could have been done using QG1 instead, and what difference that might have made. Where the QG1 design was possible, why might it not have been used?

QG2: The Separate-Sample Pretest-Posttest Design. This design can be diagrammed as follows.

G1	R	O_1	(X)
G2	R		X O_2

In some cases, there is only one group that can be studied because the event or treatment of interest is so widespread that none of the units to be studied can be prevented from being exposed to it. Perhaps all the students in a school system get a redesigned course in social science at the same time because of a state mandate, or all the workers who produce a certain automobile change to a new production technology at the same time, because design changes require it. To study the effects of the event in question, a researcher could simply assess the group's behavior before and after the group experienced it, using the one-group pretest-posttest design (PT2). Using that design, however, leaves open the possibility that the pretest might somehow alter the way that the treatment affects the behavior being studied.

In those cases, it may be possible to randomly divide in half the whole group that will be exposed to the treatment. If the pretest is administered to one of the two randomly constituted groups that result, and the posttest is administered to the other, the information about any possible change in behavior from before the treatment to after it can be obtained without risking a pretest sensitization effect. Because the groups are created by random assignment, there is no reason to believe that the pretest or posttest average for one would be any different than for the other.

I used this design myself once, to evaluate the method I was using to teach a course in organizational behavior to business students. I wanted to know if students' misconceptions about the ways in which organizations functioned were cleared up by what they learned in the course. Do you recall the discussion earlier in this chapter about the use of case studies in business education? That's where the misconceptions seem to have originated.

If I had pretested all of the students to document the existence of those misconceptions at the beginning of the course, then tested all of them with the same questions again at the end of the course, they might have been sensitized to change their answers even if their private beliefs hadn't changed. Their memory of their original answers also might have influenced their later ones. I therefore chose to pretest half, chosen at random. The other half got a different, irrelevant questionnaire at the same time, to disguise the purpose of the testing and allay suspicion. Then the other half got tested at the end of the course, with the same questionnaire the first half had filled out at the beginning. The first half got the same bogus questionnaire the other half had gotten at the beginning, again to make sure that the students weren't wondering why some were being tested and the others not. The results, at least the way I interpreted them, showed that the students benefited from the course.

● EVALUATING RESEARCH DESIGNS

By now, you should have a feeling for what research design means. It is the arrangement of the comparisons that are made in a research study to test the research hypothesis. That arrangement determines whether comparisons are made over time or among groups, whether behavior is assessed before exposure to treatments as well as after it, whether comparison groups are constituted by random assignment or by selection of pre-existing intact groups, and so on.

In this chapter, examples of three broad categories of research designs were considered. They are the pre-experimental, true experimental, and quasi-experimental designs. A notation system was introduced for use in representing variations of each of them. A few examples were given to make the diagrams come alive a little bit. The more familiar these diagrams become, the easier it is to see them as representing research instead of as a form of abstract art.

Table 6.6 catalogs all 13 research designs presented in this chapter. The next chapter will evaluate the vulnerability of each of those individual designs to threats to construct, internal, and external validity. That analysis will reveal general properties of each of the broad categories, as well as relationships among the various groups of validity criteria. What will emerge gradually is a picture of relative strengths and weaknesses rather than foolproof prescriptions for research design. When it's all over, you should be in a better position to plan new research of your own and, probably more important at this stage of your career, to evaluate published research.

TABLE 6.6   Designs for Psychological Research

Pre-Experimental Designs	
Over Time	*Among Groups*
One-shot case study: $\qquad$ X $\quad$ O	Static-group comparison design: $\qquad$ G_1 $\quad$ X $\quad$ O_1 $\qquad$ - - - - - - - - - - - - $\qquad$ G_2 $\qquad\quad$ O_2
One-group pretest-posttest design: $\qquad$ O_1 $\quad$ X $\quad$ O_2	Correlational design: $\qquad\qquad$ r_{xo}

True Experimental Designs	
Over Time	*Among Groups*
Equivalent time samples design: $\qquad$ X_1O_1 $\quad$ X_0O_2 $\quad$ X_1O_3 $\quad$ X_0O_4 $\quad$ etc.	Pretest-posttest control group design: $\qquad$ G_1 $\quad$ R $\quad$ O_1 $\quad$ X $\quad$ O_3 $\qquad$ G_2 $\quad$ R $\quad$ O_2 $\qquad\quad$ O_4
Equivalent materials samples design: $\quad$ $M_aX_1O_1$ $\quad$ $M_bX_0O_2$ $\quad$ $M_cX_1O_3$ $\quad$ $M_dX_0O_4$ $\quad$ etc.	Posttest-only control group design: $\qquad$ G_1 $\quad$ R $\quad$ X $\quad$ O_1 $\qquad$ G_2 $\quad$ R $\qquad\quad$ O_2
	Solomon four-group design: $\qquad$ G_1 $\quad$ R $\quad$ O_1 $\quad$ X $\quad$ O_3 $\qquad$ G_2 $\quad$ R $\quad$ O_2 $\qquad\quad$ O_4 $\qquad$ G_3 $\quad$ R $\qquad\quad$ X $\quad$ O_5 $\qquad$ G_4 $\quad$ R $\qquad\qquad\quad$ O_6

Quasi-Experimental Designs	
Over Time	*Among Groups*
Interrupted time series design: $\quad$ O_1 $\quad$ O_2 $\quad$ O_3 $\quad$ O_4 $\quad$ X $\quad$ O_5 $\quad$ O_6 $\quad$ O_7 $\quad$ O_8	Nonequivalent control group design: $\qquad$ G_1 $\quad$ O_1 $\quad$ X $\quad$ O_3 $\qquad$ - - - - - - - - - - - - - - $\qquad$ G_2 $\quad$ O_2 $\quad$ X $\quad$ O_4
Multiple time series design: $\quad$ G_1 $\quad$ O_1 $\quad$ O_3 $\quad$ O_5 $\quad$ O_7 $\quad$ X $\quad$ O_9 $\quad$ O_{11} $\quad$ O_{13} $\quad$ O_{15} $\quad$ - $\quad$ G_2 $\quad$ O_2 $\quad$ O_4 $\quad$ O_6 $\quad$ O_8 $\qquad$ O_{10} $\quad$ O_{12} $\quad$ O_{14} $\quad$ O_{16}	Separate-samples pretest-posttest design: $\qquad$ G_1 $\quad$ R $\quad$ O_1 $\quad$ (X) $\qquad$ G_2 $\quad$ R $\qquad\quad$ X $\quad$ O_2

Review Questions and Exercise

Review Questions

1. What are the elements of the notation system for representing the variety of designs for psychological research? What does each represent? How are they used?

2. What are the pre-experimental research designs, what are their defining characteristics, and under what conditions are they typically used?

3. What are the true experimental designs, what are their defining characteristics, and under what conditions are they typically used?

4. What are the quasi-experimental designs, what are their defining characteristics, and under what conditions are they typically used?

Exercise

Find articles in recent issues of psychological journals, diagram the research designs used in the studies they report, and categorize them as pre-, true, or quasi-experimental, and as comparisons among groups or across occasions. Try to find at least one study of each type, if you can. (Given the answers to the review questions for this chapter, in what journals would you be most likely to find examples of each type of research design?)

CHAPTER **7**

ARRANGING THE COMPARISONS III
Evaluating Research Designs

● A QUICK GUIDE TO CHAPTER 7: EVALUATING RESEARCH DESIGNS

The choice of a research design depends to some extent on the hypothesis the researcher needs to test. The effect of a lesion in a specific region of the brain would be difficult to study using anything other than a true experimental design. For the precise location of the lesion to be specified, the lesion would have to be created by the researcher. Naturally occurring lesions that result from accidental injury or disease rarely destroy neatly bounded brain structures, and very precise lesions can be created in laboratory animals. On the other hand, the effects of having one's home destroyed in a hurricane can hardly be studied in the laboratory. A hurricane cannot be created; victims and nonvictims can be chosen only by nature, not assigned randomly by researchers. A study of the effects of a hurricane therefore must be nonexperimental. And so on.

Some hypotheses, however, afford the researcher a choice of research designs. The effect of competing on one's home turf, compared to someone else's, can be studied in a true experiment. Pairs of college dormitory residents can be assigned randomly to play a game in one or the other's dorm room, or the hypothesis can be tested by comparing the won-lost records of college and professional sports teams between their home and road games.

Regardless of the researcher's degree of choice, the findings of a study must be evaluated against the strengths and weaknesses of the research design that was used. First, it is helpful to diagram the design in question and to categorize it as pre-experimental, true experimental, or quasi-experimental. Then, individual threats to internal, external, and construct validity can be evaluated. The process can and should be used prospectively in the planning of a study. It also needs to be used to evaluate the findings of completed studies.

Such an evaluation can form the basis for a summary judgment of the validity of research findings, after the fact, or for a comparison among alternative research designs before choosing one to test a particular hypothesis. It also can be used to pinpoint specific weaknesses in the conclusions a researcher might want to draw or already has drawn from his or her research results. In other words, an evaluation of the research design can be used to identify plausible rival hypotheses and specific limitations on the generalizability of the results.

The **Validity Scorecard** is a device that can be used to facilitate that evaluation. The list of threats to validity included in it has been abridged somewhat to expedite the process. If you keep in mind the longer list introduced earlier (see Chapter 7 Quick Guide A), you should see the logic behind that shorter list. Conceptual validity and statistical conclusion validity are not relevant to a researcher's choice of a research design. As has been pointed out earlier, the threats to validity can be organized into the categories of construct, internal, and external validity. Problems with individual threats often generalize to others within the same category.

Chapter 7 Quick Guide A:
Threats to the Validity of Research Findings

I. Threats to conceptual validity
    1. Unnecessary duplication
    2. Theoretical isolation
II. Threats to construct validity
  A. The independent variable
    a. Inadequate operationalization
      3. Lack of reliability of the independent variable
      4. Lack of representativeness of the independent variable
      5. Lack of impact of the independent variable
    b. Treatment artifacts
      6. Demand characteristics in the research setting
      7. Experimenter expectancy effects on the behavior being observed
      8. Pretest sensitization to the treatments
  B. The dependent variable
    a. Inadequate operationalization
      9. Lack of reliability of the dependent variable
      10. Lack of representativeness of the dependent variable
      11. Lack of sensitivity of the dependent variable
    b. Measurement artifacts
      12. Strategic responding by the research participants
      13. Linguistic/cultural bias in the dependent measure
III. Threats to internal validity
      14. Extraneous effects (history)
      15. Temporal effects (maturation)
      16. Group composition effects (selection)
      17. Interaction of temporal and group composition effects
      18. Selective sample attrition (mortality)
      19. Statistical regression effects (regression to the mean)
IV. Threats to external validity
      20. Nonrepresentative sampling
      21. Nonrepresentative research context
V. Threats to statistical conclusion validity
      22. Inappropriate use of statistical techniques
      23. Use of a statistical test lacking sufficient power
      24. Mistaking a trivial effect for support for the research hypothesis

The more you use the Validity Scorecard, the more familiar it will become. The more you evaluate each of the specific threats to validity, the more comfortable you will feel when you need to make the same evaluation again about a particular study. Evaluating research designs is a skill that can be developed only through repeated use. Knowing the threats to validity, their definitions, and how they are related to each other is a necessary foundation. Only through practice, however, can that information come alive and become truly useful.

Chapter 7 Quick Guide B:
Validity Scorecard for Pre-Experimental Research Designs

	PT1: One-Shot Case Study	PT2: One-Group Pretest-Posttest Design	PG1: Static-Group Comparison Design	PG2: Correlational Design
	X O	O_1 X O_2	G_1 X O_1 - - - - - - - - - - G_2 O_2	r_{xo}

Construct validity

Reactive arrangements

Pretest sensitization

Linguistic/cultural bias

Internal validity

Extraneous events

Temporal effects

Group composition effects

Temporal × group
 composition effects

Selective sample attrition

Statistical regression effects

External validity

Nonrepresentative sampling

Nonrepresentative research
 context

Chapter 7 Quick Guides B, C, and D are Validity Scorecards for the pre-experimental, true experimental, and quasi-experimental research designs, respectively. You can download blank forms of these tables from the Web site for this text so that you can use them more easily in practicing the analysis of research findings using published studies from the research literature.

● INTRODUCTION TO THE CHAPTER

This chapter will put together what you learned in the previous two, and add some to that. Our purpose is to understand how research design—the arrangement of the comparisons on which a test of a research hypothesis rests—affects the validity of research results. Decisions need to be made about who should be studied,

(text continued on p. 215)

Chapter 7 Quick Guide C: Validity Scorecard for True Experimental Research Designs

	TT1: Equivalent Time Samples Design	TT2: Equivalent Materials Samples Design	TG1: Pretest-Posttest Control Group Design	TG2: Posttest-Only Control Group Design	TG3: Solomon Four-Group Design
	X_1O_1 X_0O_2 X_1O_3 X_0O_4 etc.	$M_aX_1O_1$ $M_bX_0O_2$ $M_cX_1O_3$ $M_dX_0O_4$ etc.	G_1 R O_1 X O_3 G_2 R O_2 O_4	G_1 R X O_1 G_2 R O_2	G_1 R O_1 X O_3 G_2 R O_2 O_4 G_3 R X O_5 G_4 R O_6
Construct validity					
Reactive arrangements					
Pretest sensitization					
Linguistic/ cultural bias					
Internal validity					
Extraneous events					
Temporal effects					
Group composition effects					
Temporal × group composition effects					
Selective sample attrition					
Statistical regression effects					
External validity					
Nonrepresentative sampling					
Nonrepresentative research context					

Chapter 7 Quick Guide D: Validity Scorecard for Quasi-Experimental Research Designs

	QT1: Interrupted Time Series Design	QT2: Multiple Time Series Design	QG1: Nonequivalent Control Group Design	QG2: Separate-Sample Pretest-Posttest Design
	$O_1 O_2 O_3 O_4 X O_5 O_6 O_7 O_8$	$G_1 O_1 O_3 O_5 O_7 X O_9 O_{11} O_{13} O_{15}$ $G_2 O_2 O_4 O_6 O_8 \quad O_{10} O_{12} O_{14} O_{16}$	$G_1 O_1 X O_3$ $G_2 O_2 \quad O_4$	$G_1 R O_1 (X)$ $G_2 R \quad X O_2$
Construct validity				
Reactive arrangements				
Pretest sensitization				
Linguistic/cultural bias				
Internal validity				
Extraneous events				
Temporal effects				
Group composition effects				
Temporal × group composition effects				
Selective sample attrition				
Statistical regression effects				
External validity				
Nonrepresentative sampling				
Nonrepresentative research context				

when their behavior should be observed and how often, and what events or experiences participants should be exposed to and when. Those decisions play an important role in determining the conclusions that can be drawn from the observations that ultimately are made by the researcher.

If we didn't have so much else to do, we could examine every research design described in Chapter 6 for its vulnerability to every threat to construct, internal, and external validity defined in Chapters 3, 4, and 5. Of course, even those are just samples from the designs and validity issues we might have considered, not all of them, though they were selected because they are important ones. We will abbreviate our analysis somewhat to save time for other issues we must still consider.

Let's begin with a format. First, just three threats to construct validity will be considered, and issues concerning the measurement of the independent and dependent variables will be considered together. Besides saving time, this will focus our discussion on the ways research design, particularly, affects construct validity. Fortunately, it turns out that the effects of research design are fairly uniform in these cases. Then, all six threats to internal validity and both threats to external validity defined in Chapter 4 will be considered.

To keep our evaluation of these 11 threats to validity on track, we will keep score on a form called the Validity Scorecard (see Chapter 7 Quick Guides B-D). We will concentrate on the major validity issues associated with each research design, although you can learn even more if you score each of the 12 research designs, PT1 through QG2, for each of the 11 threats to validity.

In principle, you should be able to diagram any research study, planned or published, and evaluate it for its vulnerability to all of the threats to validity listed on the Validity Scorecard, along with the other threats we have considered and still others we will consider later on. The goal of this chapter is to help you build a foundation of understanding of the basic concepts we've considered so far that will enable you to go beyond the specific examples we are able to consider here.

Four symbols are used in filling out the Validity Scorecard. A "+" will be entered in a cell of the table if the design heading that column is clearly *not* vulnerable to the threat to validity listed on that row. In other words, + means "good"—the design is strong in this particular respect. A "−" (minus) will be entered if the design is clearly vulnerable to that threat. That is, − means there's a problem—the design has a weakness in this area. A "?" will be used to indicate that the design may be vulnerable or not, depending on the specific circumstances in which it may be used. In such a case, we need to explore those circumstances and their role in evaluating the design. Finally, the cell will be left blank to indicate that the threat to validity in question is not relevant to the design being evaluated, as when the **pretest sensitization** issue is considered for a design that does not include a pretest.

As you practice filling out the Validity Scorecard, if you're anything like me you'll want to work in pencil and have a good eraser handy. I'd like to tell you that you can learn to make these decisions quickly and with complete confidence, because that might make you feel better about all of this. In all honesty, however, I have always found those decisions to be difficult and to this day always have to rethink them every time I make them.

I don't feel bad about that indecision, and neither should you. This is not about having the right answer—it is about thinking through the right questions and having good reasons for your answers. If you change your mind later, that means you've been thinking, and that's good. Methodology is more like chess than checkers. It takes lots of thought, and there are no surefire right answers, but great satisfaction comes from playing the game well.

By the way, in addition to the abbreviated versions of the Validity Scorecard that you will find sprinkled throughout this chapter, at the very end of the chapter you'll find my (current) evaluations of all 12 research designs for all the major design-related threats to validity. They are shown in Tables 7.3, 7.6, 7.9, 7.12, 7.15, and 7.18 (at the ends of the sections discussing the types of research designs; see pp. 221, 226, 233, 241, 250, and 256). There, along with the +'s, −'s, and ?'s, I've included brief notes that reflect my reasons for evaluating each threat to validity as I did. You'll learn more if you do as much as you can by yourself before you look at what I did. Then you can compare your decisions with mine, including our reasons.

Most important, don't accept my reasons if you have some question about them. Talk it over with your instructor and your classmates, then make up your own mind. Learning to think for yourself is more important than learning what's in a book, even this one. Besides, by the time you read this, I might have changed my mind on one or two points, so that we might agree after all.

● EVALUATING PRE-EXPERIMENTAL RESEARCH DESIGNS

Pre-Experimental Designs That Compare Over Time (Within Subjects): PT Designs

PT1: The One-Shot Case Study. This design is diagrammed as follows.

In the typical case, the one-shot case study takes place over an extended period of time, long enough for a neurosis (O) to develop, or a new government policy (X) to filter down into people's everyday lives. In such a case, there are significant threats to internal validity. Did X cause the behavior that is observed, or was it some **extraneous event**, or some coincidental **temporal effect**? Was the economic boom of the mid-1990s caused by President Clinton's economic policies, or by the cost-cutting measures (downsizing, etc.) instituted by large corporations, or by the credit policies of the Federal Reserve Board, or by new agreements with international trading partners, or by some other event?

During a one-shot case study, a **temporal trend** can affect the behavior in question; that trend may have nothing to do with the causal construct. A young woman can go through puberty. An economic cycle can bottom out or recover. A fad can die out. Thus, a change in behavior that a researcher might want to attribute to a hypothesized cause might actually reflect a change in direction in a long-term cycle that started long before the time frame of a one-shot case study and that will continue long past it.

Group composition effects are not a matter of concern in a one-shot case study. Because only one group or one individual is being studied, no group comparison is required. It is possible, however, that the behavior that is observed reflects the intrinsic nature of that unit rather than the effects of any specific event or trend that happens to occur during the course of the study. Doomsday cultists may differ from other people in their tenacity in keeping the faith regardless of how outsiders might view the circumstances that test that faith. A psychoanalytic client might be constitutionally prone to anxiety, independent of whatever childhood experiences or repressed feelings an analyst might uncover and identify as the cause of the client's complaints. These types of factors limit the generalizability of the research results to other types of individuals, however. They don't produce group composition effects.

If a group is studied in a one-shot case study, **selective sample attrition** might cause a change in its behavior rather than the event identified as the cause by a researcher. If a historian or a psychologist looks far back in time, so that the records that remain are old and incomplete, the loss of participants may be very difficult to evaluate. A study of family values in 16th-century England may be based on diaries, books, and other written records that survive from that time. That is tantamount to studying only the educated aristocracy, because only they could have left such written evidence. The data are further limited to only those educated individuals who chose to leave samples of the behavior in question for posterity. Selective sample attrition could be said to have caused the remainder of the population to disappear, in effect, from the original complete sample of 16th-century English society. In such a case, the effect of attrition can be mistaken for the effect of the event (X) stated as the putative cause in the research hypothesis.

The fact that a one-shot case study is usually based on a single individual or group exposed to a unique set of personal or historical circumstances means that the generalizability or **external validity** of any causal relationship that might be

TABLE 7.1   Partial Validity Scorecard for One-Shot Case Study

	PT1: One-Shot Case Study
	:---:
	X O
Reactive arrangements	+
Extraneous events	−
Temporal effects	−
Selective sample attrition	−
Nonrepresentative sampling	−
Nonrepresentative research context	−

identified is often questionable. *Nonrepresentational sample (of units)* (as discussed above) and *nonrepresentative research context* are both troubling problems in interpreting the outcome of such a study.

The bright spot in this picture is in the area of **construct validity**. The researcher probably doesn't come into direct contact with the participants, and the behavior that is studied and the circumstances that influenced it are generally real, unadulterated, and significant. In other words, one-shot case studies are usually characterized by realistic measures and a lack of artifact-producing **reactivity**, even though the design doesn't require it.

A summary of the analysis of the one-shot case study can be found in Table 7.1.

PT2: The One-Group Pretest-Posttest Design. This design can be diagrammed as follows.

$$O_1 \quad X \quad O_2$$

The pretest that transforms the one-shot case study design into the one-group pretest-posttest design (O_1) brings two clear improvements in internal validity. *Selective sample attrition* is eliminated as a threat because the pretest allows the researcher to learn which participants, if any, were lost, and whether they were representative of the group as a whole. With respect to the representativeness of the sample, the pretest also reveals whether the behavior of the individual or group was intrinsic to it before the occurrence of the causal event in question. Think about Dement's study of REM rebound (1960, **E14**). Comparing subjects' REM sleep after deprivation with a baseline measure from before deprivation makes it clear that these weren't just people who dreamed a lot in the first place. The availability of a pretest measure in this design makes it clear whether the behavior observed had anything to do with X or was there all along.

Extraneous events and *temporal effects* remain threats to internal validity in spite of the pretest. This is especially true when a one-group pretest-posttest study covers a long period of time and takes place outside the controlled conditions of a laboratory, as such studies often do. There is the same opportunity as in the one-shot case study for events other than X to affect O_2, and for long-term trends to change the behavior in ways that cannot be determined from only two points of comparison, O_1 and O_2.

In the one-group pretest-posttest design, there is the potential, at least, for **statistical regression effects** to occur. In a study where participants were chosen from a much larger group because they had very extreme scores on the pretest, and where the same test was administered again as the posttest, any change between O_1 and O_2 would have to be evaluated against the expected regression toward the mean. A special education program for the very worst students in a school might show a false positive effect if the participants were chosen on the basis of a standardized achievement test and then retested with the same instrument afterward.

Potential problems with *construct validity* also are associated with the use this design, and they are both attributable to the addition of the pretest. If the pretest is administered directly to the participants, it would heighten their awareness that their response to the causal event being studied is under scrutiny. In that case, the pretest could be responsible for creating related *reactive arrangements* and producing related *pretest sensitization effects*. If a pre-X measure of the behavior in questions were obtained indirectly, or with a measure different from the post-X measure, those problems would be mitigated.

In a one-group pretest-posttest study, participants are more likely to be contacted directly than in a one-shot case study. Because of the necessity to administer the pretest, it is more likely that the researcher will intrude into participants' day-to-day lives. That requirement may limit the choice of participants and setting, thus increasing the likelihood of a *nonrepresentative sample of participants* and a *nonrepresentative research context*. The external validity or generalizability of the research results would be decreased to that degree.

Thus, in the case of the one-group pretest-posttest design, what little the pretest giveth, in the form of enhanced internal validity, it (possibly) taketh away, especially in an increased number of threats to construct and external validity. The large number of question marks among the grades for this design (see Table 7.2 for a quick summary) reflects the crucial role of research setting in determining its value. If pretest and posttest come from archival records or can be obtained otherwise from a distance, those question marks turn to pluses and the design far outstrips the one-shot case study in the quality of its evaluation of the research hypothesis. If participants are contacted directly and brought to a laboratory or other controlled setting, they turn to minuses, and much more may be lost by the use of the pretest than is gained. Table 7.3 shows a complete validity scorecard for pre-experimental research designs that compare over time (PT designs).

TABLE 7.2   Partial Validity Scorecard for One-Group Pretest-Posttest Design

	PT2: One-Group Pretest-Posttest Design $O_1 \ X \ O_2$
Reactive arrangements	?
Pretest sensitization	?
Extraneous events	–
Temporal effects	–
Selective sample attrition	+
Statistical regression effects	?
Nonrepresentative sampling	?
Nonrepresentative research context	?

Pre-Experimental Designs That Compare Among Groups (Between Subjects): PG Designs

PG1: The Static-Group Comparison Design. This design can be diagrammed as follows.

$$
\begin{array}{ccc}
G_1 & X & O_1 \\
\hline
G_2 & & O_2
\end{array}
$$

An alternative approach to eliminating some of the threats to the internal validity of research that can arise in a one-shot case study is to add a comparison group rather than a pretest. This would be another group of participants whose experiences are roughly similar to those who are exposed to X (except for X, of course). It could be a second classroom, or church, or factory, whose post-X behavior can be used to rule out *extraneous events* as an alternative explanation for that behavior.

If the two groups can also be expected to be subject to the same long-term trends or cyclical changes in the behavior being studied, this design may also be free from the threat of *temporal effects* if their relevant experiences are comparable. It is possible in some cases that there also are separate maturational trends that affect the two groups differently. In that case, the design does suffer from the additional problem of a possible **interaction of temporal and group composition effects**. In Festinger et al.'s study of a doomsday cult (1956, **E11**), for example,

TABLE 7.3   Validity Scorecard for Pre-Experimental Research Designs, PT Variety

	PT1: One-Shot Case Study X O	PT2: One-Group Pretest-Posttest Design O_1 X O_2
Construct validity		
Reactive arrangements	+ behavior evaluated after the fact of whatever its cause	? depends on whether the behavioral measure is administered directly by researcher to participants
Pretest sensitization	+ no pretest	? depends on whether the pretest is administered directly to participants
Linguistic/cultural bias	+ case studies usually involve intensive study of behavior from many different angles	? depends on nature of O; if administered in verbal form, bias can be a problem
Internal validity		
Extraneous events	– too many pre-X events that might have influenced O to draw a causal inference with confidence	– time span and naturalistic setting for X and O make extraneous events difficult to account for
Temporal effects	– too long a pre-X time span to rule out temporal trends as alternative explanation for O	– the longer the O_1 – O_2 interval, the more difficult it is to account for temporal trends that could cloud the effects of X
Group composition effects	+ one group	+ one group
Temporal × group composition effects	+ one group	+ one group
Selective sample attrition	– difficult to tell whether the historical record is preserved in an unbiased form	+ retest allows identification of lost participants and evaluation of their representativeness
Statistical regression effects	? depends on whether participants represent an extreme group (or an extreme economic or political cycle)	? if participants are extreme scorers on O at pretest, regression effects need to be taken into account in interpreting results
External validity		
Nonrepresentative sampling	– case studies typically lack generalizability, either broadly or to other cases	? depends on the method for sampling participants, but the researcher rarely has much discretion in the use of this design
Nonrepresentative research context	– case studies typically represent unique combinations of circumstances	? depends on how representative the research context in question is, versus contexts to which results might be applied

some cult members might have chosen to wait alone because they were already losing their faith gradually. Those who waited as a group might not.

Because participants are not randomly assigned to groups in this design, this nonequivalent comparison group does not rule out *group composition effects* or *selective sample attrition*. This design has two disadvantages compared to the one-group pretest posttest design. Zajonc and Markus (1975) probably were very careful to take into account differences between their participants other than family size and birth order (**E16**), but it is still possible that such differences did exist and that they were partly responsible for the differences in IQ that were observed, making them seem larger or smaller than they really were. In Triplett's (1897) comparison of performance in different kinds of bicycle races (**E3**), perhaps the racers who had less success in head-to-head competition (nerves?) gradually dropped out of those competitions, leaving behind only those best suited for that type of race.

Because there is no pretest, however, there is no threat from *statistical regression effects* or, switching now from internal validity to construct validity, from *pretest sensitization effects*. As in the other pre-experimental designs, the vulnerability of the research findings to misinterpretation because of the effects of *reactive arrangements* depends on whether or not subjects are contacted directly.

The treatment X could be an event that occurs in the natural course of everyday life, a classroom lesson, an office memo, or an interest rate increase. The participants' behavior could be measured by using data that are collected in a routine manner, such as sales figures, periodic grade reports, or employee turnover. In such cases, participants are unlikely to be aware of any unusual interest in their behavior, or to respond to the events of interest to the researcher in a different way than they ordinarily would.

On the other hand, participants could be taken out of their normal routines and questioned in an obtrusive manner. Then, reactive arrangements could be created that would make them more likely to form their own hypotheses to explain what is happening, and to respond to **demand characteristics**. Those who cause the nonroutine events to occur and who question participants about them could communicate their expectations about the outcome and thus contaminate the treatments with *experimenter expectancy effects*.

The *generalizability* of results from a static-group comparison study also depends on how the study is carried out. If the group involved and the conditions under which members are studied are representative of the people and contexts to which the results need to be generalized, or if a theory is being tested in one of many possible ways, then *external validity* is not a problem. Generalizing from one specific group to a different one, or one particular context to a different one, is problematic in this case, as it is in every other.

Although the conclusions stated above need to be qualified, as they are above, it should be said that this design is used most often at a distance and in applied re-

TABLE 7.4   Partial Validity Scorecard for Static-Group Comparison Design

	PG1: Static-Group Comparison Design G_1 X O_1 - - - - - - - - - G_2 O_2
Reactive arrangements	?
Extraneous events	?
Temporal effects	?
Group composition effects	–
Temporal mul group composition effects	–
Selective sample attrition	–
Nonrepresentative sampling	?
Nonrepresentative research context	?

search. As a consequence, reactive arrangements and generalizability of research results are more likely in practice to not threaten the validity of the results of static-group comparison studies than to be problematic in those respects. See Table 7.4 for a brief review of the properties of this design.

PG2: The Correlational Design. This very simple design can be diagrammed as follows.

$$r_{xo}$$

The correlational study, as we're using the term here, amounts to an expansion of the static-group comparison design by adding a very large number of comparison groups. For statistical reasons (see below), researchers sample as many units as they can, determining a value for the independent variable and a value for the dependent variable for each one. The units might be groups, individuals, points in time, places, or others.

There is no question that correlational studies suffer from serious weaknesses in internal validity. The calculation of a correlation coefficient (r_{xo}) based on values for the independent and dependent variables may indicate that there is a relationship between the two, meaning that they covary to a substantial degree. That does not mean, however, that the variations in the behavioral measure were caused by the variations in the independent variable.

Let's return to the hypothetical example where a large number of elementary school students are questioned to determine how violent a diet of television programs each watches (X), and observed to determine how aggressive each is when playing with his or her classmates (O). One might find that students who watched more violent programs behaved more aggressively. That would be reflected in a substantial positive correlation between the two sets of measurements. It is possible, though, that some experience other than watching violence on television is responsible for each individual's level of aggressive behavior and for that individual's choice of TV programs. It could be an *extraneous event* such as observing violence in the home. Given a sufficient interval between assessments of X and O, it could be a maturational trend such as the unfolding of a genetically uninhibited temperament—a *temporal effect*. In this case, the term **third-variable cause** (a variable besides X and O) is often used rather than the more general terms *alternative explanation*, *rival hypothesis*, or *threat to internal validity*.

It is also possible that causation is reversed from the expected direction. The designation of one of the variables as the independent variable and one as the dependent variable is arbitrary compared to a true experiment, in which the independent variable is manipulated by the researcher. People may watch violent TV programs because they behave aggressively rather than the other way around. TV programs may validate their choice of activities by showing others who do the same, or people may watch to learn more about how to behave violently. These are just two examples. This design is extremely weak in its resistance to five of the six threats to internal validity (not to statistical regression effects). It makes any causal inference drawn from research results very tenuous indeed, but it deserves discussion for a number of reasons.

First, it is in very common use. It is used in many cases because available data make it easy to use. In some of those cases, researchers and their readers are unaware of the problems inherent in the causal inferences drawn from observed correlations. In others, more careful researchers use the results of correlational studies to formulate new hypotheses they can test later using more rigorous research designs, rather than to test hypotheses about cause and effect directly.

A second reason to understand the correlational design is that it can be used as the foundation for other designs that permit more certain causal inferences to be drawn from results. Much of the next chapter is devoted to a consideration of some of the ways in which correlational research can be improved to better understand cause and effect.

Another relatively positive reason is that correlational research, as it is used most typically, avoids problems with construct validity and external validity. It is usually conducted as hands-off research that does not create *reactive arrangements*. It does not usually involve repeated administrations of a behavioral measure, thus avoiding *pretest sensitization*. It usually uses very realistic measurements of behavior and its possible causes as well. Correlational research thus

TABLE 7.5 Partial Validity Scorecard for Correlational Design

	PG2: Correlational Design r_{xo}
Reactive arrangements	+
Pretest sensitization	+
Extraneous events	–
Temporal effects	–
Statistical regression effects	+
Nonrepresentative sampling	+
Nonrepresentative research context	+

avoids the problem of *nonrepresentative research context*. It also permits the use of large, carefully chosen samples, thus avoiding the threat of *nonrepresentative sample of participants*. Finally, because for statistical reasons (see Chapter 10) correlational research must consider a wide range of variations on both independent and dependent variables (predictor and criterion, respectively), it is clearly free from the threat of *statistical regression effects*.

It also needs to be pointed out here that there are rare cases where the correlational design can be used without fear of the serious limitations discussed above. Haier et al.'s (1992) study of intelligence and brain efficiency (**E23**) is a good example. In such a carefully controlled laboratory study (very different from most correlational studies in that respect), it is difficult to imagine how extraneous events or temporal effects could have produced the differences in GMR that were observed between more and less intelligent subjects. It is possible that the high- and low-intelligence groups differed in some other crucial respect that affected how hard their brains worked while they played Tetris, but it doesn't seem plausible that group composition effects caused the result, in the absence of a specific suggestion of what that might have been. Basic processes of brain function probably don't vary as much across individuals or settings as some other behaviors we might mention. Such exceptions are not reflected, however, in the brief summary shown in Table 7.5. The two pre-experimental research designs are compared in Table 7.6.

EVALUATING TRUE EXPERIMENTAL RESEARCH DESIGNS ●

It is easy to tell at a glance from the Validity Scorecard (see Table 7.9, p. 233, and Table 7.12, p. 241) that all the true experimental designs achieve perfect or nearly

TABLE 7.6   Validity Scorecard for Pre-Experimental Research Designs, PG Variety

	PG1: Static-Group Comparison Design G_1 X O_1 - - - - - - - - - G_2 X O_2	PG2: Correlational Design r_{XO}
Construct validity		
Reactive arrangements	? depends on whether researcher and participants are in direct contact with one another	+ usually minimizes participants' awareness of purpose of research
Pretest sensitization	+ no pretest	+ data for X and O usually collected simultaneously or in a manner that disguises connection between the two
Linguistic/cultural bias	? depends on whether O is a verbal measure and, if so, on its nature	? depends on whether measures of X and O are verbal and, if so, on their nature
Internal validity		
Extraneous events	? depends on whether comparison group is exposed to same non-X events	– possible third-variable cause is always a matter for concern
Temporal effects	? subject to same limitations as extraneous events; comparability of groups' experiences key factor	? if X is measured far in advance of O, temporal trends can constitute an alternative influence on O
Group composition effects	– intact groups, not equivalent	– individuals who differ on X may differ on other variables that could influence O
Temporal × group composition effects	– even if matched at outset, groups could be influenced by unequal temporal trends	– same as PG-1 if a problematic interval passes between X and O
Selective sample attrition	– in natural settings in which this design typically is used, can't evaluate attrition or its effects on $O_1 - O_2$ comparison	? again, if X collected before O, loss of data could cause problem for evaluating relationship between X and O
Statistical regression effects	+ no pretest on which to base selection of participants with extreme standing on O	+ entire range of scores considered
External validity		
Nonrepresentative sampling	? generalization beyond groups studied in research problematic, especially with intact groups of unknown characteristics	? no problem when research based on data from large, representative samples such as census data or political polls
Nonrepresentative research context	? generalization across all settings or to different settings more problematic than to same type of groups studied in research	? no problem if based on realistic data (vs. questionnaire studies where measures tap selected aspects of variables involved)

perfect records for their resistance to threats to internal validity. The discussion therefore will just highlight the reasons for that perfection (this is a case where a lack of attention is a good sign) and deal more extensively with the questions of construct validity and external validity. All the true experimental designs are defined by the control the researcher exercises over the exposure of participants to the events (X) hypothesized to influence their behavior (O).

The researcher's ability to randomize the timing of those events, in the case of the TT designs, or the assignment of participants to different treatment conditions, in the case of the TG designs, is an important aspect of that control. The determination of exactly what participants will be required to do, the isolation of treatments and measures from unwanted interference, and the compression of more lengthy experiences in our daily lives into brief, absorbing laboratory scenarios are others. These features are what make the true experiments what they are, for better and for worse.

True Experimental Designs That Compare Over Time (Within Subjects): TT Designs

TT1: The Equivalent Time Samples Design. This design can be diagrammed as follows.

$$X_1O_1 \quad X_0O_2 \quad X_1O_3 \quad X_0O_4 \quad \text{etc.}$$

Because the same participants are exposed to all the treatments (here, X_1 and X_0), there is no problem with *group composition effects*, Because treatments are usually repeated in a randomized sequence, and presented in an isolated laboratory setting, *extraneous events* are not a threat to interfere with treatments. The same extraneous events are very unlikely to recur coincidentally in the same random sequence as the treatments. It is similarly very unlikely that *temporal effects* will match a random cycle of different treatment conditions, especially since most experimental research is conducted in brief sessions in a laboratory.

Sample attrition is unlikely in the controlled conditions of a psychological laboratory, or within the brief time frame of most experiments. If it did occur, the researcher could identify which participants were lost and determine from their early results how their loss affected the results. This would eliminate *selective sample attrition* as an alternative explanation for the research results. Finally, even if the participants in an equivalent time samples study were selected on the basis of extreme scores in the behavioral measure being used, the repetition of the treatment-measure combinations would rule out *statistical regression effects* as a problem for causal inference from the research results.

Consider Pavlov's research on the "conditioned reflex" (1927, **E20**). Given the degree of control researchers could exercise over the stimuli their canine subjects

---

Box 7.1 | *THINKING ABOUT RESEARCH*

Do Cars Kill People, or Is It the Drivers?

In the 1970s, consumer advocate Ralph Nader alerted Americans to the apparent dangers of driving the Corvair automobile. National Highway Transportation Safety Board (NHTSB) statistics showed that Corvairs were more likely to roll over than other makes of cars, per mile driven.

General Motors had introduced the Corvair during the 1960s to cater to car buyers who wanted superior handling. It was supposed to be a move away from conventional American cars like Buicks and Dodges, toward the style of European sports sedans of the period (see Figure 7.1). It was a small, light, rear-engine design, with a special type of rear suspension that allowed it to corner better at high speeds.

What research design would correspond to the comparison Nader made between rollover rates for the Corvair versus other makes? What problems would that design cause in determining whether the design of the Corvair was responsible for its rate of rollover crashes being higher? Was this sporty car driven by the same types of drivers as Buicks and Dodges? Was it driven the same way?

How do these questions affect Nader's interpretation of the results of the NHTSB's "research?" Was he right about the Corvair's radical design being responsible for its greater likelihood of being involved in rollover accidents? Or did he overlook some important threats to the validity of his "findings" based on that research? If so, what are they? Can you think of any besides the ones suggested in the previous paragraph?

---

were exposed to, and over when that exposure occurred, how could anything other than the overlapping presentation of the CS and US account for the emergence of the CR?

The same control over who gets what and when that allows us to paint such a pretty picture of the internal validity of the results of equivalent time samples research can prove its undoing when it comes to construct validity and, especially, external validity. Participants' responses to each of the treatments being compared in such a study may be affected by their exposure to the other treatments, especially if human participants are studied. If so, their experiences may be quite different from those intended by the researcher, and they may change continuously as the study goes along, creating a complex and virulent form of *pretest sensitization*, If the researcher and the participants interact directly throughout the course of the study, extremely *reactive arrangements* will be created. One of the best-known examples of the use of the equivalent time samples design illustrates these problems dramatically. Workers at a telephone equipment factory became participants in a series of experiments usually referred to as the Hawthorne studies. They were removed from their normal work stations to a controlled environment elsewhere

Figure 7.1. A print ad for the Corvair automobile. Notice that the ad emphasizes the car's sporty nature and encourages drivers to push its special handling capabilities to their limits.

on the factory grounds, where they did their usual assembly and wiring jobs while researchers varied such conditions as lighting and the timing of rest breaks.

As the study progressed, the researchers noticed a number of anomalous results. When lighting conditions were improved, workers' productivity increased, as expected. But when conditions were later changed for the worse, productivity unexpectedly increased again. Similar unexpected changes occurred in response to other assumedly negative variations in other aspects of the working conditions.

There is some controversy to this day over how to interpret these results, which is what one would expect when there are problems with a research design. It seems likely, however, that the research participants became keenly aware that their bosses were interested in how hard they were working in response to the conditions being created in their new "laboratory" surroundings, and that their awareness played an important role in determining how they responded.

Laboratory conditions foster reactivity in general. Exposing participants to repeated changes in the laboratory may make it obvious that conditions are being manipulated for the purpose of observing their effects on participants' behavior. This can magnify the problem of reactive arrangements far beyond what might occur when participants are exposed to a single treatment.

When Broverman et al. (1972) asked their research participants to describe the average male and average female (**E5**), choosing from a list of stereotypic terms, could the participants have responded without first forming their own hypotheses about the purposes of the research?

One way of avoiding these problems of interference and reactivity is by using nonhuman participants. This design is probably used more often, in practice, with rats and pigeons than with people, especially adult, intelligent people (children and adults with limited cognitive capacities, such as institutionalized developmentally disabled adults, pose less of a reactivity problem).

Even if researchers' expectancies can affect the behavior of nonhuman participants, as well as humans, they are probably less likely to do so. It also seems pretty certain that rats and pigeons don't feel the same curiosity or anxiety about researchers' motives for studying their behavior as humans do. Even nonhuman participants, however, can receive unintentional messages from researchers, as Clever Hans did from his trainer. More credit should be given to Pavlov for the ingenious laboratory setup that blocked visual contact between researcher and dog.

Of course, the use of nonhuman participants raises serious questions about a *nonrepresentative sample of participants* if the results are to be generalized to humans, as they almost always are. Equivalent time samples studies, whether conducted with nonhuman subjects or human participants, also often raise questions about a *nonrepresentative research context*.

Because the researcher must exercise such precise control over the presentation of treatments and administration of behavioral measures, the use of this design is virtually restricted to laboratory settings where the physical environment, the tasks, and the duration of the participants' experiences are likely to differ materially from the real-life context to which the results need to be generalized. How

TABLE 7.7 Partial Validity Scorecard for Equivalent Time Samples Design

	TT1: Equivalent Time Samples Design $X_1O_1 \ X_0O_2 \ X_1O_3 \ X_0O_4$ etc.
Reactive arrangements	?
Pretest sensitization	?
Internal validity	+
Nonrepresentative sampling	?
Nonrepresentative research context	?

certain can we be that the differences in cerebral hemisphere functioning observed by Gazzaniga (1967, **E21**) are found in normal people engaged in their everyday activities?

See Table 7.7 for a brief summary of the validity evaluation for the equivalent time samples design.

TT2: The Equivalent Materials Samples Design. This design can be diagrammed as follows.

$$M_a X_1 O_1 \quad M_b X_0 O_2 \quad M_c X_1 O_3 \quad M_d X_0 O_4 \quad \text{etc.}$$

Equivalent materials samples research comes very close to being the methodological twin of equivalent time samples research. The only addition is the materials sampling feature, the random assignment of different task materials to the sample of treatment-observation pairings used in an equivalent time samples study. This confers at least two advantages, one each in the areas of construct and external validity.

First, though, let's review briefly—because of the similarities to the previous design—the status of the six threats to internal validity for this design. *Group composition effects* and the *interaction of group composition and temporal effects* are ruled out by making the comparisons between treatments within a single group of participants. *Extraneous events* are ruled out as alternative explanations because of the implausibility of coincidental occurrence with randomly scheduled treatment conditions. *Temporal effects* would similarly require implausible coordination with random alternations of treatment conditions to threaten internal validity. *Selective sample attrition* is unlikely because of the brevity and the laboratory setting, and it would be able to be detected and its effects determined because the researcher can monitor the loss of participants and consult the measures of their be-

TABLE 7.8 Partial Validity Scorecard for Equivalent Materials Samples Design

	TT2: Equivalent Materials Samples Design $M_aX_1O_1 \quad M_bX_0O_2 \quad M_cX_1O_3 \quad M_dX_0O_4$ etc.
Reactive arrangements	?
Pretest sensitization	?
Internal Validity	+
Nonrepresentative sampling	?
Nonrepresentative research context	+

havior that were taken prior to their loss. *Statistical regression effects* would not occur because a series of repeated measures of treatment effects would be made.

Reactive arrangements would pose the same kinds of problems for this design as for the equivalent time samples design. Compared to that case, however, the equivalent materials samples design is more likely to be used with normal human subjects, where reactivity is an important issue, than with animal or special adult populations where it is not. Of course, *experimenter expectancy effects* can occur in either case.

At the same time, *pretest sensitization effects* are less likely to cloud the interpretation of results from an equivalent materials samples study (the first advantage). The alternation of materials makes it more difficult for participants to develop patterns of strategic responding. Participants in the Cherulnik et al. (1981) study of impressions of high and low Machs (**E17**) might have been shown just one example of each type, the two being alternated repeatedly. Even with a random sequence, participants might have become curious about what the two photos represented. That might have made it more likely for them to develop response strategies that could compromise the scientific goals of the study.

The sampling of materials gives this design a second advantage over the equivalent time samples design, the lower likelihood of a *nonrepresentative research context*. It makes it possible for researchers to determine the generality of participants' responses to the treatments across varied task materials. The use of more tasks, more stimuli, or more varied experiences makes any observed effect more likely to generalize beyond the specifics of a given study. Finally, although this design is subject to the same threat from a *nonrepresentative sample of participants*, it is less likely to require tenuous generalizations from results with nonhuman subjects to presumably parallel human behaviors.

All of this is summarized in Table 7.8. Table 7.9 compares the true experimental research designs.

TABLE 7.9 Validity Scorecard for True Experimental Research Designs, TT Variety

	TT1: Equivalent Time Samples Design $X_1O_1 \ X_0O_2 \ X_1O_3 \ X_0O_4$ etc.	TT2: Equivalent Materials Sample Design $M_aX_1O_1 \ M_bX_0O_2 \ M_cX_1O_3 \ M_dX_0O_4$ etc.
Construct validity		
Reactive arrangements	? if participants are humans and the setting is a laboratory, awareness will be high and contact with experimenter direct	? same as for TT1; as in exemplar study in text, if treatments are subtle, hypothesis may be disguised
Pretest sensitization	? with human participants, each O serves as pretest for following X, raising participants' awareness	? when participants are nonhuman species, TT1 and TT2 may be safe from reactivity and pretest sensitization threats
Linguistic/cultural bias	? depends on nature of participants and O; with humans and verbal measure, must be aware of possible bias	? see TT1
Internal validity		
Extraneous events	+ random sequence of treatments rules out coincidental events	+ see TT1
Temporal effects	+ random sequencing of treatments rules out coincidental temporal trends	+ see TT1
Group composition effects	+ within-group comparison	+ within-group comparison
Temporal × group composition effects	+ see temporal effects and group composition effects	+ see TT1
Selective sample attrition	+ repeated administration of O allows selective attrition to be detected and the results to be adjusted accordingly	+ see TT1
Statistical regression effects	+ even if group selected for extreme scores on O, repeated assessment of O will eliminate regression effects	+ see TT1
External validity		
Nonrepresentative sampling	? if participants are nonhumans or nonrandom sample of humans, generalizability might be limited	? see TT1
Nonrepresentative research context	? in animal experiments, and in laboratory, tasks and settings are often artificial, making generalizability problematic	+ materials samples provide opportunity to increase generalizability of findings to wider range of contexts

True Experimental Designs That Compare Among Groups (Between Subjects): TG Designs

TG1: The Pretest-Posttest Control Group Design. This design can be diagrammed as below.

$$
\begin{array}{llllll}
G_1 & R & O_1 & X & O_3 \\
G_2 & R & O_2 & & O_4
\end{array}
$$

In all three true experimental designs that compare across groups, the use of random assignment creates equivalent groups. This "controls for" *group composition effects*. That is, differences in behavior between the groups cannot be attributed to pre-existing differences between the participants in those (equivalent) groups. As is also true for all other true experimental designs, the question isn't so much determining whether there are problems with internal validity as understanding why there are not.

In most cases, the pretest-posttest control group design is used to conduct research in the laboratory, where participants' experiences are compressed into a fairly brief time frame. In that setting, a researcher has sufficient control over the participants' experiences to prevent the occurrence of any *extraneous events*. Unless some unexpected disturbance or equipment malfunction affects the participants in one group and not the other(s), and unless such an unforeseen event influences the behavior that is being studied, extraneous events pose no threat to internal validity.

Even if such extraneous events were to occur, the researcher would be in a good position to know that, and could repeat the affected treatment with a fresh sample to replace the contaminated group. Such an exception is made all the less likely in the typical case, in which experiments of this type test one participant at a time, so that the impact on the overall comparison between groups would be very small even if the extraneous event went undetected. Of course, if it were detected the researcher could simply discard the observations of a single participant made during such an atypical session to eliminate the problem completely.

Laboratory experiments in psychology usually are so brief that *temporal effects* of the sort discussed in connection with pre-experimental designs—economic cycles or maturational processes in human development—are not plausible threats to valid causal inference from the research results. There are briefer temporal effects, however, that might need to be accounted for. Fatigue is an example we considered in Chapter 5. If participants are required to perform difficult or repetitive tasks, even during a relatively brief laboratory experiment, their behavior might change as a result of fatigue. That change could be greater in one group than another, if that group were given more difficult problems to solve, or given discouraging instructions, or for some similar reason. If so, that change could be mistaken for the effect of a treatment, or could cover up the effect of a treatment, thus causing an invalid causal inference to be drawn from the research results. As the "+" rating on the Validity Scorecard indicates, this sort of problematic temporal effect reflects not an inherent weakness in the pretest-posttest control group design but an unlikely aberration. Still, it is a potential problem to which researchers need to be alert.

When one considers the *interaction of temporal and group composition effects*, brief intrasession temporal effects such as fatigue can be safely ignored. In the case of this threat, the only temporal effects that need to be considered are long-term maturational processes that can cause a group composition difference after the fact of the initial random assignment of participants to groups. Only that kind of temporal effect could influence the behavioral tendencies of participants unequally across the groups being compared. That does not seem a realistic possibility in most implementations of a pretest-posttest control group study.

Selective sample attrition is not a threat to the validity of causal inference from the results of a pretest-posttest control group study. Laboratory experiments typically are brief, and participants usually don't have much opportunity to wander off. If there is any attrition, the pretest makes it possible to evaluate whether the participants who are lost during the course of the study are atypical of their group as a whole. Were that to be the case, it would be possible to adjust the comparison between the groups statistically to eliminate any possible effects of sample attrition.

Again, however, this design would be used most often in a laboratory setting where attrition is unlikely because of the control the researcher is able to exercise and because of the brevity of the experiment itself. A rare exception is when participants fail to provide the required information by leaving a questionnaire or rating scale blank or responding in a way that indicates either a failure to follow directions or a lack of attention. A participant may rate every stimulus alike, for example. In such a case, it may be preferable to discard a subject's data so that "attrition" (leaving in spirit if not in body) doesn't complicate the interpretation of the comparison that is made between the groups in the experiment.

Finally, for the issue of internal validity, *statistical regression effects* are ruled out as a rival hypothesis for the results of a pretest-posttest control group study by the use of an equivalent (randomly assigned) comparison group. In most cases, this design is used with representative groups of participants. Even if participants were chosen because they did achieve extreme scores on the pretest, they would then be assigned randomly to the groups. This would ensure that any regression toward the mean would affect pretest-posttest differences in both groups equally and not confuse the comparison between the groups.

It is interesting that the lone example of a TG1 design among our exemplar studies is so atypical because it was conducted outside the laboratory over an extended period of time. Rosenthal and Jacobson's (1966) research on teacher expectancies (**E15**) ruled out *group composition effects*, *temporal effects*, any *interaction between temporal and group composition effects*, and *statistical regression* *effects* by the use of random assignment of participants to groups. The fact that bloomers and nonbloomers were from the same community, and in the same classes, with the same teachers, ruled out most *extraneous events*. Even over a period of several months, schools generally keep good track of which students stay and which leave, and the researcher had the test scores of both, thus ruling out effects of *selective sample attrition*.

The issue of *construct validity*, on the other hand, can be very troublesome for this and other true experimental designs that compare across groups. The reasons are the same ones that make internal validity so minor a concern in interpreting the results of research that utilizes these designs. They are the laboratory setting, random assignment to groups, and brevity of duration. Laboratory experiments, in particular, pose the greatest risk of creating *reactive arrangements* that arouse participants' curiosity about the research hypothesis and about their role in the research enterprise. The participants may be encouraged by the resulting feelings of self-consciousness to "cooperate" with the researcher, or they may be motivated to make themselves look good. In either case, the treatments as they experience and respond to them can be different from those intended by the researcher, tainted by *demand characteristics*.

Direct contact between researcher and participant in the laboratory makes it possible for any information the researcher has about the research hypothesis to be transmitted unintentionally to participants, causing *experimenter expectancy effects*. In the case of the pretest-posttest control group design, there is the additional problem of possible *pretest sensitization*. In a reactive laboratory setting, the pretest is especially likely to influence participants' perceptions of and responses to the treatment that follows, and to become an extraneous influence on their responses to the posttest.

Laboratory researchers have attempted to deal with these threats to construct validity in a number of ways. They have concocted elaborate "cover stories" to provide participants with a rationale for their experiences that leads them away from the actual research hypothesis. That is believed to make participants respond more spontaneously to the treatments and to the behavioral measures that are administered. Some methodologists have been skeptical about the effectiveness of these deceptions. They have wondered aloud whether researchers are fooling their participants or themselves, and even whether they have engendered a culture of disbelief among prospective research participants. This is especially problematic on the college campuses where most psychological laboratories are located and where stories about participation in psychological research to fulfill a requirement of the introductory psychology course spreads quickly through the student population. I can recall an instance in which one of our research participants was a reporter for the campus newspaper who wrote a very imaginative story about his participation that could have frightened other students about our study and other research in our department.

The use of nonhuman research participants is another way to deal with the reactivity problem. Although nonhuman subjects may be influenced by experimenters' expectancies, it is probably easier to make sure that they don't, and they probably don't develop the same self-consciousness as human participants, nor the associated desires to please the researcher or to protect their fragile self-concepts.

When human participants must be studied, because the behavior in question is difficult to approximate in other species, an effective way to minimize reactivity is to move the experiment outside the laboratory. Psychological experiments have been conducted in public places, including classrooms, bus stations, city sidewalks, and subway trains. In the **field**, as nonlaboratory settings are called, people are unaware that the situations they encounter may have been created by a researcher to evaluate their responses, or that those responses are being observed by researchers. When these **field studies** or field experiments are feasible, as in the case of Rosenthal and Jacobson's study (**E15**), they provide nonreactive alternatives to the laboratory experiment.

In the laboratory, *experimenter expectancy effects* can be minimized either by minimizing the direct contact between participant and researcher or by minimizing the researcher's knowledge about the research hypothesis. The former alternative has been made a good deal easier to achieve by recent advances in computer technology. Instructions and even tasks can be presented to participants on a computer screen. Participants can respond on the keyboard, and their responses and even information such as how long it takes them to respond can be recorded automatically for later retrieval by the researcher.

It is more difficult to keep researchers "blind" to the research hypotheses. If participants can form their own hypotheses, researchers are in a much better position to do so by virtue of their greater sophistication about psychology and the information they acquire from observing the behavior of numerous participants. Using a large number of researchers to avoid consistent influence by a single hypothesis would at least make the problem of experimenter expectancy effects less acute. Comparing the data collected by those researchers can clarify the issue even further by revealing whether the interaction between a particular researcher and research participants can influence the outcome.

External validity also can be a serious problem with the use of this and other true experimental research designs. The pool of potential participants that is handiest to the psychological laboratory is a roomful of rats, pigeons, or introductory psychology students. If the research participants are chosen from one of those groups, it may be difficult to justify generalizing the research results to factory workers, violent criminals, or people in general. If the target population the researcher wishes to understand is very different from the prospective research participants who are handy, it may be necessary to make special efforts to go farther afield to find a sample that will minimize the threat of *nonrepresentative sampling*.

TABLE 7.10 Partial Validity Scorecard for Pretest-Posttest Control Group Design

	TG1: Pretest-Posttest Control Group Design G_1 R O_1 X O_3 G_2 R O_2 O_4
Reactive arrangements	–
Pretest sensitization	–
Internal validity	+
Nonrepresentative sampling	?
Nonrepresentative research context	–

The tasks and other aspects of the research context that is created in a psychological laboratory may be convenient for the researcher but very different from those to which the research results need to be generalized. For example, a good deal of research on how juries make decisions has been carried out outside the courtroom. College students read synopses of real or fictitious cases, then decide the guilt or innocence of a fictitious defendant. Do we need to worry about how much this research tells us about what goes on in real jury deliberations?

Field settings are less likely to create problems associated with a *nonrepresentative research context* or with a *nonrepresentative sample of participants*, but they are also less amenable to the control over participants and events that are expected of true experimental designs.

It should be fairly clear by now, and this is a point to keep in mind when considering any true experimental design, that true experiments achieve very high levels of internal validity in ways that are likely to create problems for construct validity and external validity. Artificial conditions and captive populations make control over threats to internal validity easier to achieve, but they make generalization of results and observation of spontaneous and realistic behavior more difficult. Those limitations can be ameliorated to some extent. Even if they can't be eliminated entirely, that is cause to keep them in mind when evaluating research results, not to give up entirely on the use of experimentation. After all, laboratory experimentation is responsible for many of the most important discoveries in the history of psychology.

A brief survey of the evaluation of the pretest-posttest control group design can be found in Table 7.10.

TG2: The Posttest-Only Control Group Design. This design can be diagrammed as follows.

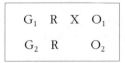

$$G_1 \quad R \quad X \quad O_1$$
$$G_2 \quad R \qquad O_2$$

The posttest-only control group design is like the pretest-posttest control group design in most respects. It shares random assignment of participants to groups, control over events other than the treatments that might influence the behavior being studied, and the brevity of a typical experiment, the features that make true experimental designs what they are. All those features work in the same way as in the pretest-posttest control group design to eliminate the threats to *internal validity*.

The lack of a pretest is the only difference. It makes it more difficult to evaluate the effects of sample attrition, though that is unlikely to be needed in the instances where this design is typically used, in the laboratory over a brief period of time. Harlow's (1958) comparison of rhesus monkeys randomly assigned to be fed by either wire or cloth surrogate mothers (**E12**), Seligman and Maier's (1967) comparison of dogs randomly assigned to receive inescapable electric shock or not before shuttle box training (**E18**), and Rosenzweig et al.'s (1972) comparison of brain development in rats reared in normal versus enriched lab cages (**E22**) all make this point very well.

Again in the case of this design, the features that enhance internal validity tend to cause problems with external validity. The design tends to be used in settings that create *reactive arrangements*, a problem when human subjects are used. Close contact between researcher and subject make *demand characteristics* and **experimenter expectancy effects** more likely. Did the subjects in the Darley and Latané (1968) study of bystander intervention (**E7**) form their own hypotheses, or did they receive unintentional clues from the researchers or even the setting? The design also risks the *nonrepresentative sample of participants*, especially with the use of nonhuman participants, as in the examples given above. It tends to suffer from a *nonrepresentative research context*. One is faced with the problem of generalizing the research results from shuttle box to depression, laboratory cages to Montessori preschools, and the like.

The elimination of the pretest helps a little in these respects. First, it eliminates *pretest sensitization* as a threat to construct validity. Second, it makes it easier to move the experiment outside the laboratory where a pretreatment measure of behavior is more difficult to obtain. This makes nonreactive use of this true experimental design easier and brings with it the potential for observing a more representative sample of participants in a more representative context for the behavior in question.

As we discussed earlier, the comparison of the posttest-only experiment with the pretest-posttest alternative reveals a case where less clearly is more. The elimination of a pretest makes the design less work for the researcher and adds to, rather than detracts from, the validity of the research results.

Why, then, would the pretest-posttest control group design even be included in this analysis? Because it is used! But why would it ever be used? One reason is that some researchers do not trust random assignment to create truly equivalent comparison groups. They should. There is far less danger that random assignment will

TABLE 7.11 **Partial Validity Scorecard for Posttest-Only Control Group Design**

	TG2: Posttest-Only Control Group Design G_1 R X O_1 G_2 R O_2
Reactive arrangements	?
Pretest sensitization	+
Internal validity	+
Nonrepresentative sampling	?
Nonrepresentative research context	?

fail them than that a pretest will make it more difficult to interpret their research results with confidence.

A second reason is that changes in behavior associated with exposure to a putative cause of that behavior seem to some researchers to provide more information about the effects of that putative cause than a simple comparison of treated and untreated (or differently treated) groups posttreatment. They rarely do provide more information. It is usually just as clear from an examination of posttest scores alone as from an examination of pretest-posttest differences whether treatments had the effect predicted in the research hypothesis. Random assignment makes pretest differences unlikely, and statistical problems make comparisons of changes more problematic than comparisons of differences at one point in time. It may still seem too good to be true, but in this case less truly is more.

The lack of value of a pretest is clear when the design is examined carefully, using a little algebra. Because of random assignment, it is reasonable to expect in a pretest-posttest control group design (TG1) that O_1 will be equal to O_2. Because G_2 is untreated, it is also reasonable to expect O_1 and O_2 to be equal to O_4. Comparing O_1 with O_2 in a posttest-only control group design (TG2) therefore is equivalent to comparing the difference between O_1 and O_3 in TG1, and the difference between O_1 and O_2 in TG2 is equivalent to the difference between O_3 and O_4 in TG1. If you do the math, you'll agree that the pretest information is essentially worthless in estimating the effect of X on O, and, as a "bonus," it makes validity-weakening artifacts more likely to occur. Anything that can be learned from a pretest-posttest control group study can be learned at less cost and with greater confidence from a posttest-only control group study, except for the magnitude of the effect of X on posttest compared to pretest. Compare Table 7.11 with Table 7.10 for a graphic representation of that conclusion; also see Table 7.12 for a full comparison.

TABLE 7.12 Validity Scorecard for True Experimental Research Designs, TG Variety

	TG1: Pretest-Posttest Control Group Design G_1 R O_1 X O_3 G_2 R O_2 O_4	TG2: Posttest-Only Control Group Design G_1 R X O_1 G_2 R O_2
Construct validity		
Reactive arrangements	– usually in a lab setting, with direct contact between participants and experimenter	? see TG1; features normally associated with random assignment and manipulation of the independent variable
Pretest sensitization	– especially in a lab setting, where pretest is administered directly to participants	+ no pretest
Linguistic/cultural bias	? depends on the nature of O; if verbal measure is administered directly to participants, problematic	? see TG1
Internal validity		
Extraneous events	+ lab setting, manipulation of independent variable, usually brief duration	+ same features as TG1 lessen likelihood of coincidental event that could affect O
Temporal effects	+ unlikely influence on O because of most experimental sessions	+ see TG1
Group composition effects	+ random assignment creates equivalent groups	+ random assignment
Temporal mul group composition effects	+ random assignment, manipulation of independent variable by experimenter	+ see TG1
Selective sample attrition	+ lab setting, brief duration usually sufficient; if not, pretest allows evaluation of those lost	+ lab setting and brief duration make it easy to account for participants and lessen likelihood of loss
Statistical regression effects	+ even if sample is selected for extreme scores on O, control group matched by random assignment	+ no pretest means no selection based on scores on O
External validity		
Nonrepresentative sampling	? depends on method of sampling participants, universality of relationship between X and O	? see TG1; in lab experiments, sample rarely random and representative
Nonrepresentative research context	– in lab experiments, task and setting usually artificial simulation of natural context of behavior	? in rare field experiments, context can be more representative of those to which results are to be generalized

TG3: The Solomon Four-Group Design. This design can be illustrated as follows.

$$
\begin{array}{llllll}
G_1 & R & O_1 & X & O_3 \\
G_2 & R & O_2 & & O_4 \\
G_3 & R & & X & O_5 \\
G_4 & R & & & O_6
\end{array}
$$

A pretest is necessary in those rare instances when it is essential to know not only whether a treatment had the predicted effect on the behavior in question, but also exactly how the behavior of those exposed to the treatment changed from before the treatment to after it. Knowing what we do about the potential problem of *pretest sensitization effects*, the pretest-posttest control group design would seem a risky choice. Fortunately, there is a better one. One can use the Solomon four-group design, although this design is used more often in pedagogy than in practice (the reason it is not included in Table 7.12).

Comparing the $O_1 - O_3$ difference with the $O_2 - O_4$ difference would tell a researcher more about the change caused by the treatment than could be learned from a posttest-only experiment. At the same time, it would be possible to compare O_3 with O_5 (the effect of X after a pretest with the effect of X without any pretest) to determine whether the pretest altered the effect of the treatment. If the behavior following the treatment were the same whether or not there was a pretest, the $O_1 - O_3$ versus $O_2 - O_4$ comparison could be taken at face value. If not, the researcher would know that any difference between $O_1 - O_3$ and $O_2 - O_4$ reflected not only the effect of the treatment but also the effect of the pretest. It would even be possible to use the results of the posttest-only half of the experiment to estimate the amount of change attributable to the treatment without the sensitizing effect of the pretest ($O_5 - O_6$).

Otherwise, the Solomon four-group design shares all the strengths and weaknesses of the other two true experimental designs that compare across groups and that make up its two halves (TG1 in G_1 and G_2, and TG2 in G_3 and G_4). It should be clear by now that if there is no good reason to include a pretest, the posttest-only control group design is a much better alternative. It provides more flexibility in sampling participants and context features representatively, and it avoids the possibility of pretest sensitization effects. It should also be clear by now that not trusting random assignment is a very poor reason for including a pretest, and being curious about the nature of participants' pre-treatment behavior is a weak one.

EVALUATING QUASI-EXPERIMENTAL RESEARCH DESIGNS ●

Psychologists and other scientists have long believed that research based on what we have been calling true experimental designs brings science closest to the truth. No less an authority than the noted paleontologist and science writer Stephen Jay Gould stated this view as recently as 1996 in a revised edition of *The Mismeasure of Man*. He wrote that the ability of the experiment to reduce the influence of confusing variables (in our terms, to increase internal validity or make possible unambiguous causal inference) by varying one potential factor at a time while holding all others constant in the "artificial simplicity" of the laboratory makes the experiment the preferred method for science.

Thanks in large part to Campbell and Stanley (1963), and to other contemporary methodologists, today we know better. In fields that study inanimate objects, like physics and Gould's paleontology, the more traditional view still makes sense, but in psychological research, experimentation may involve the creation of a reactive and artificial situation that may permit unambiguous causal inference, but at considerable cost. First, there is the ambiguity about what exactly is being studied, the problem of construct validity. We may know what causes what, but it may not be so clear what those "whats" really are, or how close they come to the problem we really want to study. Then, there is uncertainty about how the results can be generalized to organisms and conditions other than those represented in the study itself, the problem of external validity. In what units, treatment, observations, and settings will the relationship be observed?

If the researcher had to choose between the freedom from threats to internal validity of true experimental designs and the greater realism and lesser reactivity of pre-experimental research, the choice might not be very difficult. Experimentation still has a very positive cachet, and pre-experimental designs are too weak in internal validity to be taken very seriously. The choice, however, would ultimately be unsatisfying. Each of those forms has significant weaknesses that must dampen one's enthusiasm about their strengths.

Fortunately, at the same time that Campbell and other methodologists tarnished the pristine reputation of experimental research in the behavioral sciences, they offered an alternative. They showed how nonexperimental research could be designed to complement its strengths in the areas of construct validity and external validity with features that can rule out most of or even all the major threats to internal validity.

Campbell and Stanley chose to call research designs that meet that criterion "quasi-experimental." I worry that the label connotes an inferiority to "true" experimental research, that this research is almost experimental in the sense of almost as good. That is not the meaning that was intended or the one that will emerge from our analysis, which is summarized in Tables 7.15 (p. 250) and 7.18 (p. 256).

Quasi-Experimental Designs That Compare Over Time (Within Subjects): QT Designs

QT1: The Interrupted Time Series Design. This design can be diagrammed as follows.

$$O_1 \quad O_2 \quad O_3 \quad O_4 \quad X \quad O_5 \quad O_6 \quad O_7 \quad O_8$$

A time series is, in most cases, a long series of measures taken at regular intervals, that can be used to assess the behavioral construct in a research hypothesis. It is more often created to serve the purposes of a school, business, government, or other organization than for the purpose of a research study. When an event occurs during the period covered by that series of measures that is of theoretical interest to a researcher, a time series can make it possible to test a hypothesis about the effects of that event. In other words, the event interrupts the time series, or occurs somewhere within it, and the measures in the series can be examined to determine what effects, if any, that event/interruption might have caused.

The key to the freedom from threats to internal validity of the findings of time series research lies in the availability of multiple measures of the behavior in question extending for a considerable period before and after the event. *Temporal effects* can be ruled out as an alternative explanation because the series of measures would reveal any trend that began before the event occurred and make it possible to determine whether that trend was altered by the occurrence of the event. *Group composition effects* would not pose a threat to internal validity because the comparisons related to the hypothesis are made within a single group. The pre-existing (pre-X) behavior of that group is evident in the first part of the time series, which can be used to estimate pre-existing characteristics or behavioral tendencies. Following that same reasoning, it would not be possible for an *interaction between temporal and group composition effects* to be mistaken for the effects of X in a time series study.

Statistical regression effects would work themselves out long before X ever occurred, even if the group being studied had been selected on the basis of extreme scores on the first measurement (O_1). *Selective sample attrition* could be ruled out or factored into the interpretation of the results because of the availability of behavioral measures (one or more pretests) for all participants who began the study.

The explanatory power of the interrupted time series design lies primarily in its ability to reveal a group's long-term trends in the behavior being studied. Compared to the pre-experimental one-group pretest-posttest design (PT2), and

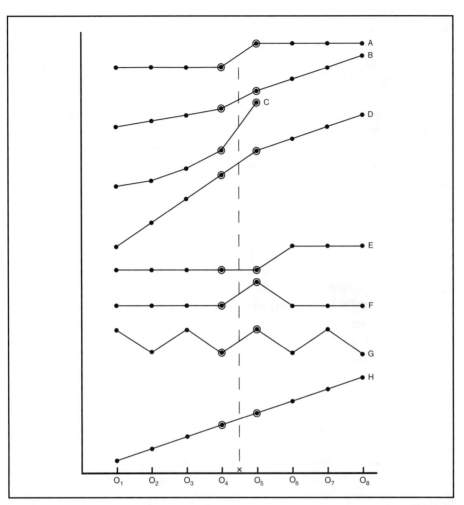

Figure 7.2. A sample of time series outcomes.

even compared to multiple-group designs, this is an important asset whose value can hardly be overstated. It can probably best be appreciated by a visual depiction such as that in Figure 7.2 (adapted broadly from Campbell and Stanley's 1963 work).

Figure 7.2 shows eight possible outcomes of a time series study (A through H). It makes clear how difficult it can be to interpret the results of a one-group pretest-posttest design, where one has only the measures just before and just after X. This is especially true when the duration of the study makes it possible for temporal effects to be mistaken for the effects of the independent variable. At the same time, it shows how the added information collected in a time series study makes the true effects of X so much clearer. In every case shown in Figure 7.2 (except for pattern E), a conclusion based solely on the information that would be provided in a one-group pretest-posttest study, the comparison between O_4 and O_5, would be identical. Based on the $O_4 - O_5$ difference alone, X seems to have an effect on O in every one of those cases.

When one examines the entire series of measures that would be collected in a time series study, O_1 to O_8 (in all patterns except C), it is clear that the conclusions should not all be the same. In study A, there is a clear effect of X; the pattern in that series is altered at the same time that X occurs and remains in the same altered state thereafter. In studies B and C, the effect of X is more ambiguous. The increase in value of O from one measurement to the next through the series seems greater after X than before, more so in C than in B. In study D there is a comparable effect, but in the opposite direction; the increase seems to be less after X than before.

Studies E and F show that a time series can provide even more crucial additional information. In E, X appears to have no effect based on a comparison of O_4 and O_5, but there is a delayed effect that shows up beginning with O_6. In F, the effect that seems to occur at O_4 is shown to be temporary when it disappears at O_6.

Finally, there are increases in O associated with the occurrence of X in studies G and H, but the time series patterns show that in both cases X does nothing to change the trends that began before it and continued afterward.

Although a long series of measures can cure a lot of internal validity ills, it can't cure all of them. No matter how extensive a series of measures is available, it is possible that some *extraneous event* occurred around the same time as X. That could cause any observed change in the series or, if no change is observed, cancel out the true effects of X. Time series research often extends over long periods of time—years' worth of monthly fertility rates or political opinion polls results, for example. Thus, the period during which X occurs is often long enough for events other than X to occur that may be overlooked as potential influences on the behavior being studied.

The most common use of time series research is to investigate the influence of historical, economic, or political events or changes on the behavior of those exposed to them. The researcher who examines a pre-existing and continuous series of institutional records is separated from the (unaware) participant widely in time and space. This makes **reactive arrangements** very unlikely, so that there are likely to be no participant hypotheses, (quasi-) *experimenter expectancy effects*, problems with *demand characteristics*, or *pretest sensitization effects*.

For the same reasons, the results of time series studies are more generalizable than most. The number and diversity of people affected by the kinds of global events studied using this design lessen the likelihood of a *nonrepresentative sample of participants*. The realism and duration of the interrupting events and of the behavior recorded in the time series lessen the likelihood of a *nonrepresentative*

| Box 7.2 | *THINKING ABOUT RESEARCH* |

When a Flu Shot Is Just a Flu Shot

Every autumn, public health officials do their best to convince Americans to get flu shots. They have their work cut out for them, because many people are reluctant to get the shots. A large number of those people believe that they risk developing a case of the flu from the shot itself, even though they are assured that the flu vaccine contains no live virus that could make them ill.

The belief that people catch the flu from flu shots illustrates one of the problems of making a valid causal inference. It is especially apparent in cases like this one, where conclusions are drawn without benefit of the necessary bases for comparison. When one thing follows another, it appears that the first caused the second.

Consider the case of flu shots being followed by illness. Quite apart from the possibility that some people who get flu shots expect the shots to make them sick, resulting in a placebo effect of illness rather than the better-known one of cure, think about how many people actually get flu shots. Even with the resistance to the shots, millions of Americans get them. Among such a large group, how many are likely to get sick in a 10-day period, with the flu or with some other disease that has flu-like symptoms? Do we know if people who don't get the flu shot are any less likely to get sick with flu-like symptoms during the same period than those who get the shot?

What does this example tell us about the need to make appropriate comparisons to rule out threats to internal validity and thus separate coincidence from cause? Which research design is being used, unwittingly, by people who conclude that flu shots give people the flu? Which research design would you use to provide a better evaluation of the hypothesis that flu shots cause the flu? Would your evidence be more effective in allaying people's fears than the earnest pleas of public health officials? Is it possible that people without training in science still appreciate methodological issues like the one we're studying here?

research context. Time series studies are used most often to study large samples of people responding sincerely and unself-consciously to significant events in their lives.

Of course, the same design could theoretically be used in a reactive laboratory setting to study a nonrepresentative sample of college students who perform a brief task devised by the researcher especially for that purpose. In such a case, the time series might elapse in a matter of minutes. Such a study would lose the significant benefits in the areas of construct and external validity described above. Given that degree of control, and the difficulty of obtaining long-term commitments from research participants, however, a researcher would probably not choose this design.

TABLE 7.13 Partial Validity Scorecard for Interrupted Time Series Design

	QT1: Interrupted Time Series Design O_1 O_2 O_3 O_4 X O_5 O_6 O_7 O_8
Reactive arrangements	+
Pretest sensitization	+
Extraneous events	−
Temporal effects	+
Group composition effects	+
Temporal × group composition effects	+
Selective sample attrition	+
Statistical regression effects	+
Nonrepresentative sampling	+
Nonrepresentative research context	+

Table 7.13 summarizes the evaluation of the interrupted time series design.

QT2: The Multiple Time Series Design. The multiple time series design is illustrated below.

$$G_1 \quad O_1 \quad O_3 \quad O_5 \quad O_7 \quad X \quad O_9 \quad O_{11} \quad O_{13} \quad O_{15}$$

$$\text{---}$$

$$G_2 \quad O_2 \quad O_4 \quad O_6 \quad O_8 \quad X \quad O_{10} \quad O_{12} \quad O_{14} \quad O_{16}$$

Sometimes, an interrupted time series study can be expanded by adding a comparison group for whom the same series of behavioral measures is available, but that has not been exposed to the event whose effects are being studied. In such cases, the single most serious threat to the validity of the research findings is eliminated. Any potent *extraneous event* that might occur coincidentally at around the same time as the event in question should affect both groups and their respective time series similarly, thus being taken into account in any comparison between the two time series.

In all other questions of validity, the multiple time series design is indistinguishable from the interrupted time series design. This can be seen by comparing Tables 7.14 and 7.15.

TABLE 7.14 Partial Validity Scorecard for Multiple Time Series Design

	QT1: Multiple Time Series Design O_1 O_3 O_5 O_7 X O_9 O_{11} O_{13} O_{15} - O_2 O_4 O_6 O_8 O_{10} O_{12} O_{14} O_{16}
Reactive arrangements	+
Pretest sensitization	+
Extraneous events	+
Temporal effects	+
Group composition effects	+
Temporal × group composition effects	+
Selective sample attrition	+
Statistical regression effects	+
Nonrepresentative sampling	+
Nonrepresentative research context	+

Quasi-Experimental Designs That Compare Among Groups (Between Subjects): QG Designs

QG1: The Nonequivalent Control Group Design. This design can be diagrammed as follows.

$$
\begin{array}{llll}
G_1 & O_1 & X & O_3 \\
\text{- - - - - - - - - - - -} \\
G_2 & O_2 & & O_4
\end{array}
$$

Random assignment of participants to treatment and nontreatment groups, or to groups exposed to various strengths or versions of a treatment, is not always possible, and an extended time series of measures of the behavior in question is not always available. In such cases, the nonequivalent control group design can provide the researcher with a useful alternative. If both groups are exposed to the same potential *extraneous events*, and subject to the same *temporal effects*, those alternative explanations for the results will be ruled out.

The groups in this design are not equivalent. The research usually is conducted in a natural setting where the researcher can't implement random assignment, but the pretest makes it possible to compare the groups' behavior before the occurrence of the treatment event in order to estimate and adjust for a *group composi-*

TABLE 7.15 Validity Scorecard for Quasi-Experimental Research Designs, QT Variety

	QT1: Interrupted Time Series Design O_1 O_2 O_3 O_4 X O_5 O_6 O_7 O_8	QT2: Multiple Time Series Design G_1 O_1 O_3 O_5 O_7 X O_9 O_{11} O_{13} O_{15} - G_2 O_2 O_4 O_6 O_8 X O_{10} O_{12} O_{14} O_{16}
Construct validity		
Reactive arrangements	+ behavioral measures are usually not administered directly to participants when this design is used	+ see QT1
Pretest sensitization	+ pretests aren't administered directly	+ see QT1
Linguistic/ cultural bias	? if behavioral measure is verbal, bias needs to be considered a potential problem	? see QT1
Internal validity		
Extraneous events	– depending on length of interval between O's, coincidental events capable of influencing behavior are problematic	+ if comparison group is exposed to same non-X events, threat is eliminated
Temporal effects	+ long sequence of measures makes it possible to separate temporal trends from the effects of X	+ see QT1
Group composition effects	+ one group	+ comparability of groups can be ascertained from the series of pretests and taken into account in results
Temporal × group composition effects	+ one group	+ temporal trends assessed via the long sequence of measures
Selective sample attrition	+ selective attrition is detectable via the long sequence of measures	+ see QT1
Statistical regression effects	+ regression effects can also be detected via the long sequence of measures	+ see QT1
External validity		
Nonrepresentative sampling	+ samples used in time series studies are usually large and representative (e.g., public opinion polls, economic indicators)	+ see QT1
Nonrepresentative research context	+ time series studies are usually based on assessments of real behaviors in natural settings (schools, factories, etc.)	+ see QT1

tion effect. For example, imagine a study comparing the effects of two different methods of teaching reading in two different elementary school classrooms. Both groups of students would be exposed to many extraneous events, including changes in the school or in the community as a whole. Similarly, normal developmental changes should be the same if the two groups are at the same grade level, as we would expect them to be. Any difference between the groups in reading ability or general scholastic aptitude should be apparent from the pretest, which probably would be a standardized achievement test administered by the school at regular intervals rather than an integral part of the research study itself.

The pretest data also make it possible to determine whether any loss of participants over the normally extensive duration of such a study (testing a new teaching method, management policy, or the like) results in *selective sample attrition*. Selective attrition might occur because a less successful or more demanding treatment makes participants in one group more likely to drop out than those in another. A particularly vulnerable subset of that group would be more likely to drop out than other members. In that case, the pretest data for those who drop out of the study (O_1 or O_2) can be used to adjust the comparison of post-X behavioral measures (O_3 vs. O_4) accordingly.

The value of the pretest measures is not unlimited. Even if the groups are comparable before X, an *interaction of group composition and temporal effects* could cause them to be different afterward, even if the treatment had no effect at all. That is because two or more nonequivalent groups may be subject to different time-linked (maturational) changes, so that even if they are matched on pretest scores, they may not still be comparable when the treatment ends and the time for the posttest comes around.

For example, adolescent girls mature faster than adolescent boys, precocious children may become bored more quickly than their more typical age-mates, students enrolled in Head Start might be developing faster than those not enrolled because of greater parental interest, and so on. Should such an interaction occur, one-time pretest data would not be very useful for adjusting posttest comparisons. An illustrative example of the problem is presented in Figure 7.3.

Figure 7.3 Illustrates the temporal × group composition interaction that might occur in a nonequivalent control group study. In this fictitious yet plausible example, the study evaluates the effectiveness of a Head Start program. The specific behavior that is at issue is the children's readiness to enter the first grade of elementary school, as measured on a 100-point scale (shown on the y-axis). The graph shows the results of assessments of school readiness made approximately every 2 weeks over the course of a year, T_1 through T_{20} (shown on the x-axis). During part of that period, between T_6 and T_{14}, the 20-week Head Start program takes place.

The graph in Figure 7.3 compares the changes in school readiness in two groups of children, the group that participates in the Head Start program (HS) and a second group that is comparable in age, socioeconomic background, and other

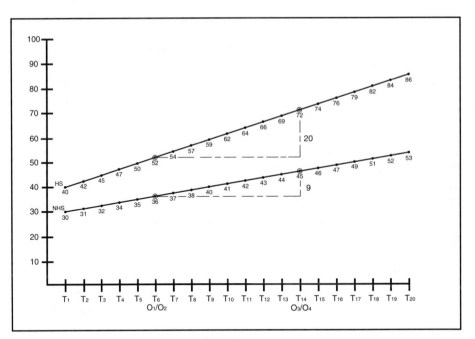

Figure 7.3. An illustration of a temporal × group composition interaction.

characteristics that seem relevant to school readiness, but that does not participate in the program (NHS). These changes represent the ongoing course of development in the children and are presumably related to their maturation and to the experiences in their lives, including the quality of interaction with caretakers. It is apparent that the HS children begin the year with a higher level of school readiness, and that their level also increases at a faster rate during the year, with their 10-point advantage at the beginning growing to a 33-point advantage by the end.

The pretest administered in a nonequivalent control group study could be used to match the two groups on the behavior being studied. One could select pairs of children for membership in the two groups, one from each group, who have identical scores on the school readiness scale at T_6, when O_1 and O_2 are administered and the Head Start Program is about to begin. This method of equating group composition would result in only lower-scoring HS children and higher-scoring NHS children being compared in the study. From the graph, it seems clear that even if the Head Start program had no effect on school readiness, it might appear to be beneficial by the time the program ended and the posttest was administered at T_{14} (O_3 and O_4). The HS children would improve 11 points more on the school readiness scale than the NHS children (20 points vs. 9), due only to the difference in the maturational rates between the groups.

Unfortunately, in a nonequivalent control group study that trend would not be known to the researchers. They would know only the pretest and posttest scores. Thus, if they found a larger gain in school readiness in the HS group than in the ini-

TABLE 7.16 Partial Validity Scorecard for Nonequivalent Control Group Design

	QG1: Nonequivalent Control Group Design G_1 O_1 X O_3 - - - - - - - - - - - - G_2 O_2 X O_4
Reactive arrangements	?
Pretest sensitization	?
Extraneous events	?
Temporal effects	?
Group composition effects	+
Temporal × group composition effects	–
Selective sample attrition	+
Nonrepresentative sampling	+
Nonrepresentative research context	+

tially matched NHS group over the course of the study, they might overestimate the contribution of Head Start to that gain. Matching the two groups at the outset of the study wouldn't eliminate the problem of temporal × group composition interaction shown in this example or its threat to the validity of the research findings. The groups wouldn't stay matched through the course of the study. How different would that problem be if the multiple time series design were used instead of the nonequivalent control group design?

A study using the nonequivalent control group design may track the effects of naturally occurring, or even natural-seeming, events in schools, factories, and other field settings. It may assess behavior that also occurs naturally in those settings. In that case, neither treatments nor behavioral measures require direct contact between participants and researchers. Thus, there is no danger of *reactive arrangements* or *pretest sensitization*. If the participants' routine is disturbed and researchers do intrude, both of those threats to construct validity will hamper the interpretation of the research results. The more the introduction of a new teaching method or new management technique and the measures of its effects seem to participants like part of their everyday routine, the less reactive the setting and the fewer problems regarding the possible occurrence of artifacts.

This design typically will make use of the normal incumbents in a natural setting, along with their usual artifacts, tasks, and avenues for response. As a consequence, neither of the potential threats to external validity, *nonrepresentative sample* and *nonrepresentative research context*, needs to concern the researcher who uses this design very much in most cases.

Table 7.16 summarizes our evaluation of the nonequivalent control group design.

QG2: The Separate-Sample Pretest-Posttest Design. This design can be diagrammed as follows.

$$
\begin{array}{llll}
G_1 & R & O_1 & (X) \\
G_2 & R & & X \quad O_2
\end{array}
$$

Sometimes a single group is exposed to some event, such as an innovative teaching method, that is suspected of being capable of having a scientifically significant effect on some aspect of their behavior. If it is possible to divide the group randomly in two, and to designate one of the randomly constituted halves to receive a pretreatment measure of that behavior and the other half to receive a posttreatment measure, the result is a surprisingly powerful design for a research study to test that suspicion.

Because there is really just one group experiencing the treatment, both "ends" of the crucial comparison between pretest and posttest (O_1 and O_2) are assessed in random samples from the same group of individuals. This eliminates the possibility of *group composition effects*. The possibility that the behavior being studied is influenced by *extraneous events* or *temporal effects* depends on the duration of the treatment and the degree to which the researcher can insulate participants from their effects. The question of an *interaction between temporal and group composition effects* isn't even relevant here because there is actually only one group involved, or two randomly constituted subgroups. Neither is the question of *statistical regression effects*, because there is no selection pretest administered to all participants that could be used to constitute a group of extreme scorers.

For internal validity, attrition can't be expected to affect both groups equally because the participants available for the posttest may be affected negatively by the treatment during the course of the study. Attrition is always possible in a study of considerable duration conducted in a natural setting, as a study utilizing this design is likely to be. When attrition does occur, the pretest can't be used to determine whether the participants who are lost change the composition of the group, because only half the sample are pretested. That information can't be used to determine whether a difference between O_1 and O_2 reflects the effect of the treatment or of *selective sample attrition*.

Pretest sensitization effects are not a potential matter of concern when using this design because the group that is evaluated for the effects of the treatment (G_2) is not pretested. It seems prudent nevertheless to administer pre-X behavioral measures to both groups (as in the example given in the previous chapter of an evaluation of an organizational behavior course), with G_1 receiving the pretest measure and G_2 some irrelevant measure. This would avoid sensitizing participants to the treatment or influencing their response to the posttest. Such a preventive measure would also lessen the likelihood of *reactive arrangements*. The measures and treatment events may resemble the natural experiences of the participants in the

TABLE 7.17 Partial Validity Scorecard for Separate-Sample Pretest-Posttest Design

	QG2: Separate-Sample Pretest-Posttest Design G_1 R O_1 (X) G_2 R X O_2
Reactive arrangements	?
Pretest sensitization	+
Extraneous events	?
Temporal effects	?
Group composition effects	+
Selective sample attrition	−
External validity	+

setting in which they are being studied—normal classroom experiences and tests, or routine job tasks and performance evaluations, for example. If so, it is unlikely the results will be influenced by artifacts that can be threats to construct validity.

In the kinds of applied research where this design is likely to be popular, there are unlikely to be serious problems with *external validity*. Ordinarily, the results of such a study will be applied to the same or similar participants in the same or a similar context. Again, this isn't an inherent feature of the design, but rather a part of its implementation.

Table 7.17 summarizes the key validity issues for the separate-sample pretest-posttest design, and Table 7.18 compares the quasi-experimental research designs.

CONCLUSIONS ABOUT EVALUATING ● RESEARCH DESIGNS

It would be comforting, at the end of a long and sometimes tortuous consideration of the various research designs and their assorted vulnerabilities to threats to the validity of the findings they produce, to be able to point to one design or one group of designs as superior to the rest. Psychologists once did that, and some scientists still do, venerating true experimental research designs above all others. Unfortunately, we cannot.

Each type of research design, if not each individual design, has its own peculiar pattern of strengths and weaknesses. None is perfect, or even clearly superior overall to the others. The goal of the researcher who is planning to test a hypothesis, or of the reader of the report of a completed study, needs to be to understand

TABLE 7.18 Validity Scorecard for Quasi-Experimental Research Designs, QG Variety

	QG1: Nonequivalent Control Group Design $G_1 \ O_1 \ X \ O_3$ ----------- $G_2 \ O_2 \qquad O_4$	QG2: Separate-Sample Pretest-Posttest Design $G_1 \ R \ O_1 \ (X)$ $G_2 \ R \qquad X \ O_2$
Construct validity		
Reactive arrangements	? if there is direct contact between researcher and participants and direct administration of O, setting is reactive	? direct contact and administration of O mitigated by examining effect of X after the fact (O_2)
Pretest sensitization	? if pretest is administered directly, rather than obtained from an archival source, sensitization is a potential problem	+ group that is assessed (G_2) is not pretested
Linguistic/cultural bias	? if O is a verbal measure, bias is a potential problem	? see QG1
Internal validity		
Extraneous events	? depends on duration of study and degree of discretion that can be exercised by researcher	? same problems as QG1; in quasi-experimental studies, they are more likely to obtain than not
Temporal effects	? problems of duration and degree of control by researcher again	? see QG1
Group composition effects	+ retest can be used to show equivalence or, in its absence, to adjust results for nonequivalence	+ random assignment renders groups equivalent
Temporal × group composition effects	– even matched groups might change at different rates if the pre-post interval is as long as is usual in quasi-experimental studies	+ random assignment precludes this threat
Selective sample attrition	+ pretest makes it possible to detect attrition and to evaluate its effects on group composition	– if attrition occurs, even as the result of X, can't evaluate its effects on group composition
Statistical regression effects	? if sample is selected via the pretest for its extreme standing on O, regression effects are a potential problem	+ no extreme group selected by pretest
External validity		
Nonrepresentative sampling	+ this design typically is used to study an intervention in the organization to which the results will be applied	+ see QG1
Nonrepresentative research context	+ again, the design typically is used in the same context in which the results of the study are to be applied	+ see QG1

how the choice of research design, along with all the other choices that need to be made in order to do psychological research, affects the interpretation of the research results.

Even if one were willing to prioritize the various validity considerations involved—ranking internal validity ahead of the rest, or ranking external validity ahead of the rest, or even conceptual validity first in order of importance—it would still be impossible to choose one type of research design over the others. That is because the choice of a research design is based on more than considerations of the validity of a study's findings. To some degree, a research design needs to conform to the nature of the research problem or hypothesis.

It might be desirable, depending on one's priorities, to design a true experiment to test the hypothesis that exposure to an accident at a nearby nuclear reactor causes people to experience stress, but it would not be possible. The random assignment of participants to treatment groups (i.e., exposure and no exposure) and the manipulation of the putative causal event in isolation from other possible influences on the behavior in question, features that confer such obvious advantages in inferring cause and effect from the results of true experimental studies, would not be feasible.

A researcher would need to study pre-existing (not randomly assigned) groups' responses to natural (not manipulated) events in a complex, natural (nonlaboratory) setting in order to test that hypothesis. No one can randomly assign people to be exposed or not to be exposed to a nuclear accident. Even if some kind of simulation could be arranged that would permit the use of a true experimental design, its use probably would raise such serious questions about construct validity and external validity that no net gain in overall validity would be realized. Very serious ethical issues also would be raised (see Chapter 11).

In much the same way, if the researcher's hypothesis concerned the specific effects on memory of the destruction of a particular region of the brain, experimental research with nonhuman subjects might be the only feasible alternative. Even if the prospect of generalizing the results from laboratory mice to human Alzheimer's patients seemed highly problematic, natural occurrences in humans of precisely the type of brain damage specified in the hypothesis might not be available for study using a nonexperimental design. Accidents, illnesses, and strokes don't usually follow lines drawn by neuroscientists on diagrams of the brain.

There are, however, hypotheses that can be tested using a variety of types of research design. Triplett's (1897) studies of the effects of coaction, utilizing quasi-experimental comparisons based on actual bicycle races and experimental comparisons based on his fishing-reel laboratory task , are one example. Not so long ago, most psychological researchers would have simply chosen or believed the experimental results and discarded the nonexperimental. Today, thanks to Campbell and other modern methodologists, those ideas are changing. The experimental and nonexperimental methods complement one another, each with its own peculiar strengths and weaknesses. Together, they increase our confidence in conclusions about the research hypothesis.

Recognizing this, Campbell and others have proposed that, where it is feasible, a research hypothesis should be tested with as many different research designs as possible. The same hypothesis could be tested in a laboratory experiment, a pre-experimental case study, and a naturalistic quasi-experiment. If the results of all those studies were consistent in the conclusions they supported about the truth of the research hypothesis—if they uniformly supported or refuted it—then the complementary strengths and weaknesses of the three research designs would together cover most of, if not all, the possible threats to internal, external, and construct validity.

Many researchers are in too much of a hurry to move on to the next interesting hypothesis to test the current one in several different ways. It may be possible, however, to put together such a set of findings from the work of multiple researchers. We'll discuss this possibility further in the following chapters. If the hypothesis is important enough, researchers should make the effort to go beyond a single study or a single research design.

Finally, it needs to be said here that methodology does not involve the search for a perfect scientific method. The goals of a researcher are to minimize as many threats to the validity of the research findings as possible and to understand those that remain. Flawed findings are not failures if the limitations are understood. Assuming perfect validity is a worse sin than admitting that research findings need to be qualified.

Measurement is never perfectly reliable or valid. Cause and effect can only be inferred; it cannot be observed directly. Generalizability is always limited to some degree. Although it might be comforting to believe that it is possible for science to produce answers that need no qualification, it wouldn't be justified in the light of what we know about the research process. Unfortunately, those who can't accept science as the best knowledge available at a given point in time have no better alternative, at least based on our current understanding of epistemology. The best science may not be perfect, but it is the closest one can come to the truth, and it is good enough to hold up our skyscrapers and bridges, find a gene that can cause breast cancer, and train a bear to ride a bicycle, among other things.

Review Questions and Exercise

Review Questions

1. How would you characterize the overall strengths and weaknesses of pre-experimental designs, and how do the various examples compare with one another for their vulnerability to the various threats to validity?

2. Answer the same questions about true experimental designs.

3. Answer the same questions about the quasi-experimental designs.

4. Given the differences in strengths and weaknesses of the three types of research designs, and the requirements for implementing each one, how can a research psychologist maximize what we know about the truth of a research hypothesis?

Exercise

Fill out the Validity Scorecard for each of the studies you found when you did the exercise at the end of Chapter 5. If you can, practice on other studies you've learned about in your psychology classes or your own research.

CHAPTER 8

BUILDING MODELS OF MULTIPLE CAUSES AND EFFECTS

● A QUICK GUIDE TO CHAPTER 8: BUILDING MODELS OF MULTIPLE CAUSES AND EFFECTS

Each of the research designs described in Chapter 6 and analyzed in Chapter 7 evaluates the effects of a single cause (X) on the behavior in question (O). Many of the behaviors about which researchers have serious questions, however, clearly have more than one cause. Why do people smoke? Why do children fail in school? Why do some people learn much faster than others? In each case—and for many, many others—there are likely to be multiple reasons.

It is possible to expand the univariate designs in Chapter 6 that study one cause and one behavior at a time. One of the most obvious benefits of doing so is the efficiency of determining the effects of two or more putative causal factors in a single study. But evaluating multiple independent and dependent variables in a single **multivariate research** study is not so much less work than conducting a number of separate **univariate research** studies. Much more important than efficiency is the opportunity to discover whether there is an **interaction** between the independent variables. The effects of a given independent variable can be different in the presence of different amounts of other independent variables, and we can learn about such interactions only by studying more than one independent variable in the same study.

The Chapter 8 Quick Guide shows the expansion of the very popular posttest-only control group design to study two independent variables simultaneously. This expanded true experimental design is known as a **factorial experiment**. That means that each of the possible combinations of the two independent variables is administered to a separate randomly assigned group. For example, four groups of children might be exposed to the four factorial combinations of violent versus nonviolent television programs (X_1) and live versus animated forms (X_2).

It is also possible to evaluate the effects of the treatments on more than one dependent variable in a single research study. There are many behaviors that are so complex that their various components can't be combined meaningfully into a single measure. Recall from our discussion of construct validity how misleading a compound measure can be. Experiments may be expanded to include multiple measures of behavior. The results of such experiments, though, are analyzed using correlational methods, in a more flexible approach to multivariate research known as **multiple correlation research**.

In this expansion of the pre-experimental correlational design, one group of participants is assessed for exposure to multiple causal factors (independent variables or predictors) and one or more behavioral measures (dependent variables or criterion measures). Powerful statistical methods based on the technique of partial correlation make it possible to study the independent and interactive effects of a large number of independent variables, if one can test a sample of sufficient size.

Chapter 8 Quick Guide: Univariate and Multivariate Research Designs Compared

Design Name	Design Diagram	Comparisons	Results
Posttest-only control group design	G_1 R X O_1 G_2 R $\quad O_2$	O_1 vs. O_2	Effect of X
Two-factor factorial posttest-only control group design	G_1 R $X_{1a}X_{2a}$ O_1 G_2 R $X_{1a}X_{2b}$ O_2 G_3 R $X_{1b}X_{2a}$ O_3 G_4 R $X_{1b}X_{2b}$ O_4	$(O_1 + O_2)$ vs. $(O_3 + O_4)$ $(O_1 + O_3)$ vs. $(O_2 + O_4)$ $(O_1$ vs. $O_2)$ vs. $(O_3$ vs. $O_4)$	Effect of X_1 (X_{1a} vs. X_{1b}) Effect of X_2 (X_{2a} vs. X_{2b}) Interaction between X_1 and X_2
Correlational design	r_{xo}	X vs. O	Statistical relationship between X and O
Multiple correlation analysis	$R_{X1X2 \ldots XnO}$	X_1 vs. O X_2 vs. O . . . X_n vs. O	Statistical relationship between each X and O with other X's "partialled out" and interactions

The Chapter 8 Quick Guide shows one example of the use of **multiple correlation analysis (MCA)**.

One example of the use of MCA would be in a study of the causes of crime. If good reasons could be found in the research literature, or in theory, one might test the hypothesis that family income, family structure, gender, and age were likely causes of a person's record of being convicted of a violent crime. A **multiple regression analysis** of the data from a large sample of participants would reveal the independent effects of each hypothesized cause, holding the others constant. It would also reveal any possible interactions, where one cause had different influences on criminality depending on the amount of one or more other causes. For example, gender might be more strongly related to criminal behavior for younger individuals than for older ones.

INTRODUCTION TO THE CHAPTER ●

It isn't too likely that anyone, instructor or student, veteran methodologist or neophyte, would think that the analysis of the research process that we've gone through thus far is too simple—but in a way it is. In all the designs and sample studies we've considered up to this point, there has been a single independent variable represented by two or more treatments, sometimes including a "no treatment" option. There also has been a single dependent variable or behavioral measure, though it is sometimes administered more than once.

Many research studies in psychology, if not most, investigate more than one independent variable and more than one dependent variable at a time. This isn't simply because researchers are in too much of a hurry to do separate studies for each combination of one independent variable and one dependent variable. There is an important advantage to considering more than one variable of either type at a time, and the main objective of this chapter is to make clear what that advantage is. Once we've done that, we can consider a few examples of how that advantage can be realized through the use of specific research designs that expand some of the designs already familiar from previous chapters.

In its various forms, research that includes multiple independent and/or dependent variables is referred to as **multivariate research**. Because this is a large and complex subject, we will only be able to scratch the surface here. This chapter will certainly not prepare you to conduct, or even to understand completely, all types of multivariate research. There are, in particular, some very complex statistical concepts involved in multivariate research. We can, however, introduce the basic concepts here. Through them, we can explore the reasons that multivariate methods are an increasingly important part of research in psychology and other disciplines.

Psychology uses two major forms of multivariate research. One of them expands the various designs that we have considered already that compare among groups, or that study a single group over time. In this type of multivariate research, the group or groups may be exposed to combinations of treatments representing multiple independent variables. These designs are generally referred to as **factorial experiments**, even though many of them are not true experiments but actually pre-experimental or quasi-experimental studies according to the classification system we've used in earlier chapters.

The second form of multivariate research expands the simple correlational design we considered earlier by adding additional predictor (X) and/or criterion (O) variables. The designs in this category are known collectively as **multiple correlation research**.

● FACTORIAL EXPERIMENTS

A Classic Example

Multivariate research that compares across groups is exemplified by a classic psychological experiment that examined the effect of arousal on task performance. If arousal had been the only independent variable to be evaluated, the researchers could have exposed different groups to treatments that created different levels of arousal. Then, while the participants all performed the same task, the researchers could have compared their levels of performance.

That would be a univariate study. It could be experimental or not, depending on how participants were assigned to the various groups or levels of arousal and how much control the researcher had over the scheduling of the treatments. That study would have one independent variable, arousal, represented by a number of different treatments that created different levels of arousal. It would also have one dependent variable, task performance. Nothing new here.

The hypothesis tested in this multivariate study was more complex. It made predictions about the effects of arousal, the first independent variable, on tasks of differing levels of complexity, the second independent variable. It included the prediction that the effect of arousal on performance would depend on the nature of the task. Some tasks are simple, meaning here that the correct response is well known or well practiced. For simple tasks, higher levels of arousal were predicted to be associated with higher levels of performance. In complex tasks, the correct response still needs to be learned better. In other words, a complex task is one in which the most likely response is one that is incorrect. For complex tasks, higher levels of arousal were predicted to be associated with lower levels of performance. What was predicted in this study is known as an **interaction**. That means that the effect of one independent variable (arousal) was predicted to differ according to the status of a second independent variable (task complexity).

This study could be based on a posttest-only control group experimental design. In the simplest form, with two levels of each independent variable, there would be four groups of randomly assigned participants. They would receive treatments that represented all possible combinations of the two levels of arousal, high and low, and the two levels of task complexity, simple and complex. This design is known as a 2×2 factorial experiment, with $2 \times 2 = 4$ groups in all. In the notation system we've been using all along, the design for this factorial experiment could be diagrammed as follows.

$$
\begin{array}{cccc}
G_1 & R & X_{sl} & O_1 \\
G_2 & R & X_{sh} & O_2 \\
G_3 & R & X_{cl} & O_3 \\
G_4 & R & X_{ch} & O_4 \\
\end{array}
$$

The first treatment subscript indicates the level of task complexity. There are two levels, s and c, for simple and complex tasks. The second treatment subscript indicates the level of arousal. Again, there are two levels, l and h, for low and high arousal. The hypothesized outcome of this study would be $O_2 > O_1$ and $O_3 > O_4$. That is, the prediction would be that performance on the simple version of the task would be better under conditions of higher arousal, while performance on the complex version would be worse under conditions of higher arousal—an interaction or interactive effect of the two independent variables.

Factorial experiments can also be represented another way. Our hypothetical experiment, with two independent variables each represented by two levels, could be diagrammed as follows.

		Task Complexity	
		Simple (s)	Complex (c)
Arousal Level	Low (l)	G_{sl}	G_{cl}
	High (h)	G_{sh}	G_{ch}

The four cells in this 2×2 table represent the four possible combinations of treatments in our 2×2 factorial experiment.

One of the most recent versions of this basic experiment was carried out by social psychologist Robert Zajonc (1965). The participants were cockroaches. The task was learning the path through a maze, for the negative reinforcer of escape from a bright light (thank goodness something gets rid of cockroaches, even if only temporarily). The simple version of the task was a straight alley. A cockroach just had to run straight ahead, starting from one end where the bright light was turned on behind it, toward the other end where the light would be far less intense and thus much less aversive for the animal. The complex version of the task required the instinct-driven insects to turn before reaching the end of the straight path, a response in clear conflict with that phototropic instinct, to travel down a side alley. That side alley had an opaque wall on the side toward the light that would block the light completely, providing the animal with faster and more complete relief (reinforcement).

The simple task was simple because the required response was the one nature built into the animal. It is an instinctive response that the animal would make under virtually any circumstances—running away from light. The complex maze was a complex task because it required the animals to learn a new response that would have to override their phototropic instinct, moreover in a setting that was unfamiliar to them.

In the low arousal condition, each animal was tested in a maze suspended above an empty terrarium. A higher level of arousal was induced by placing other cockroaches in the bottom of the terrarium. You may remember Triplett's (1897) study of coaction (**E3**), which actually started the line of research that finally reached all the way to this study by Zajonc more than 50 years later. The time required to escape from the light, either to the end of the straight alley or into the side alley of the complex maze, was the measure of performance for all groups. We'll get to the results later.

The same hypothesis could also be tested in a study that compared the performance of a single group over a number of different occasions. On different, randomly scheduled occasions, participants could be required to perform simple or complex versions of a task under conditions of high or low arousal. In its simplest form, an equivalent time samples experiment, each treatment combination would be presented just once and all participants would be tested on the task four times, until all four combinations of task complexity and arousal were presented. This version of the study could be diagrammed as follows (with the same subscripts we used for the posttest-only control group experiment above, although in practice the order of presentation of treatment combinations would be randomized):

$$X_{sl}O_1 \quad X_{sh}O_2 \quad X_{cl}O_3 \quad X_{ch}O_4$$

The Raison d'Être of Factorial Experiments

Whichever design one chose, a study where all possible combinations of the two independent variables, arousal and task complexity, can be compared in a single study has an important advantage over testing the effects of those same two independent variables in two separate studies. It tells us more about how the two independent variables, arousal and task complexity, affect task performance.

First, it tells us the effect of each independent variable individually: It tells us about the effect of arousal on performance and the effect of task complexity on performance. These are the effects we would observe in separate univariate experiments. These effects are known in statistical terms as the **main effects** of the independent variables when referring to a factorial experiment like this one. A main effect is the effect of one independent variable averaged across the levels of the other independent variable.

A single study would also tell us about the joint effects of the two independent variables, or the interaction between the two. Later, we'll get to the results of the factorial experiment described above, when we'll focus on the between-groups design actually used by Zajonc. First, we'll consider the results one might get from the two univariate studies (one independent variable each) compared with those of the combined factorial study.

We will be using a fictitious set of data I created, not Zajonc's actual data, in order to make all of this as clear as possible. These data are presented in Table 8.1.

One of these two univariate studies, the one that assessed the effect of task complexity on task performance, is labeled Study I in Table 8.1. It would be expected to yield the result that the level of performance on a simple task was higher than on a complex task. In this case, that would mean fewer seconds to comple-

TABLE 8.1 Results of Studies of Maze Performance (average time to completion, in seconds)

Study I: Task Complexity

Simple	Complex
7.6	13.1

Study II: Level of Arousal

Low Arousal	High Arousal
10.3	10.4

Study III: Task Complexity × Level of Arousal

	Simple	Complex
Low arousal	9.0	11.8
High arousal	6.2	14.4

Study IV: Task Complexity × Level of Arousal × Intelligence

	Lower IQ		Higher IQ	
	Simple	Complex	Simple	Complex
Low arousal	8.8	12.8	9.2	10.8
High arousal	6.0	16.4	6.4	12.4

tion. After all, that's pretty much the difference between simple and complex tasks. Any organisms should "learn" faster to respond instinctively. In this case, cockroaches should find it easier to run in a straight line away from a bright light in the simple maze than to fight their instincts so that they can make a different response, such as to slow down and turn into the side alley of the complex maze.

But we already suspect that the subjects' level of arousal would have something to do with their performance. In our study of the effects of task complexity, we could try to set arousal at a moderate level to make the effects of task complexity clearer. In a study of cockroaches, that might be done by varying the brightness of the light, or the animals' level of hunger, or whatever. However we chose to do that, in a univariate study, where task complexity is the only independent variable, all subjects would need to perform at approximately the same level of arousal. To compare groups performing tasks that differed in complexity and to be able to tell what effect task complexity had on their performance, we would have to hold the arousal variable constant. Of course, without knowing exactly what the level of arousal would be, given what we suspect about a possible interaction between arousal and task complexity, it would be difficult in an actual case to predict the effect of task complexity.

But what about the univariate study assessing the effect of arousal? That one is labeled Study II in Table 8.1. Would performance be better or worse under conditions of high arousal, compared to low? Again, where the only independent variable is arousal, there can be only one task. To compare groups of subjects performing under different levels of arousal, and to be able to tell what effect level of arousal had on their performance, one would have to hold the task variable constant. Again, it would probably make sense to use a task of moderate complexity, if one could find such a task, to make the effects of arousal clearer. For cockroaches, there might be some sort of maze that is more complex than a straight alley but less complex than one requiring a response that is incompatible with the phototropic instinct. What would we find if we could do such a study? Maybe that a higher level of arousal helped performance, or maybe that it hurt. Again, without knowing exactly how complex the task really is, and suspecting an interaction between task complexity and arousal, it would be difficult to predict the effect of arousal. In our hypothetical example, shown in Table 8.1, there is actually no meaningful difference between the group averages.

The uncertainty can be cleared up to some extent by going back to Zajonc's (1965) study to see what he actually found. As he predicted, on the complex maze, higher arousal produced poorer performance. On the simple task, the straight alley maze, higher arousal produced better performance. In other words, Zajonc found the interaction between arousal and task complexity that he predicted.

If our hypothetical study turned out the way Zajonc's did, the results of both of our univariate studies would be pretty meaningless. The effects of task complexity would depend on the performer's level of arousal, and the effects of arousal would depend on how complex the task happens to be.

That is made pretty clear in the results of Study III, also shown in Table 8.1. That is the study that looks at both independent variables, arousal and task complexity, in a single factorial experiment. It shows what might happen when task complexity and arousal interact. They would combine in a less-than-straightforward way to affect task performance. As in the Zajonc study, when the task is simple, higher arousal produces better (faster) performance. When the task is complex, higher arousal results in worse (slower) performance. In such a case, performance can't be predicted very well from knowing about just one of these causal factors. One really needs to know about both.

In more straightforward cases, the effects of two causal factors simply add together to influence task performance. In other words, there is an **additive relationship** between the two rather than an interactive one. This case illustrates how factorial studies are not only more efficient in studying more than one causal factor at a time but also more accurate in making it possible to detect interactions among causal factors that can't be seen at all in univariate studies, even a series of them. It would be easy in univariate studies to arrive at erroneous conclusions about arousal: for example, that increased arousal simply enhanced performance if one happened to choose a simple task for study; that increased arousal simply impaired performance if one happened to study a complex task; or that complex tasks are performed as well as simple ones, if the participants happened to have just the "right" level of arousal.

We'll consider interactions between two independent variables again in Chapter 10, from the point of view of the statistical methods used to detect them. The important point for now is that expanding a research design to include multiple independent variables in a single study produces results that are more accurate in representing the effects of all the independent variables involved than are the results of a series of studies in which each tests the effects of one of those independent variables alone.

In fact, it may be more important in some cases, such as the one discussed above, to learn about interactions between variables, should they occur, than to learn about the effects of the individual variables themselves. When we consider the results of Study II, for example, it looks like arousal makes no difference at all to performance. But when arousal is combined with task complexity in Study III, it is clear that arousal makes a big difference. The nature of that difference becomes clear, however, only when both independent variables are taken into account.

Of course, if no interaction is observed, the results of a multivariate study provide all the information of separate univariate studies of the effects of the two or more independent variables involved. Studies I and II in Table 8.1 actually show the main effects, the effect of each independent variable separately, drawn from the results of Study III. Much can be gained, therefore, with nothing lost in conducting a multivariate study if the likelihood of an interaction seems great enough to generate a conceptually valid hypothesis.

Limitations on the Use of Factorial Experiments

There is, unfortunately, one serious limitation on the use of multivariate designs such as the multivariate posttest-only control group design and the multivariate equivalent time samples design. That is exemplified in the hypothetical Study IV, whose results are shown in Table 8.1. In that study, a third independent variable, intelligence, is added to arousal level and task complexity to create a three-factor factorial study. Clearly, a multivariate study testing the effects of arousal and task complexity together, and finding that the two interact to determine task performance, provides a much better understanding of the roles of arousal and task complexity in determining task performance than do two univariate studies observing

---

Box 8.1   *THINKING ABOUT RESEARCH*

Statistical Interaction in the Classroom

It is traditional in American public schools for boys and girls to learn together in the same classrooms, but recent educational research has convinced some people that young women would be better off in classrooms of their own. Standardized achievement tests show that girls outperform boys in subjects that emphasize reading and writing, whereas boys do better in math and science. Although this might look like an even-up situation, there are reasons to be concerned for the young women involved, according to a report from the American Association of University Women (1991) titled *How Schools Shortchange Girls*.

First, occupations based on the study of math and science tend to be higher in status and pay. Second, some studies of classroom interaction show that girls' deficiencies might result from math and science teachers' bias in favor of the boys in their classes. Finally, some educators are concerned that girls in coed classes suffer from social pressures to act more feminine, pressures that hold them back from participating fully in math and science classes (math and science aren't "girl things").

These concerns have led some parents and educators to work together to create single-sex math and science classes and even gender-segregated schools. Some evidence shows that girls in single-sex classrooms do better academically than girls in traditional coed classrooms. Apart from the validity issues inherent in the research that produced that evidence (although you are encouraged to think about those issues), consider what the results look like.

The difference between boys and girls in math and science achievement that is apparent in coed classrooms shrinks or disappears when girls are taught apart from boys. What kind of statistical relationship is this between the students' gender and the gender composition of the classroom? How would the relationship look in the form of a graph? How does it change our interpretation of the original findings of a gender difference? How does it illustrate the value of considering the effects of multiple independent variables on the behavior in question? How could yet other influences on math and science achievement be added to the analysis, and which influences might those be? Finally, could this same type of argument be applied to understanding the causes of girls' superiority over boys in language skills, such as interpreting poetry?

---

the effects of arousal and task complexity separately. But consider what happens when the third independent variable, intelligence, is added to the mix.

By the way, if you've noticed already that intelligence isn't a variable than can be studied experimentally, with participants randomly assigned to different groups or levels of intelligence, or with cockroaches, more power to you. But let's disregard that problem for now and focus only on the problem of interpreting interactions among three or more variables. They're called **higher-order interactions**.

Think back to the two-factor arousal × task complexity interaction we discussed earlier, where the pattern of means for four groups needed to be understood. In a 2 × 2 × 2 three-factor factorial study, like the arousal × task complexity mul intelligence study labeled Study IV, the number of means would grow to eight (in the simplest case with two levels of each variable). What if the positive influence of high arousal on performance of a simple task was equal for all participants, regardless of their level of intelligence, while the negative influence of high arousal on performance of a complex task was much greater for participants of lower intelligence than for those of higher intelligence?

If a three-way interaction were observed, in this case among task complexity, level of arousal, and intelligence, the effect of arousal would be specified even further, and the limitations of that effect would be understood better. Now it would be seen to depend not only on task complexity but also on the intelligence of the person performing the task.

If you have the table of means in front of you (Table 8.1) and are reasonably familiar with it, a three-way interaction like this isn't so difficult to follow. But what if a fourth variable were added, or more levels of arousal, task complexity, or intelligence? The interaction, the table, and especially the meaning of the results of such a study quickly become very difficult to grasp and to explain, even for an experienced researcher.

In a study involving only three independent variables in which only two levels of each independent variable are studied, the minimum increase in complexity over a two-factor study, there would be eight possible combinations of the three independent variables—2 × 2 × 2—that would need to be represented in eight separate treatment combinations. Think how much more complicated the study itself would be if there were even more variables, or more levels of the variables, or both. A between-subjects design like the posttest-only control group design wouldn't tax individual participants with a very long series of potentially taxing experiences (sometimes referred to, appropriately in this case, as trials). It would, however, require testing more groups and more participants than many researchers would like to consider.

The independent variables in a multivariate experiment may interact with one another in determining participants' behavior as measured by the dependent variable. If so, the interpretation of the results also becomes exponentially more difficult as the number of independent variables and the number of levels of those independent variables increase. The gain in understanding of the effects of two independent variables that comes from studying them together in a multivariate experiment begins to be prohibitively costly and confusing. Its advantage can erode and eventually can even turn into a liability as more independent variables are added.

Representing Interactions in Graphic Form

One way that researchers try to make the results of their experiments easier to understand, especially for factorial experiments, is by presenting them in graphic form. If we do that for the results of the hypothetical studies whose results are presented in the form of group means in Table 8.1, we can see both the value in that approach and the rapidly increasing difficulty of understanding the results of factorial experiments as the number of independent variables grows beyond two. The results of Studies I through IV are summarized in graphic form in Figure 8.1.

One point that might be clarified by looking at the graphs rather than the tables of means concerns the concept of an interaction. The graph for Study III shows the interaction between task complexity and arousal. The fact that the two lines on that graph, for the simple and complex task groups, are not parallel to one another suggests that there is an interaction. Whether the lines diverge, converge, or even cross, whenever they aren't parallel, the variables interact. If they are parallel, then the relationship between the independent variables is an additive one. "Additive" is synonymous with the absence of a statistical interaction.

Of course, in an actual research study the lines would rarely be perfectly parallel. Fortunately, there are statistical tests (statistical inference is explained more fully in Chapter 10) that can tell us when they are close enough to parallel to indicate that there is no interaction, as well as when they deviate enough from parallel to indicate that there is an interaction.

You should also bear in mind that the points shown on the graphs in Figure 8.1 (and other similar graphs) are the group averages shown in Table 8.1. The degree of consistency within the groups of scores from which those averages are calculated can vary considerably (variability is also explained more fully in Chapter 10). Some researchers prefer to show the points with vertical bars called error bars that reflect the degree of variability among the scores from which each average was derived. We haven't done that here, but the practice is becoming increasingly popular, and deservedly so.

In Figure 8.2, the graphs labeled (a), (b), and (c) at the left side of the figure depict different types of statistical interaction. In each case, the effects of independent variable 2 (2A vs. 2B) differed depending on the value of independent variable 1 (1A vs. 1B). In (a), independent variable 2 produced the opposite effect on the dependent variable (i.e., the behavior being studied) under 1B than under 1A. Treatment 2A produced an increase over 2B when independent variable 1 took the value 1B, but 2B produced an increase over 2A under the value 1A.

In (b) and (c), independent variable 2 had an effect on the dependent variable under one value of independent variable 1, but not under the other. In (b), there was a statistically significant difference between 2A and 2B at 1B, but not at 1A. In (c), there was a significant difference between 2A and 2B at 1A, but not at 1B.

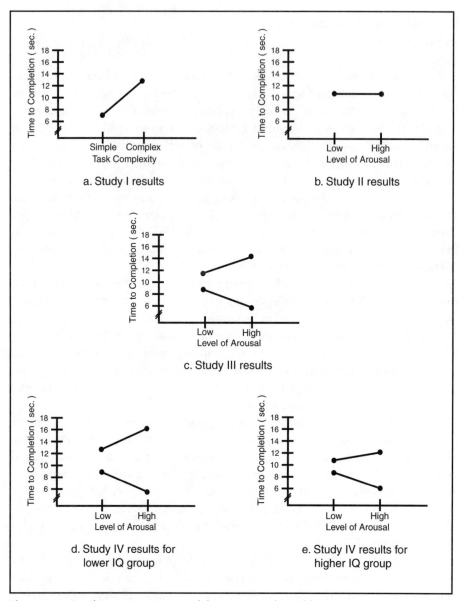

Figure 8.1. Graphic representations of data presented in Table 8.1.

In each case where there is a statistical interaction, as there is in (a), (b), and (c) in Figure 8.2, one could just as easily switch the positions of the independent variables to show the interaction. Try to do that for these examples (redraw the graphs with 2A and 2B on the x-axis and show the effects of 1A and 1B on the graph, using the same values of DV, the dependent variable). You'll see that the effects of independent variable 1 differ with the value of independent variable 2 as much as the

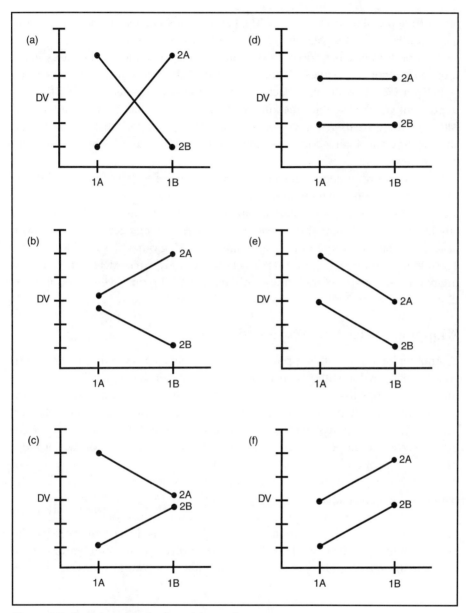

Figure 8.2. Sample results for factorial experiments.

other way around. Again, as a general rule of thumb, when the lines in a graph showing the effects of two independent variables are not parallel, that is an indication that there is a statistical interaction between those variables.

In graphs (d), (e), and (f), the effects of independent variable 2 are the same at both levels of independent variable 1. The same would be true, again, for the effects of 1 at the different levels of 2. The parallel lines suggest an additive relation-ship, or a lack of statistical interaction, in all these three cases.

A second point has to do with the rate at which complexity increases when more independent variables are added in a factorial study. As the graphs for Study IV in Figure 8.1 show (Table 8.1 actually shows the same results), adding a third in-dependent variable doubles the amount of information that must be interpreted. Although there are three-dimensional graphic representations that can be used to show a three-way interaction, they can be difficult to read unless one is used to do-ing so.

What if a fourth independent variable or factor were added in a factorial study? One factor requires a minimum of two groups. Two factors require a minimum of four groups. Three factors require a minimum of eight groups ($2 \times 2 \times 2$, or 2^3). If any factor has more than three treatments or levels, things get even worse even faster. Four factors would require a minimum of 16 groups ($2 \times 2 \times 2 \times 2$, or 2^4). The minimum number of groups for any factorial study can be determined by rais-ing two to the power of the number of factors (2^n). I won't even mention four-dimensional space.

Wrapping Up Factorial Experiments

Another limitation of this approach to multivariate research is that it is very diffi-cult to use in anything other than a true experimental design. It may be possible to find intact groups that have been exposed to varying levels of a single indepen-dent variable for the purpose of comparing some related aspect of their behavior. The likelihood is remote in most cases, however, of finding intact groups that have been exposed to all possible combinations of contrasting levels of two or more causal factors, one group to each combination.

That leaves a researcher no option but to use experimental designs that limit the nature of the participants that can be studied and the context in which the research can be conducted, usually a reactive laboratory setting with a contrived task. An al-ternative way of conducting multivariate studies places fewer limitations on the number of independent variables that can be studied and the number of depen-dent variables that can be considered at the same time. We turn next to that ap-proach.

● MULTIPLE CORRELATION RESEARCH

Introduction

The alternative to factorial experiments for studying multiple independent vari-ables is actually a family of methods that are all expansions of the correlational design discussed in Chapters 6 and 7. These multiple correlation methods or designs provide a number of advantages. They do not require that groups be exposed to particular combinations of large numbers of independent variables. Any individuals can be studied whose degree of exposure to the independent variables of interest is known. The independent variables whose possible effects are to be analyzed are usually quantitative measurements. They can also be qualitative measurements that can be represented numerically by what are called "dummy variables." For example, gender can be represented as "1" and "2," standing for female and male.

This method makes it possible to study larger numbers of potential causes or independent variables. It can be used to study exposure to influences that are produced only in nature, in natural settings where researchers have no way of controlling events. It also makes possible the study of multiple measures of the behavior in question.

Like the simple correlational design from which they come, these are nonexperimental designs, with the same advantages in external validity and construct validity. In the same way as the quasi-experimental designs build high levels of internal validity by expanding their pre-experimental counterparts, multiple correlation methods provide strong controls over threats to internal validity. They do so, however, by using statistical methods rather than the comparisons among discrete groups of people or occasions that characterize experimental research.

Correlation

To understand multiple correlation research, we need to begin with the basic concepts. The first of those is the **correlation coefficient**. It is an invention of 19th-century British mathematician Karl Pearson. Although it has been extended in various ways since that time, Pearson's original architecture has been preserved to this day. A correlation coefficient is a number that summarizes the relationship between two variables. It is based on measurements of two characteristics for each of a group of individuals or units, sometimes known as a **bivariate distribution**.

The bivariate distribution is a distribution of points determined jointly by the two measurements. Each point in a bivariate distribution represents one participant. It is determined by plotting both measurements for that individual on a graph where the two variables are represented on the two axes of the graph.

Using the same arousal-performance hypothesis we've been considering throughout this chapter, imagine that we had access to information about 50 students taking a final examination at the end of their first course in psychology. It isn't difficult to imagine how we could measure their performance on this task: We could use their score or grade on the exam. Because we're imagining, let's imagine big. What if each student had been fitted with electrodes that would transmit data on his or her level of physiological arousal? We could scale both measures, exam grade and arousal, from 0 to 100, so that we could construct a bivariate distribu-

TABLE 8.2   Bivariate Distribution of Arousal and Exam Scores

Participant Number	Arousal Score	Exam Score
1	41	82
2	38	71
3	15	55
4	42	86
5	35	67
6	53	91
7	66	83
8	37	65
9	26	73
10	44	76
11	90	51
12	76	74
13	78	66
14	52	84
15	35	75
16	54	70
17	78	61
18	65	87
19	32	72
20	67	76
21	47	68
22	60	95
23	48	77
24	29	60

tion, two measures per individual. One way to represent that distribution is shown in Table 8.2, where the two measures labeled Arousal Score and Exam Score are listed next to an arbitrary identification number assigned to each participant.

A correlation coefficient can be calculated from those 50 pairs of numbers. Theoretically, it could take a positive or negative absolute value between 0 and 1.00. The larger the coefficient, whether positive or negative, the more consistent the relationship between the two variables, usually designated X and Y, or predictor and criterion (although what one chooses to predict from what is an arbitrary choice that can go either way: X from Y, or Y from X).

If the coefficient takes a positive value between 0 and +1.00, individuals who measure higher on X will measure higher on Y, and individuals who measure higher on Y will measure higher on X. This is sometimes referred to as a **direct**

Participant Number	Arousal Score	Exam Score
25	57	81
26	53	71
27	68	78
28	8	48
29	63	90
30	18	59
31	71	73
32	58	91
33	86	54
34	57	75
35	56	88
36	14	45
37	93	63
38	57	87
39	59	96
40	82	65
41	66	76
42	74	82
43	74	69
44	87	57
45	49	79
46	65	92
47	75	67
48	68	78
49	58	89
50	86	68

relationship. If the coefficient takes a negative value, between 0 and −1.00, individuals who have higher scores on X will have lower scores on Y, and individuals who have higher scores on Y will have lower scores on X. This is sometimes referred to as an **inverse relationship**.

Some qualifications need to be kept in mind, however. For the correlation coefficient to provide an accurate measure of the relationship between X and Y, there needs to be a wide range of values on both variables. If exam scores or arousal scores (or both) were all within a narrow range or **restricted range** of the possible scores, the correlation coefficient would be very low, near 0, just because of the way it is calculated. Second, the correlation coefficient Pearson devised is appropriate only for bivariate distributions where the two variables show a **linear relationship**. That is, the direction of the relationship must be the same through-

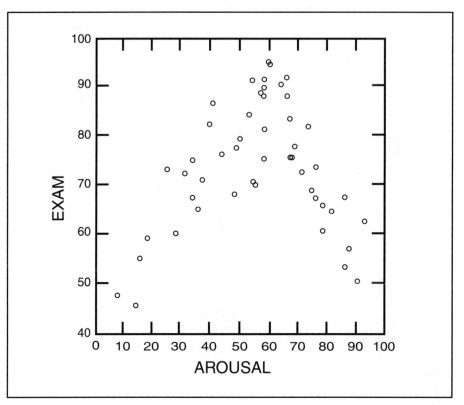

Figure 8.3. Scatterplot for bivariate distribution in Table 8.2.

out the range of the variables. We'll return to the question of how this and other statistics should be used in the next chapter. For now, let's see how the bivariate distribution in Table 8.2 stacks up.

If we calculate the correlation between exam scores and arousal scores for the 50 individuals in our hypothetical study, we find a value of +.141. But does that mean that there is only a very weak positive relationship between exam scores and arousal scores for this group? Think about our two qualifications. There does seem to be a reasonably broad range of exam scores, from 45 to 96, and an even broader range of arousal scores, from 8 to 93.

But do we know whether the relationship between these two variables is linear? One way to find out is to graph or plot them. Figure 8.3 shows how. The result is called a **scatterplot**, and it shows that the relationship between the two variables is not linear. Instead, it is a **curvilinear relationship**. That means that the direction of the relationship changes as the values of the variables change.

When arousal scores are low to moderate, from 8 up to 40 or 50, the relationship between arousal and performance is positive. In that range, higher arousal scores are associated with higher exam scores. As arousal scores increase further, however, from about 50 or 60 up to 93, exam scores decrease. In other words, the relationship between arousal and performance is negative at higher levels of arousal. That is why the Pearson correlation coefficient indicates very little relationship. It measures only the strength of linear relationships, not that of curvilinear ones.

There are ways of measuring the strength of a curvilinear relationship. They can be used when a researcher either knows (usually from looking at a scatterplot like the one in Figure 8.3) or suspects, because of some theory or previous research, that that's the kind of relationship he or she needs to look for. Those methods are far too complicated to discuss here (exceptions to the continuing widespread use of the Pearson form), but suffice it to say that if they were used for this set of data, they would indicate a strong curvilinear relationship between arousal and task performance. A coefficient designed to detect only linear relationships obviously does not show a strong relationship.

When the nature of a bivariate distribution has been determined using the appropriate means, further questions of interpretation arise. In our discussion of the correlational research design in the previous chapter, we learned that correlation is a very shaky basis on which to draw causal inferences. A strong correlation between two variables doesn't tell us which caused which, or even if there is any causal relationship at all between the two. Does watching violence on TV cause a child to behave aggressively, or does a child who behaves aggressively prefer to watch violent programs? Or does a third factor such as violence in the home cause both? We can't tell solely on the basis of a correlation, even a very strong one.

Even ignoring cause and effect, it can be tricky to judge the strength of the relationship between two variables from a correlation coefficient. Because correlation coefficients vary in magnitude between 0 and 1.00, it may seem reasonable to infer that the strength of the relationship between the two variables involved can be measured on the same scale. A correlation of .80 (positive or negative, because the direction of the relationship is a totally separate issue from its magnitude or strength) is not, as it might seem, 80% as strong as it can be.

To determine how strong a relationship is compared to its maximum possible strength, one needs to square the value of the correlation coefficient. Of course, squaring any number will remove a negative sign if there is one, so this measure of the strength of a relationship varies only from 0 to 1.00 (no negative values). For a correlation of .80 (or −.80), it is the squared value, or .64, that reflects its proportional strength. In statistical terms, the square of the correlation coefficient is known as the **coefficient of determination**. It reflects the degree to which the value of one variable determines, predicts, or accounts for the value of the other.

There is another way of saying the same thing, one that is used quite a bit in discussing multiple correlation analysis, which we are about to do. One can say that if the amount of TV violence a child watches is correlated .80 with the child's level of aggressive behavior (a purely hypothetical result, please remember), then the amount of TV violence watched *accounts for 64% of the variance in aggressive behavior*. That means that of all the factors that determine why one person is more aggressive than another (the total variance in aggressiveness), this one by itself accounts for 64% of the total determination by all those factors. In that hypothetical case, then, 36% of the variance would be left to be accounted for by other variables that might be associated with aggressive behavior. These might include gender, socioeconomic status, temperament, and a host of others.

To understand the causes of aggressive behavior in children, in a correlational sense at least, one would try to include measures of as many potential influences as possible. The proportional influence of each one would be determined by squaring the coefficient of correlation for it and the measure of aggression. If one could find all the causes, those proportions of variance would add up to 1.00, accounting together for all the variability in aggressive behavior for the sample of children observed. That would be true if all the squaring and adding were performed correctly. In this case, however, "correctly" is not as simple as the rules of arithmetic imply. The correct methods of accounting for the variance in a dependent variable are the subject of the next several sections of this chapter.

An Introduction to Multiple and Partial Correlation

What if TV violence exposure did correlate .80 with aggressive behavior in a sample of children? And what if gender, socioeconomic status, temperament, and other factors were also associated with aggressive behavior for that sample? If we could measure those variables in the same sample of children, how large would the correlations between those variables and aggressive behavior be? Does it seem from what you know now that they couldn't be too large? The squared values of the correlation coefficients—the coefficients of determination for all the possible variables associated with the levels of aggressive behavior in those children—couldn't add up to more than 1.00. Furthermore, the coefficient of determination based on the correlation with exposure to TV violence alone is .64.

Again, it's not that simple. Correlations, or the coefficients of determination derived by squaring them, don't add up in that straightforward way. That's because summed or multiple correlations have to take into account more than the relationship between each **predictor variable** (in this case, exposure to TV violence, gender, socioeconomic status, temperament, and the rest) and the **criterion variable** (in this case, aggressive behavior). They also have to take into account the relationships among the predictor variables themselves.

Let's continue with our hypothetical example of aggressive behavior in children. Imagine that in our sample of 50, exposure to TV violence correlated .80 with aggressive behavior, and that gender also correlated .80 with aggressive behavior. Gender isn't a continuous variable but a discrete one because it can take only two mutually exclusive values, male and female. A different kind of correlation coeffi-

---

Box 8.2 *THINKING ABOUT RESEARCH*

The Search for the Causes of Breast Cancer

One area where multiple correlation research is used very extensively is epidemiology, one type of research into the causes of disease. Epidemiological research is based on relationships between characteristics of groups of individuals and the groups' likelihood of developing a particular disease. Although univariate studies could tell us something about the role of one possible cause or another, understanding the development of a disease often requires considering many possible causes.

Take the case of breast cancer as an example. So far, the list of possible causes or risk factors identified in epidemiological and other research includes obesity, regular alcohol consumption, late or no childbearing, a history of breast cancer among one's mother and sisters, a history of developing lumps in the breast that need to be biopsied (even if the results are all negative), carrying one of the two known genes for breast cancer, and even a history of breast cancer on one's father's side of the family.

Because all these characteristics are known to be associated with breast cancer, how accurate a picture of the cause of the disease would evidence for just one of them provide, and how useful a basis for advising women about their need for regular screening examinations or preventive care (especially now that preventive drugs are available)? Moreover, with so many possible causes, how large a share of the variance in the incidence of the disease would a single cause likely account for? Finally, how would multiple correlation research provide information about the degree to which each of these factors posed an independent risk that multiple univariate studies would not provide? Doesn't it seem likely that family history and genotype, to take one example, tap at least some common variance rather than making entirely separate contributions to an overall explanation?

---

cient must be used to assess this relationship. That one, using gender as a dummy variable with arbitrary values like 0 and 1, still takes the traditional Pearson form.

If we simply added up the coefficients of determination for those two predictors, we'd get 1.28 (.64 plus .64). But that's impossible. As we know already, the maximum sum for all possible predictors, these two and any others, is 1.00. No set of predictors can account for more than 100% of the variance in a criterion, because 100% is all there is of anything, including the variability in aggression scores for the individuals involved.

There is an answer to this riddle. When two or more predictors are related to the same criterion measure, as exposure to televised violence and gender are in this hypothetical example, the proportion of variance in the criterion accounted for by all the predictors is not simply the sum of the proportions accounted for by each

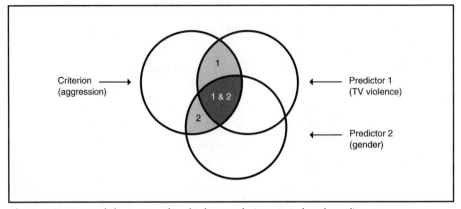

Figure 8.4. A visual depiction of multiple correlation–correlated predictors.
NOTE: 1 = variance in Criterion scores accounted for by Predictor 1, 2 = variance in
Criterion scores accounted for by Predictor 2, and 1 & 2 = variance in Criterion scores
accounted for by Predictors 1 and 2 (total shaded area).

individual predictor. When two or more predictors are considered together, their
joint contribution depends not only on their individual correlations with the criterion but also on the correlations between the predictors. To understand this, we
will examine the predictors one at a time.

In this hypothetical case, we started with exposure to TV violence. That predictor was correlated .80 with aggressive behavior in a group of children. Then we
considered gender, and that predictor was also correlated .80 with aggressive behavior for the same group of children. But what about the correlation between exposure to TV violence and gender? What is it, and why should that make a difference in adding up the contributions of the two predictors in accounting for the
variation in aggressive behavior among that group of children?

Imagine, for the sake of this argument, that gender and exposure to televised violence are also correlated .80 in this group. More specifically, let's assume that
boys are more likely to watch violent TV programs (with your permission, we'll
fight gender-role stereotypes some other time). Then part of an individual's score
for exposure to TV violence would be attributable to that person's gender: The two
predictors aren't independent of one another. When we know a child's gender, in
this hypothetical case, we also know a good deal about his or her TV viewing
choices, and vice versa. When we add gender as a second predictor, then, we don't
add an entirely different predictor. And when we add the proportion of variance in
aggressive behavior accounted for by gender, .64, it isn't an entirely separate proportion, because part of it is actually contained, so to speak, in the first predictor,
exposure to TV violence.

Figure 8.4 shows this set of relationships in a visual form. The overlap between
gender and exposure to televised violence defines their joint contribution to the

prediction of aggressive behavior in the sample. Each predictor also makes a unique contribution, represented by the smaller gray areas. Their total contribution consists of the sum of all three of those parts: the unique contributions of the two predictors and their joint contribution.

Multiple Correlation

There is a statistic that takes into account all three individual correlations—between TV violence and aggression, gender and aggression, and TV violence and gender. It combines them into a **multiple correlation**, represented by the symbol R. In this case, R, given the individual correlation coefficients we've assumed, would be equal to .84, which makes a lot more sense than 1.28. Another statistic combines the corresponding coefficients of determination into a multiple coefficient of determination, R^2, which in this case would equal .71.

To summarize, in Figure 8.4 the areas of the circle labeled Criterion that are cut off by the other two intersecting circles represent the proportions of the variance in the criterion explained by the two predictors. The smaller areas within the criterion shaded with light gray represent the unique proportions accounted for by each predictor. The larger area shaded with a darker gray represents the joint contribution of the two predictors.

Another way to try to understand how multiple predictors combine is to consider the most extreme cases. If two predictors, X_1 and X_2, were both correlated with the same criterion but totally uncorrelated with one another (r_{X1X2} = .00), the sum of the proportions of variance in the criterion accounted for by the two predictors would be the sum of their individual contributions (the sum of the individual coefficients of determination). Because they were uncorrelated predictors, there would be no joint contribution. Figure 8.5 shows an example of this set of relationships. It shows the individual proportions of variance accounted for in shaded areas.

In the opposite extreme, if two predictors were both correlated with the same criterion and perfectly correlated with one another (r_{X1X2} = 1.00), they would both account for the same variance in the criterion. It would all be joint contribution, with no unique contributions at all. Figure 8.6 shows this set of relationships, with the circles for the two predictors completely superimposed on one another. (Actually, because of the limitations of this sort of graphic depiction, they look like two concentric circles of almost the same size in the diagram.) The proportion of variance in the criterion accounted for is shown in gray shading. In this case, adding a second predictor, either one, would add nothing to the proportion of variance accounted for by the first predictor. The multiple coefficient of determination would be equal to either one of the individual coefficients of determination, which, by virtue of the perfect correlation between the two, would have to be equal. There would be the same total overlap shown in Figure 8.6.

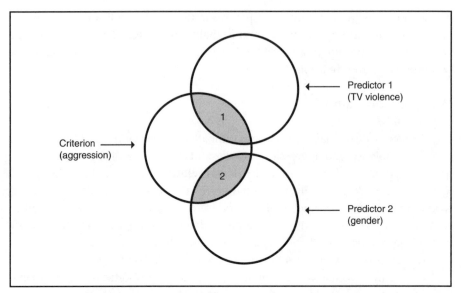

Figure 8.5. A visual depiction of multiple correlation–uncorrelated predictors.
NOTE: 1 = variance in criterion scores accounted for by Predictor 1, 2 = variance in predictor scores accounted for by Predictor 2.

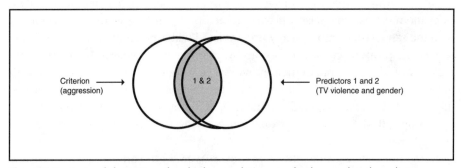

Figure 8.6. A visual depiction of multiple correlation–perfectly correlated predictors.
NOTE: 1 & 2 = variance in criterion scores accounted for jointly by Predictors 1 and 2.

By the way, remember that these pictures—in words or circles—would look exactly the same if the correlations were negative. That's because proportions of variance accounted for are all squared correlations. There is no such thing as a negative proportion, at least in the mathematics of real events that psychologists use.

Partial Correlation

Another way of understanding the contributions of multiple predictors is called **partial correlation**. Here, instead of "adding" the proportion of variance accounted for by a second predictor to that of the first, the joint influence of the two predictors on the criterion variable is, in a sense, subtracted. In the example we've been discussing, this would amount to answering the question, "What is the influence of exposure to TV violence on aggressive behavior with gender held constant?" The influence of gender is said to be "partialled out" of (in a sense, subtracted from) the relationship between TV violence and aggression.

Again, let's assume that exposure to TV violence is correlated .80 with aggressive behavior, exposure to TV violence is correlated .80 with gender, and exposure to TV violence is correlated .80 with gender. Then, the partial correlation of TV violence with aggression, controlling for gender, would be .44 (I hope you'll trust my calculations). That means that, in this hypothetical example, TV violence accounts for about 19% of the variance in aggression when gender is controlled, compared to 64% when it isn't. In other words, a large part of the relationship between watching violence on TV and behaving aggressively is due to the fact that boys watch more violence on TV. Of course, the same could be said of the relationship between gender and aggression, with respect to controlling for exposure to TV violence. Figure 8.4 shows the portions of variance accounted for by TV violence and gender alone—their unique contributions, as we referred to them earlier—in each case controlling for the other predictor. They are shown in the areas shaded in the lighter gray.

VARIETIES OF MULTIPLE CORRELATION ANALYSIS ●

From the basic mathematical building blocks of the correlation coefficient, the coefficient of determination, and the techniques of multiple correlation and partial correlation, statisticians have built a powerful family of techniques that have revolutionized research into the causes of behavior. These statistical techniques can be thought of as research designs that expand the scope and validity of the basic correlational research design in much the same way as we have already seen pre-experimental research designs expanded into much-improved experimental and quasi-experimental designs. In both cases, the expanded and improved research designs rule out many of the alternative explanations for research results. They increase their validity, to varying degrees, by adding appropriate comparisons. In the case of multiple correlation research, however, plausible rival hypotheses are ruled out statistically by adding measures or variables, rather than by adding groups or occasions.

These forms of **multiple correlation analysis (MCA)** can also be thought of as alternatives to quasi-experimental research designs. They are used very widely in some areas of research, in psychology and outside. Some of the most important, in addition to epidemiology, are educational research and criminology. They are used wherever it is necessary to consider many possible causes of an important behavioral outcome such as success in school, mortality, or criminal behavior. These methods are of particular value where that behavior and its possible causes cannot be studied in a controlled setting where a true experimental design can be used, and where so many causal variables are involved that combinations of selected values of them cannot be observed often enough in nature. In such cases, MCA is extremely important to researchers.

Because control over threats to validity is accomplished statistically in MCA, we can think of these statistical techniques as the equivalent of different research designs. We won't be considering these MCA designs in the same detail as the univariate designs covered in Chapters 5, 6, and 7. That could double the size of this book and would require the use of statistical concepts rarely studied by anyone other than advanced graduate students or researchers. Another notation system or a point-by-point analysis of threats to validity will not be presented for these designs, merely an introduction to the most basic forms (designs) and brief discussions of their advantages and disadvantages.

Multiple Regression Analysis

Multiple regression analysis (MR) evaluates the influence of two or more predictors on a single criterion. Regression is merely a different way of using correlation. Instead of expressing the relationship between two or more variables with a correlation coefficient, in regression analysis an equation is developed from a distribution of two or more scores, with one or more predictors (X's) and a criterion (Y) for a sample of individuals or units. Using this **regression equation**, it is possible to predict a criterion value for an individual (unit) when only a predictor measurement has been made.

We could start with a bivariate distribution of scores measuring children's exposure to TV violence and scores measuring their level of aggressive behavior. A regression equation could be produced that would allow the prediction of a particular child's level of aggression from a measure of his or her exposure to TV violence. The accuracy of the prediction would depend largely on the strength of the relationships between the predictor and criterion variables in the group as a whole.

More important for our present discussion, the regression equation can be expanded to accommodate multiple predictors, using multiple regression analysis. Following the logic of multiple correlation, the multiple regression equation would assign weights to the influence of the individual predictors according to their independent relationships with the criterion. The weight assigned to each predictor would reflect its partial correlation with the criterion, controlling for the influence of every other predictor in the equation. The analysis is based on the relationships among the predictors themselves as well as their individual relationships with the criterion.

It is beyond the scope of this chapter to explain how this is done mathematically, but it is still possible to appreciate what MR does. Its most useful outcome is an estimate of the proportion of variance in the criterion accounted for uniquely by each predictor. In a widely used variation of multiple correlation analysis (MCA) known as **stepwise multiple regression**, complex statistical procedures rank the predictors for the magnitude of their unique contributions to accounting for variance in the criterion. Stepwise multiple regression progresses step by step from the strongest predictor to the weakest, often applying some criterion for the minimum proportion of variance accounted for to include a predictor in the final statistical solution. Some MR analyses include a very large number of possible predictors. Stepwise multiple regression analysis resolves, albeit somewhat arbitrarily, the thorny problem that the unique contribution of each predictor to explaining the criterion can be viewed in a variety of ways, depending on the order in which other predictors are controlled in a multiple regression analysis.

MR can be used in a variety of research contexts. A sample of participants can be measured directly. In the example we have been considering, a group of children could be asked about their TV viewing habits and/or preferences and about their favorite games, as well as given personality and intelligence tests. The gender of each child could be recorded, along with age and information about the child's family structure and parents' occupations and incomes. All those variables could be entered into MR as predictors. Then their behavior in play with classmates could be observed to determine their level of aggression, perhaps combined with ratings obtained from teachers and peers. Those measures could be combined into a single criterion measure. A multiple regression analysis would determine the independent predictive value, if any, of the predictors (TV violence, individual personality traits, family background, etc.) for the criterion measure of aggression. Similarly, older individuals could be assessed for their health status, diet and other lifestyle variables, and family medical history for a study of disease etiology.

MR can also be used to study crime statistics, census data, institutional records, and other archival data that lessen concerns with response bias and reactivity because they can be collected without making direct contact with the research participants.

In effect, MR uses predictor variables in the same way that the nonequivalent control group design uses comparison groups. Each predictor provides statistical control over an alternative explanation for variance in the criterion or behavior being studied. In Haier et al.'s (1992) study of brain efficiency and intelligence (**E23**), the amount of training on the Tetris task was used along with intelligence as another predictor of GMR.

MR is especially useful in research that is aimed more at prediction than at determining cause and effect. If we want to know how certain factors are associated with aggressive behavior in children, or about the use of tobacco by adults, and we are not concerned whether those factors are causal agents, MR findings can be used to escape the logical pitfalls of using correlations to establish causality. If one predictor is actually a stand-in for some highly correlated but unmeasured variable, it still may be useful. For example, eating oat bran may be associated with a reduction in the risk of some cancers because people who eat it are not hungry for other, less healthful foods, rather than because the oat bran itself directly improves one's health. Even so, getting people to eat more oat bran would still have beneficial effects, and it wouldn't be of so much practical importance that oat bran was not the ultimate cause of those effects. The weakness of the causal inference would be much more problematic if the purpose of the research were to test a scientific theory about the causes of atherosclerosis.

MR is also especially useful when so many causal factors are suspected that it would not be feasible to set up an experiment or even a quasi-experiment because of the number of groups required to assess all possible combinations of independent variables, and because the resulting interactions among so many independent variables might be very difficult to interpret. Partial and multiple correlations are much easier to interpret than interactions, once one gets the hang of it. They can also be useful to a researcher who wants to go beyond correlational evidence of a strong causal factor. In some cases, he or she could set up a true experimental study, where the strongest factors from an MR study were manipulated as independent variables, to strengthen confidence in a causal inference.

In summary, MR offers the advantages of utilizing available data, considering large numbers of possible influential factors (predictors), and estimating the magnitude, rather than merely the probability of existence, of predictor-criterion relationships (more will be said about that subject in Chapter 10). MR is especially valuable in studying behaviors that are affected by many factors, especially when those factors are difficult to simulate in a laboratory, difficult to represent in other forms of statistical analysis, and primarily of practical rather than theoretical concern.

Multivariate Analysis of Variance (MANOVA)

The contribution that multiple regression analysis has made to psychological research is especially important in cases where the behavior being studied is likely to result from a limited number of contributing factors, none of them overwhelmingly influential by itself. It is especially vital where the required data cannot come from randomly assigned or clearly defined intact groups of individuals exposed to specific combinations of treatments, as they would need to be in a factorial study.

Where MR has made it possible to study more than one, or even many predictors, at one time, **multivariate analysis of variance (MANOVA)** provides a capability of studying multiple criterion or behavioral measures. Cases clearly exist in which many factors are likely to be responsible for variation in a particular behavior. There are also cases where an important behavioral outcome has many separate facets that cannot be combined easily into a single measure, or where those aspects of the behavior in question are of such interest in their own right that combining them into a single measure would obscure their separate effects.

Consider the question of why people differ widely in the degree to which they adopt a healthful lifestyle. There may be many determining factors, predictors, or independent variables involved, such as family background, gender, age, and personality. Many separate behaviors constitute a healthful lifestyle, such as diet, exercise, regular medical checkups, and abstinence from tobacco use. Just as it is possible to test the effects of the possible causes of healthy lifestyles one at a time in separate univariate studies, it is possible to study the effects on one component behavioral measure at a time. One could conduct separate studies that evaluate individual predictors or individual component behaviors, but that approach would ignore analogous advantages to those in considering interactions or relationships among predictors. These are made possible on the independent variable side of the hypothesis by MR analysis, with the attendant advantages discussed in the previous section of this chapter.

MANOVA provides similar advantages for the dependent variable side of the equation. MANOVA considers the relationships among behavioral measures to determine the extent to which effects of independent variables are unique to a single criterion or shared among two or more criteria. MANOVA provides a clearer picture of multiple criteria or effects in this way, just as MR provides a clearer picture of multiple predictors or causes.

MANOVA is an acronym that is an extension of **ANOVA**, which stands for **analysis of variance**, a statistical method for analyzing the results of factorial studies (see Chapter 10). It builds on the comparisons among separate observations made on groups of participants who received different treatment combinations, or who were observed on different occasions, that are at the heart of ANOVA. It adds to that base the same kinds of multiple correlational analysis used in MR analysis to evaluate the relationships among behavioral measures. That makes it both different from ANOVA and more powerful than combining separate ANOVAs for individual behavioral measures. Separate ANOVAs cannot address the question of the degree of interdependence among behavioral measures any more than they can show interdependence among predictor variables.

MANOVA is used in a wider variety of settings than is MR analysis. It can be used to extend true experiments in cases where multiple measures of participants' behavior can be made within the context of random assignment and manipulation of one or more independent variables. It can be used in the same way to extend quasi-experimental research designs that compare among groups or over time and are amenable to analysis using ANOVA, by considering multiple measures of the behavior in question.

The strengths and weaknesses of MANOVA designs are very similar to those of the experimental and quasi-experimental design on which they are based. The exception is that by considering multiple behavioral measures together, MANOVA designs can increase construct validity markedly on the dependent variable side. They can represent more separate facets of the behavior being studied than is possible with a single dependent measure. The limitations on the number of independent variables that can be considered alongside the multiple behavioral measures in MANOVA are addressed by the MCA method we will consider next, canonical analysis.

Canonical Analysis

We have seen already how MR designs permit an analysis of the independent contributions of multiple predictors to a particular behavior, as well as how MANOVA designs permit an analysis of the effects of a predictor on multiple behavioral measures that can tap separate facets of the behavior in question. Sometimes it is desirable to examine multiple predictors and multiple behavioral criteria in a single research study. Fortunately, there is a statistical technique that makes it possible to do that. It is called canonical correlation or **canonical analysis (CA)**.

The purpose of CA is much easier to understand than the mathematical procedures that make it work. It reduces almost any number of predictors and criteria to a single correlation coefficient, called the **canonical coefficient** and symbolized R_c. R_c estimates the total proportion of variance, among all the predictors and criteria involved in the analysis, that can be accounted for by the data collected in a particular study. In addition, it shows, using the same basic methods as multiple correlation, the intercorrelations among predictors and criteria and the unique contributions of individual predictors and criteria to that overall relationship.

Canonical analysis transforms the variables from their original forms into new combination forms known as *variates*. Those variates show the variables' unique contributions to the group of variables on the other side of the equation. Each predictor's relationship with the set of criterion variables and each criterion's relationship with the set of predictor variables, known as its *loading* on the variate, can be assessed separately from the relationships of other predictors or criteria.

Several years ago, I conducted a study that illustrates the value of canonical analysis. The research hypothesis was that a particular style of effective leadership, known as charismatic leadership, was the result of a leader's development of useful social skills. Those skills were hypothesized to develop out of opportunities provided, in part at least, as a result of other people's reactions to the leader's physical appearance.

In that study, some students and I explored as many aspects as we could of the behaviors exhibited by the participants in the study, who were male and female college students. They were required to videotape a simulated campaign speech for a fictitious student government election. Their behaviors served as the criteria in this study. We also explored as many relevant aspects of their background as we could manage to measure. Those were our predictors.

We chose to include five predictors in our analysis, based on past research and correlation coefficients for individual pairs of predictor and criterion variables. One was the participants' gender. A second was their degree of social confidence, as measured by a standardized questionnaire. We also assessed their level of past leadership experience. Each participant listed specific instances, and a group of judges rated each list on a 5-point scale. Then we included two aspects of their physical appearance, judged from photographs taken following their videotaping sessions. Those were their levels of physical attractiveness and baby-facedness.

We also chose five criterion measures, for the same reasons. We collected ratings by other students of the level of leadership experience evident in their performance of the campaign speech, and we determined the favorability of traits attributed to them by other students. We also used three direct behavioral measures made from the videotapes: the amount of time participants spent looking directly at the camera, the number of times they smiled, and the number of speech interruptions or nonfluencies. All the behavioral measures were adjusted for the amount of time each participant took to complete the speech.

Entered into a canonical analysis, the result was a canonical correlation of .48 between two variates. The predictor variate was composed of four of the five original variables (their loadings or correlations with the variate are in parentheses): actual leadership experience (.84), baby-facedness (−.59), physical attractiveness (.46), and social confidence (.40). The criterion variate included the favorability of attributed traits (.88), judged level of past leadership experience (.87), and directness of gaze into the camera (.38). This CA solution accounted for 52.6% of the variance in the total array of predictor and criterion variables we chose to measure in this study (R_c's aren't squared the way many correlation coefficients are to determine proportion of variance accounted for). We took this result as strong evidence that appearance and related social skill development are important factors in determining how charismatic a leader someone seems to be, at least for this sample of participants in this particular research context.

This example shows how CA can make it possible for researchers to investigate complex relationships between multiple antecedent conditions and multiple behavioral outcomes. Using R_c, CA both summarizes the degree to which a researcher's choices of measures of both causal factors and behavioral measures explain the overall relationship. In variate loadings, it also indicates the degree to which individual predictors and criteria are important to that relationship.

Other Forms of Multiple Correlation Analysis

Several other forms of MCA have proven themselves to be very useful in psychological research. Because I can't do justice here to even a limited sample of

MCA techniques, the ones remaining from the set to be discussed in this chapter will be described even more briefly than the examples considered above.

Factor analysis

Factor analysis is actually one of the earliest of these statistical techniques, having been developed by Louis Thurstone in the 1930s. It uses multiple correlation to analyze a group of variables and determine whether and, if so, how they can be reduced to a smaller number of factors, in the same way as canonical analysis reduces groups of predictors and criteria to predictor and criterion variates. Factor analysis has been a key part of research into the structure of intelligence, especially the question of how many separate "intelligences" there might be. It has also been used in studies of the structure of personality. It seems to have been more successful in the latter case, leading to the relatively recent breakthrough discovery of the "Big Five" factors of personality.

A variation of factor analysis known as **principal components analysis** can be used as an adjunct to many of the other research methods we've considered. It can be used to reduce multiple independent or dependent variables to a smaller number of factors. In a study I conducted with Kristina Donley, a student of mine, we were interested in people's nonverbal responses to charismatic leaders. The research literature gave us ideas about a large number of leader behaviors that might constitute charisma and that might affect the responses of others. We used principal components analysis to reduce the measures of those behaviors to a smaller number of factors. The analysis grouped together those that were statistically related, and it separated clusters made up of measures that were unrelated. That made it much easier for us to identify the leaders who were most and least charismatic. They were the ones to whom we wanted to expose our participants, in order to determine their emotional reactions.

Discriminant Function Analysis

Discriminant function analysis is used to determine the accuracy with which two or more predictors can be used to place individuals or events in one of a number of criterion categories. Multiple correlation is used to determine the weighted combination of predictor variables that best separates the individuals being studied into those separate groups. In some cases, the category system is dichotomous. For example, one can ask whether the predictors separate the individuals into criminal and noncriminal groups. This is one way of answering the question of what factors lead people to criminal behavior. As discussed above, causal theory is less likely to be the focus in such research than is pragmatic identification of factors that characterize at-risk individuals, for whom some intervention might prevent actual criminal behavior.

In other cases, there are more than two categories. For example, one could ask whether background variables separate individuals into several categories of psychiatric diagnosis, or several levels of socioeconomic status. There are many such questions for which discriminant function analysis is a useful research design.

Time Series Analysis

Time series analysis is a powerful statistical tool for determining whether a hypothesized causal event altered the course of a series of measurements. Without it, there would be no objective and quantitative means for determining whether a change in a time series associated with a hypothesized causal event constituted a meaningful departure from the other ongoing fluctuations in the series. For briefer series of measures, ANOVA can be used to determine trends and changes in trends. For the longer series that are used in the methodologically strong quasi-experimental time series designs, special statistical techniques for time series analysis are required.

Cluster Analysis

Cluster analysis is used to determine the best way of separating individuals (units) into groups based on a set of predictors (sort of the reverse of discriminant function analysis). Some forms of cluster analysis are hierarchical, establishing more than one level, such as a family tree or organizational chart. In a hierarchical solution, the most basic clusters may branch out into a second level, then a third, and so forth. For example, an analysis of multiple judgments of the appearance of residential streets might reveal that the most fundamental division was based on cost or wealth, but that within each of four levels of differing cost, raters secondarily distinguished three different architectural styles, and, within each of those, two different types of landscaping.

CONCLUSIONS ●

The purpose of this chapter was to introduce a variety of ways that the basic research designs considered in Chapters 5, 6, and 7 can be expanded to include multiple independent and dependent variables. The 13 basic designs considered in those chapters help us to understand how the arrangement of comparisons, across groups or over time, affects the validity of conclusions drawn from the research results about the truth of the hypothesis. A good deal of psychological research investigates more complex hypotheses about multiple causes, multiple effects, or both. Important behaviors often have more than one cause as well as more than one measurable component themselves.

Given the complexity of behavior and of its causes in nature, it is fortunate that the research designs/statistical techniques introduced in this chapter are available to research psychologists. Thanks are due to the mathematicians and mathematically sophisticated psychologists who developed them. Historically, "correlational research" has been used as a derogatory term for designs and methods that preclude valid inferences about cause and effect. This is probably because of the known problem of discerning cause and effect based on a simple correlation coefficient. That unfortunate connotation is finally being overcome by the recognition that correlation is a necessary element in many powerful research designs that produce findings that meet the very highest standards for validity. The primary impetus for the development of multiple correlation methods has been the pressing need to address important practical questions about behavior in such areas as education, health, mental health, and crime, but research psychologists are increasingly being won over by the capability of these methods to provide valid answers to basic theoretical questions about human behavior.

Review Questions and Exercise

Review Questions

1. What is a statistical interaction?

2. What is a factorial experiment, and what are its major advantages over multiple experiments with single independent variables?

3. On what statistical techniques is multiple correlation research based? How do those techniques substitute for the comparisons among groups or across occasions that are used in univariate research designs?

4. Under what conditions are multiple correlation designs used in preference to factorial experiments?

5. What opportunities does multiple correlation research offer that are not available in factorial experiments? Consider specific forms of multiple correlation research as well as the general benefits of all forms.

Exercise

Describe a study, real or imagined, that is carried out using the posttest-only control group design (TG2). Then describe a second study, using the same design, that investigates the effects of a different independent variable, representing another possible causal influence on the same behavior. Now combine those two studies into a factorial experiment with both independent variables. Compare the results of the two posttest-only control group studies with the results of the factorial experiment. Finally, add an additional independent variable, but use a multiple correlation design. Can you add additional dependent variables as well? What form of multiple correlation research could you use to analyze the results of that expanded study?

CHAPTER **9**

COLLECTING THE DATA

A Quick Guide to Chapter 9: Collecting the Data

Introduction to the Chapter

Settings for Data Collection in Psychological Research

The Laboratory

The Field

The Archives

Participants in Psychological Research

Nonhuman Participants

Human Participants

Aggregates

Data Collection Techniques

Self-Report Measures

Standardized Tests

Ad Hoc Self-Report Measures

Other Forms of Self-Report

Observer Ratings

Behavioral Observations

Unobtrusive Measures

Archival Measures

Conclusion

Review Questions and Exercise

● A QUICK GUIDE TO CHAPTER 9: COLLECTING THE DATA

There are many sources for **data**, the measures of behavior that can be used to test research hypotheses in psychology. The groups or occasions that are specified in a particular research design are compared on the basis of **observations** selected from one of those sources. The observations can be made in a variety of settings, including the **laboratory**, the **field**, and **archives** containing public or institutional records of past behavior. They can be used to study the behavior of people as well as nonhuman species.

In many studies, research participants record their own behavior. These studies are said to make use of **self-report measures**. Some studies use **standardized tests** developed for a wide variety of uses, usually through a program of extensive psychometric testing. In many cases, they respond to ad hoc instruments (designed for the specific study they are in) that ask about their attitudes after they've read a persuasive message, or their mood after they've watched a disturbing film, or the words they remember an hour after reading a paragraph. Participants may also respond to an **interview** or keep a **diary** of specific activities.

In other cases, the researcher makes use of direct observations of the participants' behavior. One alternative is **behavioral observation**. A researcher may count the number of times a specific behavior occurs, or record the time spent on a particular activity. Some observations are made with the help of instrumentation. An electronic counter can be used to record each instance of a pigeon pecking the key in an operant conditioning experiment. A clock built into a computer can be used to measure the time that elapses between a problem being presented on the screen and a research participant striking a key on the keyboard to choose among alternative solutions to the problem. The computer can also process the output from an EEG recording to determine the prevalence of alpha brain waves.

The researcher may instead make use of **observer ratings**. Either trained or naïve observers can evaluate the behavior of research participants, using rating scales or checklists. Responses can be categorized by type or judged for intensity. Such responses include facial expression, job performance, or friendliness in tone of voice, among many, many others.

Direct observation can be used outside the laboratory settings described in the previous examples. Researchers can observe how long someone sits at a study table in a college library after a stranger sits down uncomfortably close to them, whether a person helps a stranger pick up some dropped books, or how angry someone appears after being insulted.

Other studies use **unobtrusive measures**, such as the amount of litter found on the ground after an outdoor event, or how many people pass through a turnstile. Still others use **archival data** such as the results of periodic opinion polls or

---

**Chapter 9 Quick Guide: Sources of
Data for Psychological Research**

Settings
Laboratory
Field
   Archives
Participants
   Nonhumans
   Humans
   Aggregates
Data collection techniques
   Self-report measures
      ● Standardized tests
      ● Ad hoc self-report measures
      ● Other forms of self-report
   Observer ratings
   Behavioral observations
   Unobtrusive measures
   Archival measures

---

population censuses, or the information provided on applications for marriage licenses.

The choice of a source for research data depends to some extent on the nature of the hypothesis, but it has implications for psychometric quality, reactivity, and the various other construct validity criteria applied to behavioral measures in Chapters 3 and 4. Those implications should not be ignored.

The Chapter 9 Quick Guide reviews major sources of data in psychological research.

INTRODUCTION TO THE CHAPTER ●

To restate briefly what we all should know already, scientific tests of hypotheses, in psychology as well as in other sciences, are based on observation. Psychological research is a search for relationships between events in people's lives, and their physical and psychological characteristics, on one hand, and their behavior, on the other, as revealed in the vast array of measures or indicators used in that research. Throughout this text, we have seen examples of the ways in which psychological researchers measure behavior to test their hypotheses. This chapter will review those techniques of data collection, or sources of behavioral measures, more fully and more systematically.

● SETTINGS FOR DATA COLLECTION IN PSYCHOLOGICAL RESEARCH

Before I begin to attempt to enumerate a fraction of that vast array of psychological measures, I will consider the first of a number of related issues. This issue concerns the places or **settings** in which psychological researchers find their data.

The Laboratory

Most researchers can make their observations of behavior in one of three places. The first, and probably the one most people associate with psychological research, is the **laboratory**. Depending on the type of research involved, a psychological laboratory can be anything from a sterile surgical environment with a lot of expensive high-tech equipment to a college classroom containing the usual assortment of furniture and audiovisual equipment. There are endless variations in between. As we've already seen, a key feature of the laboratory setting is the discretion it affords the researcher to administer the treatments and behavioral measures of his or her own choice, to control the timing of those events, and to limit or prevent the occurrence of extraneous events—influences on the behavior in question that are not intended to be part of the treatments—that might influence the behavior being studied. It also allows control over other variables that may not be threats to internal validity but can result in greater variability in observed behavior. That variability can make it more difficult to discern meaningful patterns in the research data.

The laboratory setting also imposes significant limitations on the researcher. There are many theoretically significant behaviors, and causes of those behaviors, that are not likely to occur in a psychological laboratory. People aren't likely to be put in realistic fear of their lives, and they aren't likely to make life-or-death decisions. Neither their careers nor their significant relationships are going to be on the line. For ethical and practical reasons, it is very difficult, if not impossible, to observe in the laboratory truly dangerous, intimate, or otherwise significant events in people's lives, or their responses to them. Of course, there are exceptions, as the research of Pennebaker and colleagues (1996) on the therapeutic effects of writing about one's emotions demonstrates.

When nonhuman participants are studied in the laboratory, the range of possible events and behaviors that can be studied is expanded considerably. Hans Selye (1956) was able to poison rats almost to the point of death in his research on stress.

Shepard Siegel (1987, **E10**) was able to administer morphine to rats in order to study the process of opiate addiction. Seligman and Maier (1967, **E18**) gave dogs severe, inescapable shocks to demonstrate the phenomenon of learned helplessness. Experiments involving such extreme or dramatic stimuli and responses are rarer, but not unknown, in laboratory research involving human participants. In fact, most examples, including Milgram's obedience experiments (1974, **E9**) and Zimbardo's (Zimbardo, Banks, Haney, & Jaffe, 1973) prison simulation study, were never intended to be quite as extreme or dramatic as they turned out.

Perhaps the most significant limitation associated with the use of the laboratory setting for psychological research, however, is an unfortunate by-product of the felicitous opportunities the setting affords for the researcher to control the action. In the laboratory, researchers can physically screen out unintended events that might compromise internal validity, simply by closing the laboratory door. They can provide all the salient events that take place behind that door and create the precisely tuned variations of the independent variable (i.e., the treatments) on an arbitrary schedule that minimizes the possibility of coincidental events that might affect the behavior being studied. All of this, however, necessarily forces the researcher and the research participants into direct and continuous contact with one another.

For human research participants, at least, the laboratory is almost inevitably a reactive setting. Cover stories and elaborate scenarios involving cleverly coached actors and cleverly chosen props can succeed in misleading participants about the true purposes of the research, but it is difficult to imagine how participants can be distracted to the point of forgetting completely and permanently why they are in the laboratory in the first place: They are there to be studied. As a result, any measures of their behavior obtained in the laboratory must be considered vulnerable to taint from the hypotheses that human participants themselves form, from the cues made available to them. As we have seen, these effects can be far more subtle than many would imagine if it were not for the evidence about experimenter expectancy effects provided by Rosenthal and his colleagues (Rosenthal, 1969). Even nonhuman participants may behave differently if researchers who have hypotheses of their own are able to convey expectations for the participants' behavior by the way they handle them during the course of a laboratory experiment.

Behavioral measures in the laboratory are limited in other ways. Laboratory experiments are often brief compared to the influential events in people's and animal's lives they purport to study. Measures of participants' behavior have to be tailored to that abbreviated time frame. Rats and pigeons must learn in an hour. Memory ordinarily must be tested within a few hours (no more than days) of a participant's exposure to the material to be remembered. A group status hierarchy must develop within a few 1-hour weekly sessions at most. Behaviors, and the events that cause them, that develop over significant periods of time are not likely topics for study in the psychological laboratory. Think of the stress that results from living within sight of a damaged nuclear reactor, for example, or especially the lifelong process of human development itself.

Laboratories are also bound by constraints of the size and cost of the physical props used to create the setting in which subjects must respond. As a result, researchers often must try to create, in the laboratory, small and sparse simulations of tasks that subjects might face in the world outside. Mazes, operant conditioning chambers, and shuttle boxes are a few examples of the simulations created for learning experiments with nonhuman participants. Memory drums, reaction timers, and Triplett's (1897) fishing-reel-winding stand (**E3**) are a few examples of the apparatus used in research with human research participants.

Not only do these laboratory versions of real-life experiences provide only limited representations of the behavior being studied, but they also sometimes seem to take on a life of their own. Once an invention of this sort is publicized in the report of a successful study in the research literature, subsequent research is often planned around it even if a new simulation might better represent the behavior in question. In their zeal for scientific progress and personal success, researchers, like others, sometimes take the path of least resistance. They may turn a good solution for one study into the basis for a routinized body of research.

Although this standardization of procedure makes the results of different studies easier to compare, it limits their construct validity if they purport to study different behaviors. It also limits their generalizability if the simulation is an idiosyncratic one. One of my favorite psychology professors once wondered aloud whether operant conditioning would ever take place if experiments with rats and pigeons were conducted in a larger chamber that located the manipulandum (bar or key) at one end and the delivery of reinforcement at the other. Real-life rat and pigeon environments probably do that quite often.

Most of the exemplar studies we've been analyzing throughout this book were conducted in the laboratory. Several areas of psychological research are represented. Haier et al.'s (1992) study of brain efficiency and intelligence (**E23**) comes from neuroscience. Triplett's (1897) experiment on coaction (**E3**) and the study by Darley and Latané (1968) on bystander intervention (**E7**) represent social psychology. Seligman and Maier (1967, **E18**) made a fundamental discovery about the causes of depression in the traditional "animal lab," using the tried and true shuttle-box apparatus. Dement's research on REM rebound (1960, **E14**) was conducted in a sleep laboratory like those where many of the basic discoveries about the sleep cycle have been made. There are other examples, from other research areas within psychology, in keeping with the general and long-standing popularity of laboratory research in the discipline.

The Field

Some researchers deal with the limitations on the measurement of behavior imposed by the laboratory setting by leaving for more realistic pastures. It is possible to conduct psychological research in public places such as bus stations, subway

---

Box 9.1 | *METHODOLOGY IN EVERYDAY LIFE*

Looking for Crime in All the Right Places _____

In Oklahoma, where I live, there's been the same good news as elsewhere recently about falling crime rates in big cities. According to the Oklahoma State Bureau of Investigation (OSBI) Uniform Crime Report for 1998, the handful of cities in Oklahoma with populations greater than 50,000 are becoming safer. The two largest, Oklahoma City and Tulsa, experienced reductions in violent crime from the previous year of 7.2% and 6.0%, respectively, with total reductions of about a third compared to 1992.

The same report paints quite a different picture for communities of 10,000 or less. The rates of violent crime in those small towns increased during the same period, 1992-1998, by approximately 25% across the state. In the town of Grove, Oklahoma, with a population of 5,331, there were 3 violent crimes reported in 1997, compared to 39 in 1998.

Why are small towns in Oklahoma getting so much more dangerous? Or are they? One possible explanation for the apparent explosion in their crime rates has to do with federal programs that have funded growth in small-town police departments and improvements in their equipment and training. What police do, after all, is investigate crime, and the more police, the more investigation. Furthermore, the more police officers out looking for crime, and the better their equipment and their methods, the more crime is likely to be found.

The change in violent crime rates in small-town Oklahoma therefore may be more a matter of better, or at least more concerted, measurement than of more crimes actually being committed. What does this example tell us about the difficulties involved in using archival data? If a researcher takes the information in an archive like the OSBI Uniform Crime Report at face value, how might this affect the validity of the findings of research into the causes of crime that is based on the data in that archive?

---

cars, city sidewalks, and bars, among others. These settings are referred to collectively as the "**field**." The field is a fertile ground for psychological research if researchers have access to and can unobtrusively observe the behavior of the users of the setting. If they can create, when they wish, events that might have theoretically significant effects on behavior for randomly selected users who can be observed in a public setting, they can even conduct true experiments in the field.

The most obvious advantage of conducting experiments in the field rather than in the laboratory is the lack of reactivity. Although the researcher may be present in the scene, he or she is not in the participant's face. The lack of direct face-to-face contact makes experimenter expectancy effects easier to control. If someone does need to interact with participants, it can be a research assistant who knows much less about the purpose of the research and the research hypothesis.

Nor do participants in field experiments need to be aware that their behavior is being studied. The treatments in field experiments can be designed to resemble everyday events in the settings where they occur. A passerby (research assistant) can drop a package, or ask directions, or stumble and fall. At the same time, the participant's response can be observed, rated, or even videotaped by someone at a sufficient distance, and far enough out of the participant's direct line of sight, so that the observation is likely to be unobtrusive.

The principal disadvantage of a field setting is the limited range of behavioral measures that can be used. Participants' thoughts, moods, emotions, and other private experiences usually cannot be accessed directly. Even if participants could be stopped long enough to fill out questionnaires or rating scales, that would immediately reinstate the reactive arrangements researchers seek to escape by studying behavior in the field. Observations in the field usually are limited to overt behaviors. The researcher can observe what the participant does, or says out loud, in response to the treatment. Or how fast he or she walks. Or how long it takes participants to notice some event. Or if there is a facial expression and, if so, what it is. Even those behaviors need to be obvious enough to be observed and recorded at a distance, often in a crowded and noisy place, and within the limitations of an unobtrusive observer's capacity to make a record of them.

One way to deal with some of these limitations is to use video cameras or stop-action movie cameras. They can be mounted unobtrusively in positions where they can permanently record participants' behavior so that it can be analyzed in more detail after the fact. Even those techniques, however, limit the researcher to what can be seen about participants' behavior. Participants' subjective responses to the events whose effects are being studied, the responses that in the laboratory can be measured by questionnaires, rating scales, and even psychophysiological recordings, can only be inferred from their most public, observable consequences.

It should be pointed out, however, that these limitations are not always disadvantages of field research compared to research carried out in the laboratory. The laboratory study by Darley and Latané (1968) of bystander intervention (**E7**) used only directly observable aspects of the participants' behavior. These researchers measured how long it took participants to leave their cubicles to go to help the victim. Many other studies of bystander intervention have been carried out in public places, such as on city sidewalks and in New York City subway cars. In those field studies, in much less reactive settings, researchers were able to study the same behaviors, in response to much more realistic and involving emergencies. In addition, field research can be aided by relatively new computer chip-based technology that allows unobtrusive observers on the scene to make much more extensive records of the behavior they observed than were possible with the old-fashioned clipboard, paper, and pencil arrangement.

Our exemplar studies contain few examples of field research, but Festinger et al.'s (1956) study of expectancy disconfirmation and cognitive dissonance among doomsday cult members (**E11**) is one well-known example. Rosenthal and Jacobson's (1966) demonstration of teacher expectancy effects in the elementary school classroom (**E15**) is another. The bystander invention study by Darley and Latané (1968, **E7**), performed in a laboratory, was followed up by several field experiments conducted in New York City subway trains. Milgram's laboratory studies of obedience (1974, **E9**) were developed further in research carried out on the sidewalks of that same city. Field research is less flexible and more difficult (even dangerous) to carry out, in part because of the lack of a strong tradition in psychology that can provide good models for future studies in the field.

The Archives

A final "setting" for research is the various **archives** of behavioral measures. As we have seen on a number of occasions, many organizations and institutions in every literate society keep records that can be used to assess members', workers', students', or citizens' behavior for the purpose of testing hypotheses in psychological research. These records include detailed crime statistics, records of economic activity, census data, job performance and industrial output measures, school records, traffic accident data, the results of long-term periodic surveys of public opinion, surveys of sexual practices and of many more aspects of people's beliefs and activities, records of energy use, and far too many more to even mention here.

Although some of those archives of behavioral measurements (it should be kept in mind that most were never intended as such) remain as "hard copy" on library shelves, in file cabinets, and elsewhere, they are increasingly likely to be stored in computers. This is important for two reasons. First, it makes them much more portable. Rather than traveling to distant storage sites or having voluminous records shipped in, the researcher is able to download archival records or work with them directly from virtually any distance over a computer network, especially the Internet. Second, it makes them much easier to search. Rather than paw through files looking for page numbers, dates, or other identifying landmarks, powerful software (electronic retrieval systems analogous to those discussed in Chapter 2 for searching the psychological research literature) can be used to locate the specific information a researcher might need. The increasing ease with which archival records can be used may also have the effect of encouraging the creation of more of them, reflected in the growing use of the term **database** among researchers who access their data via computers.

Archival data have many advantages. Most of these data are collected anonymously. In many cases, the individuals represented in an archive were never aware that their behavior was being assessed. When you get a speeding ticket or buy a gas-guzzling sport utility vehicle, the possibility that some psychologist will use the fact that you did so to test a hypothesis about human learning or motivation, persuasion, or some other behavioral phenomenon is probably the farthest thing from your mind. For that reason, many of the archival measures available for use by psychological researchers can be said to be free of reactivity. People do what they do independently of what researchers might someday expect them to do, and without any concern for how future research might make use of the resulting record of their having done whatever it was.

Another positive feature of archival records as sources of data for psychological research is their scope. In the laboratory or the field, researchers are limited to studying dozens or, at most, hundreds of people over a span of minutes or maybe hours. There are only rare exceptions, such as the use of time-lapse photography in heavily used public places, that make more extensive data collection possible. In contrast, it is not unusual for archival records to reflect the behavior of thousands or even millions of people, over periods of months or years. This is the case with crime statistics, traffic accident records, health and mental health records, and the U.S. Census, among others. These archives may cover the entire population of the United States over an indefinite period. International archives such as the Human Relations Area Files and economic, health, and other statistics collected by various United Nations agencies cover virtually the whole world's population in comparable ways.

If you recall our earlier discussion of time series research designs, you may remember how well they stack up against possible threats to construct, internal, and external validity. Time series research can ordinarily only be carried out using archival data. It is difficult to conceive of a researcher having the foresight, the resources, and the patience to collect sufficient data for time series analysis that would serve only to test one particular research hypothesis. Archival records usually provide the only way to learn about murders, wars, and other behavioral phenomena that most researchers (thankfully!) will never be able to observe directly.

Unfortunately, the virtues of archival records as a source for psychological research data are counterbalanced by some significant drawbacks. The most general of these problems is that the researcher usually has no control over, and often no knowledge of, the conditions under which archival data are collected. More specifically, it is possible that archival data are biased in ways that jeopardize the validity of research findings based on analysis of them. An example is the recent disclosure that Alfred Kinsey's (Kinsey, Pomeroy, & Martin, 1948) voluminous records of interviews with Americans about their sexual behavior may have overestimated the incidence of homosexuality. It seems that Kinsey specifically sought out homosexuals as potentially interesting interviewees rather than interviewing a random sample of Americans. That revelation calls into question the long-standing estimate of the incidence of homosexuality in the general population that had been based, in large part, on Kinsey's data.

As mentioned earlier in this text, public records may underestimate the rate at which Catholics commit suicide because Catholic families may pressure authorities to not list suicide as the official cause of death of a family member because of the conflict with their religious beliefs. The number of rapes reported to the police may be far smaller than the number committed because of rape victims' fear of

---

TABLE 9.1   The Principal Advantages and Disadvantages of Three Research Settings

Setting	Advantages	Disadvantages
Laboratory	Control over extraneous events Efficiency	Reactivity Nonrepresentativeness Limited sampling of units Brevity
Field	Wider sampling of units Ecological validity Nonreactive context	Lack of control Limited range of independent variables
Archives	Lack of reactivity Extended time frame Large and representative samples of units	Hidden biases in data

---

stigmatization or retaliation. Young and African American drivers may be more likely to be stopped by police for minor traffic violations than other drivers who commit those same violations. The administration of President Ronald Reagan reported a self-congratulatory decline in the nation's unemployment rate after it chose to include military personnel, none of whom are ever unemployed, in those calculations. That was the first time that unemployment records had included military personnel since the government began keeping such records. The list of similar examples of problems with archival data could go on to fill an entire chapter.

Many of the distortions in the archival record are innocent with regard to their use in psychological research. Those who keep the records may be trying to protect vulnerable parties, or they may limit their records to the information that is most readily available to them, or they may be trying to please a narrow constituency. This does not obviate the fact that conclusions about the causes of human behavior based on those records may be in error as a result of the records being either incomplete or distortions of what actually occurred.

Researchers can trust archival records of behavior no more than they trust other measures of behavior. Just because the records say that something happened doesn't mean it actually happened. The appeal of archival data is their extensive scope and valuable lack of reactivity, but those virtues can't be allowed to blind researchers to the limitations of such data.

Among our exemplar studies are two that used archival data. Frazier's (1985) evaluation of the modular, direct-supervision jail in Contra Costa County (**E25**) was based in large part on institutional records of incidents of violence (do administrators in a "model jail" keep records the same way they do in ordinary jails?). Zajonc and Markus's (1975) study of family structure and intelligence (**E16**) was based on an analysis of existing Dutch government records.

Table 9.1 summarizes our discussion of settings for psychological research.

● PARTICIPANTS IN PSYCHOLOGICAL RESEARCH

Nonhuman Participants

Much of the classic research in psychology was conducted with "animals" or, more accurately, nonhuman organisms. Far too many species have been used to name them here, but among the exemplar studies we already have seen examples of the use of rats in Rosenzweig et al.'s (1972) research on brain development in enriched environments (**E22**) and in Calhoun's (1962) study of the effects of population density (**E19**), the use of dogs in Pavlov's (1927) studies of classical conditioning (**E20**) and in Seligman and Maier's (1967) research on learned helplessness (**E18**), and the use of monkeys in Harlow's (1958) research on the origins of mother-infant bonds (**E12**). Of course, most psychology students are well aware of B. F. Skinner's extensive research on operant conditioning with pigeons.

Nonhuman organisms provide researchers with several advantages. They are readily available. This is especially true of rats, which can be bred in psychological laboratories specifically for use in research, and of pigeons and mice that are bred commercially to be used as research subjects. In addition to ease of acquisition, nonhuman participants are chosen for their quality as animal models of human characteristics and behaviors. Many species show a striking similarity to humans in characteristics relevant to the behavior being studied. This is important because the ultimate goal of most of this "animal research" is to understand human behavior. For example, the processes involved in vision have been studied extensively in cats because the feline visual system is similar in many ways to that of humans. Harlow (1958) chose rhesus monkeys for his research on mother-infant bonds (**E12**) because the rhesus monkey lives in family arrangements similar to those of humans.

Nonhuman organisms also can be studied in ways that humans cannot. Harlow's (1958) isolation of newborn rhesus monkeys so as to study critical periods for social development (**E12** again) is an example, as is Rosenzweig et al.'s (1972) assignment of rats to richer and poorer laboratory cage environments (**E22**). Studies of experimental brain lesions in rats, such as Neil Miller's classic study (Miller, Bailey, & Stevenson, 1950) of hyperphagia (overeating due to loss of function in the ventromedial hypothalamus), are another. None of those treatments could ever be administered to humans, although nonexperimental research can take advantage of similar unfortunate experiences that may occur naturally.

There are, of course, ethical objections to such animal research, by groups that don't share the belief that human welfare is more important than that of nonhuman species. Humans and nonhumans, however, certainly have very different legal rights. As a result, such research is currently possible, under strict professional and government guidelines for the humane treatment of the animals involved, whereas comparable research on humans simply is not. The ethical treatment of research participants is discussed in much more detail in Chapter 11.

As we discussed earlier, there are important questions about the quality of inferences about the causes of human behavior that should be drawn from research with nonhuman participants. Studies in comparative psychology and neuropsychology suggest that there are important differences in behavior among species that are rooted mainly in differences in central nervous system structure. In cases where nonhuman species are similar to humans in the neural substrate for a particular behavior, those species may be good choices for research into the causes of that behavior. Where differences are apparent, they may not. Cockroaches may respond similarly to humans in the physiological changes that accompany the presence of other members of their species, because the neural mechanisms for arousal are similar in the two species, but they are quite different in the way they learn complex hierarchies of concepts to make sense of their environments—humans use language, and cockroaches don't.

Human Participants

Human beings have increasingly supplanted nonhuman organisms as the participants of choice for the research psychologist. Questions about the generalizability of research results are one reason. Another reason is growing knowledge about differences in behavioral capabilities among species, particularly about the importance of species-specific neural mechanisms that "hardwire" patterns of behavior into individual organisms. Yet another important factor is the growth of cognitive psychology. More than in the past, psychological research studies memory, decision making, verbal behavior, and other problems for which nonhuman organisms do not seem to be suitable research participants. This contrasts with research on the effects of reinforcement on responses such as bar pressing or maze running, or on the effects of Pavlovian conditioning on salivation, the subjects of so much of the classic research in experimental psychology. Today much more research addresses applied questions about learning, motivation, problem solving, and the like, in settings such as schools, factories, and hospitals where only humans can be studied.

Much research with human participants also raises questions about the generalizability of research results from humans to other humans. The label **participants** is especially appropriate when humans are the objects of study, given what we know from Orne (1959), Rosenthal (1969), and others about the active role they take in psychological research: When the behavior in question is subject to the influence of social and cultural factors, caution needs to be exercised in generalizing research results beyond those who share the relevant background characteristics with the actual research participants. Age, education, gender, and religion can all fall into that category. On the other hand, research into more basic processes, such as learning, memory, and perception, may be free from such concerns. Psychological research should not be dismissed cavalierly for being a "psychology of the college sophomore" without cogent reasons for doing so.

Important ethical issues are raised in the treatment of human research participants. Many examples exist of their being deceived, threatened psychologically and physically, and embarrassed; these have led to the imposition of severe restrictions on the use of human participants. Before they can be studied, human research participants may need to give their consent based on a prior description of the purpose of the study, although this is a recipe in some cases for the production of artifacts that threaten the validity of the research findings. They may need to be told even more about the research in a debriefing session afterward, a possible problem for evaluating the responses of subsequent participants should the information spread to prospective participants. Ethical problems become even more acute when human participants are not fully functioning adults. Research problems in psychology sometimes require the study of children, cognitively impaired individuals, institutionalized persons, and others who are not capable of giving fully informed consent or understanding subsequent explanation. How are their rights to be protected?

Aggregates

Finally, some research in psychology protects the privacy of participants because it is based not on the study of individuals at all, but on study of aggregates. Research into the effects of the Supreme Court decision striking down state segregation laws was based on fertility rates in specific states during specific months. Like studies of crime, highway safety, educational innovation, and many other problems in psychological research, the data from that study could not be traced back to any specific individual. Although there are some exceptions, that is often the case in research based on archival data. It may also be the case in studies of sensitive behaviors in which individual data could jeopardize the privacy of the research participants. In those cases, aggregating participants into classrooms, or departments, or other units, may be preferable on ethical grounds.

Privacy is an issue in all research with human participants. Researchers have an obligation to code their data so that they can't be traced back to the individuals from whom they came. In the rare cases in which the specific characteristics of an individual are an important factor in interpreting the research results, as in a clinical case study, care needs to be taken to change names of people and places to protect the privacy of participants. Again, much more will be said about research ethics in Chapter 11.

Table 9.2 reviews the main points of our discussion of the variety of participants studied in psychological research.

TABLE 9.2 The Principal Advantages and Disadvantages of Three
Types of Research Participants

Participants	Advantages	Disadvantages
Nonhumans	Availability Ethical latitude	Generalizability Limited cognitive capabilities
Humans	Generalizability Complex cognitive processes	Reactivity Ethical limitations
Aggregates	Large database Practical significance	Limited opportunities Unknown biases

DATA COLLECTION TECHNIQUES ●

The remainder of this chapter will discuss five techniques that are widely used by research psychologists to measure the behavior they are studying. Data are (remember, data is the plural form of datum) the measurements of behavior that researchers use to determine the effects of the treatments they are comparing. Sometimes referred to as dependent measures, they constitute the results of a research study. **Data collection** techniques are the specific measurement tools, tasks, or instruments that are used to acquire data.

Self-Report Measures

One of the most common ways to measure people's behavior is to simply ask them questions about it. Their answers, or reports, of their knowledge, feelings, attributes, actions, or whatever, then become the data that are collected. To better organize our analysis of **self-report measures**, we will consider two different types. The first type consists of **standardized tests** that have been developed to measure intelligence, school achievement, and personality, for use in industry, schools, clinics, and other such venues. The second type consists of measures devised strictly for use in research. We will refer to those as **ad hoc self-report measures** because, although they may be used in large numbers of studies, in similar if not identical forms, they are usually produced for use in a particular study without following the formal psychometric procedures that are used to produce standardized published tests.

Standardized Tests

In their study of the effects of teacher's expectancies on their student's academic achievement, Rosenthal and Jacobson (1966, **E15**) used a group-administered IQ test to measure achievement. They compared changes in the IQ test scores of those students who were randomly designated to their teachers as bloomers (or underachievers) and those who were not. Zajonc and Markus (1975), in their study of the effects of family structure on intelligence (**E16**), also used scores on a standardized intelligence test as the dependent measure.

Following his research on learned helplessness with dogs (**E18**), Seligman studied the effects of Introductory Psychology students' explanations for their failure on a classroom test. In that research, he measured the incidence of depression in the groups he compared by administering a standardized published test for depression. Andrew Baum (Baum, Cohen, & Hall, 1993) evaluated the effects of the accident at the Three Mile Island nuclear power plant on the people who lived nearby by administering a standardized published test of depression as well. Incidentally, both studies utilized other data collection techniques to measure additional effects on participants' behavior.

Studies of psychotherapy outcomes such as those meta-analyzed by Smith and Glass (1977, **E24**) have utilized standardized personality tests to compare the effectiveness of different therapies. Studies comparing different teaching methods, or class sizes, or teacher qualifications, among other things, have used standardized tests of academic achievement (reading, math, etc.) to evaluate their relative effectiveness and to find ways of improving public education.

Using standardized tests to measure behavior in psychological research carries some distinct advantages. First and foremost, these tests generally have met established psychometric criteria for reliability and validity after undergoing extensive and expensive programs of development. They yield stable scores that are internally consistent, and their acceptably strong criterion validity correlations with appropriate behaviors and other measures indicate that they measure what they are supposed to measure.

Standardized tests are, however, of limited use. There is a limited number of such tests, compared to the much larger number of ad hoc self-report measures research psychologists have created. Those that are available tend to measure global behaviors or traits, such as intelligence or personality, which are, additionally, assumed to be fairly stable or insensitive to the effects of transient experiences. On the other hand, the predicted effects of treatments being compared in a research study are often much more specific—a particular response, or performance of a specific task—and presumed to be caused by just such transient variations in the conditions under which they occur, particularly the independent variable and its underlying causal construct.

Box 9.2 | *THINKING ABOUT RESEARCH*

Not All Data Come From Real "Units"

Our discussion of the sources of research data has concentrated on the observation of behavior, whether in human or nonhuman species, in the lab or in the field, directly or through archival or unobtrusive measures. Recently, researchers have developed alternatives to the observation of the behavior of living organisms. These new, nonliving sources of data include computers and chemical compounds.

The computer alternative is generally referred to as modeling or simulation. In the pharmaceutical industry, for example, computers are being used to test the effects of new drugs on virtual organs or virtual patients. Computer programs can incorporate such assumptions as the fact that some patients will not take their medicine as prescribed, and the programs can be used to estimate the doses that should be administered in actual clinical trials with human patients. In the field of evolutionary psychology, the long-term outcomes of different strategies of cooperation and competition (the "dove" and "hawk" strategies) have been compared using computer simulations.

Another approach to "non-animal testing" is based on the use of chemical compounds that are similar to those in animal tissues. New chemicals that pose a threat of toxicity can be tested on those compounds rather than on laboratory animals or human research participants. This is an extension of an old approach in science, referred to as "in vitro" research, in which animal tissues are studied in test tubes or petri dishes, in contrast to "in vivo" research on living organisms. Consistent with that nomenclature, by the way, computer simulation is sometimes referred to as research "in silico."

When would these new sources of research data be most useful? What are their methodological implications? What questions do they raise about construct validity and external validity, in particular? How might ethical concerns about research with living organisms figure into researchers' decisions about whether or not to use these new sources of research data?

In addition, many standardized tests are subject to bias, notwithstanding the evidence. African American children score higher on IQ tests when the tests are administered by African American examiners, and answers to personality test questions may be motivated by a desire to appear well adjusted or to be admired, or even by a desire to appear poorly adjusted and in need of help. In either case, respondents may not describe themselves honestly.

Although standardized tests are not especially vulnerable to such biases, compared to other behavioral measures, they are generally administered directly to research participants under conditions that make the participants aware that their behavior is being studied. Under reactive arrangements such as those, response biases are a potential problem that needs to be considered. Response biases are not so problematic in cases in which standardized tests are administered as part of an ongoing institutional routine, as when standardized achievement tests are administered to students in schools. Students expect to take these tests every so often and thus may be unaware of a researcher's interest in the relationship between their test scores and changes in, for example, school policies or practices.

Ad Hoc Self-Report Measures

This is one of the largest categories of data collection techniques, both for the number of studies in which such techniques are used, particularly in social psychology and the study of emotions, and for the variety of specific measures involved. Each measure typically is tailored to the particular research study in which it is used. The category of **ad hoc self-report measures** consists of questionnaires, rating scales, and adjective checklists, among many others.

Social psychologist Donn Byrne (1971) conducted a series of experimental studies to determine the influence of attitude similarity on liking. Although the studies took a variety of forms, the basic idea was to lead subjects to believe that someone they were going to meet held attitudes that were either similar to or dissimilar from their own. To determine how similarity affected the subjects' liking for that prospective acquaintance, Byrne asked a few questions—ones that he designed himself for use in this particular research—about the subjects' anticipated feelings for the person. Together, those questions were labeled the Interpersonal Judgment Scale. Their psychometric adequacy was more assumed from the fact that they discriminated successfully among the groups compared for the effects of varying degrees of attitude similarity in Byrne's studies than it was determined from a formal psychometric evaluation.

J. L. Moreno (1934) developed a technique called *sociometry* to measure patterns of relationships within groups. Numerous researchers have used this technique, in which each group member is asked to list a small number of others in the group whom he or she likes best, or wants to work with most, or who exert the greatest influence on group decisions, or who possess whatever other characteristic might be relevant to the research hypothesis (or therapeutic goal, because this technique was developed for use in group therapy). Group members' sociometric choices can be used to test a variety of hypotheses about the factors that influence the development of relationships in a group, including similarity, quality of past task performance, and length of acquaintance.

In studies of stereotyping, such as Broverman et al.'s (1972) research on gender-role stereotypes (**E5**), a number of "target persons" to whom varied group affiliations have been ascribed are presented to the research participants. That can be accomplished by using verbal labels such as "an average adult woman" or "an average adult man," for example, or visual stimuli such as photographs of Asian

Americans or African Americans. The participants who are exposed to those target persons rate the character of each of them after being told or shown who they are.

One technique for assessing stereotypes is to present a list of descriptive terms (for example, "intelligent," "kind," "selfish," etc.) and to ask the research participants to choose some number of them that seems most appropriate for each target person (for example, the 8 most descriptive out of 20). Alternatively, as in Figure 9.1, participants can rate each target person on a number of 10-point scales (how intelligent, kind, selfish, etc.). Evidence for a stereotype could be found using either of those ad hoc self-report measures, either in different numbers of choices or in different average ratings for target persons representing different groups. The choices or ratings can be summed to create a single score that indicates the overall nature or favorability of the participants' impressions of different target persons representing different groups. Differences among the target groups would be evidence of stereotyping and/or prejudice. A very similar technique was used by Cherulnik et al. (1981, **E17**) to measure their research participants' impressions of the high and low Machiavellian men they saw on videotape or in photographs.

In studies comparing the effectiveness of different methods of persuasion, research participants' responses are measured by asking them to report their attitudes toward whatever idea, person, or object was chosen as the subject of the persuasion. They do this by completing an ad hoc questionnaire evaluating different aspects of that attitude object.

I once carried out a study to evaluate the effect of the layout of a shopping mall on the movements of shoppers. Randomly sampled shoppers were asked, as they were about to leave the mall, to indicate on a map of the mall where they had gone during their visit (see Figure 9.2). In another example, Rotter and his colleagues (Rotter, 1966) evaluated the effect of locus of control on hospital patients' knowledge of their medical conditions by administering an ad hoc test to them (**E1**).

We could continue with an even more exhaustive list of ad hoc self-report measures, but these examples are probably sufficient to suggest how varied and large a number have been used, many of them designed to meet the needs of a single study or a series of studies in one particular area of research. The flexibility to create, on the spot, a new measure or a new adaptation of one used previously is a great strength of this technique. It is also a weakness, because the limited use of these measures usually rules out the investment of time and effort required to demonstrate fully that they are reliable and valid measurement devices. As a consequence, the psychometric quality of these instruments usually is indeterminate.

Another weakness of this technique is its vulnerability to response bias. Most often, ad hoc self-report measures are administered under reactive arrangements, in laboratory experiments in which there is direct contact between participant and researcher. We know that in such cases participants may exhibit hypothesis seeking and evaluation apprehension, and those who administer the measures may have some knowledge of the research hypothesis.

No. _____

Remember, write a number from 1 to 10 in the space next to each of the adjectives below indicating how well you think that adjective applied to the child whose photograph is on the screen, based on this scale.

1	2	3	4	5	6	7	8	9	10

Definitely
Does Not
Apply

Not Sure
Whether
It Applies

Definitely
Applies

Fill in the space next to every adjective. Don't take too long on any one. If you trust your first impression, you should be able to keep up without any problem.

_____ CARELESS
_____ COLD
_____ CREATIVE
_____ KIND
_____ MOODY
_____ NEAT
_____ RELAXED
_____ SHY
_____ TALKATIVE
_____ UNINTELLIGENT

Figure 9.1. A self-report form used in research on how people draw inferences from others' physical appearance. The research participants saw a series of slides showing people who had been preselected based on some aspect of their appearance, such as attractiveness, ethnicity, or gender. After looking at each slide, they rated the person they saw on each of the traits on the list. The traits represent what are believed to be the five basic factors of human personality.

One concrete indication of response bias under such conditions comes from work by Sigall and Page (1971) using the method known as the **bogus pipeline**. Sigall and Page probed white college student participants for evidence of racist attitudes under two conditions. In one case, they simply asked them what they believed about the members of different ethnic groups, in the way that self-reports are often gathered in such research. The only difference was that the students (research participants) used a device like an automobile steering wheel to move a pointer along a scale to indicate how much they agreed with racist and nonracist statements. In the other case, participants were told an elaborate (and false) story about the steering wheel apparatus that was designed to convince them that the device was able to detect their "true" attitudes by measuring minute muscular contractions in anticipation of moving the wheel, through electrodes attached to their

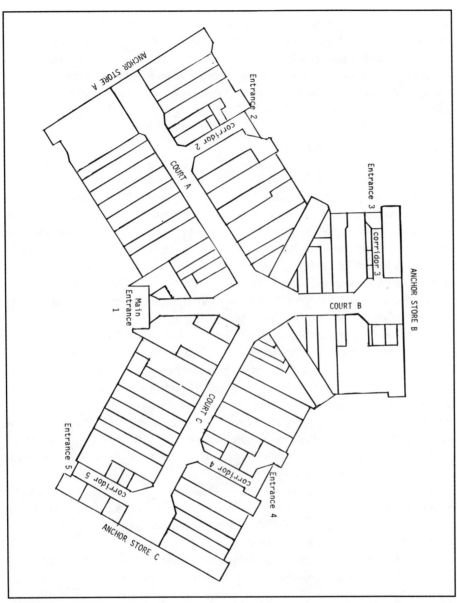

Figure 9.2. A form developed for a study of the behavior of visitors to a regional shopping mall. As they exited the mall, randomly selected shoppers were asked to draw their path through the mall on this form.

arms. The story was backed up by a rigged demonstration of this "bogus pipeline" supposedly leading to the truth.

Participants who were led to believe that the researcher had this special access to their true attitudes admitted to more racial prejudice than those who most likely believed, as is true in most cases where self-report measures are used, that their responses would be taken at face value. Of course, admitting to racism is a more sensitive, affect-laden response than most, but researchers need to be concerned about response bias in more than a few cases, as shown by Orne's (1959) work on demand characteristics and Rosenthal's (1969) work on experimenter expectancy effects.

Other Forms of Self-Report

Reports of research participants' thoughts, actions, and feelings can be obtained by means other than the tests and questionnaires, standardized or not, that we've discussed so far. One such technique is the **interview**. In many cases, it removes the requirement that participants be able to understand questions and instructions simply by reading them, and that they be able to respond in writing, even if only with a check mark or number. That's because it allows participants and questioners to expand, explain, or clarify questions and answers. Of course, bias can be introduced if questioners don't follow a prescribed interview protocol so as to present a fairly consistent stimulus for respondents' answers.

In any case, respondents usually are free to respond in their own words, although researchers eventually may have to make some judgments or categorizations of their answers in order to compare one respondent or group with another. Such category forms of analysis are popular. Raters can be trained to achieve a high level of agreement in deciding how to make the necessary category assignments. Computer software programs exist that can facilitate content analysis of interview and other verbal data. Dictionaries of key words are used to count the rates of occurrence for particular attitudes, moods, motives, or other behaviors predicted by the research hypothesis.

A **survey** is a more circumscribed form of interview. Respondents are likely to be asked whether or not, or how often, they think, or do, or feel something, rather than to describe it in their own words. The questioner is usually bound by a tighter script or protocol in posing the questions.

Interviews and surveys can be administered face to face or over the telephone. Surveys also can be administered in written form, delivered by hand or through the mail. Return rates usually are better when the questioner can contact the respondent in person. Mail surveys are especially problematic; it can be difficult to obtain a return rate large enough to ensure a representative sample of respondents.

Both interviews and surveys are more likely to be used in nonexperimental research, but because they require direct contact between researcher and participant, they usually are administered in a reactive setting. As a result, they may not be appropriate for assessing personal, intimate, or controversial behavior because of the danger of response bias. In some cases, respondents may exaggerate or minimize their true beliefs or feelings in order to avoid embarrassment or to win approval.

One ingenious solution to this problem is Greenberg's (Greenberg, Abernathy, & Horvitz, 1970) **random response technique**. If the researcher needs to know only whether or not the respondent has done, thought, or felt something that is potentially embarrassing or damaging if revealed, and not how much or how often, this technique can be invaluable. First, the respondent is asked to choose privately between two available questions, both of which can be answered yes or no. The respondent must be convinced that the researcher has no way of knowing which question is answered, only the probability of each being chosen.

Incidentally, that is true. The respondent is allowed to choose a card from a deck of playing cards without showing it to anyone before replacing it in the deck. He or she is advised of some rule to be used for that card to choose one of the two questions. A black card might mean that he or she would answer Question 1, and a red card Question 2, or a number card might mean that Question 1 would be answered, with a "picture card" meaning Question 2. Any rule would work, as long as the probability of Question 1 or Question 2 being answered over an entire sample of respondents can be determined (.50 for each if black card means 1 and red card 2, or .23 if it's picture card vs. .77 for number card, for example).

One of the two questions is the critical question that might elicit a biased answer if asked directly. For example, the question might be "Have you smoked marijuana during the past month?" The other must be a question for which the percentages of "yes" and "no" answers are known in advance. For example, that question might be "Were you born in the month of July?" (Over a large sample, which is typical for surveys, 8.33% of respondents, or 1 in 12, were, or should have been, born during the month of July.) At the end of the survey, the researcher knows how many answers overall were "yes" and how many "no," what percentages of respondents answered Question 1 and Question 2 (for example, 50% for each), and how many answered "yes" to Question 2 (for example, 1 person in 12 is born in any one month). Based on those known quantities, the percentage who answered "yes" to the question of whether they had smoked marijuana in the previous month can be calculated (try out an example yourself to see how it works).

The random response technique affords respondents complete anonymity. If they can be made to understand that, their answers should be more honest than if they think the researcher will be able to find out whether they personally use drugs. Of course, the researcher usually is interested only in learning the percentage of the population as a whole that does (assuming a representative sample, also typical for survey research).

The final self-report method in this brief review is the **diary**. Research participants can be asked to keep a record of any behavior of interest to a researcher. It might be thoughts of death, hours of television viewing, food eaten, or whatever. If the participants can be trusted to be conscientious and honest, these diary data may be useful for comparing people of different personality types, different appearance, different occupations, or a host of other such categories. The data might be used to compare groups that have and have not experienced some event whose possible effects are the subject of the research hypothesis.

Sometimes, rather than recording everything—a daunting task if the behavior occurs frequently—the researcher can sample thoughts or actions. Electronic beepers sometimes are used to signal participants at randomly selected times to report by writing a brief note or by filling out a brief form that becomes a diary entry. I suppose that palm-sized computers will be used instead before too long.

Observer Ratings

There are times when it doesn't make sense to ask research participants about themselves or their behavior. It may be that it would be difficult for them to be objective. Most people rate themselves above average for most positive traits and performances, suggesting that we may find it difficult at times to face unpleasant truths about ourselves. There are also research hypotheses that focus on others' impressions of participants' behavior rather than on the participant's point of view. For those and other reasons, researchers sometimes use **observer ratings** of participants and their behavior as a source of data.

Nisbett and Cohen (1996) conducted research on the relationship between Southern culture in the United States and violence. In one study, they arranged for Southerners and Northerners attending the University of Michigan to be insulted unexpectedly in a hallway by a stranger, who jostled them intentionally as they were walking from one session of a research study to another. To determine how angry the insult made each research participant, a third student in the hallway—who, like the jostler, was an associate of the researchers—observed the participant's reaction and recorded a judgment of it on a rating scale. The participants themselves might have been unaware of how upset they were, or might have been reluctant to admit it.

In a study of leadership, the quality of participants' performance of a leadership task (they recorded a simulated campaign speech in a television studio) was judged by a group of fellow students who guessed how much leadership experience each participant seemed to have. In this case, the "leader's" opinion of the quality of his or her performance was clearly less pertinent to the research hypothesis than were the opinions of those who watched it on tape. The research was concerned with the leader's effect on those who were exposed to his or her leadership style.

In research into the causes of aggression, the behavior of pre-adolescent boys on their school playground was rated by teachers who were observing them. Research to evaluate the effectiveness of management techniques often uses supervisors' ratings of employees' job performance as a source of data. Researchers also

---

Box 9.3 | *THINKING ABOUT RESEARCH*

When Are You Really Married?

In some important ways, archival data can be invaluable to research psychologists. We have seen the advantages in freedom from artifacts associated with the nonreactive nature of archival research. Valuable research designs like the time series and multiple time series depend on the availability of archival data. Data bearing on very important practical questions such as the causes of crime can hardly be gathered effectively in any other form.

For all their charms, however, archival data have their own peculiar Achilles heel. The researcher who uses them has no control over the manner in which they are collected. Very often, the data predate the research, or even the formulation of the research hypothesis, so that archival research may be a case of data in search of an explanation.

One of the well-worn examples of the dangers of using archival data, discussed already in this text, concerns suicide statistics. When a member of the Catholic church commits suicide, the story goes, family members and friendly clergy may conspire to influence a family doctor to identify a different cause of death on the death certificate so that the body can be buried in a Catholic cemetery with a religious ceremony.

Recently, this speculation has been bolstered by an account of an analogous situation that has been documented in the predominantly Catholic country of Chile, where divorce is illegal. When a marriage fails there, the partners seek an annulment if they can afford the hefty legal fees involved. Whether they divorce officially or not, because of the potential hassles in a country where there is little separation between church and state, if they choose to live with new partners they are likely to do so without the benefit of marriage. A Chilean woman interviewed recently for an article in the *New York Times* described herself as a mother of two and grandmother of one who has been "effectively" married for most of her adult life to two different men. According to official Chilean government (archival) records, however, she has been single all her life.

Where does this problem of falsified or distorted public records belong in our analysis of validity issues? What other archival data should a researcher use with great care? Is there any way to ensure "clean" archival data, either through trustworthy sources or through estimating possible distortions in the data? Should a researcher ask similar questions about data found on the Internet or elsewhere if their origins are unknown?

---

have measured the effects of mental hospital patients' beliefs about their chances of being released back into the community by having clinical psychology interns evaluate them on the basis of an interview.

In all these cases, the use of observers' ratings probably made more sense than using self-report measures. A child is aggressive because of what he or she does *to others*. An employee is productive if his or her contribution is valued highly *by others*. A hospital patient's treatment is based on evaluations by health care professionals. And so on. Among our exemplar studies, Festinger et al. (1956) rated their research participants' responses to the disconfirmation of their expectancies about the world coming to an end (**E11**), and Cartwright (1974) rated the content of her subjects' dreams (**E13**).

A key issue in the interpretation of observer ratings such as those described above is bias. In some cases, research participants are unaware that their behavior is under scrutiny by one or more individuals around them, as when schoolchildren play in the presence of their teachers, or when one passes a fellow student or coworker in a public hallway. In such cases, the lack of reactivity in the setting means that the behavior being studied is likely to be a spontaneous and unmanaged response to some preceding event. When the behavior that is rated takes place in a reactive setting such as a psychological laboratory, a concern about strategic responding seems warranted. The same reasons that research participants don't always answer questions honestly can apply to their displays of overt behavior in reactive settings.

A different type of bias also is at issue here. If observers are not kept ignorant of the research hypothesis or, at the least, of the independent variable or treatment status of the particular research participant being judged, the data can be compromised. One solution to this problem is to record participants' behavior, generally on videotape, so that extraneous cues such as surrounding props and people are not visible to the observers who rate the behavior. Videotape also makes it possible to show the segments of behavior to be rated out of their original temporal order, another way to lessen the likelihood that raters will be aware of the purpose of the study or the events that led up to the behavior, and to make it more likely that they will judge the behavior solely for itself. Taped behavior also can be shown to large samples of naïve observers who did not need to be present when the behavior occurred or involved in the circumstances that surrounded it.

The instruments that observers use to rate or judge research participants' behavior are the same sort of ad hoc checklists and rating scales that participants use to report about themselves. They tend to share the same psychometric uncertainty concerning their reliability and validity. Observer ratings raise an additional measurement concern. Because researchers generally believe that bias on the part of observers can be reduced by having participants' behavior rated by more than one observer (the argument for using videotaped records so that they can be shown to more observers than could be accommodated in the research setting in person), the question of agreement among observers arises. There are statistical methods for evaluating **interrater reliability**, as it's usually called, and there are normative criteria for acceptable reliability for specific ratings that have been used in past research. If found to be unacceptably low, the level of reliability can be improved by training observers to use similar criteria. Specific instructions also help, as do discussions among raters about discrepancies that arise during practice rating tasks.

Behavioral Observations

Along with ad hoc self-report measures, **behavioral observation** is one of the most common data collection techniques used in psychological research. It is probably the most varied or diverse as well. Behavioral observations usually involve timing or counting responses, or determining their strength or magnitude in some other way. They are more likely to make use of precise scales of measurement, including ratio scales, than are other categories of behavioral measures; however, they are still subject to the same psychometric concerns about reliability and validity as are other measures.

In field studies of people's reactions to invasions of personal space, participants' walking speed was measured as they passed between two people who were talking in a hallway (to be compared with those who walked down the same hallway but didn't need to walk between others). In a study of the effects of physical appearance, college students who differed in their level of attractiveness were assessed for the amount of time they spent looking at their reflections while walking past a campus building with a mirrored facade. Studies of group problem solving have compared the amount of time it takes, working under different conditions, to solve the same problems, or the number of errors groups make. In a study of achievement motivation, participants with high and low levels of that trait were compared for how long it took them to work through tasks with and without a monetary incentive.

In the bystander intervention conducted by Darley and Latané (1968, **E7**), as you'll no doubt recall, research participants were exposed to a staged emergency. They thought a fellow participant was having an epileptic seizure and needed their help. They were observed to determine how long it took them to act, depending on how many others they believed also knew about the victim's problem. In a British field study, reactions to a man dressed in either a working class or a professional manner were measured by the amount of time passersby were willing to spend answering his request for directions. In Triplett's (1897) study of competitive motivation (**E3**), the effects of performing a task alongside someone else were determined by the speed at which participants wound fishing line (the number of completed turns within a fixed period of time).

In some research in cognitive psychology, the factors that determine how people group objects into categories are evaluated by measuring how long it takes participants to decide whether two stimuli are similar or different. The effects of motivation on rats learning their way through a maze are determined by measuring how long it takes them to get from start to finish. Finally, in Dement's (1960) study of dream deprivation (**E14**), the dependent measure was the amount of time participants spent in REM sleep after deprivation, as compared to before.

In studies of operant conditioning, pigeons' and rats' responses to different reinforcement contingencies are compared by counting the number of times they

Figure 9.3. A cumulative event recorder, a device invented originally for use in Skinner's operant conditioning experiments. Each response during an experimental session is recorded by a pen on a moving roll of paper, in such a way that distinctive patterns of response to various schedules of reinforcement are apparent.

peck a key or press a bar in a given period of time (response rates). In some research on memory, groups of participants study different kinds of material, or they study the same material under different conditions or for different lengths of time. Then they have their memory tested later for the number of items they recall or can recognize. One technique for studying how members of different groups (ethnic, racial, gender, etc.) interact with one another is to count the number of times people from different groups sit next to one another in a room, such as a college classroom, where there are no assigned seats (compared statistically to a random pattern). In research on the effects of conflicting motives for competition and cooperation in the Prisoner's Dilemma game, researchers compare the numbers of competitive and cooperative choices made by the research participants. In studies of group decision making, researchers use a technique known as Interaction Process Analysis, counting the number of times participants' statements fit into each of a number of predetermined categories.

Among our exemplar studies, Friedman and Rosenman (1959) evaluated the effects of the Type A personality on cardiovascular health by comparing the number of heart attacks among different personality types (**E2**). Clark and Clark (1940) studied racial identification and racial preference among African American children by comparing the numbers of choices of white and black dolls (**E6**).

Behavioral observation also includes the recording of participants' nonverbal behavior. This can involve counting smiles, or measuring the proportion of time during a sample period that two participants look one another in the eye (eye contact), or counting the number of interruptions in their speech, to cite just a few examples. In one study of the causes of liking between mixed-gender couples who had recently met, liking was measured as the distance between the members of each couple as they stood in front of the researcher's desk after returning from a 30-minute get-acquainted "Coke date."

Even brain waves can qualify as behavior that can be observed by a researcher. In his research on dream deprivation, Dement (1960, **E14**) used EEG recordings like the ones shown in Figure 9.4 to document the hypothesized increase in REM sleep.

A good deal of behavioral observation consists of measuring the performance of research participants on standardized laboratory tasks. Some of these tasks are physical—winding fishing reels, tugging on a rope, or jumping over a barrier to escape electric shock. Some are cerebral—finding creative uses for common everyday objects such as a paper clip, deciding whether the amount of a liquid changes when it is poured from one container to another, determining which species of birds are most typical of birds in general, or remembering the path through a maze. As these examples remind us, tasks have been devised to test both human and nonhuman research participants. In Milgram's (1974) research on obedience (**E9**), participants' behavior was measured as the number of switches they were willing to throw on the apparatus shown in Figure 9.5. Participants were told that throwing a switch, on the experimenter's orders, would deliver a shock to the "learner" in Milgram's experiments. Behavioral researchers also may study performance on "natural" tasks, including classroom tests, office duties, corporate decisions, sporting events, and even those that are part of everyday life in pastures, jungles, and beehives.

In some cases, behavioral observation can be carried out in a very unobtrusive manner. In a natural setting, such as on a campus sidewalk or in a restaurant, research participants may be completely unaware that their behavior is being assessed. Even in the reactive setting of a research laboratory, participants may not be aware that researchers are measuring how long they look at one another, or how close together they stand. In the case of more reactive settings and more obtrusive observation, however, researchers need to be concerned about the degree to which participants might alter their behavior to meet perceived expectations or to influence others' impressions. As we've seen, even the behavior of nonhuman participants can be biased by contact with a researcher who has knowledge of the research hypothesis. Keeping those who have direct contact with research participants unaware of the hypothesis—or, better yet, minimizing contact between researcher and participant through the use of automated procedures—is always desirable in this regard.

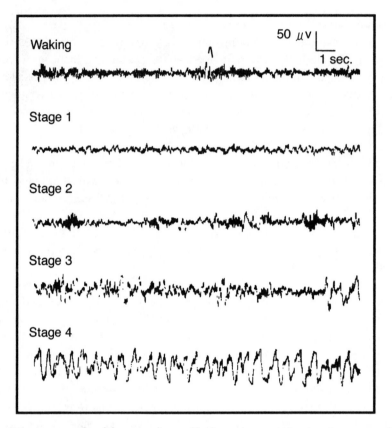

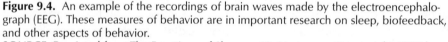

Figure 9.4. An example of the recordings of brain waves made by the electroencephalograph (EEG). These measures of behavior are in important research on sleep, biofeedback, and other aspects of behavior.
SOURCE: Reprinted from *The Functions of Sleep*, p. 22, Hartmann, © copyright 1973 by Yale University Press. Reprinted with permission.

The psychometric properties of behavioral observations are also a matter of concern. These measures need to be evaluated for precision, reliability, validity, and interobserver agreement as much as any other source of data. As mentioned earlier, the use of permanent recordings on film or videotape, especially if made without the prior knowledge of research participants, can make it easier to evaluate the data. It can make participants' behavior available again and again, to more observers, on more occasions, in varied sequences, for a variety of purposes. Of course, surreptitious recordings raise significant ethical questions. At the very least, participants deserve the right to have final control over whether and how the observations of their behavior will be used, especially if permanent recordings have been made.

Figure 9.5. The response panel used in Milgram's research on obedience to authority. In the role of "teacher," participants were led to believe that each switch caused an electric shock to be delivered to another party, the "learner." Successive errors by the learner called for increasingly severe shocks along the series of switches, from left to right. SOURCE: Reprinted from *Obedience to Authority*, Milgram, p. 25, © copyright 1974 by Stanley Milgram. Reprinted by permission of HarperCollins Publishers, Inc.

Unobtrusive Measures

Although many of the behavioral observation techniques we've discussed can be used in ways that minimize participants' awareness that their behavior is under scrutiny, there are some measures of behavior that are so unobtrusive that they deserve to be discussed as a separate category. These so-called **unobtrusive measures** utilize the impact made by people's behavior on the physical objects and landscape around them as indicators of what they have done in the course of their daily lives. These measures can be utilized by researchers long after the people in question (now research participants) have left the setting where the observations are made.

Some of these unobtrusive measures are referred to as **erosion measures**. They utilize the wear and tear on a setting to assess the behavior of that setting's users. In one case, researchers used records of the replacement of floor tiles in an art museum to measure the popularity of the various exhibits. They reasoned that greater interest in an exhibit eventually would result in more wear and tear on the floor tiles in its vicinity.

Other unobtrusive measures are known as **accretion measures**. People leave things behind (add things to a setting) that indicate what they have done. For example, gangs' defense of their territories can be studied by analyzing graffiti. The conditions that influence the likelihood of vandalism in an area can be evaluated by an assessment of the damage, and the effectiveness of different methods to control littering can be compared by counting or weighing litter.

An interesting unobtrusive measure of attitudes was developed by social psychologist Stanley Milgram (1969), with whom we're acquainted already through his research on obedience to authority (**E9**). This measure was used in Hong Kong, before the British returned it to China, to assess people's attitudes toward the Mao-led Communists on the Chinese mainland and the Chiang-led opposition on Taiwan. Researchers dropped apparently unmailed, stamped letters on streets. The letters were addressed in equal numbers to two fictitious political organizations whose names indicated support for the two opposing factions, Mao's and Chiang's. The rates at which the letters were mailed by passersby who found them (to addresses where the researchers could retrieve them) were taken as indications of the levels of support for those factions among the population. This **lost-letter technique** (mentioned in Chapter 4, pp. 130-131) has been used several times by other researchers, including once by yours truly when it worked even in small towns in rural Maine. My colleagues and I were able to assess attitudes toward the development of a potentially polluting oil transport industry.

Unobtrusive measures have the obvious advantage of low reactivity. Research participants are never observed directly, so they can be trusted to have acted spontaneously. They are unlikely to have any concern for their role in the research or for the impression their behavior might make on the researcher. There is no opportunity for the researcher's expectations to influence that behavior. Measurement is usually very precise, consisting of counting and weighing varieties (ratio scales). There are limited opportunities to use such measures, however, although researchers have found some ingenious uses for them and should be encouraged to continue doing so.

Archival Measures

Industrial-organizational (I/O) psychologists make extensive use of **archival data** in their research. Fiedler (1967) tested his contingency theory of leadership by comparing group performance under varying combinations of leadership style and favorability of situation for the leader. He examined the won-lost records of high school basketball teams as well as company records of the productivity of steel mill work crews, among other sources, to obtain his data. Other I/O psychologists have evaluated theories of worker motivation using routine organization records such as productivity, absenteeism, and turnover.

Triplett (1897, **E3**) initially used newspaper records of the performance of bicycle racers (from the sports pages) to test his theory of the effects of competitive motivation on task performance. Environmental psychologists have evaluated the effects of home field advantage on team success by analyzing similar public records for college and professional sports. They have used won-lost records as well as a variety of other sports performance statistics (and any sports fan knows how inexhaustible those are!).

Many theories about the causes of violence have been tested using records of crime kept by law enforcement agencies. Researchers have found archival measures of urban crowding, summer temperatures, and economic deprivation reflected in lower prices for cotton. In general, applied research on public policy questions such as the causes of traffic accident fatalities, violence in high schools, economic downturns, and low academic achievement has made more extensive use of archival data than has theory-driven research.

We have already discussed archival research, on a number of occasions. It shares many of the advantages of other unobtrusive measures. Records that are kept routinely in factories, offices, schools, government agencies, and elsewhere can be extremely useful for testing hypotheses in psychological research. Because those records reflect the everyday activities in people's lives, they are unlikely to have been influenced by the participants' concern about the role their behavior might play in a future research study. People don't choose to work hard, or to have children, or to commit murder because some researcher did or might hypothesize that they have been exposed to conditions that should cause them to do so. Furthermore, the researcher generally is not involved in any way in deciding which records should be kept or how they should be kept, so that his or her hypothesis about what should be found in the data cannot influence what actually is found.

Archival records are often based on very large samples, as large as the population of the United States. Earlier, we considered examples of large archival databases, including the U.S. Census, the FBI's Uniform Crime Statistics, and the National Institute of Mental Health records of mental hospital admissions. There are even larger databases, such as some United Nations agency records. In addition, these records often extend over long periods of time, and they usually make use of very precise measurement operations.

Archival data, however, do have their drawbacks. They are beyond the control of the researchers who use them. That means that researchers must often tailor their hypotheses to the data that are available, rather than pursuing freely the most theoretically significant questions, as they can when they are free to go after whatever data they like. One researcher has described this as "looking where the light is best, rather than where the object was lost."

That same lack of control also means that researchers often don't know what rules were used to make the measurements that end up in an archival database. Although the research hypothesis may not have played any part in biasing archival data, the motives of the organization that collected them might have. Business managers, government bureaucrats, and even clinical psychologists may have expectations for the performance of their organizations. They may also have strong needs to look good in the eyes of shareholders, voters, or the general public. Both

TABLE 9.3   The Principal Advantages and Disadvantages of Five Data Collection Techniques

Data Collection Technique	Advantages	Disadvantages
Self-report measures	Wide range	Reactivity
Standardized tests	Psychometric quality	Limited variety Linguistic/cultural bias
Ad hoc self-report measures	Flexibility	Lack of psychometric quality
Observer ratings	Objectivity/group agreement Assessing others' points of view	Limited access to subjective states Reactivity when observer present Rater biases
Behavioral observations	Measurement precision Variety Objectivity (instrumentation)	Limited access to subjective states Reactivity if obtrusive Observer biases
Unobtrusive measures	Lack of reactivity Measurement precision	Extremely limited variety Indirect
Archival measures	Large, representative samples Lack of reactivity Long time frames	Hidden biases Limited variety

could influence how they keep their records—what information is kept and about whom. Because those motives generally are inaccessible to researchers outside the organizations in question, possible biases may be more likely to go undetected than is the case for data collection techniques that are initiated by the researcher.

Table 9.3 reviews the issues related to a researcher's choice among data collection techniques.

● CONCLUSION

Research psychologists have been so prolific and so ingenious in devising techniques for collecting the data they need to test their hypotheses that it is impossible to produce a complete catalog of their work. Even the task of classifying those techniques in order to present a representative sample has been very difficult. Still, the sample presented in this chapter has provided an opportunity to discuss most of the major methodological issues associated with data collection in psychological research.

Some of those issues were discussed in earlier chapters, especially in connection with the subject of construct validity in Chapters 3 and 4. It is hoped that the occasion to revisit them here has reinforced some of the most important principles a researcher or consumer of research needs to keep in mind. There is so much to remember that repetition can only help.

Review Questions and Exercise

Review Questions

1. What are the major sources of data for psychological research?

2. How does the choice of a data source influence the likelihood of inadequate operationalization of the behavioral construct in a research hypothesis?

3. How does the choice of a data source influence the likelihood of measurement artifacts in the dependent variable derived from the behavioral construct in a research hypothesis?

Exercise

Identify the data sources for a sample of the exemplar studies introduced in Chapter 2. Consider alternative data sources for each study and evaluate the implications for construct validity of a choice among the alternative data sources.

CHAPTER **10**

ANALYZING THE DATA

● A QUICK GUIDE TO CHAPTER 10: ANALYZING THE DATA

Once the data are in, the researcher must be able to use them to evaluate the research hypothesis. Groups of observations, known as *distributions*, represent the effects of the various treatments on different individuals or occasions. Do those results reflect the differences predicted in the research hypothesis and, if so, to what extent? Those questions usually are answered by conducting statistical analyses.

Statistics are numbers that have been devised by mathematicians to serve the purposes of research psychologists and other scientists. They serve two important functions. **Descriptive statistics** can be used to summarize the results. **Inferential statistics** can be used to test for the differences among groups or across occasions that were predicted.

Descriptive statistics from **univariate distributions** (one measurement per research participant or unit) summarize data mainly in two ways. They describe the **central tendency** of a group of measurements, usually with the **mean** or arithmetic average. They also describe the **variability** of those measurements, usually with the **standard deviation**. When the data are in the form of a **bivariate distribution** (two measurements per unit), the **correlation coefficient** can be used to summarize the relationship, if any, that exists between the two variables. We saw in Chapter 8 how statistical techniques are used to analyze more complex **multivariate distributions**.

Inferential statistics are important because comparisons among treatment groups are complicated by **sampling error**. The groups to which a treatment is administered, or the occasions on which it is administered, are sampled from an infinite population of people or occasions. The observations or scores for the individuals involved, or the averages for the groups or occasions, would be different if the treatment were administered in exactly the same way to different individuals or on different occasions sampled from the same populations.

Inferential statistics take sampling error into account. **Significance tests** use the obtained data to estimate the probability that the results (the observed differences among treatment groups or the observed relationship between the independent and dependent variables) were due to chance or sampling error rather than the effects of the treatments. If that probability is found to be low enough (usually .05 or smaller), the results can be taken as evidence for effects of the treatments. Many such significance tests have been developed, including the *t* **test** for comparing pairs of groups of measurements, the *F* **test** of analysis of variance for larger numbers of groups, and tests for correlation coefficients and multiple correlations based on the statistic z.

Statistical conclusion validity evaluates the appropriateness of the statistics selected by the researcher to summarize and draw inferences from his or her data. Recently, some researchers have questioned the significance test as a means for

Chapter 10 Quick Guide: Statistics Used in the Analysis of Research Data in Psychology

Category	Example	Question
Descriptive Statistics		
Central tendency	Mean	What is the midpoint of the distribution, or the typical score?
Variability	Standard deviation	How widely spread out are the scores across the distribution?
Correlation	Correlation coefficient	What is the relationship between the two variables in a bivariate distribution?
Inferential Statistics		
Comparing two groups	*t* test	Can the observed difference between group means be accounted for by sampling error?
Comparing three or more groups	Analysis of variance	Can the observed differences among group variances be accounted for by sampling error?
Evaluating correlation	*z* test	Can the relationship between variables be accounted for by sampling error?

evaluating the truth of research hypotheses. They favor **estimating effect size** by taking into account the magnitude of treatment effects more directly.

The Chapter 10 Quick Guide summarizes the main forms of descriptive and inferential statistics used in psychological research, gives prominent examples of each, and reviews the questions about research data each is used to answer.

INTRODUCTION TO THE CHAPTER ●

One of the most exciting moments in any research study comes right after the last bit of data has been collected. A stack of questionnaires or rating scale booklets, a notebook full of laboratory records, or perhaps a floppy disk containing participants' responses downloaded from laboratory instruments or from a computer keyboard contains the tangible results of months of planning, preparation, and data collection. At this point, researchers are eager to learn whether their hypotheses will be borne out by the behavioral observations they have made, as well as apprehensive about the possibility that no clear-cut results will emerge.

To find out what their results are, they must take the next step in the research process: They must make the comparisons among the observations made of participants in contrasting treatment conditions, or calculate the relationship between the independent and dependent variables. Their statistical analysis of the data will provide the basis on which to make an evaluation of their research hypothesis. To do that analysis, research psychologists make use of the work of applied mathematicians called statisticians.

Over the past hundred years or so, some of those mathematicians have worked to assist researchers, while others have worked as researchers within the scientific disciplines themselves, including psychology. During that time, they have devised means of describing research data in concise and informative ways, and of using observations from a sample of research participants to draw limited conclusions, based on the results of one study, about the general truth or falsity of a research hypothesis. Those statistical techniques are known as **descriptive statistics** and **inferential statistics**, respectively.

This chapter will first review briefly some of the statistical techniques available to research psychologists. We will be more concerned with what those methods can do than with how they do it. This chapter is in no way intended to be a substitute for a course in statistics. Its goal is merely to provide a basic familiarity with the statistical methods that research psychologists use. This is necessary if we are to appreciate the implications for the validity of research findings of the decisions researchers make while planning and carrying out the analysis of their data.

Thus, the most important issue in our effort to understand the research process is whether statistical methods are used appropriately, in ways that ensure the accuracy of the conclusions drawn from research data about the truth of the research hypothesis. To that end, this chapter will add the last group of criteria for evaluating the validity of research findings. Those are the threats to **statistical conclusion validity**.

● SUMMARIZING THE RESULTS: DESCRIPTIVE STATISTICS

Univariate Distributions: One Variable at a Time

The first step in statistical analysis is to summarize what can be a very large array of measurements. It is not unusual for research studies in psychology to generate thousands of individual measurements or numbers (sometimes referred to as *data points*). It is not unheard of for a researcher to be faced with hundreds of thousands of numbers for analysis. That makes even the simplest questions about how the research turned out impossible to answer without the use of statistics.

TABLE 10.1 Frequency Distribution for Arousal Scores

X (Arousal)	Frequency	Relative Frequency	Cumulative Frequency	Cumulative Relative Frequency
0-9	1	.02	1	.02
10-19	3	.06	4	.08
20-29	2	.04	6	.12
30-39	5	.10	11	.22
40-49	6	.12	17	.34
50-59	11	.22	28	.56
60-69	9	.18	37	.74
70-79	7	.14	44	.88
80-89	4	.08	48	.96
90-100	2	.04	50	1.00

TABLE 10.2 Frequency Distribution for Exam Scores

X (Exam)	Frequency	Relative Frequency	Cumulative Frequency	Cumulative Relative Frequency
0-9	0	.00	0	.00
10-19	0	.00	0	.00
20-29	0	.00	0	.00
30-39	0	.00	0	.00
40-49	2	.04	2	.04
50-59	5	.10	7	.14
60-69	11	.22	18	.36
70-79	16	.32	34	.68
80-89	10	.20	44	.88
90-100	6	.12	50	1.00

Tabulating the Data

The first step in summarizing the results usually is to create a table. In Chapter 8, we used fictitious data consisting of arousal measurements and exam scores in our discussion of multivariate research. If we created a table of (that is, tabulated) those same data, they would be transformed from lists of numbers arranged in the order in which they were collected—in this case, from the first participant tested to the 50th and last one as shown in Table 10.3—to a more orderly form that gives a better idea of what those scores actually were. Take a look at Tables 10.1 and 10.2, and see if you don't agree.

TABLE 10.3 Bivariate Distribution of Arousal and Exam Scores

Participant Number	Arousal Score	Exam Score
1	41	82
2	38	71
3	15	55
4	42	86
5	35	67
6	53	91
7	66	83
8	37	65
9	26	73
10	44	76
11	90	51
12	76	74
13	78	66
14	52	84
15	35	75
16	54	70
17	78	61
18	65	87
19	32	72
20	67	76
21	47	68
22	60	95
23	48	77
24	29	60

In each of those tables, the scores have been arranged in the order of smallest to largest and grouped into equal intervals (X, for score or measurement) along the respective measurement scales for level of arousal and exam performance. In addition, the number of scores in each interval is listed—frequency, often abbreviated with the letter "f." Next listed is the relative frequency—the proportion of the total sample to be found in each interval (abbreviated "rel. f "). Then comes the cumulative frequency, or number of data points through each interval beginning with the lowest one ("cum. f "). Finally comes the cumulative relative frequency, or proportion of data points through the interval ("cum. rel. f "). Tables like these are known as **frequency distributions**.

Participant Number	Arousal Score	Exam Score
25	57	81
26	53	71
27	68	78
28	8	48
29	63	90
30	18	59
31	71	73
32	58	91
33	86	54
34	57	75
35	56	88
36	14	45
37	93	63
38	57	87
39	59	96
40	82	65
41	66	76
42	74	82
43	74	69
44	87	57
45	49	79
46	65	92
47	75	67
48	68	78
49	58	89
50	86	68

Note that Table 10.3 reproduces Table 8.2. Don't Tables 10.1 and 10.2 make it much easier to answer questions about the data, such as "What were the average arousal and exam scores?" and "To what degree did both those scores vary among the 50 subjects tested?" There are no hard-and-fast rules about how to construct tables like these. It is up to the researcher to choose the size and number of intervals or categories into which the scores are divided, and the ways in which the frequencies or proportions in those intervals are reported. Those choices depend on the researcher's understanding of his or her data and his or her skill in communicating that understanding to the reader, although some statistics textbooks provide useful rules of thumb for beginners.

Graphing the Data

Graphic techniques also can be used to display those same data. For example, Figures 10.1 and 10.2 are **histograms**, or bar graphs. They show some of the same properties of the distributions of arousal and test scores as Tables 10.1 and 10.2. One can see the numbers of scores in the various intervals into which the distribution was divided. Figures 10.3 and 10.4 are **cumulative histograms** that show the shapes of those distributions based on the cumulative frequencies reported in Tables 10.1 and 10.2.

Notice how these devices, both tables and graphs, allow one to answer questions about the data that one could never answer from the original lists of scores—for example, "What's the most common test score?" or "How many participants scored below 60 on arousal?" Many more similar questions could be answered from these devices.

Statistics

The tables and figures help us to better understand the data, but they still provide somewhat imprecise answers to two questions of interest to most researchers and readers. Both groups want to know what the average score is for the participants in the sample and how widely the sample members' scores vary around that average. In statistical terms, those two properties of distributions are known as **central tendency** and **variability**. The most precise ways of representing those properties (and most useful, as we'll see later on) are with numbers that summarize them much more succinctly than table or graphics can.

Central Tendency. There are three accepted ways of representing the central tendency of a distribution. The **mean**, or arithmetic average, is the most common. It is calculated by adding all the scores in the distribution and dividing by the number of scores represented in that total. A statistical formula for the mean is as follows:

$$M = \Sigma X/n.$$

M is a statistical symbol for the mean. Σ is the Greek letter sigma, used to represent summation, or adding up. X stands for each of the individual scores in the distribution. Thus, ΣX indicates the sum of the scores. Finally, the symbol n stands for the number of scores. The formula simply indicates that all the scores in the distribution should be added together, and then the total should be divided by the number of scores. This is nothing more than you would do to determine your test average going into the final exam in a course you were taking. In our example, based on the distributions shown in Table 10.3, the mean arousal score is 56.20, and the mean exam score is 73.72.

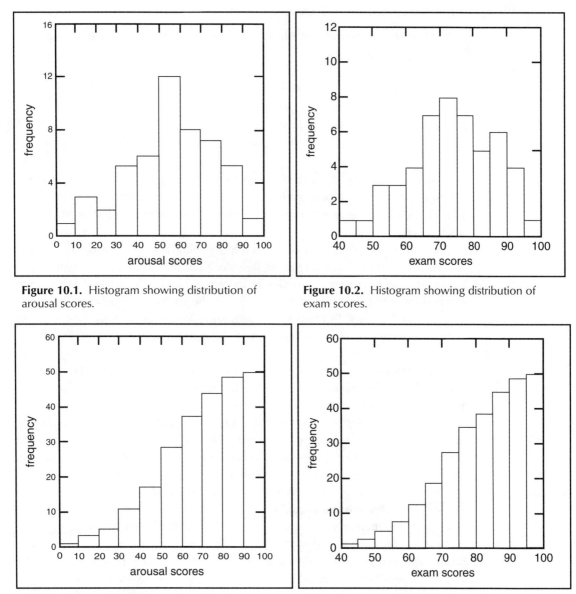

Figure 10.1. Histogram showing distribution of arousal scores.

Figure 10.2. Histogram showing distribution of exam scores.

Figure 10.3. Cumulative histogram showing distribution of arousal scores.

Figure 10.4. Cumulative histogram showing distribution of exam scores.

A second measure of central tendency is the **median**. It is the central score in the distribution, the score that has an equal number of smaller and larger scores below and above it when the scores are listed in order of their magnitude. The median of the distribution of arousal scores is 57.5. Because there are 50 scores, there is no single middle score. The two middle scores are 57 and 58, so the median is calculated as the average of those two. The median exam score is 74.5, calculated

TABLE 10.4 Comparison of Mean, Median, and Mode for Arousal and Exam Scores

Measure	Mean	Median	Mode
Arousal scores	56.20	57.50	50-59
Exam scores	73.72	74.50	70-79

exactly the same way. There are also statistical formulas for calculating medians when the data are grouped, as they are in Tables 10.1 and 10.2. Those are more complicated than we need in our nonstatistical treatment of statistics (if there is such a thing!).

The final representation of central tendency is known as the **mode**. It is simply the most frequently occurring score in a distribution. In our examples, it makes more sense to determine the modes for the arousal and exam scores based on the intervals used in Tables 10.1 and 10.2, because there is no obviously most frequent single score in either distribution. For arousal scores, the modal interval is 50-59, with a frequency of 11. For exam scores, the modal interval is 70-79, with a frequency of 16.

The mean, median, and mode are all statistics. That is, they are numbers that are used in the description and analysis of distributions of data. One reason for having more than one central tendency statistic is that distributions come in a variety of shapes. The two distributions we've considered as examples are fairly symmetrical; therefore, the three central tendency statistics are fairly similar. They are shown in Table 10.4 for purposes of comparison. In a case like this, the mean is usually preferred because it is more useful in further statistical analysis.

A distribution may not be symmetrical. If it is a **skewed distribution**, to use the statistical term for "asymmetrical," the median usually is preferred because it is not influenced so much by very extreme scores. This would be the case if one wanted to represent the central tendency of the distribution of Americans' incomes, for example. The incomes of a relatively small number of billionaire business executives and investors would cause the mean to overestimate the "average" American's income. The median would provide a more accurate description of the distribution as a whole. If you pay close attention the next time you hear or read a news report on the incomes of Americans, you should recognize the term median, because that's the measure most often used for that purpose.

Finally, the mode can be useful in some cases, even though it's based on so little information about the distribution as a whole. If the question about the distribution concerns which event is most common or which alternative is most popular, the mode may provide the best answer. In some cases, looking for the most common or modal score or interval reveals that the distribution has more than one center. Such a distribution is known as "bimodal" if there are two modes. The modes can help to identify subgroups of individuals within the larger group whose scores make up the whole distribution. If we looked at the distribution of heights for all of the students in a high school, we'd probably find two modes a few inches apart. Can you guess why?

Variability. Once the central tendency of a distribution has been established, the next most likely question concerns its **variability**. In other words, how widely dispersed around the center of the distribution are the scores?

One way to describe variability is with the **range**. One simply subtracts the smallest score from the largest and adds one to the result. For our arousal scores, the range is 86 (93 – 8 + 1). For the exam scores, the range is 52 (96 – 45 + 1).

The most commonly used and most useful statistic for assessing variability, however, is the **standard deviation**. It is calculated using a complicated formula. The formula is encoded on the memory chip in most pocket calculators (along with that for the mean), so that one can enter the scores one at a time in any order and get the standard deviation (or mean) simply by pushing the correct key. We won't concern ourselves with calculations here. Suffice it to say that the standard deviation measures variability in the same unit of measurement as the original scores.

In our example, the standard deviation for the arousal scores is 20.79 (20.79 units of arousal along the measurement scale used in this hypothetical study). For the exam scores, it is 12.53. This squares nicely with the impression one gets just from looking at the arousal and exam scores in Figures 10.1 and 10.2. The range of the exam scores is smaller, with a narrower, more concentrated histogram, compared to the distribution of arousal scores.

The Normal Distribution. Together, the mean and standard deviation can be very useful in describing a distribution of scores. One reason is that, fortunately, many of the behavioral measures used by research psychologists form fairly symmetrical distributions known as **normal distributions**. A normal distribution can be described by a mathematical formula that specifies that the proportion of scores within one standard deviation of the mean, either above or below, is approximately .34. (That is, the proportion of scores between one standard deviation below the mean and one standard deviation above is it approximately .68.) The proportion in the next standard deviation beyond that one, in either direction, is approximately .14, and so on. Figure 10.5 shows a normal distribution of IQ test scores.

The formula for the normal curve can be used to estimate the **relative standing** of a score in a distribution. Let's assume that the distribution of exam scores in our example (Table 10.2) is normal and, thus, follows the formula. Then, we can estimate that a score of 61 (approximately one standard deviation below the mean) is higher than approximately 15% of the scores in the distribution and, therefore, lower than approximately 85%.

Box 10.1 **THINKING ABOUT RESEARCH**

When Statistical Analysis Leaves Reality Behind _____

It might seem that converting frequencies to percentages would be about the most straightforward form of descriptive statistical analysis. It would be more meaningful in many cases to know the percentages of respondents who gave each of a set of alternative responses than the number. To do so would require only the simple steps of adding up the number giving a particular response and dividing that sum by the total number in the sample.

Imagine how surprised political scientist Gary King was as he listened to testimony in a federal voting rights case in 1994. According to that testimony, in one voting district after another more than 100% of black voters had cast their ballots for Democratic candidates. How can one part of a sample be greater than the total?

The reason for answers that seem so illogical is that the researchers who produced them didn't follow the simple procedure described above. They used group-level data, like the overall vote totals and percentage of black voters

in a district, to estimate what they would find if they followed the more costly approach of actually polling individual voters, even though their estimates made no sense.

King, according to a National Public Radio broadcast, was so appalled by what he heard that he developed a new method for estimating individual-level data from group data. His computer-based method incorporates a safeguard that rejects all illogical answers, such as estimates greater than 100%. In a test, he compared his method with actual polling results and found it to be highly accurate.

What lessons can we learn from this case? Does the use of computers for complex statistical analysis make it more likely that researchers will accept illogical answers as true? Are the errors always so obvious that those who hear or read the results will feel the need to look into them further? What can we learn from King's example that will make this sort of error less likely to occur?

Standardized Scores. In this case, we can see in Table 10.2 that 7 exam scores out of 50, or 14%, are below 60. But what if the distribution had thousands or even millions of scores, as is the case for IQ or SAT scores? Using the mean and standard deviation, the scores in any normal or approximately normal distribution can be converted or standardized to compare scores from different distributions that are based on different scales of measurement. One could use such scores to compare ACT and SAT college entrance tests, or different questionnaire measures of anxiety. A sample exam score of 61 could be standardized by entering it in the following formula:

$$z = X \ O \ M/s.$$

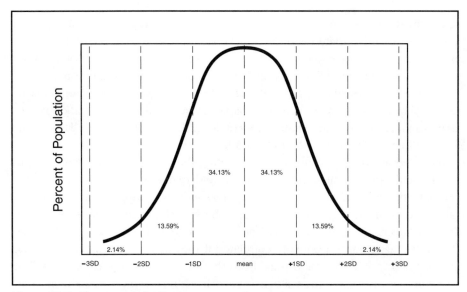

Figure 10.5. The normal distribution or normal curve.

The **standard score**, z, represents the number of standard deviations (s) between the score in question (X) and the mean (M). If it is negative, as in our example ($[61 - 73.72]/12.53 = -1.02$), one knows that the score is below the mean. If it is positive, one knows it is above the mean.

It is also possible to set arbitrary values for the mean and standard deviation, as is done in the case of many standardized test scores such as the ACT and SAT (18 and 6, respectively, for the ACT, and 500 and 100 for the SAT). In multivariate analyses, such as those discussed in Chapter 8, standard scores are often used to make very different measurement scales comparable. Then, a variety of predictors or behavioral measures can be combined into a single statistic. Although this may be far from obvious from the formulas used to calculate them, **correlation coefficients** actually compare pairs of scores from two different distributions by making use of the relative standing of scores in their respective distributions.

Bivariate Distributions: Two Scores Per Unit

You are familiar with the correlation coefficient from the previous discussion of multivariate research. It can also be thought of as another statistic used to describe a distribution. This time, the distribution is of pairs of scores rather than individual ones. This might be a distribution of two variables or scores measured for each of a sample of people or cases, such as each person's height and weight. It can be any two related scores, such as the IQ scores of a parent and child. If you recall the

scatterplot discussed in Chapter 8 (see Figure 8.3 to refresh your memory), you know that these bivariate distributions can be represented by coordinates on a graph. The value of one score in each pair is plotted against the value of the other to determine each point that is plotted on the coordinates of the graph.

A scatterplot is a visual representation of whatever degree of correspondence or relationship exists between the two variables in question. The correlation coefficient is a more precise mathematical way of doing the same thing. Recall that it varies in absolute value from 0 to 1.00, and it can be positive or negative.

As stated above, the formula for calculating this statistic (even more complicated than the one for the standard deviation and, thankfully, just as unnecessary if you have the use of a calculator or computer) actually compares standard scores calculated from the original scores. Thus, the scores are positively correlated if they tend to fall at roughly equal distances in standard deviation units on the same side of the mean, and negatively correlated if they are approximately the same number of standard deviation units from the mean but on opposite sides. The scores are uncorrelated if the relative distance from the mean of one score in a pair is unrelated to that of the other.

● INFERENTIAL STATISTICS

As useful as descriptive statistics are for understanding and communicating the results of psychological research, they are, for the research psychologist, above all a stepping-stone to further statistical analysis. That analysis, known as **statistical inference**, is aimed more directly at the heart of the matter. It addresses the question of whether the data bear out the predictions made in the research hypothesis. As you may recall from our discussion of research design, the purpose of collecting research data is to make possible comparisons across groups, comparisons over time, and determinations of relationships among variables. Each of those permits an evaluation of the independent variable–dependent variable relationship specified in the research hypothesis. Those comparisons and determinations are accomplished by means of statistical inference.

Statistical Inference: The Basic Problem

In the preceding lengthy discussions of threats to the validity of research findings in psychology, we have considered ways of ruling out alternative explanations for the results of a research study. It could be said that statistical inference is a mathematical method for ruling out yet another alternative explanation for the differences or relationships that make up those results. That alternative explanation is **sampling error**.

Statistical inference evaluates whether the treatment group differences, or the independent variable–dependent variable relationships, found for a particular sample of research participants hold true for the entire population of individuals from which that sample was drawn. In our hypothetical example, as in most cases of hypothesis-testing research, the research hypothesis postulates a relationship between variables (arousal and exam performance) that will hold in general. The research is not just a search for a relationship for the specific sample of participants on whom the test is conducted. At the time the research hypothesis is framed, the particular sample that ultimately will be studied usually has not even been identified.

Let's consider, then, how we might use our arousal and exam data to test a hypothesis about the effect of arousal on task performance. We could divide our hypothetical research participants into groups that had different measured levels of arousal and compare the average exam scores of those groups, or we could use correlation to determine the relationship between the two sets of scores. Recall that we suspect from past research that the relationship might be curvilinear. Recall also the scatterplot in Figure 8.3 that shows that the relationship is curvilinear. It is positive for some values of arousal and negative for others; specifically, in this case, it is positive for lower values and negative for higher ones. It might make sense, therefore, to divide the participants into three groups—high, moderate, and low arousal. Then one could compare group means. If we chose to use a correlational analysis, we would have to use a measure that is capable of detecting a curvilinear relationship, but that is a statistical technique used so rarely that it does not merit further discussion here.

At first blush, there doesn't seem to be much of a problem here. We could divide the 50 participants into those with the highest levels of arousal, those with moderate levels, and those with the lowest. We could constitute groups containing 17, 16, and 17 individuals, respectively. To begin with, the exam scores of those three groups could be compared using the descriptive statistics we considered earlier in this chapter, the mean and standard deviation. The calculated values of those statistics for the three arousal groups are shown in Table 10.5.

Just looking at the group means, it might seem clear enough that the expected effect of arousal on performance did occur. Those participants in the hypothetical study with moderate levels of arousal outperformed those who had low or high levels of arousal by about 17 points, on average, in both cases. But what about the variability in each of the three groups? Because of sampling error, the individuals in each group varied considerably in their level of performance. It seems likely that there were some individuals in the moderate arousal group who performed worse than some in the other groups. How do we know that the mean differences are large enough, or that the group differences are consistent enough, to warrant the conclusion we jumped to based solely on the descriptive sample statistics? More to the point of statistical inference, how do we know that the difference isn't the re-

TABLE 10.5 Exam Score Means and Standard Deviations for High, Moderate, and Low Arousal Groups

	Level of Arousal		
	High	Moderate	Low
Exam score mean	68.53	85.19	68.23
Exam score standard deviation	9.47	8.24	11.35

sult of an atypical sample? Perhaps a few more bright students, who got their usual very high test grades, found their way into the moderate arousal group than usually would be the case?

That is where the question of sampling error comes in. The participants in this study were chosen to represent the population of all the individuals who might find themselves in those same circumstances. But what if a different sample of 50 participants had been chosen? Or what if we repeated the study with a different sample, keeping every other aspect of it the same? (Because this is a hypothetical example, we can suspend disbelief and assume that is possible.) Would it be reasonable to expect that a different sample of 50 participants would produce exactly the same results?

The results of this study—the mean exam scores and associated standard deviations for the three arousal groups—are one of an infinite number of possible set of results. If we repeated the study an infinite number of times, drawing a new random sample of the same size from the same population of potential participants each time, the group means would be different each time. Let's consider one group at a time—high, moderate, and low arousal. In each case, that infinite number of repetitions (replications) could be represented as a distribution of group means that follows the shape of the normal curve. It would be perfectly symmetrical, with known proportions of means falling within specified distances (measured in standard deviation units) from the mean of the distribution as a whole.

Solving the Problem: The Sampling Distribution

Such a distribution is known as a **sampling distribution**. There would be a separate sampling distribution for each sample size that could be chosen for the infinite number of repetitions of the study. The larger the sample size, the smaller the standard deviation of the sampling distribution would be. With larger samples, the sample means would provide better estimates of the overall population mean, thus varying less around that value. Because it is not possible to conduct an infinite number of studies, sampling distributions are of necessity theoretical rather than real. They are thinking tools invented by mathematicians to create a means of evaluating the outcomes of research that is known as **null hypothesis significance testing (NHST)**.

In addition to sampling distributions of single group means, we can imagine sampling distributions of differences between group means. We could repeat the study of the effects of arousal on exam performance an infinite number of times, with groups of the same size each time. The means of the individual groups would vary, creating a distribution of means for each group. The differences between them would also vary, creating a distribution for each of the possible mean differences, high versus moderate, low versus moderate, and high versus low.

It is the differences we're really interested in, because our research hypothesis predicts differences, not actual group means, so it's the sampling distribution of mean differences that we'll look at more closely. To simplify things a little, at least to begin with, let's focus our discussion on one element of the hypothesis. We'll concentrate on the prediction that students taking the test under moderate levels of arousal will do better than those who take the test under high levels of arousal. The results on that point were, to recall our hypothetical data summarized in Table 10.5, that the average exam score for the high arousal group was 68.53, with a standard deviation of 9.47, and the average exam score of the moderate arousal group was 85.19, with a standard deviation of 8.24. Thus, the difference between those group means was 16.66, in the predicted direction of the moderate arousal group performing better on the exam.

Is this difference consistent with what we'd get if we repeated the study over and over again? Can the result from this sample be generalized to the entire population of potential participants who might be tested in order to study this question? That's the question addressed in statistical inference. To answer that question, we'll use null hypothesis significance testing (NHST), a method devised by the applied mathematicians called statisticians.

Testing the Null Hypothesis

Null hypothesis significance testing begins, logically enough, with something called the **null hypothesis**. Whereas the research hypothesis predicts differences between groups (caused by the treatments), the null hypothesis predicts no difference. In other words, in the case of NHST, we begin by asking "What would we expect if the participants' level of arousal had no effect on their exam performance?"

If that assumption were true, consider what the sampling distribution of mean differences of the study would look like. For starters, the mean of that distribution of differences would be zero (0.00). Even if arousal had no effect on exam performance, sampling error would be such that there would be differences in almost every case or sample where the comparison was made. Those differences would be distributed symmetrically around the mean of 0.00. In other words, the positive and negative differences would cancel each other out over a series of studies so that the average outcome would be zero difference.

The mean difference that was found in the only study we know about, of the infinite number of possible studies that might be done, is 16.66. So the null hypothesis is false, isn't it, because the mean difference is not zero? Remember, though, that even if the null hypothesis were true, some of the studies—almost all of them, actually—would produce differences other than zero. Given that, what can we make of a difference of 16.66? Is it reasonable to expect that such a large a difference would still be found even if the null hypothesis were true? If so, how often would it be found? In statistical terms, we ask if it is a **significant difference**. That is a difference so unlikely given a true null hypothesis that we should abandon our assumption that the null hypothesis is true. Or is it nonsignificant, that is, likely enough even if the null hypothesis is true?

Those are the questions null hypothesis significance testing was designed to answer. It does so by making some further assumptions. The first is that the sampling distribution of the mean difference will approximate the shape of the normal curve. As you will recall, the normal curve is a distribution that follows a mathematical formula. In that distribution, there are known proportions of scores (in this case, mean differences are the scores) falling at specified distances from the mean of the distribution. Those distances are measured in terms of the standard deviation of the distribution. If we know how far any score (mean difference) in the distribution is from the mean in standard deviation units, we can determine what proportion of scores falls above or below it.

For the purposes of NHST, the mean of the distribution is 0.00 because the null hypothesis sets it there. We know the score we're interested in: It is the mean difference of 16.66 that we found in our study. If we knew the standard deviation of the sampling distribution and assumed the mean differences to be normally distributed, we could determine what proportion of those mean differences would be expected to be as large or larger than 16.66, if the average of all the mean differences were 0.00.

In null hypothesis significance testing, that is essentially what is done. We use the standard deviations of the samples from which the mean difference comes. We also use the sample size because, again, the larger the samples, the more closely the means in the sample distribution can be expected to cluster around the mean. A bigger sample from a population can be expected to provide a better estimate of the characteristics of the population as a whole. With that information, the probability that the observed mean difference could occur in a sampling distribution with a mean of 0.00 can be determined.

By agreement among statisticians and the researchers who use inferential statistics in their work, if that probability is less than 1 in 20, or less than .05, the null hypothesis is rejected. That is the point, known as the **level of significance**, at which NHST users agree the observed difference is too unlikely to belong to the

TABLE 10.6 *t* Test Comparing Exam Scores Between Moderate and High Arousal Groups

Moderate arousal mean	85.19
High arousal mean	68.53
Mean difference	16.66
Standard error of the mean difference	3.086
t	5.398
p	< .001

null hypothesis sampling distribution for them to continue to believe that the null hypothesis is true. In that event, the researcher is bound by that convention to reject the null hypothesis and to conclude that the research hypothesis—the hypothesis that there is a difference (a treatment effect)—should be retained in the light of the research results.

Comparing Groups With the *t* Test

Because there are three groups to be compared in our hypothetical study—high, moderate, and low arousal—the statistical procedure that is most appropriate for use in our example is actually one called analysis of variance, or ANOVA for short. The calculations for analysis of variance are so complex that for now we will use a simpler form of inferential statistics called a ***t* test**, even though this isn't, strictly speaking, appropriate for use in this case (more about why and about ANOVA in a little while). The *t* test compares just two groups at a time, but the principles of NHST are the same for the *t* test and ANOVA, and the *t* test is easier to understand. We won't go into the calculations required, but the formula for the *t* test is as follows:

$$t = (M_1 - M_2)/s_{ed}$$

M_1 and M_2 are the means of the groups of participants being compared (in our case, again, 85.19 and 68.53) for the moderate and high groups, respectively. The numerator of the term, the difference between the two, works out to be 16.66 (just as it did earlier). The denominator is an estimate of the standard deviation of the sampling distribution of mean differences, called the **standard error of the mean difference**. It is calculated from the sample standard deviations and sample sizes (a pretty complicated formula, again, and a calculation that won't concern us here). In this example, the standard error of the mean difference works out to be 3.09, so the *t* statistic, 16.66 divided by 3.09, has a value of 5.39. See Table 10.6 for a summary of the *t* test calculation and result.

Using the calculated value of t, the sample sizes, and a table based on the formula for a normal distribution, we can determine the probability of a mean difference of 16.66 being found as the result of one study when the mean of the mean differences of all possible repetitions of the study is approximately 0.000. That probability (p) is less than 1 in 1,000 ($p < .001$). Because we, as NHST statistics users, have agreed that a result as unlikely as 1 in 20 should lead to the rejection of the null hypothesis, it is clear that we would reject the null hypothesis in this case, where the result is more than 50 times less likely than that.

That would lead us to conclude that the mean difference we found must have come from a different sampling distribution of mean differences. That alternative sampling distribution must have a mean greater than zero. In other words, we would reject the null hypothesis. In reference to our research hypothesis, this means that we would conclude that, based on our results, exam takers with moderate levels of arousal in general would perform better than those with high levels of arousal under the conditions of our research study (not perform equal to them, as maintained in the null hypothesis).

Following the same procedure, the t test comparing the moderate and low arousal groups would also be statistically significant ($t = 4.93$, $p < .001$). Thus, the null hypothesis would be rejected in that case also, and the research hypothesis that performance would be better under conditions of moderate arousal supported again. As you would probably expect, the difference between the high and low arousal groups (with almost identical means) would be nonsignificant by t test ($t = .08$, probability greater than 9 in 10).

A Bit About ANOVA

In principle, it is not appropriate to make comparisons among three or more treatments groups in a single study by using multiple t tests (in our case, high vs. moderate, low vs. moderate, and high vs. low). Now we know enough to understand something about that principle. In such a case, with multiple comparisons, the t tests could not be independent of one another; each of the groups would be involved in more than one. As a result, the estimates of the probability of occurrence of a particular mean difference, and the related decision about whether to reject the null hypothesis, based on a comparison between that probability and .05, would not be accurate. That is why multiple two-group tests cannot be carried out within a single study. If those probability estimates are not accurate, and if the decision about whether to reject the null hypothesis is based on them, that decision obviously can't be trusted.

The appropriate test in this case, as we saw in Chapter 8 and earlier in this chapter, is **analysis of variance (ANOVA)**. Now that we can follow the logic of NHST in the simpler case of the t test, we can take a closer look at how ANOVA works. In

TABLE 10.7 ANOVA Summary Table for Study of the Effects of Arousal on Exam Performance

Source of Variance	Sum of Squares	df	Mean Square	F	P
Treatments (level of arousal; between groups)	3,095.64	2	1547.82	15.84	< .001
Error (within groups)	4,592.44	47	97.71		

principle, it is conducted in the same way as a *t* test comparing two groups. A statistic is calculated that estimates the probability of some difference among the groups being compared (three groups, in this case), given the assumption that there is no difference (the null hypothesis).

In the case of ANOVA, the test statistic is symbolized by *F*. Calculating the *F* statistic is considerably more complicated than the procedure for calculating *t*, so we won't worry about it at all here, not even the formula. For our hypothetical study, though, the result of an ANOVA comparing all three treatment groups would be an *F* with a value of 15.84. The probability of that *F*, given the sizes of our groups and the number of groups compared, is—as it was for the *t* test we carried out—less than 1 in 1,000.

In the case of ANOVA, the null hypothesis is less specific than when just two groups are being compared. The null hypothesis for our hypothetical study would be that all three groups came from the same population, or that there was no difference among the mean scores of the three groups. The criterion for rejection is the same, less than 1 chance in 20 that the observed result could be one of the infinite number of results when there is no difference (when arousal has no effect on exam performance). Rejection of the null hypothesis would follow in this case just as it did in the case of the *t* test. It would mean that we would be forced to conclude that the three groups did not perform equally well.

To find out which groups differed would require further testing. In our example, that testing would reveal that both the high and low arousal groups performed at lower levels than the moderate arousal group, and that the high and low arousal groups didn't differ from each other in their level of exam performance (see Table 10.7 for a summary of the ANOVA on which this conclusion is based). This is a pretty straightforward example in which the group means pretty much tell the story and the results of the *F* test and the three separate *t* tests agree. Not all examples work out quite this easily.

The logic of analysis of variance is somewhat different from that of the *t* test. Instead of comparing observed mean differences with a hypothetical sampling distribution as the *t* test does, analysis of variance (who would guess, given its name?) compares variances or variability. In our example, as would be the case generally in the use of ANOVA, there are two kinds of variability. One kind is the variability within each group. Even though participants in a group are exposed to the same treatment or version of the independent variable, like the 17 who share the designation high arousal in our example, their behavior can vary considerably. The exam scores of the high arousal group vary from 51 to 83. There is a fairly wide range of scores in each of the other groups as well, from 45 to 86 in the low arousal group and from 70 to 96 in the moderate arousal group. The variability within the groups is known as error variance or within-groups variance in ANOVA. It reflects the unreliability or random error in the treatments and behavioral measures.

The second type of variability is that among the groups. The exam scores for both the high and the low arousal groups occupy a lower segment of the overall distribution of exam scores than those for the moderate arousal group. The variability from treatment group to treatment group is known as *treatment variance* or *between-groups variance*.

The test statistic for ANOVA, *F* (for Fisher, the creator of this method of null hypothesis statistical testing), is very flexible and very widely used in psychological research. It is a ratio that compares those two sources of variance. If treatment/ between-groups variance (among groups would be more correct grammatically, because there are more than two, but it's not the term statisticians chose for it) is sufficiently greater than within-group variance, then a probabilistic judgment to reject the null hypothesis is made, in much the same way as it is for the *t* test. In Table 10.7, treatment variance is shown as "sum of squares" and "mean square." Mean square reflects an adjustment for the number of groups being compared. Error variance is shown in the same columns, except that it is adjusted for the sizes of the treatment groups. The *F* ratio of 15.84 is derived by dividing the mean square for treatments by the mean square for error. You can see from the table that an *F* ratio of 15.84 has an associated probability of less than .001.

If the treatments (in this case, differences in the level of arousal) have no effect, participants in different groups should be no more different from one another than participants in the same group are from one another. In that case, within-group and between-group variances would be equal, and the *F* ratio would take a value of 1.00. The ratio becomes larger as the variability attributable to treatments becomes greater than the sampling variability or sampling error within groups receiving the same treatment. As the *F* ratio becomes larger than 1.00 (i.e., no effect of treatments), it becomes less probable given a true null hypothesis. When that probability becomes as small as or smaller than 1 in 20 (.05), the significance level, again, this is grounds for rejecting the null hypothesis.

The summary of our ANOVA shown in Table 10.7 is known to users of ANOVA as a summary table. If we compared the same group's performance on three separate occasions using ANOVA, instead of three separate groups, we would calculate a somewhat different F ratio. There are different arrangements for ANOVA, or *designs* as they're called, depending on the research design used to collect the data. Each one has its own distinctive summary table.

We left another detail out of the discussions of the t test and ANOVA. The size of the group involved affects the probability of the test statistic value that is calculated, for reasons that must remain obscure until you have more time to study statistics. The probability values are found in tables that provide different values depending on those sizes, which are known as degrees of freedom to statisticians (see the third column in Table 10.7 for an example).

NHST and Correlation

Null hypothesis significance testing also has been extended to correlation coefficients. The null hypothesis in that case is that there is no relationship between the variables being studied. As is true of group means and group differences, even when the null hypothesis is true, varying correlation coefficients can be expected in a series of studies based on different samples and their respective bivariate distributions of scores. As in all uses of NHST, the larger the obtained coefficient (regardless of sign), the less probable it is for samples of a given size, assuming a true null hypothesis. When that probability is .05 or smaller, the null hypothesis of no relationship is rejected in favor of the conclusion that the variables are related.

Just as there are null hypothesis statistical tests for research designs with single independent variables (t) and multiple independent variables (F/ANOVA), a multiple correlation (R) can be tested in the same way as a simple correlation (r). An associated probability value can be determined for R and compared with .05. That will determine whether the null hypothesis that a particular combination of predictors is not related to a criterion variable can be rejected in a particular study. In correlational analyses, however, the proportion of variance accounted for (r^2 or R^2) often is considered more important than the question of statistical significance, an issue to which we'll return later in this chapter.

STATISTICAL CONCLUSION VALIDITY ●

Introduction

A research psychologist makes decisions about which descriptive and inferential statistics to use in analyzing his or her research data. Those decisions need to be subjected to the same kind of critical scrutiny as all the other decisions made in

---

| Box 10.2 | *THINKING ABOUT RESEARCH* |

How Much Does It Matter? _____

Chapter 1, for the purpose of introducing our subject, included extensive discussion of the hypothesis that exposure to televised violence is a cause of aggressive behavior. In the light of several recent shootings at schools around the country, this long-standing hypothesis and the psychological research that has been carried out to test it have been the subject of much public discussion, and that discussion has generated a fair measure of controversy.

In one newspaper interview, social psychologist Jonathan Freedman argued that the small, consistent correlation between children watching television and being more aggressive does not prove cause and effect. For example, children who watch television more may also receive worse parenting. On the other side, developmental psychologist L. Rowell Huesmann pointed to more than 1,000 studies, in-

cluding both experiments and "surveys," that show, individually and via meta-analysis that combines their results statistically, a consistent relationship between exposure to television violence and aggression.

Between Freedman and Huesmann, whom do you think is right? What validity issues are raised by Freedman, and how well are they dealt with in Huesmann's response? If the effect of televised violence is real, does it matter if it is small? How do we know how small it is? If it is small, why is that? How should the magnitude of the effect be factored into policy decisions about the content of television programming? If the effect is small, how great an effort should be made to change TV program content, versus other measures that might be taken to reduce violence?

---

the course of conducting a research study. They are as important as the decisions in choosing a hypothesis, specifying the independent and dependent variables, developing a research design, and selecting the data collection techniques. Poor decisions about data analysis threaten the validity of research findings as much as poor decisions at any other point during the research process. Although it sometimes seems that the use of statistical analysis is enough of a technical problem of formulas and calculations in itself, how statistical tests are chosen is as important or even more important than how they are used.

Threats to Statistical Conclusion Validity

We will consider three potential threats to the validity of research findings associated with data analysis—that is, threats to **statistical conclusion validity**. See Table 10-8 for the list, in the context of all the other threats to validity we've considered.

Inappropriate Use of Statistical Techniques

The descriptive and inferential statistical techniques used by research psychologists in their work are based in standard mathematical operations and theories about probability. As such, there are rules governing their use that must be followed if the results are to be valid. In the case of descriptive statistics, this is necessary so that the summaries of large data sets that are provided to readers of research reports represent fairly the original measurements on which they are based. In the case of inferential statistics, the rules must be followed so that the estimates of the probability of a statistic belonging to a sampling distribution with a specified mean, and the resulting decision about whether to reject the null hypothesis, are correct.

We have reviewed only a small sample of the statistical techniques used by research psychologists. Thus, the discussion that follows can be based on only a limited number of examples of the poor choices among data analysis techniques that can threaten the validity of research findings (i.e., lead to false conclusions about the meaning of research results). It is not intended to be an exhaustive list.

One example recalls the discussion of measures of central tendency found earlier in this chapter. When a group of scores (a distribution) is symmetrical, the alternative measures of central tendency—the mean, median, and mode—give similar answers to the question of where the center of the distribution is located. In most such cases, researchers would choose the mean to describe central tendency. Its computation is straightforward, most people understand what an "average" is, and it is a useful value for further computations. As we've already seen, it is used to calculate both standard scores and *t* tests, and those are just two examples.

But some distributions are distinctly asymmetrical, or **skewed distributions**, as statisticians would say, and in those cases the mean may be a misleading measure of the central tendency of the scores. Consider again the distribution of family income in the United States. Most of the scores pile up between $20,000 and $40,000 per year. That is the middle class, as most Americans understand the term (partisan congressional debates over taxes and tax cuts notwithstanding). Below $20,000, the frequencies trail off gradually into regions of greater and greater disability and poverty. Above $40,000, scores are sprinkled across a much broader range, up to levels that many of us can barely imagine. Those are the incomes of the Bill Gateses and lesser billionaires of our world. The distribution is highly skewed. It is positively skewed, in the language of statisticians, because most of the scores pile up near the low end of the income scale, and the longer "tail" of the distribution, containing the "outlier" scores, extends toward the high or positive end. In a negatively skewed distribution, the "tail" would be at the low end of the distribution, where the scores are lowest.

If one were to calculate the mean of this skewed distribution, the very few extremely high scores (incomes) would exert more influence on the final figure than

TABLE 10.8 Threats to Statistical Conclusion Validity

I. Threats to conceptual validity
      1. Unnecessary duplication
      2. Theoretical isolation
II. Threats to construct validity
  A. The independent variable
     a. Inadequate operationalization
        3. Lack of reliability of the independent variable
        4. Lack of representativeness of the independent variable
        5. Lack of impact of the independent variable
     b. Treatment artifacts
        6. Demand characteristics in the research setting
        7. Experimenter expectancy effects on the behavior being observed
        8. Pretest sensitization to the treatments
  B. The dependent variable
     a. Inadequate operationalization
        9. Lack of reliability of the dependent variable
      10. Lack of representativeness of the dependent variable
      11. Lack of sensitivity of the dependent variable
     b. Measurement artifacts
      12. Strategic responding by the research participants
      13. Linguistic/cultural bias in the dependent measure
III. Threats to internal validity
      14. Extraneous effects (history)
      15. Temporal effects (maturation)
      16. Group composition effects (selection)
      17. Interaction of temporal and group composition effects
      18. Selective sample attrition (mortality)
      19. Statistical regression effects (regression to the mean)
IV. Threats to external validity
      20. Nonrepresentative sampling
      21. Nonrepresentative research context
V. Threats to statistical conclusion validity
      22. Inappropriate use of statistical techniques
      23. Use of a statistical test lacking sufficient power
      24. Mistaking a trivial effect for support for the research hypothesis

other scores because they are so extremely large. The result would be a number much higher than most American families' incomes. It would be a strange estimate of the "center" of the distribution. In this case, the median would be a better choice because it gives all scores equal weight in determining the middle score. The result would be a number that is relatively close to the point in the distribution where the most frequently occurring incomes are to be found. Again, the next time you read or hear a news story about the current incomes of American families, pay close attention and you'll probably see or hear "median income" because it is the most accurate measure of central tendency for such a skewed distribution.

The lesson in all of this is that all researchers need to determine the shape of a distribution of scores before they choose a measure of central tendency if they and others are to draw valid conclusions about the results of their studies. A measure of central tendency that is inappropriate for the shape of the distribution to which it is applied provides a misleading result, so that the conclusions drawn about the data and, thus, the outcome of the study are invalid.

Earlier, we discussed the choice to use a correlation coefficient like the Pearson product moment coefficient to summarize the strength and direction of the relationship between two variables in a bivariate distribution. That choice also needs to be made carefully. If there is not a wide range of scores on both of the variables represented in the bivariate distribution, or if the relationship between the variables is curvilinear rather than consistent in direction across the entire range of values in the distribution (i.e., linear), the value of any coefficient that is calculated is likely to distort the true nature of the relationship. When either of the variables takes such a narrow range of values as to make the correlation coefficient an inappropriate measure of the relationship between them, that relationship simply cannot be described accurately using a correlation coefficient. When the relationship between two variables is curvilinear, it needs to be described by some means other than a correlation coefficient like the Pearson coefficient, which was designed to describe only linear relationships.

As was also discussed earlier, the *t* test is not an appropriate means of making comparisons among three or more treatment groups. When two or more *t* tests are used to compare groups within a single study, the conventional means of estimating the probability of an obtained mean difference—and, therefore, the validity of decisions about whether or not to reject the null hypothesis—are called into question. In such a case, analysis of variance must be used to obtain accurate probability estimates and to make valid decisions about the null hypothesis.

By the same token, the analysis of variance that is conducted must be tailored to the particular characteristics of the research design used in the study. Three groups of scores may come from a single group of research participants tested on three separate occasions, or under three different sets of conditions. In that case, the analysis of variance must be conducted differently from when the comparison is among three groups of scores taken from three separate groups of participants exposed to contrasting treatments. This is just one example of many features of research design that call for their own specific approaches to ANOVA. In every case, the selection of the correct ANOVA model for the particular research design used in a study is crucial to obtaining an accurate estimate of the probability of *F* and, thus, to making a correct decision about whether to reject the null hypothesis.

The validity of null hypothesis statistical testing also depends on the underlying data meeting certain assumptions on which the mathematicians who developed these methods of statistical inference based their inventions. The measurements made of participants' behaviors must have interval scale properties (recall the discussion of measurement scales in Chapter 3) so that they can be averaged without distorting the nature of the data.

In addition, the groups of participants or other sources of data sampled by the researcher must be random samples from their respective populations. The scores obtained from those participants or sources must be distributed normally, or approximately so, and the variances within the groups compared in analysis of variance must be equal or nearly equal. Meeting these and other underlying assumptions is just as important to the validity of the statistical inferences drawn by the researcher as is the choice of an appropriate statistic.

There are disagreements among both statisticians and researchers about the degree to which deviations from these assumptions jeopardize the validity of statistical inference. Some argue that the statistical tests in question are "robust" enough to withstand considerable violation of their underlying assumptions without producing invalid conclusions. Others argue that researchers whose data fail to meet those assumptions should use alternative means of testing their hypotheses, known as *distribution-free* or *nonparametric* statistical methods. These methods, unfortunately, lack the flexibility and precision of the *parametric* methods such as *t* tests and ANOVA. Distribution-free statistical methods are based on ranks or on frequencies, so that they may be used safely with ordinal or even nominal data.

Parametric methods are based on means and standard deviations, which can be calculated only from data as precise as equal-interval or close to it. A deeper consideration of those questions must be reserved for a more advanced discussion of statistics than we are able to have here. The point to remember for now is that valid research findings depend on eliminating the threat of **inappropriate use of statistical techniques**.

Use of a Statistical Test Lacking Sufficient Power

NHST. Null hypothesis significance testing can be a difficult procedure for the researcher to evaluate because it involves a good deal of uncertainty. Judgments based on NHST are necessarily probabilistic rather than absolute judgments. Researchers also have varying interests in the results of their work, depending on the purpose for which it was done and the ethical principles in which they believe. As a result, there is a good deal of debate among methodologists about the issues raised in this section and the next. Don't be too surprised about seeming contradictions: They come with the territory of statistical inference, at least at the point in its development where we find ourselves now.

TABLE 10.9 Possible Outcomes of Null Hypothesis Statistical Testing

	Actual Status of H_0	
Decision About H_0	H_0 True	H_0 False
Reject H_0	A type I error	B correct decision
Retain H_0	D correct decision	C type II error

As we've seen already, statistical inference begins with the null hypothesis. The NHST user makes the assumption that treatments (contrasting levels of the independent variable) have no differential effect on the groups exposed to them, or that there is no relationship among two or more sets of measurements on the same or related individuals. Logically, it is possible that the null hypothesis is either true or that it is false. The results of a single research study are based on one test of the research hypothesis. That test may show that treatments do have an effect, or that bivariate measurements are correlated. As a result of the application of descriptive statistics (mean, standard deviation, correlation coefficient, etc.) and then inferential statistics (t, F, etc.), the researcher will draw one of two conclusions: either to reject the null hypothesis based on an extreme (improbable) value of the test statistic or to retain (not reject) the null hypothesis based on a test statistic that is not too inconsistent with a true null hypothesis (a probability of membership in the null hypothesis sampling distribution that is greater than .05).

Errors in NHST. This means that there are four possible outcomes of NHST, shown in Table 10.9. The four outcomes shown in the four quadrants of the table (labeled A through D, clockwise beginning with the upper left) are the products of the two possible conditions of the null hypothesis (H_0), which can be either true or false, and the two possible outcomes of NHST, either rejecting or retaining the null hypothesis.

Of course, this discussion must be hypothetical, as is often the case in statistics, because it is never possible to know whether the null hypothesis is true or false or, therefore, which quadrant of the table truly represents the outcome of a particular statistical inference. If there were some certain way of knowing whether the null hypothesis (and, therefore, the research hypothesis) were true or false, we would have no need at all for the probabilistic answer we get from inferential statistics.

The decision based on NHST may be correct. That is the case in quadrants B and D, retaining a true null hypothesis and rejecting a false null hypothesis, respectively. In those cases, there is obviously no reason for concern, on the part of either the researcher or the methodologist. They, and we, need to concentrate on understanding how NHST can go wrong. We need to understand the errors that can occur, the reasons that they occur, and what can be done to minimize the likelihood that they will occur. Only then can we plan research and interpret research findings better.

The order of the two possible errors resulting from NHST has been established by convention. **Type I error** designates the error of rejecting a true null hypothesis (Quadrant A), and **Type II error** is the error of retaining a false null hypothesis (Quadrant C).

We'll consider Type I error first. Recall that the decision to reject the null hypothesis is based on the estimate of the probability that some characteristic of the scores collected in a research study would be observed if the null hypothesis were true. That characteristic can be group mean, the difference between the means of two groups, the ratio of between-group to within-group variance, or the correlation between two variables. The null hypothesis is rejected whenever the value of that characteristic, reflected in a test statistic such as t or F, is extreme enough. In the present discussion, that means that it is sufficiently unlikely (a probability of less than .05) to be part of a distribution of such values that has a mean reflecting no relationship between independent variable and dependent variable (a distribution based on the assumption that the null hypothesis is true).

Remember that the distribution against which a mean or the test statistic (t for example) based on that mean is compared is normal in shape. (The process is analogous for every null hypothesis statistical test.) It happens that normal distributions have no real boundaries, so even the most extreme value of a mean, or a t based on that mean, could conceivably come from a sampling distribution with a mean of zero. Even a very extreme value may be found, in other words, because of sampling error. It may be the result of testing an atypical sample and not occur because the null hypothesis is false.

No matter how low the probability of such a value, determined from the test statistic (t, F, or whatever), even .001 or .0001, it is never really zero and the null hypothesis is, therefore, never proven to be false beyond any doubt. A probability of less than .05 might be thought of as the scientific equivalent of the legal concept of reasonable doubt, and we know how problematic that can be.

When a Type I error is made, a true null hypothesis (of no relationship) is rejected incorrectly. In that event, the true cause of an extreme result is sampling error rather than a real treatment effect or independent variable–dependent variable relationship. As a result, false knowledge is introduced into science. The independent variable is judged to have been a real influence on the dependent variable when it was not. Many scientists consider this type of error to be the most serious of all.

The probability of such a misleading outcome can be controlled quite directly by varying the criterion probability, known as the *level of significance*, against which the probability of an obtained test statistic is compared. We have used .05 in our discussion because it is the standard long since established by statisticians and users of statistics. The value can be set lower than .05 if the researcher chooses, in order to reduce the probability of a Type I error—to .01 or even .001. Thus, the researcher may require that there be no more than 1 chance in 1,000 (rather than 1 in 20) that a test statistic could be part of a sampling distribution with a mean of 0 before being willing to reject the null hypothesis. This doesn't eliminate the possibility of a Type I error; it is still possible that sampling error could be mistaken for an effect of the independent variable. It does, however, reduce the likelihood of a Type I error, perhaps considerably.

Reducing the level of significance has implications for the likelihood of occurrence of the Type II error, the decision to retain a false null hypothesis. The more difficult it is to reject the null hypothesis, the more willing one is to hold on to the idea that there is no treatment effect even when the data seem to indicate that there is. That is, the more difficult it is to reject the null hypothesis, because of a lower level of significance, the more likely one is to fail to reject the null hypothesis when the null hypothesis is, in fact, false—and thus commit a Type II error.

The probability of a Type I error is known. It is set by the researcher when he or she chooses the level of significance. The exact probability of a Type II error is not known; however, it is known that lowering the level of significance raises the probability of a Type II error.

Other factors also affect the probability of Type II error. They do so by affecting the shape of the normal distribution against which a test statistic is compared in order to determine the probability of a particular value of the statistic occurring when the null hypothesis is assumed to be true. The most important of these is sample size. We saw earlier that a sampling distribution, the normal distribution that is used to determine the probability of obtaining a test statistic, varies in shape depending on the size of the samples tested to calculate the means, mean differences, correlations, or other statistics that are represented in it. The standard deviation of the sampling distribution, or standard error of estimate, shrinks as the sample size increases. This is because a larger sample provides a better estimate of the mean of the distribution. The bigger the sample that is used to make each estimate, the less varied or disparate those estimates will be.

One way to understand the relationship between sample size and variability is to examine the formula for calculating the standard deviation given earlier in this chapter. The term in the denominator of that formula is the sample size, n. As n becomes larger, the value of the fraction as a whole, standard deviation, decreases.

Think about the following example. Imagine that someone hands you a sealed box containing 1,000 marbles and tells you that some of the marbles are blue, and some are red. You can make some easy money by guessing correctly how many are blue and how many are red. You can open the box and, without looking in, take out some of the marbles. You can examine a sample before you guess. How large a sample would you want to draw?

Isn't it obvious that the larger the sample you take out—the more marbles you get to see and count—the closer you're likely to come to the right answer? Think about the most extreme cases. If you "sampled" all the marbles, you'd know for sure how many were blue and how many red. If you sampled just one marble, you could never guess how many of each color were in the box. In fact, when mathematicians test that idea in what they call "Monte Carlo experiments," they find that larger samples provide better estimates. The distributions of those estimates, sampling distributions, have smaller standard deviations when they are based on larger sample sizes.

Another factor that influences the probability of making a Type II error is the magnitude of the treatment effect. The greater the difference between the group means ($M_1 - M_2$), or the greater the relationship between the two variables (r_{xy}), or whatever form of the independent variable–dependent variable relationship is being tested, the more likely the test statistic will be significant and the null hypothesis rejected. As we saw earlier, the impact and reliability of the independent variable are important factors in giving the research hypothesis a fair test. Finally, the more reliable and sensitive the dependent variable chosen by the researcher, the less the variability within groups and the sharper the contrast between groups.

The Importance of Power. The significance of all of this for our discussion is that an evaluation of any set of research findings needs to take into account the nature of the statistical tests used to analyze the data on which those findings were based, the nature of the data being analyzed, the size of the sample of observations subjected to those tests, the impact and reliability of the independent variable, and the reliability and sensitivity of the dependent variable.

Given the same group mean, or mean difference, or correlation, the higher the level of significance (.05 is higher than .01), the larger the sample of observations, and the better the measurements made of the variables, the more likely it is that the null hypothesis will be rejected and the data interpreted as support for the research hypothesis, or as evidence for a relationship between independent variable and dependent variable.

If the researcher chooses too conservative a level of significance (.01 or .001), setting a higher priority on preventing a Type I error, tests too small a sample, or constructs weak and imprecise variables, there is a greater risk of a Type II error. He or she may fail to reject a null hypothesis of no treatment effect or no relationship between independent variable and dependent variable when the null hypothesis is actually false and the independent variable does have an effect, or when the independent variable and dependent variable actually are related. In statistical terms, a more stringent level of significance, a smaller sample of observations, and weak and imprecise variables add up to the **use of a statistical test lacking sufficient power** to detect a treatment effect or independent variable–dependent variable relationship where one in fact exists.

Mistaking a Trivial Effect for Support for the Research Hypothesis

The Problem With NHST. We've already seen several examples of how an improvement in one aspect of the research process can exacerbate the problems in another. Tightening up internal validity by testing a hypothesis in a laboratory experiment can make treatment artifacts more problematic. Reducing the probability of a Type I error by making the level of significance more stringent (lower) can reduce statistical power and increase the probability of a Type II error. Unfortunately, we're now up against yet another such Hobson's choice.

When the power of a statistical test is increased, the smallest treatment effect or weakest relationship between independent variable and dependent variable can pass the test of statistical significance and be accepted as support for the research hypothesis. Where research is being conducted to solve an important problem, or might be used for some practical application, **mistaking a trivial effect for support for the research hypothesis** is especially problematic. It may cost more to change to a new teaching technique, or penal system, or medical treatment than it is worth if the advantage of the new over the old is statistically significant but so small as to be trivial.

A lively debate is now going on over this issue in psychology. It is usually characterized as a debate between the alternatives of null hypothesis significance testing and **estimating effect size**. There is no quarrel about the internal logic of NHST. We know how to estimate the probability of an observed statistic given the assumption that the null hypothesis is true, and we know whether a sufficiently rare test statistic justifies the rejection of the null hypothesis. That logic seems to have stood the test of time. The wisdom of building psychological theories or basing practical interventions on the results of NHST, however, is increasingly being called into question. This debate is even more important for those who rely on verbal descriptions of the results of psychological research, without understanding the technical details of how it's carried out, than for research psychologists who are able to understand what actually has been done by reading a research report.

Null hypothesis significance tests are based only in part on the magnitude of the effect that is observed—the size of the difference between treatment group means, the magnitude of the correlation between two sets of measurements, and so on. As we have seen, they are also based on the consistency of the effect. When two or more treatment groups are being compared and a determination made to determine whether the null hypothesis should be rejected, a lack of overlap between the scores of different groups may be more important than is the size of the differences between their scores.

This is another way of saying that the degree of variability within each group is a very important. For example, think of the *t* test. The difference between two group means (the numerator) does not have to be very large if the estimate of variability (the denominator) is very small. It is that estimate of variability that measures the degree of consistency or overlap. The smaller it is, the greater the consistency of the treatment effect and the smaller the overlap between the treatment groups.

Alternatively, think of the *F* test used in analysis of variance. Between-group variability (the numerator, again) does not need to be very great in order for *F* to be statistically significant, if within-group variability (the denominator) is very small. Small differences (little variability) among groups are found to be statistically significant if they are consistent—that is, if the overlap among the treatment groups is small.

Additionally, the sizes of the groups of observations are important. Whenever a measure of variability is involved, as it is in all statistical comparisons among treatment groups, a large sample size reduces the measure of variability used. Again, look at the denominator of the formula for *t*. Estimates based on larger samples vary less than estimates based on smaller ones. Thus, all else being equal, a larger sample size inflates the test statistic, decreases the probability value associated with it, and increases the chances of rejecting the null hypothesis. All this is without any regard for the magnitude of the differences among treatment group scores. Very small treatment effects can lead to the rejection of the null hypothesis if the effects are consistent enough and/or observed in large enough groups.

The impact of sample size is especially clear in the case of correlation. The test of statistical significance for correlation coefficients is so simple in practice that researchers can just use a table that lists the smallest coefficient that is statistically significant for any given sample size. When 20 pairs of scores are correlated, the coefficient must be at least .44 (positive or negative) to be significant at the .05 level. When 50 pairs of scores are correlated, that critical value drops to .28. For 100 pairs, a minimum coefficient of only .20 is required. Thus, when the sample size is large enough, even a very weak relationship is statistically significant. The null hypothesis of no relationship is rejected even though the relationship is very weak and the percentage of variance accounted for very small. Recalling that one needs to square the correlation coefficient to estimate the percentage of variance accounted for makes the effect of sample size seem that much more striking. When based on a correlation for 100 pairs of scores, accounting for 4% of the variance is "significant" ($.20^2 = .04$).

Thus we've seen that NHST tells us very little about the strength of an independent variable–dependent variable relationship. It tells us much more about its consistency. A statistically significant result means that if another sample were tested in the same way, chances would be very good that the same type of relationship would be observed again. It doesn't mean, necessarily, that the relationship is a strong one, or that it would be strong in another case. Again, think of the amount of variance in the dependent or criterion variable that is accounted for by a predictor variable when the correlation between the two is .20—a puny 4%! With a bivariate distribution containing 100 cases (pairs of scores), that correlation is statistically significant. The situation is similar for *t* tests, ANOVA, and other forms of inferential statistics: Very small but consistent differences can be found to be statistically significant and force rejection of the null hypothesis.

An Alternative to NHST. Based on these arguments, some people contend that we need a new approach to evaluating the strength of independent variable–dependent variable relationships from the samples of observations collected in a research study. The alternative that is suggested most often by them is known as *estimating effect size.* A variety of statistical techniques are available that are based on the magnitude of treatment effects rather than their stability or reliability. Understanding how they work is far beyond the scope of this chapter. You'll need to study statistics further to understand how they can be calculated, their advantages and disadvantages, and special applications. It is important to understand, though, that some research psychologists believe that statistical analysis based solely on null hypothesis significance testing provides an inadequate basis for judging whether or not a given set of data should be taken as empirical support for a research hypothesis. Doing so, in their view, would pose a threat to statistical conclusion validity. It would pose the threat that a trivially small effect would be taken, or mistaken, as support for the research hypothesis. That would give a weak theory or weak intervention undeserved support.

Meta-Analysis. A related issue concerns another set of statistical techniques developed more recently than most of the NHST techniques that research psychologists have traditionally used. They are known collectively as **meta-analysis**, and they go beyond estimating effect size for a single study to evaluating the magnitude of independent variable–dependent variable relationships from the data of multiple studies conducted to test the same hypothesis. Again, the nuts and bolts of how this is done can't be explained adequately here. We'll discuss other aspects of meta-analysis in the next chapter. For now, understand that meta-analysis can be used to place the evidence from a single study in the broader context of other research conducted for the same purpose, should data from other studies be available for that purpose.

Null hypothesis significance testing evaluates the reliability of results from a single study by a mathematical process of extrapolation. Meta-analysis cumulates the actual outcomes from multiple studies. In a sense, it is another way, besides estimating effect size, to reduce the likelihood that a trivial result will be falsely characterized as providing strong support for a research hypothesis. In this case, however, the result would be trivial in the sense of "nonrepresentative," rather than in the sense of "small."

● SUMMING UP DATA ANALYSIS

As anyone with a degree in psychology can tell you, and as you may already know from firsthand experience, statistics is an important and a complex subject. It is extremely important for research psychologists to know how to summarize their data accurately and fairly, and how to draw inferences from them appropriately about the truth or falsity of their research hypotheses. The results of quantitative research —most psychological research, in other words—cannot be understood or communicated clearly except through the language of statistical analysis. The research designs available to the researcher are numerous and varied, as are the statistical procedures available for analyzing the produce of those designs. The number of choices can be daunting, particularly to the beginner and the mathematically challenged.

Beyond the technical complexities of statistics lies a less obvious concern that is equally important to the researcher and to the nonresearcher who needs to learn about and use research findings. That concern is statistical conclusion validity. The inappropriate use of statistical techniques can jeopardize the conclusions that are drawn from research results. An incorrect application of descriptive statistics will result in an inaccurate, misleading summary of the data (sometimes known as "lying with statistics" if it seems to have been done intentionally). The use of an inappropriate null hypothesis significance test will mean that the test statistic misrepresents the true probability of the observed outcome, and it may lead to an incorrect decision about whether or not to reject the null hypothesis. The choice of level of statistical significance and sample size will affect the probability of Type I and Type II errors that can result from that decision.

Under some circumstances, NHST can result in the reification of a treatment effect of trivial magnitude. It can encourage faith in a theory with little explanatory power, and/or it might encourage an unjustifiable investment of time and resources in an application whose benefits are minor and may not even outweigh the costs of producing them. An atypical research result may be presented without benefit of the context of other, possibly contradictory results bearing on the same research question.

Doing statistical analysis is difficult enough in itself, but the effort deserves to be admired only if the analysis is conducted in such a way as to fairly represent the research results, to lead to valid conclusions about the truth of the research hypothesis, and to truly increase knowledge about the causes of the behavior in question.

Review Questions and Exercise

Review Questions

1. What are the most widely used descriptive statistics for univariate distributions of measurements (scores), and for what purposes are they used?

2. How does the correlation coefficient describe a bivariate distribution of measurements (scores), and under what conditions can it legitimately be used to do so?

3. What is the purpose of inferential statistics, and how, in general terms, does null hypothesis significance testing work?

4. What are the three threats to statistical conclusion validity, and what implications do they have for the use of descriptive and inferential statistics?

Exercise

Use the research designs you diagrammed for the exercise at the end of Chapter 5 as a basis for deciding how to use the descriptive and inferential statistics reviewed in this chapter. Choose the appropriate inferential statistical test for each of those designs, and for more if you have the time.

THE RESEARCHER'S RESPONSIBILITIES AS SCIENTIST, COLLEAGUE, AND CITIZEN

● **A QUICK GUIDE TO CHAPTER 11:
THE RESEARCHER'S RESPONSIBILITIES**

All the technical perfection in the world is not enough to ensure the value of psychological research. Clearly, it is very difficult to produce research findings that aren't compromised by one of the many threats to validity we've wrestled with through the previous 10 chapters. Beyond that, however, we can't ignore the issue of a scientist's responsibility to those he or she studies, works with, and works for.

Researchers owe their scientific colleagues due diligence in conducting their research to meet the highest professional standards. Methodological issues need to be addressed openly, honestly, and expertly. Unfortunately, the history of science, including psychology, includes examples of fraud and other misconduct that highlight the need for vigilance about **scientific responsibility**.

Researchers also have a professional duty to disseminate their findings widely, so that other researchers can plan their work knowledgeably. Some critics deride the "publish or perish" policies of some universities that pressure faculty members to publish research articles to achieve promotion and tenure. Publication must be a duty of the researcher, however, if science is to make cumulative progress. It is also a means of quality control. Submission of a paper for publication subjects a researcher's work to the scrutiny of other experts. This system of "peer review" helps researchers to maintain the highest standards in their disciplines.

Researchers also have a duty to help their professional colleagues when they can. Again, there is historical evidence of selfish behavior on the part of scientists that suggests a need to scrutinize carefully issues of **professional responsibility**.

Finally, researchers have ethical responsibilities to those they study and to the larger society. There will never be enough institutional safeguards to take the place of a researcher's conscience. Human and nonhuman participants in research must be treated humanely. Physical and psychological harm must be avoided whenever possible, even when the research results might seem so promising as to justify possibly harmful methods. Human and nonhuman research participants have been abused in the past, undermining public confidence in the **social responsibility** of scientists. Researchers also need to bear in mind that maintaining high scientific standards of quality in their research is one of the best ways of repaying their research participants for the time and effort they contribute.

The society at large needs to be concerned about political forces that hamper science and jeopardize the welfare of those who depend on it. Much research in psychology is costly. Expensive instruments and laboratory space, animal breeding colonies and caretakers, and highly trained research assistants may be required to conduct a research study. As a result, researchers may need to seek funding from government agencies or private sponsors. In doing so, they run the risk of incurring debts that make them and their research vulnerable to outside pressure. A medical researcher may receive large research grants from a pharmaceutical man-

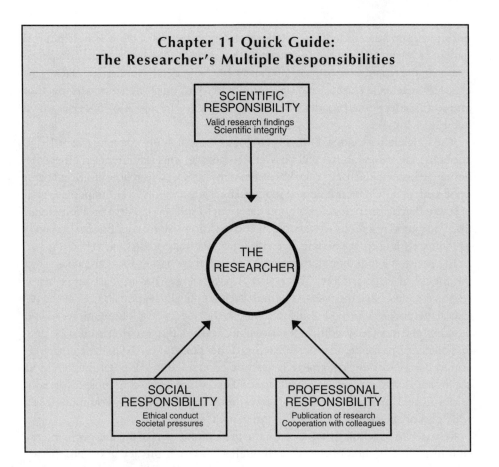

**Chapter 11 Quick Guide:
The Researcher's Multiple Responsibilities**

SCIENTIFIC
RESPONSIBILITY
Valid research findings
Scientific integrity

THE
RESEARCHER

SOCIAL
RESPONSIBILITY
Ethical conduct
Societal pressures

PROFESSIONAL
RESPONSIBILITY
Publication of research
Cooperation with colleagues

ufacturer to test a new drug or large speaking fees to inform physicians about the research results. As a result, he or she may lose objectivity when weighing the benefits of the drug against its side effects or alternative treatments or, worse yet, when planning studies to provide the data on which those judgments will be made. A researcher who seeks support from government sources may be held hostage by political interest groups.

As if validity isn't enough to be concerned about, the big picture includes many more issues, including some where answers seem far more obscure. The Chapter 11 Quick Guide provides a graphic summary of the responsibilities that weigh heavily on conscientious research psychologists.

INTRODUCTION TO THE CHAPTER ●

Have you heard the old saying about not being able to see the forest for the trees? Research methods is a field of study where there are so many terms, technical questions, and other individual details (as if you hadn't noticed!) that there is a real danger of losing track of the big picture. That includes the goals of psychological research, the reasons we are learning about all those details in the first place. This chapter presents at least a brief opportunity to try to tie all those details together and to consider some broader issues that cut across the specific concerns we've been studying.

The ultimate reason for doing psychological research is to develop knowledge about human behavior that will be useful to people. This statement isn't meant to denigrate knowledge for its own sake or to deny, as social psychologist Kurt Lewin once said, that there is nothing so practical as a good theory. The immediate goal of research may be to develop a good theory or to solve a practical problem. In either case, good research—research that adds to knowledge about human behavior —ultimately is useful to people, even though it may take some time to become so.

In order to tie together all that we've learned, this chapter is organized around the theme of responsibility. The research psychologist has at least three major responsibilities. First, the researcher must be scientifically responsible, by using research methods that provide valid findings, so that theories or interventions will be based on the most trustworthy facts possible. Second, the researcher must be professionally responsible, responsible to his or her colleagues. To make a contribution to theory or practice, research must be conducted in cooperation with, and communicated to, professional colleagues. Finally, the researcher must be socially responsible. The researcher has a responsibility to the various lay communities to which he or she belongs, including the general public.

Research in psychology is based on the use of some part of the lives of living organisms. Some of their efforts, their thoughts, and their privacy goes into the results of every study research psychologists carry out. For that and other reasons, the research psychologist has an obligation to try to give something back to those participants, and to as many others as possible.

You should be clear that the order in which these facets of the researcher's responsibilities are considered here do not reflect any judgment about their relative importance.

● BEING SCIENTIFICALLY RESPONSIBLE

The Problem

It should be clear by now that the principal theme of this book is that researchers make many choices in the course of turning their hypotheses into empirical studies, and that those choices all affect the degree to which the results of those studies are useful in deciding the truth or falsity of the researchers' underlying hypotheses. The research process has been analyzed in this book in a very logical and straightforward way. It has been divided into the five major categories of choices researchers must make and the threats to the validity of the research findings that are at stake in connection with each of those choices. The actual process is much less straightforward.

Choices that maximize validity in one of the five categories—conceptual validity, construct validity, internal validity, external validity, or statistical conclusion validity—may jeopardize validity in one of the others. Realistic quasi-experimental research based on archival data may maximize construct validity at the cost of comparing nonequivalent groups and thus raising difficult questions about internal validity. Laboratory experiments using nonhuman participants may maximize internal validity while making generalizability to human behavior problematic. These trade-offs are just examples of the basic fact that no research plan can simultaneously address all aspects of validity in an optimal manner. It is not possible to eliminate all possible threats to validity because in any specific instance, validity is a moving target.

On top of that, we have seen that researchers don't have the freedom to choose freely among the measures, research designs, participants, and other elements out of which a research plan is constructed. The research hypothesis limits the choices a researcher can make. The effects of anticipated school desegregation in 1954 on the subsequent reproductive choices made by white Southerners could not have been studied in a laboratory experiment. The effects on workers' productivity of their beliefs that they were being overpaid for their work could probably be studied only in a laboratory experiment, where those beliefs could be shaped outside of any pre-existing worker-employer relationship rooted in the real world of paying monthly bills.

The research process thus is even more complex than putting together a jigsaw puzzle. First, there are many pieces generated by individual choices among the elements of a research plan. Those choices are based, in turn, on an evaluation of the associated threats to validity of the research findings. Putting one piece into place can knock another one out of its place. Imagine that after putting a piece of a jigsaw puzzle in place, you look back at the box and the picture has changed. Add to that the problem that the researcher doesn't have a free choice of puzzles. Once the research hypothesis is set, the puzzle the researcher has to put together may not be as pretty as he or she would like.

Three Possible Solutions

There are at least three ways of understanding the difficulties posed by the incompatible demands of the choices in the research process. One was suggested, at least implicitly, by B. F. Skinner and other orthodox behaviorists. Their solution was to elevate internal validity above all other considerations. According to this view, laboratory experiments that minimize extraneous influences, conducted with nonhuman participants to minimize the likelihood of artifacts, using precise behavioral measurements that count responses and measure time, are the only acceptable forms of psychological research. Other validity considerations are secondary. In fact, they come in a distant second. According to this view, hypotheses that can't be tested in this way simply don't deserve to be part of the science of psychology. Mind you, to be fair to this view, it's not clear that there are many hypotheses that can't be shoehorned into the "proper" mold, especially considering that Skinner thought he could explain all of human behavior by studying pigeons in an isolation chamber.

A very different view was taken by Donald Campbell. His view is somewhat ironic in the light of the contributions he made toward a greater understanding of the specific technical issues involved in planning research. Campbell took a decidedly nontechnical view of the overall process. He believed that most researchers worked out of a personal desire to contribute to human knowledge and human welfare. He also believed that too strict or conservative a view of the scientific value of research, a view that emphasized its shortcomings and the need to rule out threats to validity, might discourage researchers.

As we've already seen, the task of ruling out all threats to validity is daunting if not impossible. Campbell argued that methodological criticism needed to be tempered because flawed research was better than no research, if not unavoidable in the light of the greatly expanded list of validity concerns Campbell considered. For Campbell, the prospect of researchers demoralized by criticism posed the greatest threat to the future of psychological research.

Somewhere in between the doctrinaire behaviorism of Skinner and the pragmatic attitude of Campbell is a position we can borrow from the study of human decision making. Starting out on the road to understanding the research process, one might take the view that all possible threats to validity need to be eliminated for research results to have any real value. This might be termed an **optimizing** strategy, setting the goal of optimal or perfectly valid research results. Given the vagaries and trade-offs we've learned about subsequently, optimization might seem to be too much to ask of science.

A somewhat more lenient position might be termed **maximizing**. Following this approach, the goal would be choices and trade-offs that result in the elimination of the greatest number of threats to validity, or of the most dangerous ones according to some criterion such as their plausibility in connection with a particular research hypothesis. Given the "moving target" problem, even this might be asking a lot.

An even more lenient approach might be more reasonable, in the spirit of Campbell's proposal for protecting the fragile motivation of researchers. This third alternative is known to students of human decision making as **satisficing**. In this approach, a research plan could be formulated without considering every possible choice or threat to the validity of the eventual research findings, much less every possible combination or trade-off. The research plan would aim to achieve some predetermined level of validity, or to eliminate a limited number of preselected, particularly relevant threats to validity. Then, it would be implemented without concern for the possibility of further marginal improvements that might require incommensurate levels of decision-making effort, or that might even prove to be impossible once the problem was examined more carefully.

A New Philosophy of Science?

The recognition that perfectly valid research findings may be out of reach is also consistent with recent developments in the philosophy of science. The rules that psychologists and other scientists try to follow in conducting their research are analyzed in the branch of philosophy known as **epistemology**, the study of systems for acquiring knowledge.

Since the 19th century, scientific research has been based on a set of epistemological principles known as **logical positivism**. The philosophers of science who developed logical positivism stressed the importance of basing science on observation (empiricism), of defining scientific terms unambiguously (operational definition), of building theories that rest on the confirmation of testable hypotheses (the hypothetico-deductive model), and of tying disparate phenomena together with explanations based on their most fundamental common causes (reductionism). Whether researchers are aware of it or not, the specific procedures that they use in their efforts to achieve valid research findings represent attempts to implement this coherent set of principles known as logical positivism.

During the 100 years or so that psychologists have been trying to perfect this "scientific method" that is based on logical positivism, philosophers have moved on (it shouldn't surprise us that philosophy is as dynamic a field as psychology). Logical positivism has come under increasing criticism in philosophy as philosophers have studied what scientists, including research psychologists, actually have done in their efforts to unravel the mysteries they study. They concluded that science should not, has not, and probably cannot conform to the prescriptions of logical positivism.

Gradually, then, logical positivism has given way to an approach known as **post-positivism**. It is a combination of new prescriptions for scientific research and attempts to come to grips with the realities of research that logical positivism could not possibly appreciate when it emerged so early in the development of modern science.

Post-positivist philosophers have argued that observation and precise measurement have failed to guarantee objectivity in science (the "positive" in logical positivism). They have also made the point that the hypothetico-deductive model for building scientific theories (an important part of the "logic" of logical positivism) is a poor one. No matter how many hypotheses derived from a particular theory are confirmed by research, the theory is always just one test away from possible destruction by a single disconfirming research finding. Philosopher Karl Popper (1965), in particular, has stressed the importance of putting greater effort into looking for disconfirming data so that weak theories will be exposed as such early on.

By the way, cognitive psychologists have discovered that we are all poor testers of theory, layperson and research psychologist alike. We tend to seek out confirming instances that don't add much to what we already know, or think we know, rather than seeking disconfirming ones that would really test our theories. Consider the classic "four-card problem" from cognitive psychology. In it, you need to test a rule. One example is the rule that if a card has an "A" on one side, it has a "3" on the other side. In that case, you would be given four cards to work with, each of which is known to have a letter on one side and a one-digit number on the other. The following four cards could constitute this example of a four-card problem.

Which one(s) should you turn over to determine whether any of the cards violates the rule? (I can never solve these things, so skip to the answer on the next line with my blessings if you like.)

The correct answer is cards (a) and (d). Even if the P had a 3 on the other side, or the 3 had some letter other than A on the other side, the rule would not be violated, so there is nothing to be gained from turning over card (b) or card (c). The rule doesn't say that a 3 can appear *only* on the reverse side of card (a) or any card with an A on the other side, so any letter on the reverse side of card (c) is consistent with the rule. Cards (a) and (d) do test the theory. If the A on card (a) had a number other than 3 on the other side, or the 7 on card (d) had an A on the other side, the rule would be violated.

In any case, the defining characteristic of post-positivism is that it takes a historical rather than a normative approach to the problem of epistemology. In other words, whereas logical-positivist philosophers prescribed a set of rules by which scientists ought to play their game, post-positivist philosophers studied how the game was actually played.

What they found was that scientists don't really reject their theories when contradictory evidence turns up. First, they design their research from the outset to make confirmation of their theories more likely than disconfirmation. Then, if necessary, they modify their theories to avoid having to reject them on the basis of contrary facts. In addition, the studies they conduct tend to describe phenomena more than they provide critical tests of theory that might explain them. Think about Milgram's obedience research (1974, **E9**), Broverman et al.'s (1972) research on gender-role stereotypes (**E5**), or other examples from our list of 25 exemplar studies in this light.

Layered above all of this, according to philosopher Thomas Kuhn (see Kuhn, 1962), scientists generally conform to an accepted set of general principles, known as a **paradigm**, in pursuing their science. They tend to change their approach only after being confronted with the overwhelming superiority of a revolutionary new way of thinking.

The post-positivist analysis of scientific research seems wholly consistent with recent historical analyses of particular research problems in psychology that are discussed at length later in this chapter. They include the study of genetic influences on intelligence and the search for the causes of homosexuality, and they reveal how larger social and political forces influence psychological research. The post-positivist philosophy of science explodes the myth that scientists have ever been able to preserve objectivity in isolation from the larger society, including the scientific community, in which they work.

Insights From the History of Science

The historical relativism stressed by post-positivist philosophy of science is also supported by historical studies that show how radically scientific thought can change over time. For example, it seems beyond question today that science is and must be based on observation and measurement. To test a scientific research hypothesis, one must know precisely how much of a suspected causal factor is at work and precisely how much change occurs in the phenomenon being studied. But is this scientific approach a natural way of thinking about the world around us? Have people always thought about how much of "this" is happening and how much of "that" results from it? Or did this quantitative way of thinking about things develop at some point in human history, and if so, why?

Those questions are addressed by historian Alfred W. Crosby in his 1997 book *The Measure of Reality*. Crosby describes how European thought changed from qualitative to quantitative. It happened around the time that the Middle Ages were giving way to the Renaissance, the year 1300 or thereabouts. He explains why the change took place at that time and in the way it did.

One of the most interesting of his discoveries was that during the Middle Ages and before, Europeans' failure to think in quantitative terms went far beyond the unavailability of accurate measuring instruments. Even after the invention of accurate clocks, scales, and mapping methods, pre-existing tendencies to think in qualitative terms persisted. It was more important that accounts of the natural world agree with Biblical texts, or with the work of respected ancient Greek philosophers, than with precise measurements of natural phenomena themselves. Recall

Galileo's famous tussle with the Roman Catholic Church over our solar system, in which stories from the Bible were given greater weight than the observations he made through his telescope.

Eventually, though, according to Crosby, three somewhat surprising inventions facilitated a particular kind of precise measurement that changed Europeans' "habits of thought" (*la mentalité* in French) from qualitative to quantitative. According to Crosby, they were the invention of methods of musical notation, of visual perspective in painting, and of double-entry bookkeeping. These encouraged people to visualize their worlds, bringing about a new general tendency to think in quantitative terms, a tendency known as **pantometry** (literally, measure everything). On the musical staff, one can see time and pitch. In the ledger, one can see profit and loss. On the two-dimensional canvas, geometric perspective makes it possible to see distance, or depth, and spatial orientation.

In the modern world, we all want to know—need to know—precisely what time it is, what the temperature is outside, how much money is in our checking accounts, how fast our cars are going, and how much chocolate to use in our favorite brownie recipe. In fact, we need to know to the exact minute, degree, penny, mile per hour, and ounce. That "quantificatory appreciation of reality" is pantometry. We demand universal measurement or quantification. Each of those measurements can be seen or visualized, on a clock, or a thermometer, or a checkbook register, or a speedometer, or some sort of scale dial (even better on a digital display).

According to Crosby, it is that habit of thought that developed about 700 years ago. That habit of thought made modern science and technology possible, aided by inventions such as Hindu-Arabic numerals (0, 1, 2, etc.), the printing press, and accurate clocks. It made science possible because it made it possible to use mathematics to understand reality. Every aspect of the world would and could be described using a universal abstract quantum, or unit of measurement. Units such as the second, or penny, or degree Fahrenheit could be manipulated mathematically, instead of with some vague, tradition-inspired verbal description. This quantification replaced what Crosby calls the Venerable Model, which was used in Europe throughout recorded history up through the end of the Middle Ages.

Europe was actually the last place in the civilized world where pantometry and mathematics caught on. The Chinese and the Arabs of North Africa had adopted a quantitative world view before Europeans did. The natural resources of Europe, the industry (ruthlessness?) with which Europeans used their mental advantage to exploit resources elsewhere in the world (colonialism), and the inventiveness of Gutenberg, Galileo, and other individual Europeans are what made Europe the place where quantification gave birth to the scientific revolution that modern research psychologists are still carrying on today. If history could change science that much in the case of pantometry, doesn't it stand to reason that revolutionary change can occur again and again, making the notion of absolute rules or a perfect scientific method very dubious indeed?

Science and Society

We have seen that the post-positivist view of science stresses its social and historical nature. It should also be recognized, consistent with that view, that what goes on in science inevitably is influenced by what goes on outside it. This occurs not only in closely related fields such as philosophy and mathematics but also outside the scientific community itself.

In particular, some of the biases that threaten the validity of psychological (and other) research are not introduced by individual researchers who fail to observe proper scientific protocol. Rather, they come ultimately from the social institutions of the larger society in which the research is carried out.

Throughout the hundred-year-or-so history of psychology as a science, the overwhelming majority of scientific contributions to the field have been made by white "European" men. In the United States, in particular—the world's center for research in psychology and one of its most diverse societies during the past century—African Americans have been systematically excluded from psychological science, as they have been from so many other venues and opportunities in American society.

As Robert V. Guthrie points out in his book *Even the Rat Was White* (1998), for most of the history of psychology in America, segregation in public schools and in institutions of higher education meant that most African Americans were excluded from opportunities to enter any of the professions, including psychology. Outside the black colleges in the South, few African Americans had the chance to receive a college education. For those with undergraduate degrees, graduate training proved to be a further barrier to becoming a professional psychologist.

Most black colleges lacked sufficient resources to support graduate programs, and only a small number of the many Northern universities that had established graduate programs violated the social norm of exclusion. With the assistance of a few philanthropic organizations, they made some room for the graduates of black colleges in their programs. Even so, most African Americans who did manage to complete their undergraduate studies and find places in those graduate programs gravitated toward applied programs in education and social services because of the great needs in the African American community. Thus, only a few of the few pursued careers in research.

The absence of people of color from the field of psychological research made it that much easier to maintain a Eurocentric view of human beings and human behavior. Racist views of group differences in abilities and traits, backed up by biased tests of intelligence and other measures, dominated psychological research for most of its history. The result was research that justified the absence of African Americans, along with women and other minorities, from the ranks of research psychologists.

Even more important for this discussion, white male research psychologists were less likely to question results supporting the superiority of white men and its genetic basis. Nor were they very likely to be concerned about the degree to which members of other groups were included in samples of research participants. They were even less likely to take a strong interest in the unique experiences of the descendants of slaves or in the effects of those experiences on the survivors' behavior.

Guthrie points out that much of the above discussion could be applied as easily to women, or to poor, culturally disadvantaged white Americans, male and female, as to people of color. Recent efforts by the educational establishment and the profession of psychology are beginning to overturn the historical patterns in psychology of exclusion and bias. Our society and our profession, however, continue to pay the price for their racist past. The longer these problems are left to fester, the more intractable they seem to become.

The Challenge of Scientific Responsibility

Consistent with Donald Campbell's views, the above analysis has stressed the impossibility of achieving certainty or complete objectivity. Taken together, Post-Positivist philosophy, the work of Crosby and Guthrie, and Campbell alert us to the limitations of psychological research. They broaden the basis for the conclusion that our knowledge about research methods should guide our decisions in planning research and our evaluation of the findings of previous research.

That knowledge should not cripple us in our efforts to plan research when we cannot solve all the problems we see. Nor should it destroy our faith in others' research. Like every other social endeavor, scientific research, including research in psychology, has never been perfect, and it never will be. Research methods should be judged and valued for the contributions they can make to future knowledge and human welfare. That includes methods that may not stand up to scrutiny on every possible criterion. They should not be rejected out of hand for their possible shortcomings but instead should be evaluated in the light of all we know about the uncertainties of scientific inquiry. We can strive for perfection without being daunted by it.

● BEING PROFESSIONALLY RESPONSIBLE

Conflict and Cooperation Among Scientists

Publish or Perish

The academic world, where most psychological research is done by professors, graduate students, and some undergraduates, is sometimes referred to as a world

Figure 11.1. The cover of one of the scientific journals in which research psychologists publish their work. This one is dedicated to research on personality and social behavior, as the title indicates. Reprinted with permission of Sage Publications, Inc.

of "publish or perish." That means that professors, especially those in large research universities, are evaluated for retention, tenure, promotion, and pay raises largely on the basis of how many articles they publish in the professional periodicals known as journals, as well as on their ability to win research grants (which may be enhanced by a successful record of publication and make possible still more publications).

As the phrase "publish or perish" suggests, there is ample room for debate on the wisdom of evaluating college professors on their ability to amass large numbers of published research articles (academic research psychologists also publish theoretical articles and books, but usually in later stages of their careers, after they have achieved their tenure and promotion goals). Some believe that the system minimizes the importance of their teaching responsibilities, especially in undergraduate courses, or even encourages them to ignore them as much as they can.

There has also been some controversy over the editorial process, through which a small percentage of the articles submitted for publication in psychological journals is finally accepted—a very small percentage by the most selective journals. Some research psychologists have tested the process for bias by submitting identical articles to several journals, sometimes varying the level of prestige associated with the author's institutional affiliation. Some of these studies have shown that the researchers who evaluate papers submitted to scientific journals don't agree very well on the quality of the articles they read. Do you remember the discussion of the importance of interrater reliability to valid measurement in Chapter 3?

Other studies of the review process have shown bias based on the identity and reputation of the author of an article. A growing recognition of this problem has led many leading journals today to adopt a policy of blind review. Submissions are identified to reviewers only by code numbers, not by author or institution. This procedure probably reduces the likelihood of a biased evaluation, except in cases where a particular research technique or references to previous research make it possible for sophisticated reviewers to identify the author anyway.

Some fear that publishing may have become less a scientific endeavor and more a game with selfish prizes at stake for the winners. Researchers, they believe, may be motivated by a desire to enhance their reputations and to reap the rewards of success. They may pursue research they believe is timely or attractive to the editors and reviewers who decide what will and will not get published, rather than the research they believe to have the greatest scientific value.

Personal Conflict Among Scientists: Isaac Newton

In fact, this problem of gamesmanship among scientists is as old as science itself. No less a figure than Isaac Newton experienced and created rivalry and ruthless competition with his scientific peers. Newton is regarded by many as the originator of modern empirical science. He entered Cambridge University at the age of 19, in 1661, after receiving only minimal tutoring in the rural community where he grew up. Within 2 years, he had invented the calculus, without much help from anyone at Cambridge. It was a tool he needed to prove his universal law of gravitation, which explained the motion of the planets in the solar system.

To prove that his explanation of planetary motion was correct, Newton needed the raw data to which to apply his calculus. For those, he turned to the director of the Royal Observatory at Greenwich, John Flamsteed, who had diligently, even compulsively, mapped movements across the night sky for many years. Newton saw Flamsteed as a mere technician who was obligated to provide him with whatever he needed to do the really important work of science. Flamsteed, predictably, saw Newton as an arrogant man who wanted to exploit the fruits of his many years of hard labor without giving him the credit he felt was his due.

Undoubtedly, both men contributed their share to the feud that delayed by several years the publication of Newton's theory in his 1687 masterwork, the historic *Mathematical Principles of Natural Philosophy*, or *Principia*, as it came to be known. At least one biographer (White, 1997), however, attributes the lion's share of the blame to Newton. A difficult, reclusive man, Newton feuded with other scientists, not just Flamsteed, throughout his career. As a member of the Royal Society, he was in almost constant conflict with other members over his and competing theories of gravitation and optics, among other things. Although he might well have been justified in favoring his own work, given his extraordinary record of accomplishment, Newton clearly saw himself as far superior to his contemporaries, and he took every opportunity to let them know that he did.

Driven by a need to hide unorthodox religious beliefs and his clandestine practice of alchemy, Newton was unwilling or unable to work cooperatively with other scientists. He refused to help them, or even to provide constructive criticism. He also wouldn't seek help from others with his own work. In short, Newton adopted a competitive, disputatious attitude toward his peers. In fact, based on White's telling of the story, I'm quite sure Newton would have disapproved of my calling them peers at all. His relationships with his colleagues exemplified the antithesis of the responsible relationships necessary to facilitate scientific discovery.

More Conflict: The Longitude Problem

Another example of destructive conflict in science is to be found in the case of John Harrison, described by Dava Sobel in her popular book *Longitude* (1995). Early in the 18th century, Harrison was a young man in Yorkshire, England, developing his considerable talents for music, carpentry, and especially clockmaking. Like other worldly people of his time, he was well aware of possibly the thorniest technological problem of the age, particularly for seafaring nations like England. That was the longitude problem. At the time, sailors had no reliable way of determining their east-west location at sea. For lack of accurate navigation, thousands of men at a time were drowned when their ships ran aground, or died of scurvy when delayed by weeks or even months of wandering, lost at sea.

Two competing approaches were tried to solve the longitude problem. In fact, they were competing for a prize offered first in 1714 by the British Parliament in the amount of 20 thousand pounds (millions of dollars in our current frame of reference). One approach used measurements of the positions of the moon, sun, and stars, acquired through tedious observations and calculations from complex tables. The other was much more straightforward, based on the difference in time of day between a fixed location, such as the ship's home port, and the ship's current location (think of time zones).

Figure 11.2. Two of the marine chronometers made by John Harrison in his quest for a solution to the longitude problem. On the left is his first functional model, called H1 (this clock was designed to go to sea!). On the right is the almost pocket-sized model, H4, that eventually won him part of the prize offered by the British Parliament for the first successful invention. Reprinted with permission of the National Maritime Museum.

Harrison spent most of his life pursuing the timekeeping solution. He built the first clock, then watch, capable of keeping accurate time at sea on a rolling and pitching ship, with the extreme changes in temperature and humidity (see Figure 11.2). They're called marine chronometers. When he finally succeeded, he had created a more accurate and an easier method of determining longitude than the opposing lunar approach could even promise.

Did Harrison receive the prize and the thanks of a grateful nation? Not exactly. Eventually, he got half the prize, after years of wrangling, and some other small grants and awards. The full prize and the recognition he expected along with it were blocked by influential astronomers who wanted the glory that was rightfully his. Sailors ultimately proved the superiority of the timekeeping method, by using it in overwhelming preference to all others. The best solution was never fully recognized officially because Harrison's superior science couldn't overcome pride, politics, and greed until long after his death.

Scientific Fraud: The Case of Cyril Burt

There is an even worse sort of irresponsibility toward scientific peers. Researchers may falsify data or misrepresent their findings to increase their chances of having a research article accepted for publication and of receiving recognition as scientists. One of the most famous cases in psychology is that of Cyril Burt, a British researcher who studied genetic influences on intelligence. Burt was a British psychologist whose work on the effect of heredity on intelligence showed the influence of his countrymen Francis Galton and Karl Pearson. They had created many of the pioneering statistical techniques Burt used, for their own investigations into the same subject. Although Burt may have been at the cutting edge of psychological science in his use of factor analysis, his research was guided by some questionable assumptions that had their own history in England, elsewhere in Europe, and America.

During the previous century or so, researchers had been busy measuring facial features, mapping the surface of living skulls, and estimating the size of brains by filling skeleton skulls with lead shot, among other things. Their purpose was to identify groups of people whose purported levels of intelligence, morality, and other distinctive psychological traits were hypothesized to have been inherited from their ancestors. Many of these studies, whose methods were admittedly primitive by comparison with those of modern science, were based on racist theories. Aristocratic white European researchers, and their relatives in the New World, set out to prove that they and their kind were superior to non-whites and to other "genetically inferior" groups, even poor and criminal fellow Europeans.

Burt gained a lofty reputation by publishing convincing evidence that intelligence was highly heritable. Shortly after his death, however, in the early 1970s, he was accused of engaging in unethical misrepresentation of his research results. Over a period of more than a decade, from 1943 to 1958, Burt published the results of what he claimed to be an ongoing study comparing the correlation between intelligence test scores for pairs of identical twins reared apart (MZA twins) with that for other kinship groups. Based on the presumption among behavior geneticists that a high correlation between MZA twins reflects a strong influence of heredity relative to environment (they are identical genetically but presumably are reared in different environments by their adoptive or foster families), Burt's results seemed to provide strong evidence for the heritability of intelligence. Eventually, though, it was noticed that Burt's data were not only good, but too good, and that his methods were ambiguous at best, flawed at worst.

In his articles, Burt reported data from a growing sample of MZA twins that increased in several stages from 15 to 53 pairs. In each case, though, he reported the same correlation coefficient. In three cases, it was identical to the third decimal place, .771. Those who believed in the importance of heredity to intelligence cited Burt's research as the best evidence on the subject. His final sample was the largest of any such study, and his correlation between the IQs of pairs of MZA twins the highest. Burt also reported zero correlation between the twins' IQs and the socioeconomic status (environment) of their families.

Burt's research was first called into question by Leon Kamin (1974), a specialist in animal learning who became embroiled in a controversy over academic freedom when, as chair of the psychology department at Princeton, he was forced to cancel a speech by Richard Herrnstein of Harvard. Herrnstein had used Burt's data to argue against the usefulness of government programs to create equal opportunity for minorities, and some students threatened to disrupt his talk. To educate himself about the issue afterward, and possibly to assuage his guilt, Kamin began by reading Burt's work. He soon discovered problems with the methods and the data. When those problems were publicized, Kamin's discoveries triggered other attacks on Burt, especially by Leslie Hearnshaw (1979) in an authorized and otherwise sympathetic biography of Burt.

Those who accused Burt of scientific fraud—of making up his data, in effect—relied on a statistical argument. First, the odds of a correlation coefficient being identical in three separate samples were astronomically low (recall our discussion in Chapter 10 of sampling distributions and the role of low probabilities in scientific decision making). Second, given a real relationship between two variables in a population (such as the population of all MZA twins), the larger the sample drawn from the population, the less likely the observed correlation coefficient will take an extreme value. This is because the sampling distribution has less variability (a phenomenon also discussed in Chapter 10). The size of Burt's sample more than tripled without any decrease in the size of the correlation coefficients he reported.

There were reasons to give Burt the benefit of the doubt. The first was his professional status. He was the first British psychologist to be knighted (from that point on, Sir Cyril Burt), he chaired an influential psychology department at University College London, he received a prestigious award from the American Psychological Association, and he edited two major professional journals for more than 25 years, among other honors. Second was the circumstantial nature of the charges against him. It is not surprising that some prominent psychologists disbelieved the charges of fraud made against him.

It didn't help his case, however, that his research articles were vague and confusing regarding the origins of his data, that he published articles using the names of collaborators who did not write them (to avoid the [accurate] perception that he used the journals he edited to "outshout" his critics), that he made false claims about his own contributions to the development of factor analysis, that he is identified in the light of current sensibilities (certainly not those of Galton's time) with the politically incorrect side of a controversial issue, that his raw research data were destroyed by a trusted colleague immediately after his death, and that his primary defenders are partisans who engage in personal attacks on those who question his work. In sum, Burt's supporters have argued that proven inaccuracies in his work were innocent errors rather than intentional misrepresentations (they seem to argue that his research is worthless rather than fraudulent). Some of the attacks on him were politically motivated. Still, it seems more likely than not that Burt violated his scientific responsibilities by fabricating data to verify a hypothesis he "knew" to be true rather than investigate the relationship between heredity and intelligence objectively (scientifically).

Burt's actions appear to have been politically motivated. The ascension of egalitarian values in Britain goaded him into providing (unfortunately, by falsifying) better and better proof to bolster his own elitist position. To that end, he perpetrated a fraud. That makes the offense of using an inappropriate method that results in a deficiency in the validity of research findings pale by comparison, although Burt was guilty of plenty of that as well. He was also guilty of carelessness and of making misleading claims of multiple authorship of his papers to lend unjustified credence to his work.

Even though the heritability of intelligence stands solidly confirmed today, even without Burt's research, the Burt affair demonstrates clearly the importance of not taking any researcher's claims at face value, even one with a seemingly impeccable scientific reputation. Burt intentionally misled his colleagues by advocating a questionable theory (at the time) based on fraudulent data.

The Cyril Burt case raises some very troubling questions about the trustworthiness of psychological research and science in general. We know that Burt was more protected from outside scrutiny than most researchers are, by virtue of his exalted professional status and his position as a journal editor. One wonders, though, how other overzealous researchers can be prevented from committing the same type of fraud and engaging in the same type of self-serving manipulation as he did.

Would anyone know if a researcher made up data instead of collecting it, or changed just a few numbers to manufacture a desired or a clearer result? If a researcher did succumb to the temptation to enhance his or her status, or to earn a promotion, or to win a large research grant, it would almost certainly be possible to do a better job of covering up than Burt did.

Although we can all hope that these "lapses from acceptable scientific standards" are rare events, we can't be sure, given the private and decentralized nature of most scientific research. Effective oversight would be possible only if the research were sponsored by a large organization that could provide the required infrastructure and funding. Even then, unless the research focused on an issue that engaged strong public interest, as Burt's did, little attention might be paid to charges or even evidence of misconduct.

Some see the solution to the problem of scientific misconduct, from carelessness to fraud, as more institutionalized, vigorous oversight. Others see abuses of the oversight function as potentially more dangerous to science than unfettered misconduct by the scientists themselves. As the history of the Burt case makes clear, researchers and their critics are vulnerable to politically inspired and even personal attacks on their integrity. Although the evidence in the Burt case seems to this observer to support the accusations of fraud beyond a reasonable doubt, both

---

| Box 11.1 | *THINKING ABOUT RESEARCH* |

How Much Choice Do Researchers Have in Their Ethical Decisions? _____

As many of the examples cited in this chapter make abundantly clear, behavioral research can be very threatening to people and organizations. Other kinds of scientific research can be equally threatening. If research were to show that video games spawn violence, or that cigarette smoking causes cancer, or that pesticides kill people, the companies that make those products could be subjected to government regulation or costly litigation, or they could suffer a catastrophic loss of sales.

For that reason, the United States Chamber of Commerce reportedly is pleased by a new federal law, sponsored by Senator Richard C. Shelby of Alabama. The law requires that all researchers who receive any federal funds provide access to all their data to anyone who files a Freedom of Information Act request for it.

The Chamber's interest in the new law is clarified by the experience of a researcher at the Medical College of Georgia, Dr. Paul Fisher, who studies children's knowledge about tobacco brands. Fisher found in his research that as many

6-year-olds know Joe Camel as know Mickey Mouse. Concerned about those findings, cigarette maker R. J. Reynolds asked to see his data, including the names and addresses of the children who participated in his study. After a long dispute that led to his college president agreeing to provide the information, Dr. Fisher resigned his faculty position and R. J. Reynolds got what it asked for.

How much research would get done if participants knew that their data, even their names and addresses, might become public knowledge? Why would Chamber of Commerce members want a law like this? Do they want better science, as some have claimed, or less science? If the new law were to make cases like Dr. Fisher's the norm, could it have a chilling effect on future research? Finally, how could such a law be passed, as it was, without any public debate or media coverage, as a one-sentence amendment to a complex 4,000-page appropriations bill?

---

those who attacked Burt and his defenders were motivated to some extent by political disagreement and personal dislike.

Scientific Fraud?: The Baltimore Case

It may be too easy for researchers to get away with fraud. After all, Burt was caught as the result of an unlikely accident, even though evidence of his misconduct was available for a considerable period to anyone who would look at his published papers carefully. Researchers may also be too vulnerable to false accusations. This disturbing possibility seems to have victimized Thereza Imanishi-Kari, a medical researcher in the field of immunology (Kevles, 1998).

This case is often referred to as the Baltimore case because of the involvement of a high-profile scientist and collaborator of Imanishi-Kari, Nobel laureate in Medicine David Baltimore. It began in 1986, when a postdoctoral student in Imanishi-Kari's laboratory first raised questions about her integrity. It continued until 1996, when she finally was cleared of charges of scientific misconduct. During that time, a complex pageant played itself out in two major universities, in the scientific research bureaucracy of the federal government, in the U.S. House of Representatives, and in the scientific and mass media.

Imanishi-Kari, Baltimore, and a few other coauthors (Weaver et al., 1986) published what was regarded as an important article in the journal *Cell* to get this all started. Margot O'Toole, the postdoctoral researcher in Imanishi-Kari's lab at the Massachusetts Institute of Technology (MIT), happened to see one of the notebooks that contained the data on which the *Cell* article had been based. O'Toole saw what she thought were discrepancies between those raw data and claims made in the *Cell* article for the findings of the study. She took the unusual step, for such a junior and recent member of the lab, of filing a complaint against Imanishi-Kari with the MIT administration.

There is some disagreement about O'Toole's motives for doing so. Some believe that she was a courageous whistle-blower who risked her future as a scientist to expose a case of scientific misconduct. Others believe that she was frustrated at her failure to make progress on the research problem Imanishi-Kari had assigned to her (not coincidentally, following up on the work reported in the *Cell* paper) and angry over what she perceived to be inconsiderate criticism of that failure by Imanishi-Kari.

What seems pretty clear is that O'Toole's questions about Imanishi-Kari's integrity set off a long, complicated, and painful chain of events. Imanishi-Kari was forced to move from MIT to Tufts University, and eventually she was charged formally with fraud by the Office of Research Integrity (ORI) at the National Institutes of Health (NIH), the agency that sponsored her research. At various times, she was investigated by Congress and by a federal prosecutor, she was judged guilty by the ORI, and she was disqualified from receiving federal research grants.

David Baltimore was chastised publicly for supporting Imanishi-Kari and for lending his name to fraudulent research. He was forced to resign as president of Rockefeller University. O'Toole was hailed as a hero by members of Congress, by the media, and by crusaders for scientific integrity, but she suffered professionally and personally in the process.

In the end, Imanishi-Kari managed to have her day in court, in a hearing of an appeal of the ORI report that condemned her. Her lawyers had the report overturned, as an appeals board at NIH agreed with her, Baltimore, and others who had argued that she had committed no fraud. In the view of the besieged researchers and their supporters, and finally in that of the authorities, she had merely exercised normal professional judgment in interpreting the data collected in her research.

During the period of controversy, Imanishi-Kari's claim of a groundbreaking discovery in the use of gene transplantation to alter immune function in mice was ignored by the scientific community. Researchers recently have begun to extend her work and, in the process, finally validate it in the lab rather than in the courts. One can only wonder how much consolation Imanishi-Kari draws at this point from any of the vindication she has received.

This case shows the other face of the problem of scientific misconduct. Research career can be ruined by false accusations and valuable research brought to a standstill by misunderstanding or even personal animus.

Communication Among Scientists

The Role of Publication

In spite of the debate, the controversy, and the documented problems associated with the publication of research articles, the communication of research findings within the professional community of psychologists remains an essential capstone to the research process. With the exception of research that is conducted by or for profit-making companies that consider the findings proprietary assets that they don't want to share with others, researchers have a professional responsibility to disseminate their work to their colleagues, both researchers and practitioners.

The practice of psychology, whether by clinical psychologists, educational psychologists, industrial/organizational psychologists, or other applied psychologists, gets its legitimacy from the scientific literature on which it is based. The professional journals, many published by organizations to which the subscribers belong, such as the American Psychological Association and the American Psychological Society, make it possible for practitioners to learn about the latest scientific discoveries. To the extent that the editors and reviewers do their jobs well, journal readers can expect articles that describe studies that satisfy (or at least satisfice) the methodological criteria discussed in the earlier chapters of this book.

The other audience for the scientific literature, and the more important one from the point of view of the discussion here of the research process, is the community of research psychologists. In our earlier discussion of conceptual validity, we saw that the value of research findings depends to some extent on the development of the research hypothesis. First, the hypothesis should be original. It should not engender unnecessary duplication of past research. Second, the hypothesis should be tied to existing research and theory, so that it makes a cumulative contribution to knowledge of the behavior in question. For a researcher to plan a study whose findings are not compromised by the two threats to conceptual validity, unnecessary duplication and theoretical isolation, he or she needs to know what relevant research already has been done.

The published research literature is the best guide, for two reasons. First, it has survived a peer-review selection process that should ensure that it meets the test of methodological soundness. Research that has been published has received the imprimatur of the scientific establishment. Second, the published research literature is accessible through the various electronic databases discussed in Chapter 2. That makes it much more likely that a researcher will find the relevant past research if it exists.

It should be noted that, to a somewhat lesser degree, researchers in academia gain professional status and disseminate the findings of their research through their participation at professional conferences. Conferences are held at a variety of levels—international, national, regional, and state. They are sponsored by organizations such as the American Psychological Society, the International Association of Applied Psychologists, and the Society for Research in Child Development, as well as dozens of others. On an annual basis, in most cases, the organization's members and guests share the results of their scientific work. Some presentations are made in paper sessions, where researchers give oral presentations of their work, often 10 to 15 minutes long with 5 additional minutes for questions. Others are made in poster sessions, lasting an hour or longer, where dozens of researchers simultaneously provide bulletin-board visual presentations while conference attendees circulate among them, stopping at those that interest them the most to discuss the work with the researcher.

The Research Article: A Primer

Now that a case has been made for publishing reports of psychological research, we'll take a brief look at the format used for research articles by most research psychologists. It is known as "APA format" because it was developed and is maintained by a standing committee of the American Psychological Association. There have been several versions over several decades, and the latest one is described in the *Publication Manual of the American Psychological Association*, fourth edition, published in 1994. It specifies in great detail every aspect of a research article. It describes how references are to be cited, what types of headings are to be used, how tables and figures are to be presented, and much more, in a book of almost 400 pages.

We won't be able to deal with all those technical details here. The best source for that is the *Manual*, or software that provides a template to which the details of a study can be added. We will be concerned in a more general way with what a research article is supposed to communicate to those who read it, as well as how and why.

A research article has five main parts. In the order in which they are encountered by the reader, they are the **abstract**, the **introduction**, the **method section**, the **results section**, and the **discussion** (or conclusion). It will be easier to discuss the abstract last, because that section is usually is written after the other sections are completed, so that's what we'll do.

Introduction. This section of a research article is (should be, at any rate) a logical argument. Its purpose is to persuade the reader that the research hypothesis is worth testing. Without necessarily using the same terms we learned in Chapter 2, we can describe the introduction is an argument for the conceptual validity of the research findings. It usually begins with a discussion of the general area or areas to which the current research problem belongs. Then the discussion narrows down progressively to the specific problem at hand. It often ends with a statement of the research hypothesis itself.

The argument that needs to be made in the introduction of a research article can be stated in general terms as follows: This is what we know about the question this research is intended to answer; thus, this is what we most need to know at the present time to understand the behavior in question better; and therefore, we tested this particular research hypothesis. Included in the argument are the two elements of conceptual validity, though they may appear in the opposite order from that in Chapter 2. The argument in the introduction shows how the research hypothesis ties into existing research and theory. In a well-written introduction, the reader is led gradually to what seems like an inevitable conclusion that the research hypothesis fills the most apparent and important gap left in knowledge about the behavior in question. Thus, the introduction documents the researcher's efforts to avoid theoretical isolation and unnecessary duplication, in that order.

If you look at a published research article (and that would probably be the most useful thing you could do to help you to understand the present discussion) you will see that the argument we've been discussing is made in a very brief form. Brevity is a key element in writing a research article. That is both because researchers have a need to keep up with a large and rapidly growing literature that doesn't afford them the time to read lengthy papers and because the high cost of publishing professional journals generally sets strict limits on the number of pages they can publish annually.

Short articles make it possible for researchers to read more research and for journals to publish more of it. The argument therefore cannot be presented in great detail. If the reader is not a specialist in the area that is being discussed, he or she may need to consult previously published papers or articles cited in the introduction (a list of references is included following the discussion section) to make sense out of the author's argument. Those papers are likely to be described briefly in a research article, rather than explained in detail.

Conceptual validity is not only a technical requirement imposed by methodologists or textbook writers but also a prerequisite for making a convincing argument for the research hypothesis in the introduction to a research article. If a reader, or a reviewer or editor for that matter, is not persuaded by that argument, he or she may choose to forgo reading the rest of the article and move on to a more productive activity. If a test of the research hypothesis does not promise to make an important and original contribution to existing knowledge about the behavior in question, how much can anyone be expected to care about how it was tested or the results of that test?

Method. The next section of the research article is the method section. As the title implies, it describes the way in which the test of the research hypothesis was carried out. Traditionally, the method section is divided into three parts—participants, apparatus, and procedure. In the participants part, the author describes the human or nonhuman participants, including the number that were tested and any relevant characteristics of them. In the case of human participants, information about age, gender, ethnicity, and other demographic characteristics might be considered relevant to the behavior being studied, depending on the hypothesis being tested. In the case of personality research, participants' scores on a personality test might be reported. Information about participants gives the reader some basis for estimating the generalizability of the research results.

In the apparatus part, the reader can expect to find information about tasks performed by participants, the physical setting in which the study took place, and instruments used to record participants' behavior (including mechanical, electronic, and paper-and-pencil devices). If any of those elements is a standardized model that was used in previous research, the reader might be referred to more detailed descriptions in the published research literature. Everyday objects such as tables, chairs, or stopwatches might simply be identified as such. If specialized pieces of equipment or behavioral measures created for use in the particular study being reported are used, more detail might be provided for the reader, within the space limitations discussed already. Whether by reference to previous research or by description, the reader should be provided with enough information to evaluate the construct validity of the causal events and behavioral measures used to elicit and to assess the research participants' behavior.

The procedure part of the method section describes the step-by-step sequence of events that constituted a participant's experience in the study being reported. This would include the research design, the arrangement of groups, the timing of events, the instructions given to participants (if any), and the actions of the researcher and any other individuals who might be present. This information would allow the reader to evaluate the research design, including the reactivity of the research setting, and to estimate the potential for artifacts to intrude into the treatments or the behavioral measures.

The goal of the method section of a research article is the presentation of a clear, accurate, and complete account of the participants, apparatus, and procedure used to carry out the study being reported. This presentation makes it possible for the reader to judge the methodological adequacy of the study—the ways in which the researcher dealt with potential threats to the construct, internal, and external validity of the research findings. There can be no more basic principle in the evaluation of psychological research than that the methods used in a research study are the key to understanding the meaning of the results.

The method section additionally should provide readers with the information they would need to replicate (repeat) the study. Exact replications are rare, but it is not uncommon for researchers to want to repeat a previous study with variations or additions. This may be done to test competing explanations for the original results or to carry research on the behavior in question a step further. To compare across variations or "generations" in a particular line of research, it is necessary to have sufficient relevant detail about how the research is carried out.

Again, the space limitations imposed by the volume of research, the number of articles submitted, and the economics of publishing professional journals make it difficult for even the researcher/author with the best intentions and greatest skill to accomplish that goal. I can recall a letter I received from a journal editor in response to my submission of a paper describing some research I was pretty proud of at the time. It said that the article would be published if I reduced its length by half. I began with the hopeful interpretation that the editor's instructions didn't apply to tables, figures, or the reference list, but only the text. Still, by accepting this offer, which at the time I didn't feel I could refuse, I was forced to make the final published article much less clear on the details of the research methods than the paper I submitted originally. I suspect that many published articles are briefer than their authors wanted them to be, although perhaps not so much briefer as by half.

Results. The results section of a research article presents the statistical analyses used to describe and to make comparisons among the groups of data collected in the study. These are produced by the descriptive and inferential statistical methods described in Chapter 10. They are often presented in the form of tables and figures (mostly graphs) through which the reader is guided by brief summaries in the text.

One key element in those summaries is the identification of the statistical tests used to make comparisons across the treatment groups or over the occasions specified by the research design. It is those comparisons that allow the reader to determine whether the obtained data support or contradict the research hypothesis. This makes the results section the most exciting part of a research article for many readers, not to mention for the researchers who carried out the study in question.

An equally important aspect of the results section is the provision of information that makes it possible for the reader to assess the vulnerability of the analyses of the results to threats to statistical conclusion validity. Such a judgment is based on knowledge about the research design and information about the nature of the behavioral measures, both obtained from the method section. If the author clearly identifies the statistical procedures used in the analyses, readers should be able to determine the appropriateness of the statistical methods employed and the accuracy with which the results presented portray the outcome of the study vis-à-vis the research hypothesis.

Discussion. We began with the introduction to the research article, a very brief essay that calls on the author to organize information into a logical and persuasive argument. That is a task requiring considerable skill and creativity. Then we considered the method and results sections, both of which are based on more straightforward and factual descriptions of how the study was carried out, and of the observations of participants' behavior that were obtained in the process. Next, we move on to the discussion or conclusion section, and back to the essay form.

This final section of a research article is a second opportunity for the researcher to construct a persuasive argument. This time, the argument is about the implications of the research results for the truth or falsity of the research hypothesis, and about its contribution to the body of knowledge about the behavior in question, in the light of the limitations imposed by the methods used to conduct the study. The purpose of this section is to tie the entire article together for the reader.

In a way, the author of a research article does for the reader, in the discussion or conclusion section, some of what we've described the reader doing for himself or herself during the reading of it. The author draws conclusions about the truth of the hypothesis from the results of the data analyses, as well as evaluating possible qualifications of the conclusions based on the methods used (limitations on generalizability, other possible causal factors not taken into account in the research design, measurement ambiguities, etc.).

For the informed reader, this may be an empty exercise, because the reader should already have taken note of those methodological limitations. The researcher, however, may have thought more about the study over an extended period of time and may have firsthand knowledge that would be difficult to convey to the reader, especially in the previous sections of a brief research article. Thus, he or she might have additional insights about these issues that would benefit the reader.

The discussion or conclusion section often ends with the author's view of the likely future of the research problem at hand. There may be suggestions for methodological improvements in future studies and for new studies that could resolve questions raised by the results of the current study or address additional questions about the behavior being studied. There may also be suggestions about the possible use of the research findings by practitioners, particularly if the study had an applied focus. Conclusions may be drawn about existing theories that are supported or called into question by the research findings. This is the best chance for researchers to prosecute their own favorite agendas—intellectual, scientific, and personal. Yet again, however, this section must be very brief.

Abstract. Usually, it is only after the main body of a research article has been written—introduction, method, results, and conclusion—that the first piece of the final paper will be added. It is usually called the abstract (sometimes the summary). It summarizes the entire paper in a brief paragraph. It usually is between 100 and 150 words in length, although in this computer age, the length may be specified as the maximum number of characters allowed. This may amount to no more than a sentence or two to summarize each of the four major sections of the article. Thus, it cannot and is not expected to provide a basis for judging the research findings critically in the ways that the entire article can.

The abstract has two main functions. The first is to allow readers to choose quickly, from all the articles in all the journals that address their scientific or practical interests, those that seem likely to afford them the greatest benefit from a complete, thoughtful reading. The second is to allow electronic databases to store a manageable amount of information that still allows their users to decide which articles to seek out in their full form. The abstract should include carefully chosen key words that would be used by potential readers to conduct electronic searches of those databases.

Tables, Figures, and References. A final aspect of the research article that needs to be addressed concerns the three ancillary items of **tables**, **figures**, and **references**. Tables are, as the label implies, used to present numbers or lists of items to the reader. They are usually summaries of the tabulations of data collected in the course of a study, or summaries of the statistical analyses conducted. They may summarize ANOVAs, multiple regression analyses, and the like. Figures may be graphs presented to clarify the research results, diagrams of the research apparatus or the laboratory setting, or depictions of theoretical models that were tested or that explain the research results, among other things.

In the manuscript prepared by the author, tables and figures are prepared on separate pages, not integrated within the text. The author directs the printer to insert tables and figures in the text, at or near the points where the information they contain is needed. When an article is published, the tables and figures are placed within the text, as close as possible to the points where they are mentioned, given the need to compose filled and attractive pages. Detailed instructions for the preparation of tables and figures can be found in the APA publication manual.

A research article usually will cite, throughout its text, references to published research articles, theoretical papers, books, and other sources that can provide the reader with detailed information relevant to the arguments, materials, statistical techniques, or other subjects addressed in article. These are treated according to APA style. The details, again, are available in the APA publication manual, which explains references for a wide variety of sources, including professional journals, books, newspaper articles, personal interviews, Internet listings, and many more.

In general, citations are made in the text of the article, using the author's or authors' names and the date of the publication. Depending on the author's grammatical taste, the author's name can be used in the text, with the date following in parentheses—for example, "Skinner (1948) argued. . . ." Alternatively, the author's name and date both can be put in parentheses—for example, "It has been argued (Skinner, 1948). . . ." Both are acceptable. An article or book is quoted directly only when the author's words are so well chosen as to bear repeating. In those rare cases, the page number is added to the citation—for example, "Smith (1948) wrote 'extremely relevant quotation' (p. 351)." (Other formats can be used for placement of the author's name, the date of the reference, and the page source for the passage quoted.) At the end of the research article, following the discussion section, all the references included in the paper are listed in alphabetical order according to the first author's last name.

Cumulative Analysis

A final issue concerning communicating research findings to professional colleagues is that of literature review. The sheer volume of studies produced by research psychologists imposes a difficult burden on any researcher or practitioner who tries to keep up with the state of knowledge on any but the most obscure research problem. In the past, a specialized type of professional publication, notably the journal *Psychological Bulletin* and the book series *Annual Review of Psychology*, published articles that reviewed areas of research either because authors independently chose to do so or because editors solicited specific reviews from authors who were known to be experts in the particular areas. The resulting articles drew conclusions concerning the overall state of knowledge about a particular behavior or research hypothesis at the time.

In the last two decades or so, a family of statistical techniques has been developed that makes it possible to quantify the status of a research hypothesis based on the combined results of numerous research studies. These techniques, known collectively as meta-analysis, were introduced earlier. One example of meta-analysis is the exemplar study of psychotherapy outcome research by Smith and Glass (1977, **E24**).

The point of this discussion is that many researchers now believe that it is not sufficient for the scientific community to continue producing individual research studies to add to knowledge about human behavior (and other scientific phenomena). It is also necessary to take active steps to aggregate those individual studies into generalizations that carry more weight by virtue of their numbers. This can be done by means of meta-analysis, which may become, for research psychologists, the analog of the collaborative process more characteristic of the physical sciences, in which the research community agrees to collectively investigate selected research questions exhaustively, rather than follow their individual interests, before moving on to other questions.

● BEING SOCIALLY RESPONSIBLE

As you probably can appreciate fully by now, understanding how to do psychological research properly is quite a challenge. Besides the complex questions of methodology we've considered, a competent researcher must master statistics, study the always growing literature of research and theory in the area he or she chooses to study, and establish a network of professional colleagues who can provide informal advice on scientific matters, publication tactics, and employment strategies. Beyond all these tasks within the profession, there are important relationships to consider with those outside.

Research Ethics

Ethical Treatment of Animals

One question that has occupied research psychologists in recent decades, particularly since the rise of the civil rights and environmental movements of the 1960s, is the ethical treatment of those human and nonhuman organisms whose behavior is studied in psychological research. Research psychologists who study nonhuman organisms ("animals") have come under increasing attack for exploiting their research subjects. Those who study people have been criticized for lying to research participants, placing them in stressful situations, and invading their privacy, among other things.

Nonhuman research participants often are bred by researchers for the sole purpose of being studied. Among the reasons that mice and rats are used so often in research is that they can be bred quickly and economically by researchers, and their genetic backgrounds and pre-experiment experience can be controlled in the process.

Researchers are constrained by local, state, and federal laws to maintain clean, healthful environments for those animals. Lab animals, however, typically are kept in small cages with little space or stimulation, and they may be subjected to food deprivation, electric shock, drugs, and even major surgery in the course of the research in which they are used.

In every case, ethical researchers minimize the animals' discomfort. Surgery is carried out with anesthetic and under sterile conditions, much as it would be in a hospital, but there is sometimes discomfort, perhaps even suffering. For those who believe that the potential benefits to humans, such as effective treatments for drug

---

Research in the Public Interest

The experimental method developed by philosophers and scientists over the past few centuries, and so prized by researchers, has become part of our culture. It is used to test the effectiveness of consumer products and government programs, as well as to build scientific theories. It is even used by TV news magazines and private research organizations to reveal practices usually kept secret by those who carry them out.

An experiment of this sort was reported recently by the Urban Institute, a private research organization working under contract for the U.S. Department of Housing and Urban Development (better known as HUD). Its purpose was to test the hypothesis that mortgage lenders throughout the United States discriminated against African American and Hispanic home buyers. Pairs of white and minority individuals—who provided evidence of similar incomes, assets, jobs, and credit histories —sought identical mortgages for house purchases in the same neighborhoods.

In their interactions with lenders, minority group members received less information and

briefer consultations than whites, and they were quoted higher interest rates. Minorities also were more likely to be denied loans. African Americans were almost four times as likely to be turned down in Chicago than were whites, and Hispanics almost twice as likely to be rejected in New York City, despite their similarities to white applicants in financial and other characteristics. Overall, African Americans were twice as likely to be denied a home loan, and Hispanic Americans about 1.5 times as likely.

According to HUD Secretary Andrew Cuomo, the differences in treatment received by the loan applicants in this study had to be caused by their race because the only difference was the color of their skin. Do you agree? Was this really an experiment? Why? What are the most obvious threats to the validity of Cuomo's conclusions from the research results? Is there reason to question the propriety of government policies intended to end discrimination by mortgage lenders? Can you think of other uses for this kind of research?

---

addiction or mental illness, outweigh the cost to the animals, the research is ethically defensible. For those who believe that humans and laboratory rats have equal rights, it is not.

There are many vagaries in the debate over the ethical treatment of nonhuman subjects in psychological research. Many people believe in a hierarchy of animal rights that places humans at the top, with the greatest protection from exploitation for the benefit of others. For many, insects, rodents, and other species that are sometimes referred to as pests or vermin are at the bottom. They may be killed just because they happen to turn up in our houses, or even in our gardens. Other species, including those kept as pets (dogs and cats, in particular) and those that resemble humans most (monkeys and apes), fall in between.

I can recall passing a militant group of animal rights protesters outside an APA convention in Washington, D.C., on my way to a convenience store to buy a soft drink. While the protesters were vilifying psychologists for exploiting rats in their research (among other things), only a few yards away the convenience store was selling poison to kill rats without any protesters in sight.

Just as ironic is the fact that researchers who breed and keep mice and rats for use in their laboratories often attract feral rodents from outside with the scents of the lab animals and their feed. The researchers are required to keep their laboratory animals healthy and clean, to treat them as humanely as they can, and to dispose of them painlessly when the research is over. But they can kill the feral animals using any means necessary, including painful traps and sticky patches. To complicate matters further, some research promises a direct and imminent benefit to humans—medical research, for example. Such research justifies, for many people, more exploitative and injurious treatment of nonhuman research subjects than does research carried out to test scientific theories.

Researchers who dare to use cats and dogs in their experiments, because those species have physical or behavioral characteristics that make them good models of human characteristics or behavior, risk outrage from those who cherish the same species as pets. Selling such animals to researchers, or allowing researchers to collect those that run wild in back alleys and fields, is considered barbaric by many. It would matter little to most critics that these animals are so valuable to researchers that they usually are not euthanized once their service as research subjects is completed, but used in further research (remember the "problem" this caused for Seligman and Maier in their research with dogs [1967, **E18**]), and are often treated as pets by their laboratory caretakers. It should be noted that organizations that claim to prevent cruelty to animals and that call themselves humane societies kill 10 million or more dogs and cats each year. They do so merely because the animals are the unwanted products of unintended breeding by family pets. Their actions hardly ever draw a public complaint; in fact, these organizations usually are funded by charitable gifts and tax dollars (although, to be fair, "no-kill" animal shelters are slowly gaining in popularity around the country).

Research psychologists have a much more difficult time using nonhuman participants today than in the past. They face stringent government regulations and organized public opposition that extends from lobbying and peaceful protest to the destruction of research facilities and kidnapping of research animals. Those obstacles can't help but discourage some researchers. Only medical research (which more often causes pain and harm to participants) and research by the cosmetics industry that is seen as less beneficial to human welfare seem to pose greater ethical difficulties in today's political climate.

Ethical Treatment of Humans in Medical Research

Ironically, the history of research with human participants is arguably more shocking than any legitimate research that is presently done using nonhuman species. Immediately following World War II, the victorious Allies took steps to punish the conquered Nazis for atrocities they had committed during the previous decade or so. An international tribunal was convened at Nuremberg, Germany, to try war criminals. One of the trials held there was known as the Doctors Trial. In it, approximately 20 German physicians were accused of conducting painful, dangerous, and even lethal experiments on Jews, prisoners of war, and others under their control during the Nazi regime.

During the defense of the German doctors accused of those crimes against humanity, their attorneys raised the point that dangerous medical research on captive populations had been taking place in the United States for at least the previous 50 years. Prisoners in county jails, state prisons, and federal penitentiaries; institutionalized developmentally disabled individuals; and even medical hospital patients had been subjected to chemical warfare agents, intestinal parasites, live cancer cells, radioactive materials, dioxin, mind-altering drugs, malaria, and much more. Furthermore, they had only limited freedom to refuse participation and little knowledge of the dangers to which they were being exposed. The evidence regarding that American medical research was so strong that some of the Nazi defendants escaped the death penalty or were even acquitted.

Ultimately, one outcome of the Doctors Trial was a set of ethical guidelines for future medical research. Foremost among them was the requirement that participants give their informed consent, meaning that they had to be made aware of the risks involved and had to be free to choose whether or not to participate. This Nuremberg Code was a clear repudiation of what the Nazis had done, but also of much of the medical research conducted in the United States prior to that time. Nonetheless, over the following three decades or more, American medical researchers carried out thousands of experiments on prisoners and patients without bothering to follow its provisions.

In fact, during the 1960s, after the U.S. Food and Drug Administration (FDA) established tough new requirements for approving new drugs, the scale of this unethical research escalated greatly. The new FDA regulations required a first phase of testing on human participants to determine whether a new drug was toxic. This required administering the drug to healthy people. The cheapest, easiest, and most private way to do that was for researchers to forge cooperative relationships with the administrators of prisons, jails, and other institutions who could approve the research. Jails and prisons were especially favored by medical researchers because prisoners typically were more impoverished, less educated, and more willing to take risks than people "on the outside." This made them more vulnerable to offers of money, better treatment, leniency, or just simple relief from monotony. They also were legally competent to sign releases freeing the researchers and prison officials from responsibility for any harm that might be done.

Prisoners were eager to have the opportunity to be participants in medical experiments. They earned money to buy things they needed, even to use for bail. They also had increased freedom to move around the institution, a privilege that otherwise was not available to them. At the same time, administrators gained a more motivated population inside the institution and some resources to make improvements in staffing and facilities. The researchers, whose work was funded by pharmaceutical companies, government agencies, and the U.S. military, among others, gained professional status from their research (although most of it was pretty mundane stuff that wouldn't excite their professional colleagues very much) and, of course, a great deal of money.

One of the most prominent medical researchers during that 1960s era was a dermatologist, Dr. Albert Kligman of the University of Pennsylvania. He supervised thousands of studies for dozens of drug companies, testing products ranging from skin lotions to dandruff shampoos on prisoners in three Philadelphia jails. He was first called to one of those jails, Holmesburg Prison, in 1961 to advise jail officials on treatments for athlete's foot, an infection that was rampant in the inmate population. According to a newspaper interview in 1966, Kligman recalled his first impression of the place this way: "All I saw before me were acres of skin. It was like a farmer seeing a fertile field for the first time." This quotation furnished the title for a recent book about the ethical questions in medical research, *Acres of Skin* by Allen M. Hornblum (1998).

It can't be denied that some good came of all this medical research. Advances were made in understanding infectious diseases and other serious health problems, and new drugs were developed. Kligman himself developed Retin-A, a successful acne and wrinkle treatment. Prisoners, universities, and jails were enriched, monetarily and otherwise.

Considerable damage also was done. Prisoners suffered pain and permanent damage to their health. Jails were corrupted, as they allowed their charges to be exploited. Some inmates and corrections officials gained power over others that was used to promote sexual exploitation and other nefarious practices. Important social institutions were corrupted, such as medicine, higher education, and government, including the U.S. military and the Atomic Energy Commission.

The research itself was even compromised. Inmates who were skilled in evading the law and jail regulations, as a result of considerable practice, found ways to circumvent the research protocols they were supposed to be observing. It was not until the mid-1970s that lawsuits by inmates, Congressional investigations, and media exposure combined to stimulate new laws and new guidelines for ethical research within universities and government agencies that put a stop to the long-standing horrors of medical research in Holmesburg Prison and throughout the United States.

Ethical Treatment of Humans in Psychological Research

There may be no direct parallels between the outrageous actions of medical researchers and the treatment human subjects receive in psychological research. That is not to say that research psychologists have no ethical lapses to answer for. Much psychological research is straightforward, and participants get a clear and accurate picture of what is happening to them. Memory and perception research, in which participants are asked what they remember or what they see, are good examples. That sort of research seems to pose no extraordinary threat to the welfare of research participants, either. At worst, they may have to work hard or face up to poor performance on some task. Not all psychological research, however, is so benign.

For example, a good deal of social-psychological research is based on deception. Studies are based on comparisons between groups of people who are led to very different beliefs about the events taking place in a particular setting by untruthful instructions provided by a researcher. They could be led to believe that they succeeded or failed at an ambiguous task, through false feedback regarding their performance, or that others making the same judgments as they made agree or disagree with them, through use of confederates of the experimenter posing as fellow participants.

Researchers who rely on deception to create variations in the independent variables they are studying (treatments) generally have argued that they cannot obtain informed consent from participants. That would require them to expose the deception prematurely. Moreover, their experimental manipulations often create discomfort in participants, such as a loss of self-esteem or a conflict about whether to remain independent in their judgments and risk the disapproval of others.

One very widely publicized example of research that raises these ethical issues is Stanley Milgram's research on obedience to authority (1974, **E9**). The participants were led to believe that they were playing the role of a teacher in a study of learning. They could not be fully informed in advance because, for the study to be carried out, they had to believe that they were really administering electric shocks to a learner. They reported, and showed in their overt reactions, severe anxiety over the decision that they were forced to make about whether or not to continue to obey the experimenter. Most of them were induced by Milgram's very effective, though not entirely intentional, protocol to deliver what they believed to be very painful and even life-threatening electric shocks to an innocent stranger.

When Milgram was criticized for the way he treated the participants in his obedience studies, he and his supporters made two main arguments in his defense.

One was that the participants were questioned, informed, and counseled afterward to detect and remedy any harm that might have been done. Second, they argued that the importance of the research justified any residual risks that might have been created.

Neither of these arguments seems an acceptable substitute for the informed consent required by the Nuremberg Code. No one can be sure that any harm done to Milgram's participants could have been detected or, if it were detected, that it could have been reversed by Milgram or anyone else. "The end justifies the means" probably is not an argument one wants to use against a code of ethical behavior that was formulated in response to the Nazis' atrocities, even if one could trust researchers or even disinterested third parties to judge accurately the balance between the potential costs to research participants in a particular study and the ultimate value of that research to society.

Another well-known social-psychological study, this one done by Philip Zimbardo (Zimbardo et al., 1973), raises similar questions about research ethics. He tested the hypothesis that brutal treatment of prison inmates can result from the way the role of prison guard is defined. Male Stanford University undergraduate volunteers were randomly assigned to the roles of guard and inmate in a simulated prison that was created in the basement of a psychology building. Whether Zimbardo could have foreseen it or not, the experience had such a profound effect on his research participants that the study had to be terminated prematurely. "Guards" exhibited frighteningly brutal behavior toward "inmates," who displayed equally frightening symptoms of stress. The criticisms leveled at Zimbardo, and his responses to those criticisms, were very similar to those that were exchanged over Milgram's obedience research. The disregard for the potential risks to research subjects by a zealous, if well-meaning, researcher were very similar also.

In some ways, human participants in psychological research may be even more vulnerable than their nonhuman counterparts, even though few researchers would subject them to the physical dangers or challenges that they might face in medical research. Humans can suffer humiliation, damaged self-esteem, and invasion of privacy, in addition to physical exhaustion and pain. As a result, research psychologists probably face even greater ethical challenges in planning and conducting research with human participants than they do with nonhuman ones, especially given the prevailing value system in our society that elevates the rights of humans above those of other species.

Protecting Human Research Participants

The Institutional Review Board. Research with humans that is carried out with the support of government research grants and/or in a well-organized university setting ordinarily must be approved by a group of scientists, other professionals (doctors and lawyers in many cases), and representatives of the lay community. Such a group is known as an **Institutional Review Board (IRB)**. Its function is to review detailed plans submitted by researchers, seeking to ensure that there are minimal threats to human participants, maximum safeguards for participants' rights, and sufficient potential benefits from the research findings.

One target of those who review research proposals or plans to ensure ethical treatment of human participants is any aspect of the procedure that might cause harm. This would include such things as causing some participants to fail at a task by including insoluble problems or causing participants to believe they failed by providing false feedback on their performance. It also would include embarrassing or insulting subjects. Milgram's obedience studies (1974, **E9**) subjected participants to high levels of stress that probably would be considered too harmful by a modern-day IRB. Even intense competition, or demands for strenuous performance, or confronting participants with something that frightened them, might fail to pass muster with an IRB, not to speak of asking participants to drink alcohol or take other drugs.

Reviewers could reject a proposal if they thought it threatened participants with too much harm, or they could ask for modifications if they believed that the researcher's purpose could be achieved through the use of a less dangerous procedure. They also could ask for safeguards such as prescreening to eliminate particularly vulnerable participants, close supervision by medical or other personnel during the study, or the ready availability of counseling services afterward.

Debriefing. One way of ameliorating the damage that might be done by making dangerous demands on research participants is to talk with them afterward about the procedures and their effects. In so-called **debriefing** sessions, researchers can correct false information (intended or otherwise), explain more fully the purpose of events, and probe for possible harmful changes in participants' self-perceptions or other beliefs.

To rely too credulously on debriefing is risky, however. A friend of mine once conducted a study in which he manipulated self-esteem by persuading some student nurses that they had "failed" a psychological test of empathy. Afterward, he debriefed each one of them individually, reassuring them that the test feedback they had received was false. One student nurse was almost out the door when she stopped to thank him for trying to spare her feelings and stated her intention to abandon her nursing career because she had learned from the experiment that she lacked the requisite empathy to be a good nurse. My friend quickly got her back into the room and talked with her until he was satisfied that he had corrected her misconceptions. This case points out that where participants' well-being is at stake, avoiding harm is safer than trying to detect and correct it afterward. This is true especially when deception is used, because it may destroy the trust on which effective debriefing must be based.

Informed Consent. IRBs may require researchers to protect participants' rights preventatively by obtaining their **informed consent**, as required by the Nuremberg Code that was discussed earlier. To do so, researchers must inform prospective participants fully about the nature and purposes of the study being conducted, then allow them to decide for themselves whether they want to participate. In this form, at least, informed consent prevents the use of deceptive instructions, hidden observation, or other techniques that mislead participants or invade their privacy. It also makes research in field settings extremely difficult, especially experimental studies that create events that are not intrinsically part of the setting. Participants usually are not, and sometimes cannot be, fully informed in field settings.

In some areas of psychological research, in which participants' perceptions and thoughts are the focus of study, it is difficult to conceive of research that can proceed when participants know everything about the researcher's purpose in advance. This would create such an extreme level of reactivity and thus compromise construct validity to such a degree that the research results would be essentially useless. Certainly, most of the laboratory experiments and field research conducted by social psychologists could never survive a strict requirement of informed consent. Giving participants more limited information would make it easier to conduct meaningful research but wouldn't fully protect the participants' rights.

As we have seen, since Milgram's obedience research in the 1960s and Zimbardo's prison simulation study in the 1970s, new safeguards have been put in place. Informed consent and evaluation of research proposals by IRBs probably mean that those studies wouldn't be conducted today, at least if the researchers were working in major research universities or with government grant support. Some psychologists see that as a great loss to the profession and to society, and Dr. Arthur Kligman and others probably would have felt the same way if similar restrictions had been placed on their medical research. The Nuremberg Code and ethical guidelines that are similar to it place the welfare of the research participant first and reject the argument that the ends justify the means. These codes and guidelines severely restrict the kind of research psychologists can do. That is a position that seems easier to maintain for someone else's work than for one's own, at least for many researchers.

Redeeming Social Value. The value of the research findings is one of the most difficult issues to factor into judgments of research ethics. Research might promise to advance knowledge, or human welfare, to a degree that outweighs the cost or

| Box 11.3 | *THINKING ABOUT RESEARCH* |

Does Science Have a Future?

To attempt the difficult task of understanding the overwhelming complexity of scientific research —or psychological research, for that matter—one needs to believe in the value of doing research and of understanding the research others have done. It is no wonder that researchers who have devoted their lives to understanding the "logic" of the scientific method that is the main subject of this book, and to acquiring the technical expertise required to implement it, were somewhat disconcerted by a recent book by science writer John Horgan titled *The End of Science* (1997).

In that book, Horgan argues that scientists have reached the limits of human knowledge. According to him, we know so much about the natural world—its chemical composition, the structure and function of DNA, quantum physics, and so on—that all that is left is to work out the relatively minor details.

Needless to say, not all scientists agreed with Horgan (I suspect that very few did). One of the most articulate to disagree was John Maddox, who answered Horgan in a book of his own, *What Remains to be Discovered?* (1998). Maddox cited several unsolved problems he felt were much more than minor details as evidence that science was not close to its end, but still just beginning. These problems included the way neurons accomplish human thought, the basis for the evolutionary advantage of *Homo sapiens*, external influences on the activity of genes, and a definitive explanation of the origins of the universe.

In the case of psychology, in particular, does it seem to you that recent discoveries are more trivial than earlier ones? Do most important human behaviors seem to be well understood already? Are researchers in psychology just mopping up what's left after the major discoveries of the past? Make up your own mind, but I, for one, doubt it.

even the likely harm to the research participants. In such a case, it may be judged ethical even if there is an obvious risk of harm or a considerable cost to participants. This seems the most problematic of the three elements of ethical research. It is very difficult to predict the value of research findings in advance, and the judgment of whether their value does or doesn't outweigh the risks of harm to participants is very subjective. A study that might seem a pure indulgence of the researcher's curiosity, in advance of its actually being carried out, could turn out to have enormous theoretical or practical value once the results are in, or even many years later.

Perhaps the most solid ground on which the potential value of research findings can be judged is the methodological rigor with which it is carried out. That must be judged on the basis of the criteria that we have considered for the quality of a research hypothesis, the faithfulness with which treatments and behavioral measures represent the constructs that make up that hypothesis, the degree to which the research design allows confident judgments of cause and effect, the degree to which meaningful generalization of the results is possible, and the appropriateness of the statistical treatment of the data. All those elements of validity together determine the baseline potential for the research findings to have sufficient value to justify even the most benign demands being placed on the research participants. Without validity, there can be no value and no justification for the resources expended, material or human.

The Researcher and Society

Psychologists and Society

Besides the ethical responsibility a researcher has to the participants in his or her study, there is a relationship between researchers, psychological and other, and the larger society. In the light of the contributions that psychological research has made already, it seems beyond question that it has the potential to change people's lives, and even society as a whole, for the better. Psychological research can claim some credit for helping to improve teaching in our schools, for making jails safer, for making psychotherapy more effective, and even for inspiring the establishment of alternative communities that foster equality and equanimity among their members, among many other benefits. Of course, it must also accept some blame for changing society for the worse. Research findings have been used to justify prejudice, to assist in the development of deceptive advertising and dispiriting political campaigns, and to develop exploitative management techniques, among other selfish and greedy applications.

Giving Psychology Away

Some psychologists have argued that the greatest ethical failing of research psychologists may not be the harm that has been done using their work. After all, the scientist has only limited control, at best, over how others use his or her work. In spite of his best efforts, Albert Einstein couldn't prevent the dropping of atomic bombs on innocent Japanese civilians in Hiroshima and Nagasaki, weapons whose development was based on his theories. The greatest failure might instead be the failure to adequately disseminate research findings to those who might benefit from them, and this harm can be avoided. In his presidential address to the American Psychological Association, George Miller (Miller, 1969), a prominent cognitive psychologist, urged his colleagues to "give psychology away." Rather than assuming that only professional practitioners could put into use the work of their scientist colleagues, Miller believed that the fruits of psychological science should be made available to the general public, preferably in a form that they would understand and be able to use.

Robert Sommer, a social and environmental psychologist, takes a unique approach to giving his research away. For example, Sommer (1990) found in his research that patrons of farmers' markets and food co-ops had more pleasant shopping experiences than customers in traditional supermarkets. He published his findings simultaneously in professional psychological journals and in publications for those in the grocery business. He makes a practice of writing parallel reports of all his work, one for his scientific colleagues who read professional journals and one for those outside psychology who read organization newsletters, trade magazines, and other such publications.

Of course, the parallel versions must be quite different in some respects. Journal articles emphasize technical details and statistical analyses. Publications for nonpsychologists feature nontechnical descriptions and illustrative photographs. If you've read an article in a psychological journal, and I hope you have by now, you know how different it is from an article in a popular magazine. Most psychologists would need to work hard to be able to produce both types of writing the way Sommer does. Their professional colleagues are accustomed to cryptic articles, heavily edited for length and filled with numbers, symbols, and references. The general public, or even professionals in fields outside scientific psychology, expect a more lively writing style, with colorful examples and engaging graphic design.

Program Evaluation and Politics

It must be recognized that there are other obstacles to bringing the findings of psychological research to constituencies outside the scientific community, besides the limited experience most research psychologists have in doing so. A case in point concerns one of the most valuable contributions research psychologists are able to offer those outside the profession, one called **program evaluation**. Researchers can design studies and develop measures that make it possible to determine whether smaller classes improve the quality of education, whether employee participation in management decisions enhances productivity, or whether community policing reduces crime. Research also can be used to evaluate other public programs and organizational policies too numerous to mention.

The school administrators, corporate executives, police chiefs, and mayors who implement those programs and policies may not actually want so precise an answer about their effectiveness as research psychologists are able to provide. Researchers generally want as much certainty as possible about the meaning of their results. They agonize mightily over planning their research to achieve the greatest possible degree of certainty. Administrators in the public and private sectors, on the other hand, may actually fear clear evidence: It can show that their pet programs are not working as well as expected. They may feel that they will be blamed for any failure, even if economic trends or other factors beyond their control are responsible.

Donald Campbell (1969) referred to such individuals as **trapped administrators**. He pointed out that, for their sakes and ours, program evaluation evidence would be better used to decide whether or how to continue the program in question than whether to reward or punish the administrator who implemented it in good faith. In any case, clear research evidence may be perceived as dangerous because it makes it more difficult to put a "spin" on events that will protect the executive or politician from the wrath of stockholders or voters.

The Politics of Research

Politics also interferes with the use of research evidence in another way. Political ideology may lead to the rejection of valid research findings in favor of nonscientific speculation. In today's political climate, good evidence that income disparity contributes to high rates of violent crime may be rejected in favor of demagogic exhortations about morality. Researchers who know something about the causes of crime may find themselves excluded from the debate, while crime victims who know little take center stage. There's no use having a valid answer if no one wants to hear it. There may even be some harm in it. A researcher who follows the research data to a behavioral explanation for drug use may lose a professional career if those who decide on research funding prefer to search for an elusive biochemical explanation that would better fit their political ideology.

Research psychologists have a long and proud history of dedicating themselves to finding solutions for society's problems. There are many examples just among the studies we have used in this text to provide cases for methodological analysis. Friedman and Rosenman's (1959) research on the Type A heart-attack-prone personality syndrome (**E2**) revolutionized the treatment of heart disease. Broverman et al.'s (1972, **E5**; see Figure 11.3) and Clark and Clark's (1940, **E6**) studies highlighted the prevalence of stereotyping as well as its damaging consequences. The Clarks' research played a prominent role in the 1954 Supreme Court decision in *Brown v. Board of Education* that ended legal racial segregation in the United States. The experiments by Darley and Latané (1968) on bystander intervention (**E7**), Milgram's (1974) research on obedience to authority (**E9**), and Rosenthal and Jacobson's (1966) study of the effects of teachers' expectations for their students (**E15**) informed professionals and lay people about hidden dangers in society. Frazier's (1985) evaluation of the modular direct-supervision jail design (**E25**) influenced corrections policy across the United States. These are clear examples of research psychologists' efforts to use their talents for the benefit of society, and one could make a case for some of the other studies in our list of 25 as well. Of course, there are more examples than anyone could count to be found among the rest of the psychological research literature.

STEREOTYPIC SEX-ROLE ITEMS
(RESPONSES FROM 74 COLLEGE MEN AND 80 COLLEGE WOMEN)

Competency Cluster: Masculine pole is more desirable

Feminine	Masculine
Not at all aggressive	Very aggressive
Not at all independent	Very independent
Very emotional	Not at all emotional
Does not hide emotions at all	Almost always hides emotions
Very subjective	Very objective
Very easily influenced	Not at all easily influenced
Very submissive	Very dominant
Dislikes math and science very much	Likes math and science very much
Very excitable in a minor crisis	Not at all excitable in a minor crisis
Very passive	Very active
Not at all competitive	Very competitive
Very illogical	Very logical
Very home oriented	Very worldly
Not at all skilled in business	Very skilled in business
Very sneaky	Very direct
Does not know the way of the world	Knows the way of the world
Feelings easily hurt	Feelings not easily hurt
Not at all adventurous	Very adventurous
Has difficulty making decisions	Can make decisions easily
Cries very easily	Never cries
Almost never acts as a leader	Almost always acts as a leader
Not at all self-confident	Very self-confident
Very uncomfortable about being aggressive	Not at all uncomfortable about being aggressive
Not at all ambitious	Very ambitious
Unable to separate feelings from ideas	Easily able to separate feelings from ideas
Very dependent	Not at all dependent
Very conceited about appearance	Never conceited about appearance
Thinks women are always superior to men	Thinks men are always superior to women
Does not talk freely about sex with men	Talks freely about sex with men

Warmth-Expressiveness Cluster: Feminine pole is more desirable

Feminine	Masculine
Doesn't use harsh language at all	Uses very harsh language
Very talkative	Not at all talkative
Very tactful	Very blunt
Very gentle	Very rough
Very aware of feelings of others	Not at all aware of feelings of others
Very religious	Not at all religious
Very interested in own appearance	Not at all interested in own appearance
Very neat in habits	Very sloppy in habits
Very quiet	Very loud
Very strong need for security	Very little need for security
Enjoys art and literature	Does not enjoy art and literature at all
Easily expresses tender feelings	Does not express tender feelings at all easily

Figure 11.3. A summary of the results of research on gender-role stereotypes by Inge Broverman and her colleagues.
SOURCE: Reprinted from "Sex-Role Stereotypes: A Current Appraisal," *Journal of Social Issues, 28,* p. 63 (Table 1), Broverman, Vogel, Broverman, Clarkson, and Rosenkrantz, © copyright 1978 by Blackwell Publishers.

The relationship between the researcher and society is a two-way street. In his recent book *The New Know-Nothings* (1999), Morton Hunt describes the animosity of many disparate groups toward psychological research. A layperson who has written prolifically and eloquently about psychology, Hunt documents how researchers in psychology and other scientific disciplines have faced serious and sometimes even brutal opposition to work that is relevant to social problems. Neither Hunt nor the researchers involved in the cases he reviews complains about opposition based on scientific differences of opinion. They reserve their complaints for opposition based on political ideology that ignores the scientific merits of research or even distorts them intentionally to further the interests of a particular group or belief system. As Hunt makes very clear, many researchers have faced this politicization of their work, which includes everything from lobbying to cut off their research funding, to organizing protests that disrupt their classes, to shouting them down at professional conferences, to death threats against them and their families, from all points on the political spectrum.

Those who have a liberal political agenda have been especially vehement in opposing and attacking researchers studying the role of genetic influences on intelligence, personality development, criminal behavior, and sexual orientation. Researchers have been attacked generally because their work suggested that group differences based on heredity are more important than individual differences within groups. African Americans, in particular, have been singled out as being genetically inferior in intelligence to whites by such scientists as Arthur Jensen of the University of California at Berkeley and J. Philippe Rushton of the University of Western Ontario. This has aroused spirited and, at times, acrimonious responses from minority group members and their supporters, who charge the researchers with contributing to racism and discrimination.

Advocates for the mentally ill have been just as disturbed by evidence for genetic influence on schizophrenia. By 1935, researchers already had produced convincing evidence linking schizophrenia to genetic endowment. After the Nazis shocked the world with their brutal version of eugenics, attempting to exterminate the mentally ill to eradicate their disease, researchers were discouraged from further inquiry into the genetic roots of mental illness. By the 1960s, adoption agencies were withholding information about family history of schizophrenia on the grounds that schizophrenia was so totally the result of environmental conditions that information about a child's relatives could only cause unwarranted prejudice on the part of prospective adoptive parents. As one might imagine, there were tragic consequences for some adoptive families of that policy bred of politically inspired willful ignorance.

Minority groups and civil rights advocates have also opposed the use of aptitude and achievement tests in schools and workplaces on the grounds that they are biased against minority group members. Linda Gottfredson, of the University of Delaware, was the target of strong protests against her research when she reported evidence of a relationship between IQ scores and job performance.

Camilla Benbow, of the University of Iowa, has experienced a similar response from feminists to her research showing men to be more gifted in mathematics than women. Feminists have also attacked researchers such as Jay Belsky of the Pennsylvania State University for reporting research showing harmful effects of extensive use of day care for very young children. In both cases, the findings of the disputed research were perceived by feminists as likely to cause harm to women and their political interests.

Conservative political groups have been just as outspoken and disruptive in their opposition to research that threatens their interests. Surveys of adult and teenage sexual practices have been attacked since the latter days of Alfred Kinsey's research program in the 1950s. More recently, public health problems such as the AIDS epidemic and social problems such as high teenage pregnancy rates have motivated government agencies and researchers to obtain up-to-date survey data.

Researchers Harris Rubin of Southern Illinois University and J. Richard Udry of the University of North Carolina have faced stiff opposition from conservative religious groups who argue that documenting sexual practices they believe to be immoral is tantamount to endorsing them. Lobbying by the Family Research Council and the actions of their conservative allies in Congress have succeeded in delaying or eliminating funding for nationwide surveys that are too costly to be carried out otherwise, at least with samples large enough to provide valid population estimates. Despite pressing public health needs, those lobbying efforts have in some cases delayed, compromised, or even stopped the research.

Conservative groups also have lined up against researchers attempting to conduct surveys of drug use in the public schools. Despite the interest of the U.S. Public Health Service in acquiring information it needs to plan and improve services to victims of drug abuse and related diseases, lobbyists and conservative members of Congress almost succeeded in passing legislation that would have prohibited altogether federal funding of school surveys of sensitive behaviors.

In addition to their opposition to specific research studies and topics that offend their personal beliefs, conservative lobbying groups and sympathetic members of Congress recently have made attempts to end all government funding for research in psychology and the other social sciences. Over the years, advances in the social sciences, along with growing recognition of their potential contributions to solving societal problems, have resulted in increased prominence of social sciences within the government research establishment. These trends led eventually to the creation of a separate directorate or department of Social, Behavioral, and Economic Sciences (SBE) within the National Science Foundation (NSF).

With the election of Ronald Reagan as president in 1980 and the increasing strength of conservative forces in Congress, repeated attempts were made to eliminate not only the SBE but all social science research funding at the NSF and other government agencies. Some of those involved stated a belief that the natural sciences were the only valid approach to understanding health and other problems. Many observers believe that a more fundamental opposition to liberal policies, such as fighting racism and poverty, that social science research often supports was the real reason behind those efforts.

Some of the most violent opposition to psychological research has come from groups whose political agendas are neither liberal nor conservative, at least not in the usual sense. Animal rights groups such as People for the Ethical Treatment of Animals (PETA) and the Animal Liberation Front (ALF) have protested the work of, vandalized the laboratories of, and threatened the lives of researchers who study nonhuman subjects.

Edward Taub's research focused on retraining monkeys to control arm movements by substituting different nerves for nerves that were severed. It has led to the development of techniques for the successful rehabilitation of human stroke victims. PETA infiltrated his lab and misrepresented evidence stolen from it to cause bogus criminal charges to be brought against him (he was exonerated of all but one trivial charge). Ronald Wood of New York University suffered through campus demonstrations and defamation of his character, based on similar distortions of his research, which involved monkeys inhaling aerosol drugs. The research was shut down temporarily and damaged irreparably as a result before an investigation could clear him of any wrongdoing.

Proponents of needle exchange programs for intravenous drug users attacked researcher Mary Utne O'Brien of the University of Chicago. She found that a program in Chicago did not reduce needle sharing and may even have caused increased drug use by allowing addicts to sell excess needles for money to buy drugs. When she resisted pressure from her university to stop reporting her research data, she was forced to turn back a large research grant. Eventually, she was fired from her job.

Mark and Linda Sobell found in their research that problem drinkers fared better if trained to control their drinking rather than to abstain from alcohol completely. This outraged medical researchers and members of Alcoholics Anonymous who believe that recovery from alcoholism is possible only by total abstinence. The Sobells were ostracized by the alcoholism research community and accused of fraud by their detractors. After considerable damage had been done to their scientific careers, several independent investigations of the Sobells' research failed to uncover any evidence that they had acted incompetently or unethically.

Scientific Criticism Versus Political Criticism

None of this is to say that scientific research, in psychology or any other discipline, should be immune from criticism. Criticism is the lifeblood of science. Several of the studies described above that were attacked so strongly on political grounds also could be criticized on purely scientific grounds.

In some cases, there is credible evidence to contradict the research results. Good quality day care has been shown in some studies to have positive effects on child development. Twelve-step abstinence programs have been shown to be effective in treating alcoholism. And so on.

In other cases, findings are subject to methodological criticisms. There is evidence that some psychological tests are culturally biased. Minority students who were admitted to California law schools despite failing to achieve high admission test scores performed as well in law school and afterward (passing bar exams, for example) as their white counterparts with higher test scores. In some evaluation studies, needle exchange programs have been credited with reducing the spread of infectious diseases without increasing drug use.

There is a world of difference between attacking science on scientific grounds and attacking science on political grounds. The former aids in the search for truth, while the latter impedes it. Furthermore, debates based in science try to improve research, not to stop it. Scientific disagreements may get contentious, but they rarely involve attempts to destroy a person's work or threats to a person's life.

Fear of the truth has no place in science, or in a society that hopes to solve its social or economic problems successfully. While the "new know-nothings" don't burn churches or riot against immigrants the way the original Know-Nothings did more than a century ago, there is ample reason to fear them if science or society is to be truly free.

Another example of the political heat that research psychologists sometimes face is described by Simon LeVay in the recent book *Queer Science* (1996). Numerous court cases concerning discrimination against gays and lesbians, including some that have been heard by the United States Supreme Court, have hinged to an important extent on a debate about immutability. The central question in that debate is whether homosexuals are "born that way." The answer to that question depends on the interpretation of scientific findings from behavior genetics, neuroscience, endocrinology, and personality psychology.

Researchers in those fields have compared heterosexual and homosexual subjects, including members of nonhuman species that exhibit homosexual behavior naturally or as the result of experimental manipulation. The differences they have found, including differences in brain structure and prenatal exposure to sex hormones, as well the results of twin studies and other evidence of heritability, have led some to conclude that homosexuality is an innate characteristic. Others have challenged that conclusion as an overstatement or even a distortion of the evidence as they have argued for environmental theories.

A scientific finding that homosexuality is a biological legacy rather than a choice or environmental accident has important implications for the law, public policy, and public opinion. According to LeVay (1996), a prominent researcher in the field himself, that makes research which attempts to find the cause of homosexuality inherently both a social and a political enterprise as well as a scientific one. Ever since the debate over the possibility that homosexuality is a fact of nature began in the 1800s in Germany, it has been part and parcel of the social and political struggle over rights for homosexuals.

It is probably no accident that many of the scientists who have searched for evidence of a biological cause have been homosexuals themselves or sympathetic to the cause of homosexual rights, or that many who have attacked their work have been mental health professionals or members of the religious right whose livelihoods or personal beliefs are threatened by such evidence. The former have sometimes been prone to speculation unbecoming of scientists. The latter have opposed incorporating good science into professional practice and public policy. Caught in the middle have been unbiased scientists such as LeVay, as well as gays and lesbians. Their growing pride in their sexual identities and growing stature in the society at large may well turn out to be the most important factor of all, even as the scientific evidence comes closer and closer to settling the debate.

Being socially responsible is obviously much more than a matter of interest or effort. In some cases it takes considerable political skill, at the very least. A social science researcher named Janet Reizenstein Carpman, who participated in the design of a new hospital complex at the University of Michigan in Ann Arbor, provides an instructive example. Her research suggested ways to help visitors and patients find their way around, to design more comfortable patient rooms and visitor areas, and to solve other design problems. She succeeded in influencing the decisions made by administrators and architects only to the extent that she was able to forge political alliances with nurses, doctors, and other groups within the hospital. Competing interests in costs, aesthetics, and professional status often stood in the way of her findings reaching the patients and visitors to whom she wanted to give them.

● A VERY BRIEF CONCLUSION

Research is very serious business. It is hard work, often both mentally and physically. It is important to progress both in science and in civilization, and it is important to the lives of ordinary people. Research entails an awesome responsibility on the part of the researcher, to those with whom he or she collaborates, to the participants in his or her research, to the scientific community, to dedicated practitioners, and to the public.

Research also is a lot of fun. Doing it is fun, from watching the behavior of research participants to solving the intricate intellectual puzzles research presents. The personal relationships among those who do research and those who care about it are an important source of satisfaction in many researchers' lives.

Don't be dissuaded from doing research because it is difficult. You can overcome the difficulties and derive great satisfaction from doing so. To quote a phrase we've all seen and heard so often that it has become a part of our culture, "just do it!"

Review Questions and Exercise

Review Questions

1. What are a researcher's responsibilities to science?

2. What are a researcher's professional responsibilities?

3. What are a researcher's responsibilities to society?

4. In what ways do researchers sometimes fail in the fulfillment of their responsibilities, and what can be done to minimize the likelihood of such failures?

5. What barriers to scientific progress are put in the way of researchers by their colleagues and by interested parties in the larger society?

Exercise

What do you see as the greatest challenges to a research psychologist? The greatest opportunities? Would you consider a career as a research psychologist? Why or why not?

APPENDIX A

Study Analysis Forms for the 25 Exemplar Studies Introduced in Chapter 2

The Validity Scorecard is one device that can make it easier to learn how to evaluate the validity of research findings. In this appendix, another useful device is introduced—the Study Analysis Form (SAF). Filling it out creates a summary of a research study that is especially helpful for methodological analysis. In fact, although the order of presentation is reversed here, a completed Study Analysis Form would be a good preliminary step toward completing the Validity Scorecard for a particular study.

First, it requires clarification of the research hypothesis, then clarification of the forms in which the hypothesis constructs of cause and effect are operationalized as the independent and dependent variables. Next, it prompts the classification and representation of the research design. It then asks for identification of the statistical methods used to analyze the research data and a statement of the results of those analyses. Finally, it provides the opportunity to consider how the elements specified above answer the key questions, for that particular study, about the validity of the research findings.

In this appendix, you will find 25 completed SAFs, one for each of the exemplar studies that were introduced in Chapter 2 and then referred to repeatedly in subsequent chapters. These examples are intended to serve two functions. First, they can help you to learn more about those exemplar studies. In addition, they can give you a feel for how you can use the SAF in the methodological analysis of other studies reported in the research literature, another way of becoming more proficient in using the concepts presented in the text.

As with the Validity Scorecard introduced in Chapter 7, you can print blank versions of the SAF from the Web site for this book.

STUDY ANALYSIS FORM 1

Study No. **E1**

Seeman, M., & Evans, J. W. (1962). Alienation and learning in a hospital setting. *American Sociological Review*, *27*, 772-783, as reported in Rotter (1966).

Hypothesis: Hospital patients who are internals will acquire more behavior-relevant information regarding their medical conditions than will Externals.

Causal Construct: locus of control (I-E)	**Behavioral Construct:** behavior-relevant information seeking

Variables

    IV: scores on variation of Rotter's I-E Scale; high and low groups split at mean

    DVs: 20-item patient information test of subjects' knowledge about their medical conditions, number of questions asked of nurses and doctors about patients' conditions, patients' satisfaction with the amount of information received (subjective knowledge)

Design: PG1—Static-Group Comparison Design

    G1 X_I O_1

    - - - - - - - -

    G2 X_E O_2

Pairs of males matched for occupational status, education, ward placement

Analysis: *t* tests

Results: $O_1 > O_2$ for each dependent measure

Key Validity Issues

1. Construct Validity: reliability and validity of ad hoc dependent measures
2. Internal Validity: selection/possible group composition differences, including subjective illness experience, length and severity of illness (not reflected in diagnosis), etc.

STUDY ANALYSIS FORM 2

Study No. **E2**

Friedman, M., & Rosenman, R. H. (1959). Association of specific overt behavior pattern with blood and cardiovascular findings. *Journal of the American Medical Association, 96,* 1286-1296.

Hypothesis: Behavior and personality influence cardiovascular health.

Causal Construct: behavior pattern in work	**Behavioral Construct:** coronary artery disease

Variables

IV: Type A personality vs. Type B personality (opposite pattern) vs. unemployed, blind, chronically anxious, and insecure

DV: incidence of "clinical coronary artery disease"

Design: PG1—Static-Group Comparison Design

G_1 X_A O_1

- - - - - - -

G_2 X_B O_2

- - - - - - -

G_3 X_C O_3

X_A = 83 Type A males; X_B = 83 Type B males; X_C = 46 unemployed, blind, chronically anxious, and insecure males

Analysis: descriptive statistics only

Results: $O_1 > O_2 = O_3$

Key Validity Issues

1. Internal Validity: history/extraneous events such as alcohol use, smoking, diet, other factors relevant to coronary artery disease (including possibly some not known to be at this time)
2. Statistical Conclusion Validity: lack of inferential statistical analysis; lack of formal effect size estimates

STUDY ANALYSIS FORM 3

Study No. **E3**
Triplett, N. (1897). The dynamogenic factors in pacemaking and competition. *American Journal of Psychology, 9,* 507-533.

Hypothesis: Competition enhances performance.

Causal Construct: competitive performance setting	**Behavioral Construct:** enhanced task performance

Variables

- **IV:** 1. race format; bicycle races
  2. alone vs. together format; fishing reel task

- **DV:** 1. time/distance; % gain, one race format vs. another
  2. number of "laps" on fishing reel apparatus during allotted time

Design

1. PG1—Static-Group Comparison Design

   G1 X_A O_1 (X_A = racing alone against the clock)

   - - - - - -

   G2 X_P O_2 (X_P = racing with pacemaker)

   - - - - - -

   G3 X_R O   (X_R = true/competitive race)

2. TT1—Equivalent Time Samples Design

   X_A O_{A1} X_T O_{T1} X_A O_{A2} X_T O_{T2} etc.   (subscripts: A = performance alone, T = performance together)

Analysis

1. descriptive statistics only; % gain   2. descriptive statistics only

Results

1. $O_3 > O_2 > O_1$ 2. $O_T > O_A$

Key Validity Issues

1. Internal Validity: selection/group composition differences in skill, training; history/extraneous events such as crowd reaction
2. External Validity: generalization to other tasks, settings; feedback *re* performance, individual and comparative; reactive arrangements and construct validity (perceived purpose of alternating alone and together arrangements; cf. use of multiple-treatment designs with human subjects)
3. Statistical Conclusion Validity: lack of inferential statistical analysis

STUDY ANALYSIS FORM 4

Study No. **E4**

Aserinsky, E., & Kleitman, N. (1953). Regularly occurring periods of eye mobility and concomitant phenomena during sleep. *Science, 118*, 273-274.

Hypothesis: REM sleep is associated with dreaming.

Causal Construct: REM sleep	**Behavioral Construct:** dreaming

---

Variables

    IV: REM vs. NREM sleep

    DV: frequencies of reports of no dream, feeling of having dreamed without specific recall,
detailed report of dream

Design: TT1—Equivalent Time Samples Design

    $X_R O_{R1}$ $X_{NR} O_{NR1}$ $X_R O_{R2}$ $X_{NR} O_{NR2}$ etc.   (subscripts: R = REM sleep, NR = non-REM sleep)

Analysis: chi-squared; REM vs. NREM, incidence of three different kinds of dream report

---

Results: "the ability to recall dreams is significantly associated with the presence of the eye
movements noted"; chi-squared probability < .01

Key Validity Issues: none?

STUDY ANALYSIS FORM 5

Study No. **E5**

Broverman, I. K., Vogel, S. R., Broverman, D. M., Clarkson, F. E., & Rosenkrantz, P. S. (1972). Sex-role stereotypes: A current appraisal. *Journal of Social Issues, 28*(2), 59-78.

Hypothesis: People hold stereotypic beliefs about the attributes and behaviors of men and women.

Causal Construct: male or female target person

Behavioral Construct: stereotypic trait and behavior attributions

Variables

    IV: adult man, adult woman, self

    DV: list of 122 characteristics nominated by undergraduate psychology students as differing between men and women, rated on bipolar 60-point scales

Design: TT1—Equivalent Time Samples Design

    $X_M O_M \quad X_W O_W \quad X_S O_S$ (subscripts: M = adult man, W = adult woman, S = self)

Analysis: *t* tests between masculinity response (average response to adult male instruction) and femininity response; 75% agreement on which pole more descriptive (75% of responses on one side of midpoint of scale)

Results: 41 stereotypic items, grouped afterward into "agency" and "communion" subgroups

Key Validity Issues

1. Construct Validity: reactive arrangements; demand characteristics/stereotypic responses are suggested by scales and instructions (vs. personal beliefs?)
2. External Validity: possible changes in gender roles over the past quarter century or so

STUDY ANALYSIS FORM 6

Study No. **E6**

Clark, K. B., & Clark, M. K. (1940). Skin color as a factor in racial identification of Negro preschool children. *Journal of Social Psychology, 11*, 159-169.

Hypothesis: African American children have measurable racial identification and racial preference.

Causal Construct: racism in American society

Behavioral Construct: racial identification and preference of African American children

Variables

IVs: black vs. white dolls; northern and southern subjects; age groups 2 through 7 years; light, medium, and dark skin groups

DVs: answers to 8 interview questions *re* dolls: like best, is nice, looks bad, is nice color, looks like white child, looks like colored child, looks like Negro child, looks like you

Design: TT2—Equivalent Materials Samples Design

$$MaX_BO_{B1} \quad MbX_WO_{W1} \quad McX_BO_{B2} \quad MdX_WO_{W2} \quad \text{(subscripts: B = black, W = white)}$$

Analysis: descriptive statistics (%'s); references to significance tests, but no tests reported

Results: majority of sample, across northern and southern, age, and skin color groups, made accurate identifications of race of doll and expressed preference for white over black dolls

Key Validity Issues
1. Construct Validity: reactive arrangements; experimenter expectancy effects (no practical way of keeping experimenters blind to hypothesis)
2. Statistical Conclusion Validity: lack of inferential statistical analysis

STUDY ANALYSIS FORM 7

Study No. **E7**

Darley, J. M., & Latané, B. (1968). Bystander intervention in emergencies: Diffusion of responsibility. *Journal of Personality and Social Psychology, 8*, 377-383.

Hypothesis: Diffusion of responsibility inhibits helping behavior in emergencies.

Causal Construct: presence of other observers/diffusion of responsibility	**Behavioral Construct:** readiness to help

Variables

IV: number of other bystanders; 0 (only subject and victim), 1 (subject, victim, and one other bystander), or 4 (6 individuals in total)

DV: speed of reporting (6-minute time limit)

Design: TG2—Posttest-Only Control Group Design

G1 R X_2 O_2
G2 R X_3 O_3
G3 R X_6 O_6

(subscript = size of group; subject plus victim plus other bystanders, if any)

Analysis: ANOVA; group size

Results: *F* significant; $O_2 = O_3 > O_6$

Key Validity Issues
1. External Validity: representativeness of research setting, ecological validity vs. Kitty Genovese case (danger perceived by subjects, difficult of helping, ambiguity of events, access to other bystanders' responses)
2. Statistical Conclusion Validity: no analysis of latency for first offer of help (average latency of five helpers less relevant than latency for first response)

STUDY ANALYSIS FORM 8

Study No. **E8**

Ceci, S. J., Loftus, E. F., Leichtman, M. D., & Bruck, M. (1994). The possible role of source misattributions in the creation of false beliefs among preschoolers. *International Journal of Experimental Hypnosis, 42*, 304-320.

Hypothesis: Source misattribution is a factor in children's false beliefs about having experienced fictitious events

---

Causal Construct: source misattribution	**Behavioral Construct:** false beliefs

---

Variables

IVs: age, event type (from parent interviews: positive participant = PP, negative participant = NP, neutral participant = NEP, neutral nonparticipant = NENP)

DV: assent to fictional event during first and last (12th) session/interview

---

Design: 2 × 4 × 2: age × events × time

hybrid; one-group pretest-posttest, nonequivalent control group, multiple time series

---

Analysis: ANCOVA (a variation on ANOVA) with initial false assents as covariate

---

Results: younger children had more false assents; neutral nonparticipant events highest in false assents, negative participant events lowest; increase in false assents over sessions

---

Key Validity Issue

Construct Validity: forming picture in head procedure?

STUDY ANALYSIS FORM 9

Study No. **E9**

Milgram, S. (1974). *Obedience to authority*. New York: Harper & Row.

Hypothesis: System of authority elicits obedience, overriding individual's moral principles.

Causal Construct: authority	**Behavioral Construct:** obedience

Variables:

    IV: experimenter/task requirements

    DV: shock level reached by subject

Design: PG1—Static-Group Comparison Design (replicated with various groups [student, non-student, female], procedures [distance between subject and experimenter, distance between subject and victim, presence of disobedient model, etc.])

    G1 X O_1

    - - - - - - -

    G2 O_2 (assumed or predicted by experts, subjects)

Or:

    PT1—One-Shot Case Study

    X O

Analysis: descriptive statistics; percentages reaching various shock levels

Results: high level of obedience (approximately 2/3 of subjects followed experimenter's orders to the end)

Key Validity Issues

1. Construct Validity: reactive arrangements/demand characteristics; perception of setting as safe under control of experimenter (*in loco parentis* status of university, research lab)
2. Statistical Conclusion Validity: lack of inferential statistical analysis (formal comparison between level of shock administered by research participants to level without orders from authority)

STUDY ANALYSIS FORM 10

Study No. **E10**

MacRae, J. R., Scoles, M. I., & Siegel, S. (1987). The contribution of Pavlovian conditioning to drug tolerance and dependence. *British Journal of Addiction, 82*, 371-380.

Hypothesis: Pavlovian conditioning is responsible for the tolerance that is observed in users of morphine.

Causal Construct: Pavlovian conditioning	**Behavioral Construct:** morphine tolerance

---

Variables

IV: association of injection sensations with morphine administration, in the presence of distinct contextual stimuli

DV: pain tolerance, shown in the latency of the paw-lick response to heat

---

Design: TT1—Equivalent Time Samples Design

$X_1O_1 \quad X_0O_2 \quad X_1O_3 \quad X_0O_4$ etc.

Analysis: *t* test for paw-lick latencies

Results: latencies significantly shorter (less analgesic effect of the drug) following fourth administration of standard dose than following first administration

---

Key Validity Issues

External Validity: generalization from rats to humans, and from morphine to other opiates

STUDY ANALYSIS FORM 11

Study No. **E11**
Festinger, L., Riecken, H., & Schachter, S. (1956). *When prophecy fails.* Minneapolis:
University of Minnesota Press.

Hypothesis: The disconfirmation of a doomsday cult's members' expectancies will arouse cognitive dissonance, which will lead to attempts at dissonance reduction that will depend on tactics available to the members.

Causal Construct: disconfirmation of expectancy	**Behavioral Construct:** cognitive dissonance and dissonance-reducing behaviors

Variables

    IV: disconfirmation of expectancy that the world would end

    DVs: variety of dissonance-reducing tactics

Design: PG1—Static-Group Comparison Design

    G1 X_L O_1
    G2 X_C O_2

(subscripts: L = Lake City, where group of believers experienced disconfirmation together; C = Collegeville, where believers separated from the group experienced disconfirmation separately)

Analysis: qualitative description of actions of individual cult members; no numbers or statistics

Results: as predicted, the members at Lake City engaged in a variety of dissonance-reducing behaviors that amounted to a strengthening of their original beliefs, including seeking publicity to proselytize new members (abandoning previous secrecy) and expressing increased confidence in their beliefs; the members in Collegeville became less committed to their original beliefs, some abandoning them altogether

Key Validity Issues
1. External Validity: generalizability beyond the atypical individuals who would join a doomsday cult; possible reactivity due to the presence of experimenter-observers; selection/group composition differences between those members who made a point of being with the group at the critical moment and those who were apart from it
2. Construct Validity: use of qualitative measurement
3. Statistical Conclusion Validity: lack of inferential statistical analysis

STUDY ANALYSIS FORM 12

Study No. **E12**

Harlow, H. F. (1958). The nature of love. *American Psychologist, 13,* 673-685.

Hypothesis: The love/affectional responses of an infant toward a mother are innate.

Causal Construct: innate need for contact comfort	**Behavioral Construct:** infant's love for mother

Variables

> **IV:** infant rhesus monkey fed by wire or cloth surrogate mother

> **DV:** time spent on wire and cloth surrogate mothers

Design: TG2—Posttest-Only Control Group Design

> G1 R X_W O_1
> G2 R X_C O_2

> (subscripts: W = fed by wire surrogate mother, C = fed by cloth surrogate mother)

Analysis: descriptive statistics

Results: both groups spent more time on cloth than wire surrogate mother (negative results)

Key Validity Issues

1. External Validity: generalizability to other species, especially human
2. Construct Validity: operationalization of love as clinging to surrogate mother
3. Statistical Conclusion Validity: lack of inferential statistical analysis to rule out sampling error

STUDY ANALYSIS FORM 13

Study No. **E13**
Cartwright, R. D. (1974). The influence of a conscious wish on dreams: A methodological study of dream meaning and function. *Journal of Abnormal Psychology, 83,* 387-393.

Hypothesis: Subjects instructed while awake to change a target trait (identified as discrepant from desired trait by Q-sort) will dream about that trait.

Causal Construct: conscious wish	**Behavioral Construct:** dream content

Variables

  IV: Q-sort–based induction prior to sleep

  DV: ratings of dream content (subjects woken during REM sleep) for target trait vs. 2 other "control" traits

Design: PT1—One-Shot Case Study

  X   O   (X = induction; O = rated dream content for induced trait)

Analysis: sign test; number of subjects with evidence of incorporation of target trait into dream vs. control trait 1 vs. control trait 2

Results: significant effect in predicted direction

Key Validity Issue
Construct Validity: reactive arrangements/demand characteristics; dream content reported vulnerable to manipulation by subjects (?)

STUDY ANALYSIS FORM 14

Study No. **E14**

Dement, W. (1960). The effect of dream deprivation. *Science, 131*, 1705-1707.

Hypothesis: The opportunity to dream is necessary.

Causal Construct: dream (REM sleep) deprivation	**Behavioral Construct:** disruption of psychological and/or physical well-being

Variables

    IV: deprivation of REM sleep

    DV: REM sleep after deprivation

Design: PT2—One-Group Pretest-Posttest Design

    O_B X_{RD} O_{PD}

(subscripts: B =baseline level of REM, RD = REM deprivation, PD = post-deprivation level 1 of REM)

Analysis: Wilcoxon test; number of subjects showing increase vs. no increase

Results: $O_{PD} > O_B$ (significantly more subjects showed increase in REM post-deprivation than did not; a.k.a. REM rebound)

Key Validity Issues

1. external validity: generalizability from male subjects
2. internal validity: control minimizes threats to internal validity
3. construct validity: dependent measures obviate threats from reactive arrangements; does REM rebound indicate disruption of psychological or physical well-being as consequence of REM deprivation?

STUDY ANALYSIS FORM 15

Study No. **E15**
Rosenthal, R., & Jacobson, L. (1966). Teachers' expectancies: Determinants of pupils' IQ
gains. *Psychological Reports, 19,* 115-118.

Hypothesis: Experimenter expectancy effects will generalize to teacher-pupil relationships/
interactions.

Causal Construct: expectancies for student performance	**Behavioral Construct:** student performance

Variables

IV: random identification of pupils as about to bloom (vs. not)

DV: IQ scores

Design: TG1—Pretest-Posttest Control Group Design (separate replications for grades 1 to 6)

G1   R O_{PR1} X O_{PO1}
G2   R O_{PR2} O_{PO2}

(subscripts: PR = pretest, PO = posttest)

Analysis: *t* tests for differences in gain (bloomers vs. nonbloomers), pretest to posttest
(8 months later)

Results: $(O_{PO1} - O_{PR1}) > (O_{PO2} - O_{PR2})$; bloomers showed greater gains in IQ

Key Validity Issues
1. Construct Validity: reactive arrangements or normal classroom routine?
2. External Validity: generalizability across age; significant differences for grades 1 and 2 and
   overall, but not for grades 3, 4, 5, or 6.

STUDY ANALYSIS FORM 16

Study No. **E16**

Zajonc, R. B., & Markus, G. B. (1975). Birth order and intellectual development. *Psychological Review, 82,* 74-88.

Hypothesis: The confluence of birth order and family size influences intelligence.

Causal Construct: confluence model	**Behavioral Construct:** intelligence

Variables

    IVs: family size, birth order, last born vs. others

    DV: Raven Progressive Matrices scores (for 386,114 Dutch males, obtained at age 19 between 1963 and 1966)

Design

1. PG1—Static-Group Comparison Design

    G1 X O

    - - - - - - - -

    G2 X O

    - - - - - - - -

    G3 X O

    - - - - - - - -

    etc.

    (X = family structure variable, O = IQ score)

2. PG2—Correlational Design (multiple correlation analysis)

Analysis: tests for individual variables and description of joint relationships between family structure variables and intelligence in equation/model; % variance accounted for

Results: a powerful model of the effects of birth order and family size on intelligence, based on the data set

Key Validity Issues

Internal Validity: group composition effects? Socioeconomic factors controlled statistically, but were there other differences among intact groups?

STUDY ANALYSIS FORM 17

Study No. **E17**

Cherulnik, P. D., Way, J. H., Ames, S., & Hutto, D. B. (1981). Impressions of high and low Machiavellian men. *Journal of Personality, 49*, 388-400.

Hypothesis: High and low Machiavellian men will be identified accurately as such and will be attributed traits consistent with their high vs. low Mach status.

Causal Construct: appearance of high and low Machs

Behavioral Construct: judgments of Mach status, attribution of relevant traits

Variables

IV: photos and videotape interview excerpts for 10 high Mach and 8 low Mach men, based on extreme scores on Mach V Scale

DV: identification judgments (high or low), frequency of attribution of 24 relevant traits

Design: TG2—Equivalent Materials Samples Design

$M_a X_H O_1$ $M_b X_L O_2$ $M_c X_H O_3$ $M_d X_L O_4$ etc.

(subscripts: a through d = individual target photos or videotape excerpts; H = high Mach, L = low Mach)

Analysis: z tests for significance of differences between proportions (proportion identifications correct vs. chance/.50; proportion attributions to high Mach vs. low Mach targets, adjusted for number of each)

Results: significant accuracy from photos and tape excerpts, significant attribution patterns in predicted direction for most traits

Key Validity Issues:

External Validity: representativeness of targets (research context) and judges (sample)

STUDY ANALYSIS FORM 18

Study No. **E18**
Seligman, M.E.P., & Maier, S. F. (1967). Failure to escape traumatic shock. *Journal of Experimental Psychology, 74,* 1-9.

Hypothesis: Exposure to inescapable shock impairs normal acquisition of escape/avoidance behavior in a shuttle box.

Causal Construct: experiencing helplessness	**Behavioral Construct:** learned helplessness

Variables

    IV: exposure to inescapable shock vs. access to panel-pressing response to escape (yoked pairs; panel pressing terminated shock for both animals)

    DV: escape acquisition in shuttle box, as mean latency of response

Design: TG2—Posttest-Only Control Group Design

    G1 R X_E O_1
    G2 R X_I O_2

    (subscripts: E = escapable shock, I = inescapable shock)

Analysis: sign test; between-pairs comparison (was X_I animal slower to escape?)

Results: $O_1 > O_2$

Key Validity Issues
External Validity: generalizability from learned helplessness in dogs to depression in humans

STUDY ANALYSIS FORM 19

Study No. **E19**
Calhoun, J. (1962). Population density and social pathology. *Scientific American, 206,*
139-148.

Hypothesis: When a population of laboratory rats is allowed to increase in a confined space, the rats will develop abnormal behavior patterns that threaten the extinction of the population.

Causal Construct: high population density	**Behavioral Construct:** social pathology

Variables

   IV: population density (number of animals, given that area is fixed)

   DVs: miscarriage, maternal neglect, male sexual deviance, cannibalism, overactivity, withdrawal, behavioral sink

Design: PT1—One-Shot Case Study (6 replications)

   X   O (X = population growth/density increase; O = social behaviors)

Analysis: qualitative observations

Results: as predicted, social pathology/disruption of normal social instincts accompanied increase in population density

Key Validity Issues
1. External Validity: nonrepresentativeness of research setting (high-rise nesting structures, limited-access feeders)
2. Internal Validity: history/extraneous events accompanying population density increase, such as illness
3. Statistical Conclusion Validity: lack of statistical analysis of any kind

STUDY ANALYSIS FORM 20

Study No. **E20**

Pavlov, I. P. (1927). *Conditioned reflexes*. London: Oxford University Press.

Hypothesis: The association of a conditioned stimulus with a "direct" stimulus results in the establishment of a conditioned reflex.

Causal Construct: association between stimuli	**Behavioral Construct:** establishment of conditioned reflex

Variables

 IV: pair CS (tone) with US (food)

 DV: CR, salivation to tone, measured for magnitude as number of drops of saliva

Design: TT1—Equivalent Time Samples Design

 $X_1O_1 \quad X_0O_2 \quad X_1O_3 \quad X_0O_4$ etc.

 (subscripts: 1 = CS paired with US, 0 = CS not paired with US/extinction)

Analysis: descriptive statistics; numbers of drops of saliva observed

Results: evidence of (Pavlovian) conditioning

Key Validity Issues

1. External Validity: generalizability to other species, responses
2. Statistical Conclusion Validity: lack of inferential statistical analysis

STUDY ANALYSIS FORM 21

Study No. **E21**
Gazzaniga, M. S. (1967). The split brain in man. *Scientific American, 217* (2), 24-29.

Hypothesis: There are differences in brain function between the left and right cerebral hemispheres.

Causal Construct: anatomical division of cerebral cortex into left and right hemispheres

Behavioral Construct: cognition

Variables

    IV: information to left or right cerebral hemisphere only

    DVs: linguistic responses, tactile identification of objects and other nonverbal responses

Design: TT1—Equivalent Time Samples Design

$$X_L O_1 \quad X_R O_2 \quad X_L O_3 \quad X_R O_4 \text{ etc.}$$

Analysis: descriptive statistics only

Results: language function centered in left hemisphere, spatial in right

Key Validity Issues
1. External Validity: generalizability to non-epileptic individuals (epilepsy is a brain abnormality) and to individuals with intact cerebral cortex vs. those who have undergone callectomy
2. Internal Validity: history/extraneous events experienced by patients with severe epilepsy, including drugs taken

STUDY ANALYSIS FORM 22

Study No. **E22**

Rosenzweig, M. R., Bennett, E. L., & Diamond, M. C. (1972). Brain changes in response to experience. *Scientific American, 226*(2), 22-29.

Hypothesis: Cognitive experience produces changes in the brain.

Causal Construct: training/intellectual activity	**Behavioral Construct:** brain development

Variables

IV: standard laboratory cage environment vs. enriched environment (several rats in larger cage, with rotating set of playthings)

DVs: weight of cerebral cortex, thickness of cortex, AChE activity, ChE activity, number of glial cells

Design: TG2—Posttest-Only Control Group Design

$$G1 \quad R \quad X_S \quad O_1$$
$$G2 \quad R \quad X_E \quad O_2$$

(subscripts: S = standard lab environment, E = enriched environment)

Analysis: bar graphs of differences on individual dependent measures

Results: specific hypothesized differences found that indicate greater brain development in enriched environments

Key Validity Issues

1. External Validity: generalizability from rats to humans (rat's cerebral cortex easier to separate from rest of brain); littermates randomly assigned to two cage conditions; blind autopsy
2. Statistical Conclusion Validity: lack of inferential statistical analysis to rule out sampling error

STUDY ANALYSIS FORM 23

Study No. **E23**

Haier, R. J., Siegel, B., Tang, C., Abel, L., & Buchsbaum, M. S. (1992). Intelligence and changes in regional glucose metabolic rate following learning. *Intelligence, 16,* 415-426.

Hypothesis: The greater the level of intelligence, the lower the brain glucose metabolic rate (GMR).

Causal Construct: intelligence	**Behavioral Construct:** brain efficiency

Variables

   IVs: Raven's Advanced Progressive Matrices, WAIS

   DV: GMR following learning of Tetris computer game

Design: PG2—Correlational Design

   $r_{IQ \times GMR}$

Analysis: partial correlation; intelligence vs. GMR change, controlling for days of practice

Results: significant correlation between magnitude of GMR change (decrease) and intelligence test scores in areas of brain that are changed with learning

Key Validity Issues

External Validity: generalization from sample of 8 participants

STUDY ANALYSIS FORM 24

Study No. **E24**

Smith, M. L., & Glass, G. V. (1977). Meta-analysis of psychotherapy outcome studies. *American Psychologist, 32*, 752-760.

Hypothesis: Psychotherapy is effective.

Causal Construct: psychotherapy	**Behavioral Construct:** improvement in psychopathology

---

Variables

IVs: therapy type and duration, therapist and client characteristics, study design, etc.

DV: effect size = mean difference between treated and control subjects divided by standard deviation of control group (many outcome variables, including self-esteem, anxiety, school achievement, etc.)

Design: many different designs, including pre-experimental (PT2—One-Group Pretest-Posttest Design and PG1—Static-Group Comparison Design), experimental (TG1 and TG2; waiting-list control), and quasi-experimental (QG1—Nonequivalent Control Group Design)

Analysis: meta-analysis

Results: overall, .68 standard deviation superiority of treated group over controls (average treated client better off than 75% of untreated, vs. 50% if treatment had no effect)

Key Validity Issues

External Validity: approximately 400 studies reviewed; very strong example of Brunswik's representative research design, and of the implementation Cronbach's UTOS schema (subjects, therapies/independent variables, outcome measures/dependent variables, settings); a strength of meta-analytic research generally

STUDY ANALYSIS FORM 25

Study No. **E25**

Frazier, F. W. (1985). *A postoccupancy evaluation of Contra Costa County's Main Detention Facility: An analysis of the first new-generation, modular, direct supervision county jail.* Unpublished doctoral dissertation, Golden Gate University, San Francisco.

Hypothesis: Modular, direct supervision design (a constitutional jail) reduces violence.

Causal Construct: modular direct supervision jail design

Behavioral Construct: violence

Variables

   IV: modular direct supervision design vs. traditional remote supervision design (cells along corridors)

   DVs: incidence of violence against inmates and corrections officers, interview-based judgments of safety by both

---

Design: PG1—Static-Group Comparison Design

   G1 X_M O_1

   - - - - - - - - -

   G2 X_R O_2

(subscripts: M = modular direct supervision design, R = remote supervision/traditional design)

Analysis: descriptive statistics

Results: CCCMDF received high marks for safety and satisfaction

---

Key Validity Issues
1. External Validity: generalizability to more diverse inmate population, less professional corrections staff
2. Internal Validity: history/extraneous influences including staff performance (training); selection/group composition differences, especially absence of more violent, intractable inmates from CCCMDF population (or are staff and inmate differences actually features of the modular direct-supervision design?)
3. Statistical Conclusion Validity: lack of appropriate statistical analysis

APPENDIX B
GLOSSARY

Abstract (11) A summary of a research article that appears at the beginning of the article and in listings of the research literature, either in print or electronic form; allows prospective readers to estimate in advance the value to them of reading the article.

Accretion measures (9) Unobtrusive measures based on evidence of the research participants' behavior having left additions to the environment, such as litter left after a political rally or crack vials in areas of heavy drug trafficking.

Ad hoc self-report measures (9) Behavioral measures devised for a particular research study that are provided directly by research participants on a variety of rating forms and questionnaires.

Additive relationship (5, 8) A relationship between two independent variables such that both independently affect the behavior being studied; that is, the effect of each one is constant across levels of the other.

Alternative explanation (5) An explanation for the observed differences among treatment groups (or the observed relationship between the independent and dependent variables) other than the influence of the treatments (or independent variable).

Analysis of variance (ANOVA) (8, 10) A statistical method used to draw inferences about possible differences among three or more treatment groups in scores on a dependent measure.

Archival data (4, 9) Behavioral measures that are extracted from pre-existing records for use as data in research (see archives).

Archives (9) Records kept by private organizations or government agencies that can be used as sources of research data.

Artifacts (1, 4) Unintended influences on the properties of an independent or dependent variable resulting from the reactivity of the research setting.

Behavioral construct (1)   The element in a research hypothesis that identifies the behavior to be studied.

Behavioral observation (9)   A method of data collection in which the behavior of research participants is counted or classified either directly or through the use of scientific instruments.

Between-subjects designs (5)   Research designs in which different groups of participants are compared for their responses to different treatments. *See* **comparisons over time**.

Bias (3)   Systematic errors of measurement that cause the observed score to systematically misrepresent the property being measured.

Bivariate distribution (8, 10)   A set of data consisting of a pair of measures for each of a sample of units (often the basis for calculating a correlation coefficient).

Bogus pipeline (9)   A method of obtaining truthful self-reports of sensitive behaviors that is based on deceiving research participants into believing that a polygraph-like device can reveal the truthfulness of their responses.

Canonical analysis (CA) (8)   A form of multiple correlation analysis (MCA) that determines the effects of multiple predictor variables on multiple criterion variables by establishing combinations of both, known as variates, that allow the calculation of a single canonical coefficient (R_c) that estimates the overall degree of relationship among the original set of predictor and criterion variables.

Canonical coefficient (R_c) (8)   *See* **canonical analysis**.

Causal construct (1)   The element in a research hypothesis that identifies a possible cause of the behavior being studied.

Causal inference (1, 5)   A judgment that there is a causal relationship between the independent and dependent variables in a research study.

Central tendency (10)   A statistical description of the middle or center of a group or distribution of scores.

Central tendency bias (3)   A stable tendency for a particular individual to avoid extreme evaluations when using rating scales.

Cluster analysis (8)   A form of multiple correlation analysis (MCA) that uses multiple independent variables to separate a sample of units into smaller groups or clusters.

Coefficient of determination (8)   A statistic that estimates the proportion of variance in one variable accounted for by another; the square of the correlation coefficient calculated for the two variables.

Coefficient of stability (3)   The correlation coefficient used to evaluate reliability with the test-retest method (via the correlation between test score and retest score).

Comparison among groups (1, 5)   A type of research design specifying comparison of two or more groups of participants exposed to varied treatments representing the independent variable.

Comparison over time (1, 5)   A type of research design specifying comparison of two or more occasions when a single group of participants is exposed to varied treatments representing the independent variable.

Conceptual priming (4)   A method of instilling a cognitive bias or predisposition through the presentation of subtle cues, without the target's conscious awareness.

Conceptual validity (1, 2)   The degree to which the test of a particular research hypothesis promises to make a valuable addition to existing knowledge about the behavior in question.

Concurrent validity (3)   A form of criterion-related validity in which the measurement operation being evaluated is carried out simultaneously with the acquisition of criterion measures.

Confounded (4)   The condition in which the effects of two or more potential causes of a behavior cannot be separated.

Confounding (1, 4)   A lack of separability among multiple potential causes of the behavior being studied.

Confounds (1)   The combinations of intended variables and unintended influences whose effects on the treatments or the behavior being studied cannot be separated.

Construct validity (1, 3, 7)   The overall quality of the measurement operations used to transform the constructs in a research hypothesis into the variables in a research study.

Constructs (1, 2, 4)   The causal and behavioral factors whose relationship is the subject of a research hypothesis.

Content validity (3, 4)   The extent to which a measurement instrument assesses all aspects of the domain of the construct being measured (*see* **domain**).

Control (6)   Any decision by a researcher about research design that is intended to lessen a threat to internal validity (i.e., make more certain a causal inference drawn from the research results).

Correlation coefficient (3, 8, 10)   A statistic that summarizes the direction and strength of the relationship between two variables.

Criterion variable (8)   One variable in a correlational relationship that is predicted by the other (the "predictor variable").

Criterion-related validity (3)   The extent to which the measurement of a property is related to other measurements that are tied to it by theory (i.e., criteria).

Cumulative histogram (10)   A graphic presentation of a group of data as bars of various heights showing the cumulative frequencies of the scores (*see* **histogram**).

Curvilinear relationship (8)   When the direction of the relationship between two variables (i.e., direct, inverse, or no relationship) changes with the values of the variables; indicated by a scatterplot in which the points seem to cluster around a curved line, rather than having the straight-line appearance of a linear relationship (*see* **direct relationship, inverse relationship, scatterplot**).

Data (1, 9)   The observations or measurements on which the test of a research hypothesis is based.

Data collection (1, 9)   The process by which observations of behavior are made.

Database (9)   A collection of stored measurements that might be useful in testing a research hypothesis.

Debriefing (4, 11)   A period of discussion between researcher and research participant after the latter's participation in the study has been completed, for the purpose of uncovering any suspicions or working hypotheses on the part of participants that might constitute artifacts, and to explain the purpose of the research to the participants and detect any deleterious effects of participation that would need to be addressed.

Demand characteristics (1, 4, 7)   Stimuli in a research study that suggest to participants the nature of the hypothesis being tested.

Dependent variable (1, 3)   The measurable form of the behavioral construct in a research hypothesis.

Descriptive statistics (1, 10)   Mathematical procedures that are used to summarize the data collected in a research study.

Diary (9)   A method of data collection in which research participants keep records of their daily activities, either in their entirety or for randomly sampled time periods that are sometimes signaled remotely by electronic devices.

Direct relationship (8)   When two variables are related in such a way that as the value of one increases, the value of the other increases, as indicated by a positive correlation coefficient.

Discriminant function analysis (8)   A form of multiple correlation analysis (MCA) in which two or more predictor variables are used to determine in which of a set of categories each case should be placed (i.e., likely to succeed or fail, diagnostic categories, etc.)

Discussion section (1, 11)   The final section of a research article; it considers the conclusions about the research results, including possible limitations, as well as directions for future research.

Domain (3)   The totality of the elements represented by a construct (*see* **content validity**).

Double-blind procedure (4)   The administration of a treatment or placebo without the research participant or researcher being aware of which one is being administered, particularly to avoid placebo effects.

Ecological validity (5)   The ability to generalize research results to settings where the putative cause and the behavior being studied occur in nature.

Empirical method (3)   The use of observation (broadly construed) to answer questions about natural phenomena, including behavior.

Epistemology (3, 11)   A branch of philosophy concerned with how to arrive at an accurate understanding of the natural world.

Equal-interval scales (3)   *See* **interval scales**.

Erosion measures (9)   Unobtrusive measures based on evidence of the research participants' behavior having eroded or worn their environment, such as worn out floor tiles at a popular museum exhibit or a dog-eared textbook that is obviously well used.

Error (of measurement) (3)   The discrepancy between the measurement made of a property of some event and the actual property.

Estimating effect size (10)   A family of statistical methods for estimating the magnitude of treatment effects or of the relationship between the independent and dependent variables from the research results (something null hypothesis significance testing does not do).

Experiment (4)   A form of research design characterized by random assignment of participants to groups or random introduction of treatments across occasions and, consistent with that, the manipulation of the independent variable by the researcher.

Experimental demand (4)   A cue in the research setting that alerts participants to expectations for their behavior. *See* **demand characteristics**.

Experimenter expectancy effects (1, 4, 7)   Communication from researcher to participant (presumed to be unintentional) regarding the behavior that is expected of the latter by the former.

External validity (1, 5, 7)   The extent to which research results can be generalized beyond the specific sample and context of a particular research study (*see* **generalizability**).

Extraneous events (history) (1, 5, 7)   Events other than treatments that can influence the behavior of participants in a research study and can lead to an incorrect inference about the causal relationship between the independent and dependent variables (i.e., a threat to internal validity).

Extraneous variables (1)   Influences on the behavior in a research study that are not intended by the researcher.

Face validity (3)   The extent to which the purpose of a behavioral measurement is clear to an observer.

Factor analysis (8)   A form of multiple correlation analysis (MCA) that uses a matrix of correlations among a set of variables to define subsets of those variables, known as factors, that are both interrelated and unrelated to others of the original set of variables.

Factorial experiments (8)   Studies that evaluate the effects of two or more independent variables, in which each possible combination of treatments is administered to a separate randomly constituted group of participants.

Field (7, 9)   A natural setting where research can be carried out, such as a workplace, school, or public park.

Field study (7)   A research study conducted in a natural setting, generally without participants being aware of it.

Figures (11)   Graphs, diagrams, and drawings that are included in a research article to clarify the method and results.

Frequency distribution (10)   A table that presents a group of data or scores in a way that makes the results of a research study easier to understand.

Generalizability (5, 7)   The extent to which research results can be expected to hold in samples and contexts other than those of the particular study in which they were obtained (*see* **external validity**).

Group composition effects (selection) (1, 5, 7)   Pre-existing differences between the members of the treatment groups in a research study that can influence their behavior and can lead to an incorrect inference about the causal relationship between the independent and dependent variables (a threat to internal validity).

Higher-order interaction (8)   Statistical interaction among three or more independent variables (*see* **interaction**).

Histogram (10)   A graphic representation of a group of data or distribution of scores, as bars of various heights showing the frequencies of the scores on a graph whose axes represent the range of scores and the frequencies with which the scores were obtained, to make the results of a research study easier to understand.

History (1)   *See* **extraneous events**.

Hypothesis (1)   The statement of a possible relationship between causal influence and behavior which forms the basis for a research study.

Inadequate operationalization of the dependent variable (1, 3)   Faulty measurement of the behavioral construct in the research hypothesis that threatens the construct validity of the research findings.

Inadequate operationalization of the independent variable (1, 3)   Faulty measurement of the causal construct of the research hypothesis that threatens the construct validity of the research findings.

Inappropriate use of statistical techniques (1, 10)   The use of methods of statistical analysis that are not appropriate for the research design and thus can lead to an inaccurate judgment about the truth of the research hypothesis (a threat to statistical conclusion validity).

Independent variable (1, 3)   The measurable form of the causal construct in a research hypothesis.

Inferential statistics (1, 10)   Mathematical procedures that are used to determine whether the observed differences among treatment groups or the observed relationship between the independent and dependent variables is consistent enough to hold in other samples drawn from the same population as the participants in the research study.

Informed consent (11)   Agreement in advance to participate in a research study, based on a full disclosure of any available information about the potential risks and benefits of participation.

Institutional Review Board (IRB) (10)   A group entrusted with the responsibility for evaluating research proposals for their protection of the rights of research participants and other ethical considerations.

Intact groups (6)   Pre-existing groups of people whose exposure to different treatments may be compared in a study utilizing a pre-experimental or quasi-experimental research design.

Interaction (5, 8)   A relationship between two independent variables such that the effect of each one on a particular behavior varies with the level of the other.

Interaction of temporal and group composition effects (maturation × selection interaction) (1, 5, 7)   Time-related changes in research participants' behavior that can lead to differences between the members of treatment groups that influence their behavior and may lead to an incorrect inference about the causal relationship between the independent and dependent variables (a threat to internal validity).

Internal consistency (3)   The degree of consistency among the components of a measurement (e.g., individual items on a questionnaire).

Internal validity (1, 5)   The extent to which a causal inference can be drawn with confidence from the research results about the relationship between the independent and dependent variables.

Interrater reliability (4, 9)   The degree of agreement among multiple raters whose ratings are used to measure or establish values of the independent or dependent variable; assessed by a form of correlation coefficient.

Interval scales (equal-interval scales) (3)   Systems of measurement in which all adjacent points on the measurement scale represent equal differences in the magnitude of the property being measured.

Interview (9)   A method of data collection based on asking research participants a standardized list of questions, usually face to face or over the telephone.

Introduction (1, 11)   The first section of a research article; it presents the rationale for selecting the research hypothesis.

Inverse relationship (8)   When two variables are related in such a way that as the value of one increases, the value of the other decreases, as indicated by a negative correlation coefficient.

Laboratory (4, 9)   A setting used exclusively for research, usually isolated from people and events extraneous to the treatments and measures chosen for study by the researcher.

Lack of impact (of treatments) (1, 3, 4)   Insufficient differential effect on behavior on the part of the values of the independent variable (i. e., treatments) created or chosen for a research study.

Lack of reliability (1)   An excess of random error or inconsistency in the measurement of a variable investigated in a research study.

Lack of reliability of behavioral measures (1, 4)   Inconsistencies in the administration of the behavioral measure(s) over the course of a research study (a threat to construct validity).

Lack of reliability of treatments (4)   Inconsistencies in the administration of the various forms of the independent variable over the course of a research study (a threat to construct validity).

Lack of representativeness (1)   The failure of an independent or a dependent variable to capture all relevant aspects of the construct it purports to represent.

Lack of representativeness of behavioral measures (4)   Failure of the behavioral measures to sample all relevant aspects of the domain of the behavioral construct in the research hypothesis.

Lack of representativeness of treatments (4)   Failure of the variations in the independent variables to sample all relevant aspects of the domain of the causal construct in the research hypothesis.

Lack of sensitivity (of behavioral measures) (1, 3, 4)   The inability of a behavioral measure to detect changes in the behavior being studied that might be caused by exposure to the treatments in a research study.

Leniency bias (3)   A stable tendency for an individual to favor positive evaluations when using rating scales.

Level of significance (10)   The probability of a Type I error in null hypothesis significance testing; chosen by the researcher.

Linear relationship (8)   A relationship between variables that is consistent in direction (positive, negative, or no relationship) across the entire range of values of each.

Linguistic/cultural bias (1, 4)   Inaccurate measurement of a behavior because of misunderstanding of the measure caused by differences in language or culture between the researcher and the research participant.

Literature review (2)   An examination of published research and theory that permits an evaluation of the conceptual validity of a possible research hypothesis and/or an enhancement of same.

Logical positivism (3, 11)   A school of philosophy that stressed objectivity in science, including the definition of constructs in terms of observable phenomena (i.e., operational definition).

Lost-letter technique (9)   A method of measuring public attitudes by deliberately placing stamped unmailed letters addressed to contrasting groups and comparing the number that are mailed by the passersby who find them.

Main effects (8)   In research studies that evaluate the effects of multiple independent variables, main effects are the separate effects of each independent variable on the behavior being studied, with the others held constant.

Manipulation (4, 6)   Creation by the researcher of the treatments that are compared in a research study.

Matching (5)   Selecting research participants from pre-existing or intact groups based on equal scores or status on some characteristic(s) relevant to the behavior being studied.

Maturation (1, 5)   *See* **temporal effects**.

Maturation × selection interaction (5)   *See* **interaction of temporal and group composition effects**.

Maximizing (11)   A decision-making strategy that seeks the best outcome available at any cost.

Mean (1, 10)   The arithmetic average of a group of data; used to estimate the central tendency of that distribution.

Measurement (3)   The use of symbols to represent properties of objects or events.

Measurement artifacts (1, 4)   Unintended influences on responses to the behavioral measures used in a research study.

Measurement scales (3)   Alternative means of identifying the properties of natural phenomena.

Median (10)   The middle score among a group of scores that are arranged in order of magnitude (ranked); used to estimate the central tendency of the distribution.

Meta-analysis (10)   A statistical technique for combining the results of separate studies into an overall evaluation of the magnitude or consistency of the effect of their common independent variable.

Method section (1, 11)   The second section of a research article; it describes the participants, the independent and dependent variables, the research design, and the procedures used to carry out the study.

Method variance (3)   The portion of obtained scores or measurements attributable to the method of measurement used to acquire them.

Methodology (1)   The study of the methods used in psychological and other research.

Mistaking a trivial effect for support of the research hypothesis (1, 10) Concluding from a statistically significant result of a statistical test that a very small treatment effect is evidence for the truth of the research hypothesis.

Mode (10)   The most frequently occurring score in a group of data; used to estimate the central tendency of the distribution.

Mortality (1, 5)   *See* **Selective sample attrition**.

Multiple correlation (8)   A statistical procedure that extends correlational analysis to more than two variables, allowing the determination of the relationship between any combination of those variables independent of their relationships with the other(s).

Multiple correlation analysis (MCA) (8) Any statistical analysis based on the use of multiple correlation (*see* **multiple correlation**).

Multiple correlation research (8) Studies with multiple independent and/or dependent variables in which the actual value of each variable is entered into a form of correlational analysis to evaluate relationships among all the independent and dependent variables.

Multiple regression analysis (MR) (8) Statistical analysis based on the techniques of correlation and regression that shows the independent contributions of each of two or more predictors in accounting for the variance in a criterion measure.

Multitrait-multimethod matrix (3) A method for evaluating the construct validity of a measurement operation by estimating the relative contributions of trait variance and method variance to the obtained scores/measurements.

Multivariate analysis of variance (MANOVA) (8) A statistical method of analyzing the results of research studies comparing groups exposed to treatments representing a single independent variable or combination of multiple independent variables, for their effects on multiple behavioral measures.

Multivariate distribution (10) A distribution consisting of three or more measures for each of a sample of units (often the basis for multivariate research).

Multivariate research (8) Research that studies two or more independent variables, dependent variables, or both in a single study.

Mundane realism (4) The degree to which the research context resembles a natural setting in which the behavior in question and its putative cause are found.

Nominal scales (3) Systems of measurement that categorize or name the properties of natural phenomena, disregarding their amount or magnitude (*see* **qualitative measurement**).

Nonrepresentative research context (1, 5, 6) The choice of a time and place in which to conduct a research study that are substantially different from those to which the research results are to be generalized (a threat to external validity).

Nonrepresentative sampling of units (1, 5, 7) The choice of participants (units) in a research study that are substantially different from those to which the research results are to be generalized (a threat to external validity).

Normal distribution (10) A symmetrical distribution of scores whose shape follows a mathematical equation that specifies the proportions of the distribution for each score or interval of scores.

Null hypothesis (10) The hypothesis that no treatment effects occurred, or that there was no relationship between the independent and dependent variables, that is tested by methods of statistical inference (*see* **null hypothesis significance testing**).

Null hypothesis significance testing (NHST) (10) The method of statistical inference that is used most often to draw conclusions from behavioral measures of samples in a research study about the effects of treatment or the relationship between the independent and dependent variables in the populations from which those samples were drawn.

Observations (5, 9)   The measurements of participants' behavior or data collected in the course of a research study.

Observer ratings (9)   Measures of behavior based on the evaluations made by people who have seen or heard it, either live or via a recording.

Obtained score (3)   The measurement made of the behavior being measured.

Operational definition (1, 3)   The process of specifying the measurement operations by which the causal and behavioral constructs in a research hypothesis will become the independent and dependent variables, respectively.

Operationalization (1, 3)   *See* **operational definition**.

Optimizing (11)   A decision-making strategy that seeks the best outcome against the balance of a specified cost.

Ordinal scales (ranks) (3)   Systems of measurement that assign ranks to, or rank-order, phenomena on the basis of the magnitude of the property being measured.

Pantometry (11)   A historical term for the relatively modern tendency to measure everything as precisely as possible.

Paradigm (11)   An overall approach to the scientific study of a particular phenomenon, usually one that has gained wide acceptance among researchers and influences the way they do their work.

Parallel forms (3)   Alternative forms of a measuring instrument, consisting of similar items, used in the test-retest method of evaluating reliability.

Partial correlation (8)   A statistical procedure that allows the determination of the relationship between one variable (a predictor) and another (a criterion), independent of the relationship between that predictor and another (i.e., with the relationship between the second predictor and the criterion "partialed out").

Participants (units) (1, 9)   Those whose behavior is studied in psychological research, whether as individuals, as groups, or as aggregates representing different times or places.

Pilot research (4)   A preliminary run-through of a research study that is conducted to test its procedures and measures.

Placebo effects (4, 5)   The influence on a research participant's behavior of his or her expectation of receiving a particular treatment, especially in medical research (an "artifact").

Plausible rival hypotheses (5)   Alternative explanations for the observed relationship between the independent and dependent variable(s) (i.e., the research results) that are not only possible given the methods used but also likely according to the existing knowledge about the causes of the behavior being studied (*see* **alternative explanation**).

Post-positivism (11)   A school of philosophy that uses analysis of the history of science to understand the methods that researchers use.

Posttest (6)   The administration of a dependent measure to research participants following their exposure to the treatment to which they are assigned.

Precision (3)   The amount of information provided by a measurement about the property being measured.

Predictive validity (3)   A form of criterion-related validity in which the measurement operation being evaluated precedes the acquisition of criterion measures.

Predictor variable (8)   One variable in a correlational relationship that is used to predict the other (the "criterion variable").

Pre-experimental research designs (6)   Arrangements for testing research hypotheses that lack sufficient comparison, among groups or over time, to support valid causal inferences regarding the observed relationship between independent and dependent variables.

Pretest (6)   The administration of a dependent measure to research participants before they are exposed to the treatment to which they are assigned.

Pretest-posttest research design (4)   An arrangement in which the behavioral measure is administered to research participants before and after they are exposed to their respective treatments.

Pretest sensitization (1, 4, 7)   An alteration in research participants' responses to a treatment caused by the pretreatment administration of a measure of the behavior being studied.

Primary sources (2)   Original research articles that provide information about past research.

Principal components analysis (8)   A form of factor analysis that is used to reduce a large set of possible predictor variables to a smaller, more manageable set of predictor variates or factors for subsequent use in establishing relationships with one or more criterion variables.

Professional responsibility (11)   A researcher's obligation to meet the highest methodological standards in planning and carrying out his or her research.

Program evaluation (11)   A specialized use of behavioral research to test the efficiency of policies in public- and private-sector organizations that are aimed at influencing the behavior of those affected by them.

Psychometric criteria (3)   Standards by which the adequacy of psychological measurements can be evaluated.

Putative cause (1)   The suspected cause of some behavior; the causal construct specified in a research hypothesis.

Qualitative measurement (1, 3)   The process by which properties of a phenomena are measured by grouping instances together under verbal labels.

Quantitative measurement (1, 3)   The process by which numbers are assigned to represent specific properties of the phenomenon being measured.

Quasi-experimental research designs (6)   Arrangements for testing research hypotheses that substitute long series of behavioral measures and nonequivalent comparison groups for the manipulation and random assignment of true experiments (typically where the latter cannot be achieved), so as to achieve reasonably certain causal inferences along with high levels of construct and external validity.

Random assignment (5, 6)   The process of creating treatment groups by dividing the pool of research participants available to be studied randomly among the treatments to be administered.

Random error (3)   Fluctuations in the observed score caused by temporary influences on the behavior being measured; these misrepresent the property being measured but cancel each other out over repeated measurements.

Random response technique (9)   A method of obtaining truthful self-reports of sensitive behaviors by using known probabilities to ensure the anonymity of respondents.

Random sample (5)   A group drawn from a larger population of units using a procedure that gives each unit in the population an equal chance of being selected.

Range (10)   The distance, along the measuring scale being used, from the smallest score in a distribution to the largest; an estimate of variability.

Ranks (3)   Numbers used to measure the relative amounts of a given property among a number of events (a rank of 1 usually indicates the greatest amount, 2 the next greatest, and so on).

Ratio scales (3)   Systems of measurement in which a value of zero denotes a complete absence of the property being measured (a true zero point), providing for the construction of meaningful ratios of scale values.

Reactive arrangements (4, 7)   Conditions in a research study that make the participants aware that their behavior is under scrutiny by the researcher.

Reactivity (4, 7)   A condition of the research setting that promotes awareness on the part of research participants that their behavior is being studied.

References (11)   A list of the prior research and resources cited in the text of a research article; this list (alphabetized by author name) follows the main text and includes the author, title, date, and publication information relevant to each cited resource.

Regression equation (8)   An equation that allows the prediction of the unknown value of one variable from the known value of another, based on the correlation between the two variables in a sample containing cases similar to the one in question.

Regression to the mean (1, 5)   *See* **statistical regression effects**.

Relative standing (10)   The magnitude of a score compared to that of other scores in a distribution.

Reliability (3)   The extent to which measurements are repeatable across occasions and internally consistent.

Reliability criteria (3)   Standards by which the reliability of a measurement can be evaluated.

Replication (1)   The intentional repetition of a research study for the purpose of verifying its results.

Representativeness (3)   The degree to which a variable includes all facets of the construct it measures.

Research article (1)   A report of a research study published in a scientific journal.

Research context (5)   *See* **research settings**.

Research designs (1, 5, 6)   Alternative arrangements for comparing the effects of variations in the independent variable (treatments) in a research study.

Research findings (1)   The conclusions drawn from research results about the truth of the research hypothesis.

Research hypothesis (2)   A presumed causal relationship between some event or experience and some behavior (the causal and behavioral constructs, respectively) that is tested in a research study.

Research results (1)   The outcome of the statistical analysis of research data summarizing the outcomes of treatments or relationships between independent and dependent variables.

Research settings (5)   The combinations of time and place in which research studies are carried out, including the apparatus, tasks, and people to which the research participants respond.

Restricted range (8)   So narrow a range of values of a variable that the variable is not appropriate for use in a correlational analysis.

Results section (1, 11)   The third section of a research article; it presents the results of the statistical analysis carried out on the data collected for the study.

Rival hypothesis (1, 4)   A hypothesis for the observed differences among treatment groups, or the observed relationship between the independent and dependent variables, other than the research hypothesis (*see* **alternative explanation**).

Sampling distribution (10)   A theoretical or hypothetical distribution of statistics (e.g., mean, standard deviation) for all possible samples of a given size from the same population who were exposed to a particular treatment or who were grouped together based on some independent variable.

Sampling error (10)   The variability in research results among different random samples from a population of interest, usually estimated from the sample results.

Satisficing (11)   A decision-making strategy based on the selection of the first available outcome that meets or exceeds an established standard of minimal acceptability.

Scatterplot (3, 8, 10)   A visual depiction of the relationship between two variables in which the two values for each participant are plotted as points or Cartesian coordinates on a graph.

Scientific journal (1)   A periodical that publishes reports of scientific research studies.

Scientific responsibility (11)   A researcher's obligation to disseminate the results of his or her research to interested scientific and practitioner colleagues and to assist other researchers with their work whenever called on to do so.

Secondary sources (2)   Summaries of published research and theoretical articles that can lead a researcher to relevant original sources during a literature search.

Selection (1, 5)   *See* **group composition effects**.

Selective sample attrition (mortality) (1, 5, 7)   A loss of participants from treatment groups that produces differences between the groups that can influence their behavior and can lead to an incorrect inference about the causal relationship between the independent and dependent variables (a threat to internal validity).

Self-report measures (9)   Behavioral measures that are provided directly by research participants on a variety of questionnaires and rating forms.

Sensitivity (3)   The degree to which a behavioral measure will detect the effect of a treatment or a difference between treatments, should that treatment or difference affect the behavior being studied.

Settings (5, 9)   *See* **research settings**.

Significance tests (10)   A family of inferential statistical procedures that evaluate the probability that an observed difference among treatment groups or a relationship between independent and dependent variables was the result of sampling error; if that probability falls below a preset criterion (usually .05 or smaller), the difference or relationship is attributed to the effects of the independent variable(s) on the behavior(s) being studied.

Significant difference (10)   A difference between treatment groups that is so unlikely to have been caused by sampling error that it leads to the rejection of the null hypothesis (*see* **null hypothesis**, **null hypothesis statistical testing**, and **sampling error**).

Skewed distribution (10)   A group of scores that is asymmetrical, ranging much farther away from the center of the distribution on one side (lowest or highest scores) than the other.

Social responsibility (11)   A researcher's obligation to meet the highest ethical standards in the treatment of research participants and in respect to his or her society as a whole.

Stability (3)   The extent to which repeated measurements of a particular property of a phenomenon are consistent.

Standard deviation (1, 10)   The statistic that is used most often to estimate the variability of a distribution of scores.

Standard error of the mean difference (10)   An estimate of the variability or the differences between the means of groups exposed to contrasting treatments in the sampling distribution of those mean differences (*see* **sampling distribution**).

Standard score (10)   A statistic that shows the magnitude of a score compared to other scores in the distribution (a measure of "relative standing").

Standardized tests (9)   Measures of behavior that have been evaluated extensively for psychometric criteria, that have extensive norms against which new scores can be compared, and that have well-established scoring procedures; examples include published intelligence and personality tests.

Statistical conclusion validity (1, 10)   The degree to which the statistical analysis of the research results contributes to an accurate understanding of the truth of the research hypothesis.

Statistical inference (10)   A family of statistical techniques that are used to make probabilistic judgments about the effects of treatments or the relationship between the independent and dependent variables in the populations of interest from the results of a research study carried out with samples from those populations.

Statistical regression effects (regression to the mean) (1, 5, 7)   Changes from pretest to posttest in the scores of extreme-scoring groups of research participants that can lead to an incorrect inference about the causal relationship between the independent and dependent variables (a threat to internal validity).

Statistical techniques (1)   Mathematical operations that describe research data or permit inferences from research data about the status of the research hypothesis (descriptive and inferential statistical techniques, respectively).

Statistics (1, 10)   Mathematical procedures used to summarize research data (descriptive statistics) and to infer relationships among variables in populations from the samples studied in research studies (inferential statistics).

Stepwise multiple regression (8)   A variation of multiple correlational analysis (MCA) that calculates the independent relationships between multiple predictors and a single criterion variable in order of their magnitude, beginning with the strongest.

Strategic responding (1, 4)   Responses by research participants that are intended to support the research hypothesis or to protect their self-esteem, rather than being spontaneous responses to the treatments administered to them.

Stratified random sample (5)   A group drawn from a larger population of units that represents proportionally a number of subgroups, or strata, within the population, while giving each unit in a subgroup an equal chance of being selected.

Strictness bias (3)   A stable tendency of an individual to favor negative evaluations when using rating scales.

Subjects (1)   The outdated label for those whose behavior is studied in research (replaced by "participants"), although sometimes used to refer to nonhumans.

Survey (9)   A method of data collection based on administering a standardized list of questions to research participants, through the mail, in person, over the Internet, or otherwise.

Systematic error (3)   *See* **bias**.

t **test** (10)   A statistical method used to draw inferences from the means of two treatment groups about the difference between populations that might be exposed to contrasting treatments.

Tables (11)   Compilations of numbers such as group means and standard deviations, or correlation coefficients, that are included in a research article to clarify the research results.

Temporal effects (maturation) (1, 5, 7)   Changes in the environment or in the participants resulting from the passage of time that can influence the behavior of participants in a research study and can lead to an incorrect inference about the causal relationship between the independent and dependent variables (a threat to internal validity).

Temporal trends (7)   Changes in behavior attributable to the passage of time (*see* **temporal effects**).

Test-retest method (3)   The use of repeated administrations of a measurement instrument (or of similar alternative forms of the instrument) to evaluate the stability of measurements made using that instrument.

Theoretical isolation (1, 2)   Lack of relevance of the research hypothesis to existing knowledge about the behavior in question.

Third-variable cause (7)   A factor whose independent effects on two others is responsible for a spurious relationship between those two (i.e., the third variable is the cause of the observed relationship between the other two).

Threats to validity (1)   Problems with hypothesis selection, operationalization of constructs, research design, or statistical analysis that can detract from the meaningfulness of the research results.

Time series analysis (8)   An extension of correlational analysis that is used to evaluate research studies using time series designs for the effect of an independent variable or treatment, over and above any temporal trends in the data.

Trait variance (3)   The portion of obtained scores or measurements attributable to the trait (property) being measured.

Trapped administrators (11)   Managers in private- and public-sector organizations who fear and avoid objective evaluations of their policies because any failures that are uncovered might be blamed on them personally.

Treatment artifacts (1, 4)   Unintended influences on participants' behavior that accompany the treatments administered in a research study.

Treatment effects (5)   The differences in observed behavior between research participants who were exposed to different variations of the independent variable (i.e., "treatments").

Treatments (3, 5)   Variations of the independent variable whose effects are compared to test a research hypothesis.

True experimental research designs (6)   Arrangements for testing research hypotheses that utilize manipulation of the independent variable by the researcher, along with random assignment of participants to groups or treatments to occasions, to permit valid causal inferences regarding the observed relationship between independent and dependent variables, often to the detriment of construct validity and generalizability of results.

True score (3)   The actual property of the behavior that is being measured.

True score test theory (3)   A symbolic representation of the measurement process that shows how random and systematic error contaminate obtained scores or measurements.

Type I error (10)   An incorrect probabilistic judgment to reject a true null hypothesis based on some form of null hypothesis significance testing.

Type II error (10)   An incorrect probabilistic judgment to not reject a false null hypothesis based on some form of null hypothesis significance testing.

Units (5)   *See* **participants**.

Univariate distribution (10)   A distribution consisting of a single measure for each of a sample of units.

Univariate research (8)   Research that studies the relationship between a single independent variable and a single dependent variable.

Unnecessary duplication (1, 2)   Unintentionally selecting a research hypothesis that was tested in previous research.

Unobtrusive measures (4, 9)   Behavioral measures that are obtained by examining tangible effects of the research participants' behavior on their environment.

Use of a statistical test lacking sufficient power (1, 10)   The application of a method of statistical inference that lacks the sensitivity to detect treatment effects that might occur (i.e., has too high a probability of a Type II error); a threat to statistical conclusion validity.

UTOS (5)   Methodologist Lee Cronbach's acronym for four elements of a research study that can affect the generalizability of the research results (units, treatments, observations, and settings).

Validity (1)   The degree to which the results of a research study provide trustworthy information about the truth or falsity of the hypothesis.

Validity coefficients (3) Correlation coefficients used to assess criterion-related validity via the relationships between a measurement and each of its relevant criteria.

Validity criteria (3) Standards by which the validity of a measurement can be evaluated.

Validity Scorecard (1, 7) A form that facilitates the evaluation of the validity of research findings for each of the possible threats to validity.

Variability (10) A statistical description of the extent of spread among a group of data or scores.

Variables (1) The measurable factors specified from the constructs of a research hypothesis.

Violation of test assumptions (1) The application of statistical methods to data for which they are not appropriate; such violations can lead to an inaccurate judgment about the truth of the research hypothesis (a threat to statistical conclusion validity).

Within-subjects designs (5) A research design in which the same group of participants or units is observed on multiple occasions. *See* **comparisons among groups**.

REFERENCES

American Association of University Women. (1991). *The AAUW report: How schools shortchange girls.* Washington, DC: Author.

American Psychological Association. (1994). *Publication manual of the American Psychological Association* (4th ed.). Washington, DC: Author.

Aserinsky, E., & Kleitman, N. (1953). Regularly occurring periods of eye mobility and concomitant phenomena during sleep. *Science, 118,* 273-274.

Bargh, J. A., Chen, M., & Burrows, L. (1996). Automaticity of social behavior: Direct effects of trait construct and stereotype activation on action. *Journal of Personality and Social Psychology, 71,* 230-244.

Baum, A., Cohen, L., & Hall, M. (1993). Control and intrusive memories as possible determinants of chronic stress. *Psychosomatic Medicine, 55,* 274-286.

Broverman, I. K., Vogel, S. R., Broverman, D. M., Clarkson, F. E., & Rosenkrantz, P. S. (1972). Sex-role stereotypes: A current appraisal. *Journal of Social Issues, 28*(2), 59-78.

Brown v. Board of Education (1954). 347 U.S. 483.

Brunswik, E. (1956). *Perception and the representative design of psychological experiments.* Berkeley: University of California Press.

Byrne, D. (1971). *The attraction paradigm.* New York: Academic Press.

Calhoun, J. B. (1962). Population density and social pathology. *Scientific American, 206,* 139-148.

Campbell, D. T. (1969). Reforms as experiments. *American Psychologist, 24,* 409-429.

Campbell, D. T., & Fiske, D. W. (1959). Convergent and discriminant validation by the multitrait-multimethod matrix. *Psychological Bulletin, 56,* 81-105.

Campbell, D. T., & Stanley, J.C. (1963). *Experimental and quasi-experimental designs for research.* Chicago: Rand McNally.

Cartwright, R. D. (1974). The influence of a conscious wish on dreams: A methodological study of dream meaning and function. *Journal of Abnormal Psychology, 83,* 387-393.

Ceci, S. J., Loftus, E. F., Leichtman, M. D., & Bruck, M. (1994). The possible role of source misattributions in the creation of false beliefs among preschoolers. *Journal of Clinical and Experimental Hypnosis, 42,* 304-320.

Cherulnik, P. D., Way, J. H., Ames, S., & Hutto, D. B. (1981). Impressions of high and low Machiavellian men. *Journal of Personality, 49,* 388-400.

Clark, K. B., & Clark, M. K. (1940). Skin color as a factor in the identification of Negro pre-school children. *Journal of Social Psychology, 11*, 159-169.

Cook, T. D., & Campbell, D. T. (1979). *Quasi-experimentation: Design and analysis for field settings.* Chicago: Rand McNally.

Cronbach, L. J. (1982). *Designing evaluations of educational and social programs.* San Francisco: Jossey-Bass.

Crosby, A. W. (1997). *The measure of reality.* New York: Cambridge University Press.

Darley, J. M., & Latané, B. (1968). Bystander intervention in emergencies: Diffusion of responsibility. *Journal of Personality and Social Psychology, 8*, 377-383.

Dement, W. (1960). The effect of dream deprivation. *Science, 131*, 1705-1707.

Devlin, K. J. (1997). *Mathematics: The science of patterns.* New York: W. H. Freeman.

Festinger, L., Riecken, H., & Schachter, S. (1956). *When prophecy fails.* Minneapolis: University of Minnesota Press.

Fiedler, F. E. (1967). *A theory of leadership effectiveness.* New York: McGraw-Hill.

Frazier, F. W. (1985). *A postoccupancy evaluation of Contra Costa County's Main Detention Facility: An analysis of the first new-generation, modular, direct supervision county jail.* Unpublished doctoral dissertation, Golden Gate University, San Francisco.

Friedman, M., & Rosenman, R. H. (1959). Association of specific overt behavior pattern with blood and cardiovascular findings. *Journal of the American Medical Association, 96*, 1286-1296.

Gazzaniga, M. S. (1967). The split brain in man. *Scientific American, 217*(2), 24-29.

Gibson, E. J., & Walk, R. D. (1960). The "visual cliff." *Scientific American, 202*(4), 64-71.

Gould, S. J. (1996). *The mismeasure of man.* New York: W. W. Norton.

Greenberg, B. G., Abernathy, J. R., & Horvitz, D. G. (1970). A new survey technique and its application in the field of public health. *Milbank Memorial Fund Quarterly, 48*, 39-55.

Guthrie, R. V. (1998). *Even the rat was white* (2nd ed.). Needham Heights, MA: Allyn & Bacon.

Haier, R. J., Siegel, B., Tang, C., Abel, L., & Buchsbaum, M. S. (1992). Intelligence and changes in regional cerebral glucose metabolic rate following learning. *Intelligence, 16*, 415-426.

Harlow, H. F. (1958). The nature of love. *American Psychologist, 13*, 673-685.

Harlow, H. F. (1986). *Learning to love.* Westport, CN: Greenwood.

Hartmann, E. L. (1973). *The functions of sleep.* New Haven, CT: Yale University Press.

Hearnshaw, L. S. (1979). *Cyril Burt: Psychologist.* London: Hodder & Stoughton.

Horgan, J. (1997). *The end of science.* Boston: Little, Brown.

Hornblum, A. M. (1998). *Acres of skin.* New York: Routledge.

Hunt, M. (1999). *The new know-nothings.* New Brunswick, NJ: Transaction.

Kamin, L. J. (1974). *The science and politics of IQ.* Potomac, MD: Lawrence Erlbaum.

Kevles, D. J. (1998). *The Baltimore case.* New York: W. W. Norton.

Kinsey, A. C., Pomeroy, W. B., & Martin, C. E. (1948). *Sexual behavior in the human male.* Philadelphia: Saunders.

Kuhn, T. S. (1962). *The structure of scientific revolutions.* Chicago: University of Chicago Press.

LeVay, S. (1996). *Queer science.* Cambridge: MIT Press.

MacRae, J. R., Scoles, M. I., & Siegel, S. (1987). The contribution of Pavlovian conditioning to drug tolerance and dependence. *British Journal of Addiction, 82*, 371-380.

Maddox, J. R. (1998). *What remains to be discovered?* New York: Free Press.

McKibben, B. (1998). *Maybe one.* New York: Simon & Schuster.

Milgram, S. (1969). The lost letter technique. *Psychology Today, 3* (3), 30-33, 66, 68.

Milgram, S. (1974). *Obedience to authority.* New York: Harper & Row.

Miller, G. A. (1969). Psychology as a means of promoting human welfare. *American Psychologist, 24,* 1063-1075.

Miller, N. E., Bailey, C. J., & Stevenson, J.A.F. (1950). Decreased "hunger" but increased intake resulting from hypothalamic lesions. *Science, 112,* 256-259.

Mook, D. G. (1983). In defense of external validity. *American Psychologist, 38,* 379-387.

Moreno, J. L. (1934). *Who shall survive?* Washington, DC: *Nervous and Mental Disease Monograph,* No. 38.

Nisbett, R. E., & Cohen, D. (1996). *Culture of honor.* Boulder, CO: Westview.

Orne, M. (1959). The nature of hypnosis: Artifact and essence. *Journal of Abnormal and Social Psychology, 58,* 277-299.

Pavlov, I. P. (1927). *Conditioned reflexes.* London: Oxford University Press.

Pavlov, I. P. (1928). *Lectures on conditioned reflexes* (Vol. 1). London: Lawrence and Wishart.

Pennebaker, J. W., Kiecolt-Glaser, J. K., & Glaser, R. (1996). Disclosures of trauma and immune function: Health implications for psychotherapy. *Journal of Consulting and Clinical Psychology, 56,* 239-245.

Peterson, C., & Seligman, M.E.P. (1984). Causal explanations as a risk factor for depression: Theory and evidence. *Psychological Review, 91,* 347-374.

Pfungst, O. (1965). *Clever Hans (the horse of Mr. von Osten)* (Trans. 1911; reprint, R. Rosenthal, ed.). New York: Holt, Rinehart & Winston. (Original work published 1906)

Popper, K. R. (1965). *Conjectures and refutations: The growth of scientific knowledge* (2nd ed.). New York: Harper & Row.

Prieto, J. M., Fernandez-Ballesteros, R., & Carpintero, H. (1994). Contemporary psychology in Spain. *Annual Review of Psychology, 45,* 51-78.

Rindfuss, R. R., Reed, J. S., & St. John, C. (1978, July 14). A fertility reaction to a historical event. *Science,* pp. 178-180.

Rosenthal, R. (1969). Interpersonal expectations: Effects of the experimenter's hypothesis. In R. Rosenthal & R. L. Rosnow (Eds.), *Artifact in behavioral research* (pp. 181-277). New York: Academic Press.

Rosenthal, R., & Jacobson, L. (1966). Teachers' expectancies: Determinants of pupils' IQ gains. *Psychological Reports, 19,* 115-118.

Rosenzweig, M. R., Bennett, E. L., & Diamond, M. C. (1972). Brain changes in response to experience. *Scientific American, 226*(2), 22-29.

Rosnow, R. L., & Rosenthal, R. (1997). *People studying people.* New York: Freeman.

Rosnow, R. L., & Suls, J. M. (1970). Reactive effects of pretesting in attitude research. *Journal of Personality and Social Psychology, 15,* 338-343.

Rotter, J. B. (1966). Generalized expectancies for internal vs. external control of reinforcement. *Psychological Monographs, 80,* 1-28.

Seligman, M.E.P., & Maier, S. F. (1967). Failure to escape traumatic shock. *Journal of Experimental Psychology, 74,* 1-9.

Selye, H. (1956). *The stress of life.* New York: McGraw-Hill.

Sigall, J., & Page, R. (1971). Current stereotypes: A little fading, a little faking. *Journal of Personality and Social Psychology, 24,* 14-21.

Smith, M. L., & Glass, G. V. (1977). Meta-analysis of psychotherapy outcome studies. *American Psychologist, 32,* 752-760.

Sobel, D. (1995). *Longitude.* New York: Walker and Company.

Sommer, R. (1990, April). *Research on utilization.* Keynote address at the 21st annual conference of the Environmental Design Research Association, University of Illinois at Urbana-Champaign.

Stevens, S. S. (1951). *Handbook of experimental psychology.* New York: Wiley.

Terman, L. M., & Oden, M. H. (1959). *The gifted group at midlife.* Stanford, CA: Stanford University Press.

Triplett, N. (1897). The dynamogenic factors in pacemaking and competition. *American Journal of Psychology, 9,* 507-533.

Weaver, D., Reis, M. H., Albanese, C., Constantini, F., Baltimore, D., & Imanishi-Kari, T. (1986). Altered repertoire of endogenous immunoglobulin gene expression in transgenetic mice containing a rearranged mu heavy chain cell. *Cell, 45,* 247-259.

Wener, R., Frazier, W., & Farbstein, J. (1987, June). Building better jails. *Psychology Today,* pp. 40-44, 48-49.

White, M. (1997). *Isaac Newton: The last sorcerer.* Boston: Addison-Wesley.

Zajonc, R. B. (1965). Social facilitation. *Science, 149,* 269-274.

Zajonc, R. B., & Markus, G. B. (1975). Birth order and intellectual development. *Psychological Review, 82,* 74-88.

Zimbardo, P. G., Banks, W. C., Haney, C., & Jaffe, D. (1973, April 8). The mind is a formidable jailer: A Pirendellian prison. *The New York Times Magazine,* pp. 38-60.

INDEX

ABOUT THE AUTHOR

Paul D. Cherulnik, PhD, has taught psychology for more than 30 years, at a number of colleges and universities. This is his third book. The first was a research methods text and the second a collection of case studies of the application of behavioral research in design fields such as architecture, interior design, and landscape architecture. He has also published more than two dozen research papers, most of them dealing with relationships between physical appearance and social behavior. Recently, he has been developing and validating a scale that measures people's beliefs about the Culture of Honor.